# Using Media to Make Kids Feel Good:

## Resources and Activities for Successful Programs in Hospitals

# Using Media to Make Kids Feel Good:

## Resources and Activities for Successful Programs in Hospitals

by Maureen Gaffney

Phoenix ● New York

ORYX PRESS

1988

The rare Arabian Oryx is believed to have inspired the myth of the unicorn. This desert antelope became virtually extinct in the early 1960s. At that time several groups of international conservationists arranged to have 9 animals sent to the Phoenix Zoo to be the nucleus of a captive breeding herd. Today the Oryx population is over 400, and herds have been returned to reserves in Israel, Jordan, and Oman.

Copyright © 1988 by Media Center for Children, Inc.
Published by The Oryx Press
2214 North Central at Encanto
Phoenix, AZ 85004-1483

Published simultaneously in Canada

Printed and Bound in the United States of America

∞ The paper used for this publication meets the minimum requirements of American National Standard for Information Science—Permanence of Paper for Printed Library Materials, ANSI Z39.48, 1984.

Library of Congress Cataloging-in-Publication Data

Gaffney, Maureen.
  Using media to make kids feel good.

  Results of a four-year hospitalized children's media project carried out by the Media Center for Children.
    1. Children—Hospital care—Psychological aspects.
2. Mass media and children.  3. Sick children—Recreation.
I. Media Center for Children (New York, N.Y.)  II. Title.
[DNLM: 1. Audio-Visual Aids.  2. Child, Hospitalized—psychology.  3. Hospital Administration.  4. Recreation.
WS 105.5.H7 G131u]
RJ242.G34  1988    362.1'9892    86-43113
ISBN 0-89774-345-8 (alk. paper)

# CONTENTS

# PRINCIPAL PROJECT CONSULTANTS

Maddie Appell
Chief, Child Development Section
Pediatric Service
St. Luke's/Roosevelt Medical Center

Karen Ballard
Clinical Nurse Specialist
Pediatric Mental Health Unit
New York Hospital

Joan Chan
Director, Child Life Program
Downstate Medical Center/SUNY

Kirsten De Bear
Playroom Coordinator
St. Luke's/Roosevelt Medical Center

Carol Longman
Child Life In-Patient Coordinator
Bellevue Hospital

Betty Mogtadu
Assistant Director, Child Life Program
Downstate Medical Center/SUNY

Fran Tellner
Director, Child Life Program
New York Hospital

Susan Wojtasik
Director, Child Life Program
Bellevue Hospital

# PREFACE

This is a handbook for hospital programmers, Child Life specialists, activity therapists, play therapists, recreation therapists, pediatricians, pediatric nurses, educators, and volunteers or others who work with pediatric patients. Likewise, it is a handbook for those who buy, rent, produce, or distribute pediatric media. A practical resource for anyone who wants to develop participatory media programs for children in hospitals, it discusses film and video, as well as closed-circuit TV, and provides information about how to use or produce programs in which related arts activities are followups to viewing. Its primary goal is to foster hospital-controlled programming that is beneficial to pediatric patients.

With some adjustment for the debilitation caused by illness, the book could also be used in other institutions, notably by educators who work with children in preschool and the primary grades, both in regular and special educational settings. Besides being accessible to children for whom English is a second language, many programs should work with learning disabled children.

## THE SCOPE OF THE BOOK

The Hospitalized Children's Media Project is the result of years of research in a number of hospitals. This book describes the content and summarizes the results of that project. Information about what happened as well as our thinking behind it is quite detailed in order to give readers sufficient data so they can generalize from the materials or activities recorded herein to others not covered in the course of the project. In addition to write-ups of specific programs for preschoolers through preadolescents, the book includes a number of related reports.

Several distinct sections follow the definition of terms: the introduction, the film/tape annotations, the program descriptions/evaluations, and the appendices, resources, and indexes.

## Introduction

This section explains the philosophy behind and gives an overview of the project on which the book is based. In addition, it offers summaries and programming guidelines that are not found elsewhere.

## Film/Tape Annotations

This section describes and analyzes the films that were used for research. It includes over 60 films, most of which are available in video and legally available for use on a nonprofit hospital's closed-circuit television system, provided the following conditions are met:

- Permission to use a film or tape on CCTV is obtained in writing from the distributor prior to purchase. The letter should mention the title and give some details about the type of programming it will be part of and the number of beds it will reach.
- The CCTV system is an in-house system, using hard cable and operating in one hospital and in one building only. Should a system cover more than one building, discuss the particulars with the distributor to clear use of the title.
- There is no charge to patients for viewing the CCTV programming. This may mean not charging rental fees for TV sets in order to get educational rates, which are cheaper than those for which a fee is charged.

The descriptive annotation of each film is rather detailed so that programmers can have some idea of what they will get when they schedule or purchase a film. The descriptions should also be informative for media makers. Each annotation includes the director's name, the country and year it was made in, the running time, and production details such as the use of sound or color and whether it is liveaction or animated.

Additionally, each film annotation includes a discussion of the following: attributes of its visual imagery as well as its soundtrack; its legibility and audibility on video monitors; its pace and structure;

its themes; relevant comments; suggested follow-up activities; related children's books, poems, or recordings (if any); its recommended age range in hospitals; an MCC rating for hospital-appropriateness; and its distribution source and price.

## Program Descriptions/Evaluations

In this section, program write-ups are listed in chronological order of development. They include participatory film programs designed for the playroom, for closed-circuit television, and for videocassettes in the playroom. Generally, all CCTV or video programs would work as film programs and, except when there is information to the contrary, video programs could also be used as closed-circuit television programs.

Video introductions (to both the tapes and the activities) were documented in full. Hospital staff and others who work in nonprofit organizations (excepting those involved in media production or distribution) may freely reproduce these video introductions for staff or volunteers to use in face-to-face programs with children. However, they cannot be used on television or in prerecorded programs of any sort without prior permission in writing from the Media Center for Children (MCC).

## Appendices, Resources, and Indexes

The Appendices include an MCC survey on the overall use of media with children in hospitals, a report on the use of television in children's wards and hospitals by Elizabeth Crocker, the MCC evaluation form, and a listing and percentage breakdown of children's illnesses. The Selected Resources section contains a list of children's books and recordings mentioned in the annotations, a recommended list of print resources for adults, and a directory (with addresses and phone numbers) of distributors whose works are documented in this book. The Indexes include an index of themes from the annotated films, an activities index, age indexes for the programs as well as the films, and an index of titles in each program as well as the programs each title is in.

## HOW TO USE THE BOOK

Anyone planning a comprehensive approach to pediatric programming should read the entire book since relevant issues came up in every phase of research. To get a real sense of the project, however, the reader should go through the program write-ups in chronological order (film, CCTV, then video) and should read about the failures as well as the successes, since our failures often define what would and would not work with the pediatric popu-

lation. Such a reader might also want to contact some of the people listed at the end of the MCC survey; they may be able to offer resources and insights not available in this book.

For readers interested only in CCTV programming, it would also be helpful to read the whole book. Those interested only in playroom programs could probably skip Crocker's report, but they should read everything else. Readers developing a proposal to get funding for either playroom or CCTV programming may find that the introduction, the MCC survey, Crocker's report, and a few print resources provide enough material.

Once they have gone through the book, readers will find the index of themes helpful for planning programs thematically. Readers who want to plan programs on an activity basis should start with that index. In either case, it may be helpful to cross-check them using the age indexes. To locate additional films or tapes, request children's catalogs from the distributors listed in the resources section.

Whatever the reader does, let the staff of the Media Center for Children know. We may be able to help or we may know people you could help.

## WHERE TO GET MORE INFORMATION

The Media Center for Children is a nonprofit educational organization which compiles books such as this. If you want more information about using media with children (whether hospitalized or not), write us.

Information Director
Media Center for Children
3 West 29th Street (11th Floor)
New York, NY 10001

For information about health-related and general pediatric media as well as Child Life programs in hospitals, contact the ACCH.

Public Information Coordinator
Assoc. for the Care of Children's Health
3615 Wisconsin Avenue NW
Washington, DC 20016
(202) 244-1801

For general media information, write or call the American Film and Video Association, formerly the Educational Film Library Association (EFLA), which was considering a move to La Grange Park, IL, near Chicago as this book went to press.

Information Librarian
American Film and Video Association
45 John Street (3rd Floor)
New York, NY 10038
(212) 227-5599

# ACKNOWLEDGMENTS

This book and the project on which it was based are the result of many people's work and I am extremely grateful for their time and effort.

Anne Munzer Bourne began the project in 1981 and continued as Director of Research through 1983, after which she worked as a field researcher in our Westchester site. Mary Ann Renz Bonarti, who worked as a researcher for the film programs, assumed the role of Director of Research for the CCTV and video evaluations. Both compiled excellent summaries of those field tests, with Bourne doing the pilot and film programs and Bonarti the CCTV and video programs. Gil Coyle, who did a special evaluaton of the film and CCTV activities, also worked as a field researcher. Additional field research was conducted by Maureen Gaffney, Margo Cornelius, Susan Delson, and Sylvia Santiago.

We could not have done this at all without the Child Life specialists and playroom staff at our hospital sites. We were inspired by their concern for the children and indebted by their professional assistance. Not only did they guide and advise us, they helped us analyze each screening in depth. Their commitment was a prime factor in the project's success. At Bellevue Hospital, we worked with Susan Wojtasik, Mary Jacobs, Nancy Lewis, Carol Longman, Irma Ramirez, Sally Sanborn, and Ann Touhey. At Children's Hospital/National Medical Center, we worked with Susan Eidenberg and Tom Thompson. At Downstate Medical Center we worked with Joan Chan and Betty Mogtadu. At the Eastern Maine Medical Center, we worked with Cathy Anderson. At Kings County Hospital we worked with Bernadette Mineo. At New York Hospital, we worked with Fran Tellner, Karen Ballard, Pat Livingston, and Nancy McFarland. At St. Luke's/Roosevelt Hospital we worked with Maddie Appell, Kirsten De Bear, Wayne Ver Hoeve, and Maria Scaros. And, at the Westchester County Medical Center, we worked with Trudy Weiss.

Initial activity sheets were prepared by Gil Coyle, Maureen Gaffney, and Rick Olivo. The video program activity sheets for this book were prepared by Marge Noyes. The first MCC hospital survey was conducted by Deirdre Boyle, the second by Jane Rayleigh. The third one (which appears in appendix) resulted from the work of Deirdre Boyle, Merrill Lee Fuchs, Michael Gaffney, Jane Rayleigh, and Maureen Gaffney. Editorial research and assistance in preparing the manuscript was provided by Judy Balsamo, Robert Braun, Eduardo Duarte, Merrill Lee Fuchs, Michael Gaffney, Barbara Greer, and Adrienne Wolff. The bulk of the manuscript was transcribed by Barbara Shusterman, transferred to computer by Michael Gaffney, and edited on a word processor by Maureen Gaffney.

Films/tapes were provided for our research by the following distributors and/or filmmakers: AIMS Instructional Media, Dan Bailey, Barr Films, Beacon Films, Billy Budd Films, CBC/French Services Division, Churchill Films, Tom Davenport, Encyclopaedia Britannica Educational Corporation, Films Incorporated, Hill-Gatu Productions, International Film Bureau, International Film Foundation, Karen Johnson, Learning Corporation of America, Made-to-Order Library Productions, the Museum of Modern Art, National Film Board of Canada, Eli Noyes, Perspective/Coronet Films, Phoenix Films & Video, Pyramid Films, Susan Rubin, Charles Samu, Texture Films, Alfred Wallace, Weston Woods Studios, and Wombat Productions. Children's books were donated by Greenwillow Books and Weston Woods Studios.

Many people worked on the CCTV productions used in our research. They include writer/director Maureen Gaffney; production manager Michael Gaffney; on-camera hosts Mary Ann Renz Bonarti and Rick Olivo; director of photography John Hazard; lighting director Kevin Jones; sound engineer Daniel Epstein; editor/mixer Eric Lewis; translator (of English script into Spanish) Esilda Buxbaum; and production assistants Gregory Casey, John La Fleur, Tyler Kim, and Wendy Ellen Frey. Transportation was provided by Sam Wiener, and the production was shot at Young Filmakers/Video Arts with the help of YF/VA staff Calvin Tyler and Carol Ruthberg.

The Director of Development was Sandra Edwards who, along with MCC's Executive Director, helped secure funding for the project. Grants and contributions were received from the following: the Association for the Care of Children's Health; the Jones Foundation; the Louis B. Mayer Foundation; McDonald's Corporation; the Ruth Mott Fund; the National Endowment for the Arts; the New York State Council on the Arts; several individual donors; and the United Hospital Fund of New York, which specifically funded the production of this book.

I am indebted to the Board of Directors of the Media Center for Children for their help and encouragement. Throughout this project they included Marshall Beil, Eric Breitbart, Bruce Eaken, David Crocker, Lynne Hofer, Geraldine Bond Laybourne, Richard Lewis, Eileen Newman, and Stanley Stillman. I am also grateful to Dr. Michael Rothenberg, Stephanie Steele, Dirk Wales, and—in particular—Sam Wiener (my husband) for their enthusiastic support and assistance. And I am deeply indebted to Robert Braun, MCC's Information Director, who ran the Media Center during the summer sabbaticals I took over the past few years to work on this book; without that uninterrupted time, this book would never have seen the light of day. Finally, my colleagues and I are especially grateful to the over 1,000 children with whom we evaluated the programs. Without their input this book would not have been possible.

On a personal note, this project stands now and will doubtless endure as one of the most meaningful and rewarding undertakings of my life. Everyone who worked on the research for it was remarkable—from the dedicated staff of the Media Center to the pioneering Child Life specialists who were our on-site consultants. But even more than the inspiration such colleagues provided, it was the children who made this project so compelling.

Often, the first time pediatric patients came to a program, their eyes would be full of terror and distrust. Other aspects of their appearance were disquieting—what with intravenous needles in small hands as well as dressings, sutures, or other signs of medical procedures visible here and there. But it was the cold and alien look in their eyes that was most disturbing. It haunted me until I remembered where I had seen a look like that before: in photos of the children from Terezin, a World War II concentration camp.

Conversational chitchat was out of the question. I couldn't breeze over to such children and say, "How are things going?" So I was quite nervous, at least initially, about how to make contact. I managed, in part, by explaining what was going to happen.

Once a program was underway, however, the look in their eyes got better. By the time it was over—having enjoyed a moment of pleasure or release and having been reassured by person-to-person contact—the eyes of those youngsters looked like children's eyes and somehow the world seemed right again.

At some point in the future, when pending projects are completed, I hope to return to the hospital and resume the role of "film lady" if only on a voluntary basis. I can think of few other media-related endeavors I could do that would be so humanly satisfying or so needed.

**Maureen Gaffney**
**Executive Director**
**Media Center for Children**

# DEFINITION OF TERMS

**Associative Structure.** A fairly unfocused chain of images with casual connections to an idea.

**Audibility.** The degree to which the soundtrack of a film/video can be heard and understood.

**Audio Density.** The quantity of sound usually heard throughout a particular film or tape. Unless it is packed with nonstop dialog, a work that uses predominantly natural sounds (that is, has little or no narration or music) has a low audio density. Similarly, a work in which the only sound is a simple musical score has low audio density. In contrast, a work in which the music and vocal tracks are heard simultaneously has a high audio density, a factor which often makes the sound difficult to follow. Generally, only high and low densities are mentioned.

**Box Art.** Constructing three-dimensional environments in boxes, especially shoe boxes that are placed sideways and used as a diorama or stage for the environment. The term can also mean any manipulation/alteration of boxes, but we use it almost exclusively in the first sense.

**Cameraless Animation.** A film animation technique whereby sequential images are inked or painted on clear leader, or scratched into raw film stock, frame-by-frame to give the illusion of motion when the film is projected. As the name implies, no camera is involved in the production of the film images. This is also known as *scratch and doodle* animation.

**Catalog.** An often wordless film/video in which a series of images focuses narrowly on one subject (such as barnyard fowl, positions of the human hand, or billboard ads) or juxtaposes aspects of 2 or more related subjects (for example, contrasting hand- and machine-made glass or comparing human and animal faces).

**Cel Animation.** A film animation technique which derives its name from the transparent sheets of celluloid that are layered one on top of the other under the camera; characters and backgrounds are painted on different acetate cels and are often developed by different artists. This division of labor is one reason why the technique is used by large cartoon studios such as Disney, Warner Brothers, and UPA (United Producers of America).

**Child Life.** A specific type of program found in health care settings, especially hospitals. Focusing on children, adolescents, and families, such programs endeavor to promote optimal development, maintain normal living patterns, and minimize the psycho-social trauma of hospitalization. Child Life Programs may exist under that name or a variety of different titles, including Activity Therapy, Play Therapy, and Recreation Therapy Programs.

**Child Life Specialist.** As an integral member of the health care team, the Child Life Specialist focuses on the developmental and emotional needs of children and works to humanize the hospital environment. Child Life staff use a range of means to achieve their goals including familiarizing the child and her/his family with the institution, preparing children psychologically and emotionally for medical procedures, offering therapeutic play activities, counseling children and their families, and encouraging active school programs. In ambulatory and inpatient settings, Child Life therapists provide opportunities for children to gain a sense of mastery through activities that incorporate play, learning, self-expression, family involvement, and peer interaction.

**Circular Closure.** The conclusion of a film/video in which the opening images repeat themselves or the main character in a narrative ends up where s/he began. If one were to map such a character's progress on paper, the resulting image would resemble a circle or a similarly closed form.

**Clay Animation.** A form of three-dimensional animation which uses clay, playdough, or plasticine to create characters and environments that are photographed in a manner similar to object animation.

**Closed Circuit.** A television system, often confined to a single building or institution, in which programs are transmitted by direct wire hookup from a central source to a limited number of receivers. Closed-circuit transmission is distinct from both cable television (which serves a larger universe) and broadcast television (which is transmitted by radio waves or satellite signal). Radio signals can also be transmitted by closed-circuit systems.

**Compression.** Packing too much information—aural, visual, or both—into too short a time. The opposite of allowing a narrative to be told through actions.

**Contrapuntal Audiovisual Technique.** A mismatched combination of images and sounds, as in contrapuntal music where 2 or more independent melodies are played simultaneously.

**Cutout Animation.** Flat cutout materials such as paper or cloth are photographed, frame by frame, and moved slightly between frames to create the illusion of motion; unlike clay or object animation, there is little or no dimensionality.

**Dialog.** Words spoken by characters or subjects in conversation.

**Documentary.** A liveaction film/video narrative that shows and/or analyzes people, places, processes, or events with little or no fictionalization.

**Dramatic Narrative.** A film/video story that focuses on the conflict within/among one or more characters.

**Embellishment.** Cinematic emphasis on actions, events, or objects incidental to the central storyline. An example of embellishment is when the camera pans around a room to give socioeconomic and psychological "background" on characters.

**Found Sound.** The audio equivalent of the *objet trouve* in which everyday sounds (fog horns, factory whistles, dripping water, applause, cheers, segments from familiar commercials, etc.) are "orchestrated" to form a music track for a film/video.

**Frame.** A structural device which marks the beginning and/or end of a film/video. There are several common frames, for example: the traditional folktale frame of *once upon a time... happily ever after* used often in narratives; the *sunrise/sunset* chronological frame used in both narratives and documentaries; and the lyrical or rondel frame in which the same imagery starts and ends the film/video.

**Iconographic Animation.** A limited or fairly static type of animation made by photographing two-dimensional graphic art. At times, the camera may pan across or zoom in/out; otherwise, the animation consists of a changing series of stills.

**Illustrative Music.** Programmatic music which sets a mood, evokes an emotion, or mimics real-world sounds. When such music is carefully integrated with events or images it helps viewers, especially the very young, to better interpret a film/video.

**Image/Sound Skim.** A discussion-opening technique which follows a screening. Originated by Richard Lacey, it was designed to help children savor the film or tape and share what they remember with each other in a nonjudgmental way. (For details see the introduction to the book and the video program write-ups.)

**Interactive Programming.** Media programs which are actually affected by children's responses, for example, call-in programs on "live" closed-circuit television productions.

**Kinesthetic.** Having a strong sensation of movement. A sympathetic and almost involuntary muscular response is often stimulated—especially in very young viewers—by the images or a combination of image/sound rhythm in a highly kinesthetic film or video.

**Legibility.** Clarity and decipherability of film/video images.

**Line Animation.** A film animation technique in which a series of simple drawings is created on registered sheets of paper and photographed on an animation stand. Unlike cel animation, the entire image (including background, if any) must be redrawn for each successive sheet of paper.

**List.** A series of film/video images without evident focus.

**Lyric.** A sensuous, emotionally expressive film/video—often brief and without words, the images of which are structured in a way that resembles poetic or musical, rather than narrative, forms.

**Narrative.** A film/video story or account which involves a series of connected events and which can be either true or fictitious.

**Object Animation.** A form of animation whereby three-dimensional objects (such as blocks, peanuts, or *objet trouve*) are photographed one or 2 frames at a time and moved little by little between each shot to create the illusion of continuous motion on film.

**Participatory Programming.** Media programming designed to elicit responses from viewers, vocal or otherwise. In this book the term is used to mean a combination of films or tapes followed by a related arts activity. Prerecorded TV programs may be participatory if they foster follow-up activities that children can share with staff, visitors, and fellow patients.

**Play Therapist.** A psychiatric professional who conducts individual play therapy sessions with pediatric patients.

**Play Therapy.** A technique used to assess a child's conflicts and her/his methods for coping with those conflicts. By means of this technique, a qualified specialist analyzes the child and, using dolls or other toys to play out the disturbing situation/s, directs the child to express his/her feelings about and accept or attempt to resolve those conflicts. Play therapy is one of the many techniques that Child Life Specialists use.

**Pixillation.** A form of animation (used most often with people) in which movement is shot one frame at a time resulting in a twitchy, speeded-up type of motion, an effect which mimics old silent movies and which makes the technique suitable primarily for zany and/or humorous subjects.

**Puppet Animation.** A form of three-dimensional animation using rod puppets, marionettes, or doll-like figures in a manner similar to object animation.

**Reprise.** A summary which involves the repetition of earlier images (and sometimes sounds) in a film/video.

**Scratch and Doodle Animation.** See Cameraless Animation.

**Sound Effects.** Fabricated sounds that are distinct from narration, dialog, and music. Sound effects in liveaction works are usually naturalistic. Cartoon effects are the exaggerated and conventionalized system of sound effects associated with humorous animated shorts.

**Storyteller's Delivery.** A style of voiceover narration in which one person says the narrator's lines as well as the characters' dialog, much the way an old-fashioned storyteller would—distinct from the situation in which one person delivers the narration while others speak the characters' lines.

**Video Wallpaper.** A meditative and minimally edited video recording of such phenomena as tropical fish in a tank, songbirds on a feeder, or various landscapes. Video wallpaper, like a natural environmental sound recording, is designed to be relaxing and soothing.

**Visual Density.** The usual degree of visual crowdedness in a particular film or tape. The amount of background detail, as well as the size and complexity of images, are roughly calculated to indicate how difficult the work will be to read. Simple line animations with no background detail, for example, have low visual density. Liveaction segments shot from a great distance usually have a high degree of visual density. High density (especially of unfamiliar images) is generally difficult for the very young. High visual density can also pose problems for any age when the television screen is far from the viewer. Generally, only high and low densities are discussed.

**Voiceover.** Voice of an unseen narrator or a *thought monolog* by a character who is heard speaking and may even be shown on-screen but does not appear to be talking.

**Wraparound Production.** Studio-shot introductions that precede a film/video, much the way Alistaire Cooke introduces "Masterpiece Theater." In this book, the wraparound described also includes the demonstration of one or more follow-up activities.

*Captain Silas.* Courtesy: Ron McAdow.

*The Princess and the Pea.* Courtesy: Hill-Gatu.

*Curious George Goes to the Hospital.* Courtesy: Churchill Films.

# Introduction

## by Maureen Gaffney

"...the majority of child patients in the hospital, whether acutely or chronically ill, will benefit greatly from any plan under which the needs of their minds are considered to be as important as the needs of their bodies."

**Anna Freud**
*Children in the Hospital*

# TOPIC OUTLINE

# OVERVIEW

There is more to providing quality health care for children in hospitals than attendance to the physical aspects of their illness. Media has become a contributing factor and, depending on what is shown and how it is used, can either help or hinder the complicated process of getting well. Responding to this development, the Media Center for Children (MCC) undertook the Hospitalized Children's Media Project in order to develop ways of using media to make hospitalized children feel good.

To accomplish this, MCC investigated the needs and media preferences of hospitalized children and explored the mechanics of using film, video, and closed-circuit TV programs in hospitals. We worked with health care professionals in developing a model for participatory children's programs and in determining how they could be used to help pediatric patients get better. The results are collected in this handbook for hospital programmers and media producers.

Research and documentation for the project took over 4 years and involved 1,000 children in 8 East Coast hospitals: Belleview Hospital in New York City; Children's Hospital/National Medical Center in Washington DC; Downstate Medical Center in Brooklyn NY; Eastern Maine Medical Center in Bangor ME; Kings County Hospital in Brooklyn NY; New York Hospital in New York City; St. Luke's/Roosevelt Medical Center in New York City; and Westchester County Medical Center in Valhalla NY.

Anne Munzer Bourne was Director of Research during the pilot and film program evaluations, while Mary Ann Renz Bonarti served in that capacity during the evaluations of the closed-circuit television and video programs. Maureen Gaffney, MCC's Executive Director, designed and administered the overall project, gaining first-hand experience for this documentation by working as a researcher at several sites. Other project staff consisted of MCC-based educators with a strong background in the arts and Child Life specialists at participating hospitals. The latter are nonmedical staff who offer "emotional first aid" to help children cope with the effects of being hospitalized.[1] Their knowledge about both the institution and the developmental needs of pediatric patients was indispensable, consequently we worked only in hospitals with active Child Life Programs.

## Why Alternative Media in Hospitals?

One of the chief impediments to appropriate children's programming is the myth of a homogeneous mass child audience. This marketing fiction ignores vast developmental differences that occur in several observable stages up to the age of 14. It ignores ethnic, socioeconomic, geographic, and sexual differences. Likewise, it ignores significant contextual differences that institutions, ranging from schools and museums to libraries and private homes, have for using media with young people. In short, to consider the child audience as a uniform entity is to ignore the needs and expectations of both the child and the institution in which media is used.

Children in hospitals are a special case. Unlike those in schools, children in health care institutions are generally not treated as a group. Every year one child in 15 is hospitalized in the United States and each is given individualized medical treatment. But while it can save the child's life or improve his/her health, the process exacts a serious emotional toll.

By virtue of being hospitalized, children are separated from everything familiar to them—from family, friends, and home. This separation, which many youngsters perceive as abandonment, gives rise to intense anxiety, emotional stress, and often mortal fears. Children's psychological well-being is further undermined by the physical consequences of hospitalization: shots and blood tests often hurt; medications can cause nausea; the intravenous (IV) apparatus restricts movement; and the first effects of an operation could be immobility and intense pain. Added to their own anguish and discomfort, pediatric patients are casually exposed to others' pain—from their parents' distress to the suffering and sometimes death of room- or wardmates. Because of their mental and physical vulnerability, media programs for such children should be designed with their special needs and limitations in mind.

Appropriate programming is the exception rather than the rule in most pediatric facilities. With TV sets now standard equipment in their rooms, young patients spend a great part of each day watching television. Truly a captive audience, they watch TV for many more hours than the disturbingly high national average and they watch programs children were never expected to see, inasmuch as those over 5 would normally be in school.

Daytime soap operas exemplify the problem: not only do characters constantly get into trouble, but apparent progress is always thwarted by an unforeseen setback. Their nerve-wracking lack of resolution generates a mood of frustration and tension that mirrors, perhaps too closely, the hospitalized child's state of mind. In both format and content, soaps hinder recovery by adding to the child's emotional stress.

Reruns of movies with scary or tensely dramatic plots can also be upsetting to pediatric patients. So can movies with behavior, such as rough language, that children know their parents would not approve of. Even apparently benign programs can have unanticipated and undesired consequences in a hospital. For example, a burning barn episode in the "Lassie" series was extremely disturbing to youngsters in a burn ward.

But what does a child know about this? Confined to bed and cut off from almost every other activity, the pediatric patient of today often turns to a TV set for solace. It may be the one thing in the environment that looks familiar. But because the child's perspective has been radically altered as a result of hospitalization, regular television fare (especially during the day) offers small comfort, and solitary viewing may do little except aggravate his/her sense of isolation.

## How MCC Got Involved

Health care professionals have been aware of the need for alternative pediatric programming for some time. Staff from a number of hospitals contacted the Media Center during the late 1970s for assistance in locating appropriate, user-controlled media. However, it was not until 1980 that MCC took a look at hospital programming needs. In the fall of that year pediatric staff from Kings County Hospital asked for help in designing playroom programs that would be both therapeutic and enriching for young psychiatric patients. They were interested in 16mm film screenings, a type of programming about which we were knowledgeable, and the hospital was located within commuting distance of our office.

Before initiating a limited research and development pilot project at Kings County, MCC enlisted a second site since prior experience suggested that single-site research would not provide suffi-

cient data about either the children's or the institution's needs. Then in the spring of 1981, the pilot was incorporated into MCC's ongoing evaluation program, which was supported in part by public funds from the New York State Council on the Arts. For six weeks beginning in April, MCC staff conducted screenings with 6- to 12-year-olds at both the child psychiatric in-patient center of Kings County Hospital and the pediatric medical ward of Downstate Medical Center. We usually worked at one site on Tuesdays, the other on Thursdays.

## MCC's Programming Rationale

The Media Center's programming philosophy is based on the tenet that, in order to integrate new material into his/her store of existing knowledge, a child must act on it in some way. If neither expected nor encouraged to respond, the child's film experience might remain undifferentiated from the ocean of material s/he is exposed to on TV. If unexplored, fleeting impressions of the event might wash over his/her mind and its meaning could become muddled or never be fully absorbed.

We also believed that one of media's best assets was its capacity to be a simultaneously shared, group experience. The last thing we wanted our programs to do was to replace human interaction. To the contrary, we wanted media to foster it!

As an outcome of these convictions, one of MCC's goals for the pilot was to develop a model for participatory group programming in hospitals. We also intended to identify some characteristics of the films that would be most beneficial for patients, as well as to develop an institution-specific evaluation form for documenting the programs' impact. (The form as it finally evolved is in Appendix C.)

To do this, we would build on what we knew. Our research for *What to Do When the Lights Go On* confirmed that a combination of good short films and carefully integrated arts activities could stimulate discovery-based learning and be powerful motivators of children's self-expression.[2] Although our approach had originally been developed for use in museums and libraries, we believed it could be adapted to work in hospitals.

The films would attract participants and focus the group. This would be important because hospitalized children are often strangers to each other. Although their rooms could well be in the same area, patients may have had no opportunity to interact with each other before meeting at a film program. But if films were to be more than mere entertainment, if they were to affect youngsters in a meaningful way, children would have to do something with them.

One course of action would be to talk about them. Such discussions, however, could not be adult-imposed; they would have to be child-centered to be effective.

Another course of action would be to make art in response to the film experience. When germane to the films' content or formal aspects, arts activities allow children to explore the films' meanings in their own terms and on their own levels. But the reciprocity between viewing and making art produces other benefits as well: the direct esthetic stimulation of the films is capable of fostering perseverance and of motivating children to work in more imaginative ways than if they had seen no films at all.

Perseverance and motivation would be essential for success with pediatric patients. So would the manner in which related activities were organized: if appropriately structured, such endeavors would give children both reasonable limits and reachable objectives in an environment that was generally overwhelming.

## Our Format for the Pilot Programs

All pilot programs followed the same basic pattern in that 2 short 16mm films were combined on the basis of some formal or thematic link and introduced by a member of the Media Center's staff. After each film, MCC staff asked children a few questions. Discussion of the second film was followed by an activity that related to the films' content or appearance. Collage, for example, might be the follow-up when one or both films used cutout animation. Other film-complementary arts included drawing and puppet-making. If well matched to what children (not adults) regarded as the films' dominant aspects, the activities would succeed.

We learned from working outside the hospital that a well-selected pair of films was the best lead-in to an expressive arts activity. On the one hand, too many films would deplete the group's energy and the arts activity would suffer. On the other hand, if they saw only one, children sometimes assumed they were supposed to copy it. Consequently, we deliberately used 2 films and selected pairs with contrasts and similarities, hoping that in doing the activity children would personalize and synthesize their experience of both films.

Pairing films had another advantage. Because the odds were against our being able to work with the same group for more than one session, each program had to stand on its own. Pairing allowed for enough variety to reach almost everyone in a given group. One film could appeal more to girls, the other to boys. One could be liveaction, the other animation. One could be funny, the other sweet. One could be a documentary, the other a story. One could be fast, the other slow. And one could have words, the other none—an important factor for children who did not speak English or for whom English was a second language.

## Film Selection Criteria

All the works we chose were in distribution as educational films and were legally available for exhibition to groups if no admission fee was charged. We used films made specifically for children as well as general audience films that were appropriate for and appealing to young viewers. They consisted of dramatic narratives with themes, such as separation and survival, that seemed relevant to hospitalized children; general interest or simple informational films, such as documentary portraits of people or animals; and lyrics—brief and highly cinematic works such as nonnarrative essays or improvisational animations edited to existing music.[3] We avoided "how-to" films because our programming goal was to motivate self-expression, not instruct children in arts and crafts techniques.

In selecting films for the pilot and later, we used the following criteria: first, each was a work of art, enriching rather than didactic and more like good literature than a school text; second, each had been tested and found appealing to nonhospitalized children of the same age range as the patient population; and third, after having been described in writing, discussed, and sometimes screened in advance by Child Life specialists from participating sites, each was deemed appropriate by hospital staff for the children in their care.

Because we worked only with films that MCC had already tested outside the hospital, even broader criteria were implicit in our selections. Among them were that films should excite children about themselves, other people, and the world around them; stimulate their imaginations as well as inform them about reality; and avoid what can be most concisely described as ageism, brutalism, materialism, racism, and sexism.

Although it made no difference in the pilot where we only used 16mm films, the word *film* generally encompasses both film and video. Moreover, since all the titles we used on closed-circuit TV and in the video programs were film transfers, we were able to observe how many of them worked as videos.

## Method of Evaluation

Naturalistic observation/participation, or observation with inquiry, was our means of research. Children's behavior, both verbal and nonverbal, was monitored during a screening; that and their responses to questions, as well as their artwork were documented in writing and analyzed by staff from the Media Center and participating hospitals. During screenings, MCC staff were observed and assisted by Child Life personnel. After every screening we met with hospital staff to discuss the films and activities and their impact on the children.

In both the pilot and later playroom programs, children were selected by Child Life staff, based on information from that day's census. We worked in small groups that were conducive to normal adult-child interaction and which allowed for rapid termination of a film or discussion if anyone became upset. The group situation not only put the least amount of pressure on individuals, it also offered excellent possibilities for comparison in that small-group observation was the method MCC employed with children outside the hospital.

## Results of the Pilot

As expected, pediatric patients were regressed due to the trauma of hospitalization, and seemed to prefer films that otherwise would have been considered young for their ages. We were surprised, however, at the degree to which illness, medication, diminished physical activity, and the stressful overstimulation of the environment hindered their enjoyment of highly kinesthetic films loved by healthy children. Works with a rapid editing pace and a loud musical score were overwhelming for many, particularly for the chronically ill. And although it required further study, it seemed that films without a recognizable structure were unable to hold patients' interest.

Confirming Bergmann's observation that an inhibition of verbal expression often accompanied hospital-induced bed rest, there was a general lack of oral communication among the children with whom we worked.[4] Their minimal response following a screening made children's comments, and discussions in particular, unreliable as a means of evaluating the films. Nonetheless, showing films to a small group elicited children's active participation and, perhaps because their verbalization was so subdued, arts activities became an important vehicle for patients' self-expression.

## Some Necessary Modifications

We tested only 6 programs in the pilot.[5] Each was evaluated with 2 groups, the population of which was diagnostically different. Evidently, we had to conduct further evaluations with diagnostically similar groups and a larger test population before drawing any substantive conclusions. After considering the possibilities, we decided to focus on children in medical wards and hospitals, rather than psychiatric patients, since they were more like the children we worked with outside of hospitals and we thought that comparisons between those populations would be instructive. We then enlisted additional sites and sought funding for an expanded project.

In planning for the next round of playroom evaluations, we added programs for preschool children since they were a sizable part of the pediatric population. While there was also a need for adolescent programming, we had no experience with that age level. The revised playroom film programs were designed with the consultation of Child Life staff at participating sites. Preschool programs were intended for children between the ages of 3 and 6–7, while school age programs were intended for children from 6–7 to 12–13. Both ranges were broad enough to accommodate hospital-induced regression.

The format seemed effective, so the new programs followed the same structure as those in the pilot, with the addition of bilingual, English-Spanish introductions to accommodate the large Hispanic population in our Manhattan sites. We decided, however, to modify our method of evaluation. MCC and hospital staff concurred that less emphasis on children's verbal responses and an increased emphasis on observation (during screenings, afterwards as children did the activities, and in the weeks following) would provide the best information about the programs' effectiveness.

We also modified our criteria for determining which films to use. Affirmatively, films had to foster a sense of hope or successful coping with difficulties. Prohibitively, they had to avoid images that would make hospitalized children feel bad about themselves, such as those in which people with disfiguring scar tissue or amputated limbs were presented in a negative or demeaning manner.

One of the films we tried in the pilot, but not afterwards, illustrates these issues. HANSEL AND GRETEL, AN APPALACHIAN VERSION is a 16-minute, liveaction adaptation of the Grimm folktale which is made and distributed by Tom Davenport in Delaplane, Virginia. Shot in a gripping, documentary style with realistic sets and actors, it was (and still is) one of the most successful films we had ever shown to nonhospitalized children between the ages of four and twelve. Because of this, because its child protagonists successfully cope with and survive a terrible ordeal, and because the filmmaker made it as a consequence of his preschool child's hospitalization, we thought it would be relevant to pediatric patients.

Although the film seemed to work better in the psychiatric ward than in the medical ward, we got no satisfactory reading of children's responses from the pilot. Yet when we proposed it to consultants who worked with us subsequently, they thought that its theme of abandonment in a life-threatening environment was too close an analogy to children's view of hospitalization, and that it generated a mood of too much tension and contained too many threatening images—from skulls and bones to a "butchering" knife and a "cremating" oven. In addition, the witch's make-up made her look like a burn victim, and being associated with an evil witch would not help the self-esteem of children who happened to be scarred by burns. All of this, they felt, outweighed the film's positive theme. While agreeing that HANSEL AND GRETEL, AN APPALACHIAN VERSION could have therapeutic potential once children left the hospital, most of our Child Life consultants did not consider it appropriate for in-hospital viewing, so we dropped it from subsequent programming.

Another pilot film that we decided not to use later in the project illuminates a different aspect of depiction. The film was CECILY by Pavla Reznickova which is distributed by Coronet/MTI. This 7-minute cutout animation tells the story of an abused child whose ears become enlarged—even elephantine—as a result of her grandmother's constant pulling. When Cecily can take no more, she runs away (actually she flies, using her huge ears) and finds happiness as the leader of an elephant chorus. Although she is eventually reconciled and reunited with her repentant grandmother and father, our consultants did not want to try the film because of a scene in which Cecily is mocked by the local townspeople. Since a child in one of our sites had been severely abused and beaten about the head until his ears were flat and over-large, staff there were afraid the film might stimulate other patients to mock the boy who not only looked different (because of his elephantine ears) but acted strange (because he had been locked in a closet for 6 years). Not everyone was convinced that children would imitate the scene's negative behavior and it would have been interesting to find out, but we were not willing to risk it. If we could have cut the problematic scene, we might have tried CECILY with school age children; since we could not, we dropped it.

## The Pediatric Programming Challenge

Planning pediatric programs was made complex, not only by children's psychological vulnerability, but also by their ethnic composition and economic levels. As in many large cities throughout the country, the greatest percentage of children in our New York and District of Columbia sites were minorities. Moreover, except in Bangor and Westchester, our sites had sizable chronic populations despite being designated acute-care facilities. Interestingly, the largest number of chronically ill children were indigent.

Such a population profile assumes critical significance when one sees that the majority of media productions focus on people of upper socioeconomic levels and do not begin to address the needs of indigent, minority youngsters. In response, we included as many films as possible that depicted minority children or dealt with the cultures of African- and Asian-Americans, as well as those of Native Peoples. (Although we wanted to include them, we knew of no good, hospital-appropriate films dealing with Latin-American culture; the ones that might have been appropriate in terms of content or theme suffered from being either culturally inaccurate or substandard productions. To compensate for this lack, we decided to use Spanish in our introductions.) We also avoided films with gratuitous affluence.

The fact that children's states of health varied greatly simply added to the programming challenge. Over and above injuries caused by accidents such as falls, burns, or being hit by an automobile, the nearly 1,000 children we observed and documented following the pilot had a range of illnesses that included kidney disease, cancer, blood disorders, Hodgkins Disease, spina bifida, sickle cell anemia, and child abuse. (An illness breakdown appears in Appendix D.) Since there was no way we could address the entire range of illness, we strove for a level of programming that would be accessible to children in fair or better physical and mental condition.

A great number of our programs were designed to furnish general enrichment experiences. They dealt with seasons, animals or adventures and we hoped they would offer children a pleasant escape from the hospital. Our goal for this type of programming was to reinforce everyday "normalcy." With the exception of CURIOUS GEORGE GOES TO THE HOSPITAL, MADELINE, and PIERRE, the remaining programs used folktales or stories with themes that paralleled but did not directly touch on issues related to hospitalization or illness. Our goal for the latter was to offer children metaphors for their problems, fears, and hopes. We expected the programs to provide symbolic support that, together with sympathetic human interaction, would mitigate the pediatric patient's terrible sense of aloneness.

## A Fully Developed Project Followed

The full-scale project began in August 1982 with start-up funding of $25,000 from the Louis B. Mayer Foundation. This was matched by an initial Ruth Mott Fund grant of $25,000 and a renewal grant of $15,000. Additional funding came from the Association for the Care of Children's Health, the Jones Foundation, the McDonald's Corporation, the National Endowment for the Arts, the New York State Council on the Arts, the United Hospital Fund of New York, and several individuals. While the contributions made by our Child Life consultants are inestimable, services from other individuals and goods from filmmakers or distributors amounted to nearly $24,000. This brought the overall level of support for the entire project (including the pilot, development, and final documentation phases) to just over $200,000.

Following several months of planning, we evaluated 30 playroom film programs during the first third of 1983 at 3 New York City sites. Then, using those programs as our model, we produced a closed-circuit TV series which was evaluated in May, June, and August 1983 at 4 sites, one in Washington DC, one in Bangor, and 2 in New York City.

In testing the film programs it became evident that daytime screenings presented unique problems in a hospital. Although film had esthetic advantages and was a better large-group format, we began to think that video might have significant advantages, psychological as well as mechanical. Not only was darkening the playroom to view films upsetting to some children, but at certain sites it was virtually impossible. The idea of using video seemed compelling, both because it could be watched in a well-lit environment and because the TV set was a familiar "piece of furniture" about which children had generally positive associations. On top of this, cassettes were easy to handle in terms of loading and rewinding. (The few difficulties we had were caused by poor maintenance of playroom video-cassette players or VCRs.) Although it is only a recent development, price differences now make video considerably more appealing than film.

Consequently, after documenting both the film and CCTV programs, we planned a series of 24 playroom video programs which were made with films transferred to tape. The video programs incorporated all we had learned. From January through April 1984, they were evaluated at 5 sites in the metropolitan New York area.

Besides the field tests just mentioned, we also undertook several surveys among hospitals in the US and Canada to determine how they were using media with pediatric patients. (A report on our findings is in Appendix A.)

## A Sketch of Pediatric Needs & Preferences

In the course of the project we discovered that hospitalized children were more susceptible to media than we had imagined. Chronically ill preschoolers were under-socialized and so under-exposed to real life that TV programs often became their most significant experience of the outside world. This profoundly increased the impact of both appropriate and inappropriate media on children of this age range, and increased the importance of group screenings for preschoolers hospitalized on a long-term basis.

Our testing also highlighted children's likes and dislikes, as well as some of their needs in terms of production styles. For one thing, many pediatric patients found structurally complex films incomprehensible. And because of their high levels of distraction (physical, psychological, and environmental), they only attended to productions in which the soundtrack and visual imagery were well integrated. It was easier for them to follow a narrative if actions, not dialog or narration alone, were used to move the plot along. Put another way, stories worked best when actions visually reinforced what was said. Hospitalized children also seemed to lack the whatever-it-takes to correct editing errors (the cinematic equivalent of typos) or fill in gaps in a film.

Besides a clear and well-defined structure, productions required a closure recognizable as such to the pediatric audience. Lack of closure was one of the things that made L'AGE DOOR and perhaps to some extent ARROW TO THE SUN less than appealing to this audience. Until s/he is released from the hospital, the "story" of a child's illness does not come to a satisfactory close. For this reason it was important to avoid narrative structures that, like TV soaps, too closely resembled the patient's experience.

Doubtless due to their high levels of anxiety, children exhibited a marked preference for material that reassured, consoled, or relaxed them. They responded extremely well to pleasant, nonnarrative lyrics (dubbed music videos) such as HOMMAGE A FRANCOIS COUPERIN, ISLE OF JOY, TANGRAM, and WORM DANCES. And certain themes or content areas met with universal approval from both the children and the Child Life specialists with whom we worked; the most noteworthy were narratives about overcoming obstacles, stories with safe-return-home endings, and works in which tenderness and nurturing were emphasized.

# THE PLAYROOM PROGRAMS

Children enter a hospital for treatment so they can get better and go home. At best, they are ambivalent about being there. Even with adult explanations, youngsters who are seriously ill seldom fully understand what is happening to them or why. As a result, they become confused, frightened, and angry. Worse yet, many become depressed.

Aggravating all of this is the fact that hospitalization severely disrupts children's patterns of living. Removed from their homes and usual activities, they are placed in an unfamiliar institution where unpleasant things happen as a matter of course. Wards are full of veritable strangers, so young patients get little or no privacy. And despite good intentions, medical personnel often handle children like laboratory specimens, applying medications and conducting treatments with little regard for what the child is doing or how s/he feels.

To help remedy this, the playroom is set up as a safety zone. In such rooms, patients are given outlets for self-expression by means of free play, arts and crafts, or other activities that allow them to gain a sense of control. Children are also protected there, in that medical procedures, shots, etc. are forbidden and hospital staff cannot remove youngsters from the playroom without their consent.

Besides their positive, nonmedical associations, playrooms often had the advantage of being located in areas with minimal traffic and noise. Consequently, programs conducted there were less subject to distraction or interruption than elsewhere in the ward. Because of this, we conducted our programs in playrooms whenever possible; although, at times, we worked in a lounge or a library if the playroom was not available.

## Screening Arrangements

Both film and video programs were conducted once a week on the same day (Tuesday, Wednesday, or Thursday), in the same room, for a period of 12 weeks to avoid the effect of a "one shot" event and to get a sense of how our approach would work over time. Programs for preschoolers started at about 10:00, after morning rounds were done, while those for children of school age began at 2:30 in the afternoon.

Sessions for both age groups were planned to last between 70 and 90 minutes. Films ranged in length from 3 to 17 minutes each and the total running time for a pair never exceeded half an hour. Introductions and follow-up discussions took from 5 to 20 minutes. The arts activities used the time remaining.

Groups were generally small. We worked with anywhere from 2 to 10 children, often all the patients on a floor who were not undergoing tests or medical procedures yet who were well enough to come to the playroom. Although the age range 6-7 usually divided preschool and school age programs, those boundaries were not rigidly enforced. If a preadolescent wanted to attend a preschool program, we did not stop her/him. For lack of anything better to do we often had teenagers in school age programs. And sometimes children under 7 came to a school age program, particularly if they had missed the one in the morning. While this muddied our results a bit, we did not refuse children admittance unless the program would be frightening (as with SOLO) or otherwise inappropriate. Generally, it was our philosophy to "go with the flow" since we wanted the programs to work under real hospital conditions—not be an ideal impossible to replicate.

A typical group included about 5 children and sometimes, especially with preschoolers, a parent or two. Evaluation personnel included one or two MCC staffers and one or more Child Life specialists. With small groups, the minimal adult-child ratio was 2 to 5; sometimes it was 1 to 1. When groups were large, we recruited sufficient help to keep the ratio at around 1 to 3. However, we avoided having more adults than children since it worked against group dynamics.

In addition to screening the children, Child Life staff explained the programs to parents. This was made somewhat easier by a press release describing the project that we distributed to nursing staff and posted in the ward prior to the first screening. Copies were also available for parents. The release explained that while not invited to participate during the research phase (since their presence significantly altered children's responses), parents would be welcomed to subsequent programs.

Their exclusion presented no problems for children of school age, but it did for preschoolers, a number of whom would not come to a program without their mothers. Consequently, some parents participated in the screenings. Most were fine and the interaction between parent and child was beneficial to both. It may be helpful, however, to mention the few "problem parents" who coerced their children—possibly to perform well for us. One insisted that her child watch a film he was obviously upset by. A few others either told their children how to do the activity "correctly" or did it for them. Naturally, this went against everything we were trying to do but there was not much we could say. A better explanation of our objectives might have helped; but perhaps not, since the parents of hospitalized children are often stretched to their emotional limits. As it was, we managed despite these few anomalies.

## Introductions

In the course of our research, we learned it was absolutely essential to initiate some sort of dialog with children before a program began. Compared to nonhospitalized children, pediatric patients needed significant encouragement to respond and interact. We therefore did a great deal of reaching out, making eye-to-eye and sometimes hand-to-hand contact with each child, and introducing ourselves as soon as they or we entered the room.

After clarifying that we were not doctors, we explained that the group was going to watch two short films or videos, discuss them briefly, and do an arts activity. We did not say "movies" because to children that meant feature-length films and set up expectations we could not fulfill. Before projecting a film, we warned very young or infirm patients that we were going to turn the lights off to see the film, but would put them on again when it was done.

In introducing each film or tape, we simply told children what to expect. This was indispensable with works that were unconventional. Accordingly, we told them when a film had no words and whether or not it had a story. If there was no story, we explained by analogy what it was like, such as a song, a dream, a journey, and so on. We described its pace if it was unusually fast or slow. And we summarized what it was about if that would not be immediately obvious to children of their age, experience, or condition. In essence, we focused on a film's distinctive characteristics or aspects.

| Subject | What is it about? |
|---|---|
| Technique | How does it look or sound? |
| Length | Is it short or very short? |
| Pace | Is it very fast or very slow? |
| Genre | If it's a story, what type is it? |
| | If it has no story, what's it like? |
| Mood | Is it quiet, funny, scary, etc.? |

Too much information was overwhelming. For this reason, we did not mention some aspects if they were fairly conventional. If the production was a normal looking and sounding liveaction, we did not elaborate about its technique. If it was neither fast nor slow, we did not refer to pace. And taking into account our earlier explanation that we were going to see shorts, we did not mention length unless a film was extremely brief.

With dramatic stories, we told preschoolers who the featured characters were. If such stories were gripping, we always told everyone—even older children—that things would work out all right in the end. We learned early on that this sort of reassurance was vital for an audience as beset with fears and anxieties as pediatric patients are.

The right kind and amount of preparation helped children correctly interpret what they would see and hear, yet our failures taught us not to make introductions didactic or overlong. The introduction to THE STORY OF CHRISTMAS (in Playroom Video Program #11) is a perfect example of what *not* to do. From it and others we learned that introductions had to be more involving than factual. Likewise, we discovered that we had to reinforce what we said with demonstrations or hands-on activities. For the very young or the very ill, this was an absolute requirement.

In addition to essential facts (from the box above), our best introductions matched the film's tone and set children thinking in ways that had some bearing on its content. The introductions to TANGRAM (in Playroom Film Program #4) and to ISLE OF JOY (in Playroom Film Program #14) are good examples of how we introduced lyrics, the hardest type of film to develop an introduction for.

Often we used simple, interactive games (some as basic as labeling) that continued during the screening. Sometimes, for example, when introducing a detective film, we would use a riddle to involve children in the process of problem-solving. However, it was important to use riddles of instrumentality, avoiding riddles of motivation (*Why did the chicken cross the road?*) or attribution (*What is black and white and red all over?*). Riddles of instrumentality, which deal with cause and effect and use the *"How do you...?"* format, more closely parallel the type of thinking a detective uses. Introductions are modeled in the video program write-ups that follow in this book.

## Talking During a Screening

We always encouraged children to talk out loud while they watched a film. Parents sometimes considered this a breach of etiquette, but our experience confirmed that such talking fostered a more active mental processing of the film. If one child expressed confusion, for instance, another often volunteered an explanation of what was happening. Talking also allowed us to monitor children's responses. If one expressed fear, we could reassure the child, take her/him out of the room until the film was over, or stop the film—whichever seemed appropriate.

Before a film began, we told children they could talk when it was on, and often reassured them throughout the screening that it was okay to talk aloud. Due partly to self-consciousness and partly to socialization, school age children were generally taciturn and required considerable coaxing; it was relatively easy to get preschoolers to respond. Regardless of age, if a group was silent as they watched, we prompted them with nonrestrictive questions. At timely moments we would ask, "What's that?" or "What's happening now?" or "Why is s/he doing that?"

Aside from their condition, children's level of verbalization was most affected by whether or not a film had words and they tended to be more vocal during nonverbal films. Typical responses involved labeling or evaluating what they saw, asking questions about or explaining what was happening, and talking directly to characters. Sometimes children anticipated events, both correctly and incorrectly.

Talking this way never became a problem. If one child spoke too loud for the comfort of a neighbor, we asked the child to talk a little quieter. With preschoolers, an adult moved closer to or held a particularly noisy child so s/he would know we were listening. As a rule, having access to others' comments and explanations throughout a screening helped younger or less-well children stay with films they would otherwise have had trouble following. At the same time, the process loosened children up for subsequent interaction. And with nonnarrative or nonverbal films, talking during the screening was often essential to their success.

## Repeat Screenings

Normally children like to see appealing films again and again, the same way they like to reread or have someone reread them well-liked stories. But in an environment where everything is changing and not always for the better, repeating a pleasant experience has special significance. We thus found it highly effective to repeat films or entire programs if pediatric patients enjoyed the experience, particularly if they requested it.

It has been our experience in schools and other screening situations outside the hospital that chil-

dren will spontaneously ask to see very short films again. Because of this, we had planned to repeat them in our playroom programs (as well as on CCTV). The only time we did not do so was when children responded negatively to our inquiry, but, interestingly, they almost always said yes. Sometimes they asked to see a film again before we even mentioned it and sometimes they asked to see the same film over and over. Usually, each time they saw it—whether for the second, third, or fourth time, children enjoyed the film more and got more out of it. Frequently, they became more vocal each time.

In playroom programs, we repeated very short works immediately. With films over 10 minutes in duration, we had to consider children's energy levels, how much time was left, how many actually wanted to see it again, and similar issues. Sometimes we did it later the same day, sometimes another day. If it was at all possible, however, we rescreened whatever children wanted to see. Such child/user-control was regarded by hospital staff as a special benefit of this type of programming.

## Discussions & the Image/Sound Skim

The level of discussion pediatric patients reached was far short of what healthy children were capable of. But to whatever extent possible, we held a group discussion following each film. Preschoolers often did their most film-related talking during a screening, but they were sometimes capable of doing the image/sound skim (described below). After that, what talk there was often lapsed into individual and sometimes simultaneous monologs. Older children could usually do the image/sound skim, but the extent of subsequent discussion depended on their states of health, their cohesion as a group, and the issues a film raised.

What could be called the formal discussion began in the same way each time. Its predictability seemed reassuring and responses often increased after the second film, so we followed every film with an image/sound skim.[6] In addition to allowing them to share personal recollections and observations without fear of giving a wrong answer, the image/sound skim revealed which aspects of a film were most salient to children.

The process itself was begun by asking some version of: "What images or sounds do you remember most clearly from the film?" Before children could actually reply, we often repeated the question, rephrasing and amplifying it to make sure they understood what we meant: "Was there anything you saw or heard in the film that sticks out in your mind?" After a few responses (if any), we would go on if coaxing elicited no more.

When young children seemed up to it, we might follow the image/sound skim by asking them to tell us what happened in the film. With older children, we might ask how it made them feel, and which characters (if it had any) they liked best or least. Sometimes we asked film-specific questions (which are modeled in the video program write-ups). But if nothing else, we made sure to ask children whether there was anything they did not understand, or whether anyone had questions about the film.

Except that it began with a predictable opening and closing (see below), we were not rigid about how the discussion progressed. Quite the contrary. We followed children's leads when they were interested in talking about particular aspects of a film or the associations it produced. If it raised issues they considered important, we explored them. If not, we asked a few questions, then stopped, leaving the door open for one-to-one conversations with children while they did their art.

To terminate our formal discussion period, however long, we asked children to rate each film using one of 5 ratings: super, good, okay, bad, and terrible. Children, especially those of school age, thoroughly enjoyed the ratings which served as a tangible indication to them that their opinions counted. (The ratings were also a gauge of each film's emotional appeal. However, to adjust for the fact that children did not consider motivational aspects and were biased in favor of stories, we discounted low ratings of a nonnarrative film if youngsters had been positively involved as they watched and had followed it with a meaningful activity.)

## Arts Activities

Evident responses might be minimal during a screening or in the time set aside for a group discussion, but children manifested strong expressions of feeling (both verbal and nonverbal) when they did their arts activities. Both because of and to encourage this, the greatest amount of time in each program (anywhere from 45 to 60 minutes) was dedicated to the activity. And despite our consultants' concerns about children's endurance, the entire allocation was used most of the time. Although older children might work for a relatively longer period, when preschoolers finished an activity they often stayed in the room, playing until the program officially ended.

In general, follow-ups to the films were mechanically simple. For one thing, they had to be feasible for pediatric patients, nearly half of whom (in our experience) had one hand hampered by an IV needle. For another, we wanted them to be manageable for adults, especially volunteers, with little or no training in the arts. Thus in developing activities, we avoided difficult ones, such as group movement, and concentrated on visual arts, such as collage and drawing; plastic arts, such as sculpture and box art; and language arts, such as talking and storytelling. Some programs, however, were followed with block play, dramatic play, mask-making, puppetry, music, board games, and puzzles. (A complete listing is found in the Index of Follow-up Activities.)

Most activities called for typical art supplies and materials, although some also used found objects. (Required supplies are listed in each program write-up.) As a rule, it was not essential to have a sink in the room. However, paper towels and a basin of water, as well as some form of hand wipes were necessary, since hospitalized children often became fastidious and many insisted on cleaning their hands at regular intervals while doing the activities. It was also a good idea to have paper, pencils, and crayons (or the much-coveted markers) on hand as back-ups no matter what else was planned; that way, if a child did not like the proposed activity, s/he could draw. And somehow or another, we always seemed to find a use for masking tape, but more as equipment than as material for making art. When glue cups tipped too easily, masking tape kept them upright; when a child's drawing slid around the table because s/he had a cast on the arm that would otherwise have held it, masking tape fixed the paper in place. (If you can afford them, glue-sticks are much easier for hospitalized children to handle than liquid glue.)

To succeed, activities had to be both stimulating and reassuring. Films generally provided the stimulation (of a subject or a new approach to design), while familiar materials and a well-defined structure for doing the follow-ups provided the reassurance. In addition to selecting appropriate materials, we focused children's energies by developing a predictable routine that was followed with each and every activity, no matter how varied.

When the second film discussion was through, we explained and demonstrated what children were going to do. We found it helpful to have at least 2 samples of the activity to model, one in the early stages of development and the other finished. Both were kept quite basic in order to be nonthreatening. As they observed, we would add a few details to the work in progress, often soliciting children's advice about which color to use or where to place an element. Then, before going on to the nuts and bolts of what they were to do, we asked if there were any questions.

Following that, we indicated which materials children would work with, and where. Since groups were small, everybody usually fit around one large table. If not on the table in front of them, we showed them where supplies were, and explained any limitations. When children made box art, for example, we said that initially they could take only ten objects from the supply table, but they could go back later if they needed more. Then, once again, we asked if anyone had questions. When they were ready to begin work, we told children (especially those of school age) how long they had before the program was scheduled to end. If they were still working as the time to stop drew near, we gave them a 15-minute warning. Subsequently, we gave them 10- and 5-minute warnings. After the last, we asked them to finish and suggested they start to clean up if they could.

While they worked, each adult sat near one or more children and asked if anyone needed help. We regularly asked children to tell us about their artwork as it progressed. And we praised their various modes of self-expression, admiring colors, shapes, and designs when there were not more specific aspects to discuss.

Except when a child was incapacitated, we generally ignored the *moment of terror* children exhibited as they considered what to do. Whenever possible, we encouraged them to solve their own creative problems. If a child seemed blocked, we asked open-ended questions about alternative approaches. *Could you do that another way? How about trying something you're more familiar with?* But assistance was crucial in situations that involved mechanical difficulties. If a child's IV apparatus was fixed to her dominant hand, for instance, she might be unable to use scissors to make a collage; so we would cut out shapes following the child's instructions or show her how to tear the paper.

Children often seemed apprehensive at the start of an activity if it was their first time at a program, but we were constantly amazed at their resilience. A burn patient of about 6 is a classic example of this phenomenon. When the boy came to his first program, clay sculpture was the follow-up, and we were totally nonplussed to discover that he could work with neither of his hands. He seemed quite subdued as the activity began, but he did it by telling an adult, who worked one-on-one with him, what shapes to make and what colors to use. However, the real surprise was yet to come. Once the adult had lined up a row of small clay animals on the table in front of him, the boy spontaneously smashed them, one by one, with his chin. On a certain level he was venting his anger, but on another level he was having fun. After the first one, everybody at the table applauded as he smashed the remaining creatures. It is interesting to consider that in so doing, he was touching the clay with the only part of his body he could use. And if the expression on his face was any indication, it felt good.

## Therapeutic Impact

Certain films and some activities worked better than others, but as a whole, children enjoyed the combination of screenings, arts activities, and fellowship.

On one hand, the programs fostered a closeness among participants. But at the same time, successful programs seemed to allow patients a certain distance from their predicament. That distance, coupled with the supportive presence of peers and adults, produced a situation in which children felt free to express, either directly or symbolically through their artwork, many things that were on their minds, including concerns about their illnesses, confusions about hospitalization, and fears of abandonment.

The focus and group structure of the programs had a positive impact. For preschoolers who slept in cage-like cribs, it was highly beneficial. "The film/activity program would be the first thing children did on Thursday morning, so it was a real coming out of isolation," noted Ann Touhey, who ran the preschool playroom at Bellevue. "For the very youngest," she added, "the group structure was the most gratifying aspect of the program." It was equally important for school age patients, and once the focus had been established, even shy children joined in.

Fran Tellner, Director of the Child Life Program at New York Hospital, concluded that the normalcy of the group situation reinforced the idea that children were getting well. It also facilitated subsequent socialization. "When children go back to their rooms," observed Kirsten De Bear, who ran St. Luke's playroom, "the fact that they were once in a group with so-and-so makes it easier for them to form relationships on their own."

The regularity and continuity of the programs gave children something to look forward to. Older children, particularly those hospitalized for a few weeks, kept track of when the next program would be, and, at sites where it was closed after lunch, a queue would form outside the playroom just before the afternoon session was scheduled to begin. Ranging in age from 6 to 16, patients would line up in wheelchairs and on foot, with mobile IV units in tow, eagerly awaiting "the film ladies."

Children of all ages who had attended one program looked forward to coming again. "Once they knew what to expect, they seemed to gain control over what was happening," noted Nancy McFarland, a Child Life specialist from New York Hospital. "Some even acted as leaders with newer kids." When there was a broad age span, older children often helped younger ones with their artwork.

Not unimportantly, programs also had the beneficial effect of increasing hospital staff's awareness of children's feelings, attitudes, and abilities. At times they gave rise to meaningful diagnostic information.

In considering how they could use them, the majority of our consultants believed that a regular and consistent schedule for the playroom programs would be most effective. However, staff at one site thought it might work better, at least with preadolescents, to offer them on a spontaneous basis.

## A Word about Volunteers

The success of a playroom screening depends to a large extent on the rapport facilitators can develop with children. Based on MCC's criteria for hiring program staff and on our somewhat limited experience with volunteers and college interns (one of whom was dismissed after a few days as unacceptable), we will outline what we regard as the basic requirements for an effective facilitator. First, s/he must like children and be able to relax with as well as relate to them. Second, s/he must be a good observer and a sensitive listener. Third, s/he must be willing to follow children's leads—not rigidly impose an adult schema; among other things, this means s/he must be able to assist, not instruct, children in expressing themselves through art. Fourth, s/he must not be afraid to get a little artistic mess on his/her clothes (which is why jeans and such were invented). Fifth, although s/he need not know much about media, s/he should not be afraid of technology. And last, the ironic duo, while s/he must be patient with the inevitable hospital delays, s/he must show up well in advance of when a program is scheduled in order to set up the room, the equipment, and the art supplies as well as to review who might attend with the Child Life and/or nursing staff. Facilitators do not need any artistic skills to speak of, but a sense of humor is invaluable.

Before someone actually conducts a program it is essential to rehearse with them how to operate the equipment and discuss the things that can go wrong technically. With film, preparation involves learning how to darken the room; load the projector (with auto-load projectors that may include clipping the leader and unlocking the load mechanism after the film has worked its way through); secure the take-up reels so they do not fly off the machine; make sure the film is correctly looped and all gates are locked in manual-load machines (then run the film while doing the following); check the bulb that projects the image; check the bulb that triggers the sound (and know where to find spares for both); adjust the volume; focus the image and center the frame (if needed); rewind the film so it stops just before the title; play the film all the way through; rewind it tails-out; tape the end down with masking tape (never cellophane tape) so it will not unwind and get scratched; and replace it in its can.

Video preparation involves learning how to turn on both the player and the monitor (selecting the video or VCR mode if the player also has TV capabilities); choose the correct video channel (check with your technical staff, but it is usually channel 3 or 4); load the cassette (and run it while doing the following); select the appropriate audio track if you do not hear any sound (some ¾-inch machines offer 3, one of which may be a mix of tracks #1 and #2); adjust the image tracking and/or skew devices (if the tape has funny lines in it); adjust the volume, brightness, tint, and contrast (if needed); rewind the cassette so it stops just before the titles come up; play the cassette; rewind it completely; and eject it.

Although it probably goes without saying, it is best to model one or more sessions and let the would-be facilitator assist during them. It also helps if someone can assist a facilitator during his/her first few sessions—at least until s/he feels comfortable enough with the equipment, the art supplies, and the children to tackle a program alone.

It did not come up in relation to a volunteer, but there is one more thing to consider—one which arose for us at the beginning of the project. When Mary Ann Renz Bonarti was asked to participate in the research, she was afraid she might not be able to work with hospitalized children. To determine whether she could or not, she visited one of our sites and toured the wards and playrooms. The director of Child Life remarked during that visit that she worried more about people who were not concerned about whether they could work with hospitalized children than with those who confronted the issue up-front. Thus reassured, Mary Ann took the job and even became Director of Research for the latter half of the project. But this sort of work is not for everyone.

# THE CCTV PROGRAMS

Closed-circuit television programs can reach a greater proportion of the pediatric population with less staff than playroom programs, and Elizabeth Crocker makes a compelling argument for "live" CCTV programming in her report in Appendix B. Such programming, however, can only be televised each day for a few hours, so how is a hospital to occupy the rest of the day with appropriate alternatives to regular TV fare?

It was in response to this question that the Media Center developed the model for its CCTV programs. As in our playroom programs, we were concerned about the programs' social and environmental impact. Unless programs were interactive or participatory, they would do little to counteract the isolation TV viewing itself imposed. Thus we designed participatory programs that would facilitate socialization. But, due to the differing viewing situations, our CCTV programs did not have the same impact as the playroom programs, although many were highly beneficial and the series was better than the alternative of daytime TV.

To our chagrin we learned that one of the biggest differences between the film and TV formats is the programmer's control or lack of control over what happens during a show. When children watch TV programs in their rooms, no adult is there to help focus attention distracted by roommates, visitors, and the dozen or more unpredictable hospital noises from the paging of staff over public address systems to phone calls, crying wardmates, and the sounds of other programs on different monitors. And no adult is there to postpone shots, painful procedures, or other medical business that interrupts patients' viewing. While ward distractions are not all negative, they do pose special problems for CCTV programs—especially for those that go beyond mindless entertainment or simple diversion and depend on a more active response from children. Moreover, they make both careful scheduling and the support of the nursing/medical staff requisites for success.

## Program Design and Evaluation

In our closed-circuit television programming, we wanted to replicate as closely as possible the type of participation developed in our original playroom film programs. With this objective in mind, we designed an experimental series and produced 13 programs, each of which ran for about 30 minutes and generally followed the playroom model. Some used the same combination of films (transferred to video), while others were variations on the earlier pairings.

In addition to the fact that one was prerecorded and one was live, there were other differences between the CCTV and the film programs. First was the audience; the overall series was roughly targeted for children aged 5 to 10, the broadest audience we thought we could reach. Second, each program had two hosts, instead of one facilitator, which was an attempt on our part to determine children's preferences for the host's sex and personality type, as well as to see if two hosts might have a broader appeal than one. And third, a special activity sheet was designed for each program in order to encourage viewers to do the activity.

Occasionally we used CCTV programs in a playroom or lounge with small groups, especially at one site which had minuscule 7″ monitors in children's rooms. However, a typical CCTV screening involved one child who watched a program from bed in his/her room. Sometimes 2 or 3 children in a room would watch together. This being the case, our approach to evaluation was different from that of the playroom in that selected children from the target audience were observed and interviewed, each in her/his own room by one MCC researcher.

The screening schedule was also distinct in that we evaluated from 2 to 4 programs a day. At some sites, we did one program in the morning and one in the afternoon. At others, we did 2 each in the morning and afternoon. In one site we experimented with repeating the most appealing programs later the same day or a few days later.

In so doing, we learned that the ideal time for our series was during the rest period following lunch. Scheduling programs too early, before morning rounds were done, was disastrous. But late morning was not a great time either because those who would have been our best audience (that is, school age children in fairly good condition) were usually in the hospital school. And lunch time was no good because the arrival and removal of food was highly distracting; furthermore, there was not enough room on children's bed trays for both the food and the art materials. We also observed that, besides not minding when programs were repeated, children liked seeing the more appealing ones again, and often did better activities the second time they saw a program.

Because viewers would not have the reinforcement of a group, we generally expected the CCTV activities to last for half an hour at most. To facilitate this, we sometimes repeated a program immediately after it was televised, so children could watch it—not something entirely unrelated—while they did the activity. (This was not the same as the rescreenings mentioned above which were separated by substantial amounts of time.) Sometimes nothing was televised following our programs. And although we did not try it in this context, it might have worked to follow our programs with "video wallpaper."

Children had to be able to see the programs in order to get what they offered, so their impact was determined to some degree by the condition of the television equipment, including how large the monitor was and where it was placed. In one hospital, TV sets were located near the ceiling about 12 or 14 feet from children's heads; it did not help that the best way to see the angled screen was to lie down. At another site, monitors were so small (7″) that children practically needed a magnifying glass to see details, but at least the TVs were mounted near children's beds and could be brought close by means of a jointed metal arm. The tiny size of these "personal" sets, however, worked against making the viewing experience social.

After 9 weeks of testing, our data indicated that some things worked and some did not. Aspects of the overall series, as well as a number of programs, needed revision. While many succeeded in encouraging children to do the activity demonstrated in the telecast, only half were successful with the full target audience.

## Proposed Revisions

The fairly experimental CCTV series was the Media Center's initial attempt at television production. In designing it we made what hindsight informs us were a number of errors. However, since they had no notably adverse effects on our audience, they were not particularly troublesome. Rather, as can happen, our mistakes sometimes taught us more than our successes. At the very least, they helped clarify our thinking about how to do this sort of programming.

Although its shortcomings will be corrected if we produce a revised series (as we hope to do), much of what we learned was actually incorporated into our video playroom programs. Still, whether or not we do a revision, the insights resulting from the original series may be useful to others. Thus ʿthe first thing we would alter is our studio-shot introductions and activity demonstrations (the wraparound). These segments featured a gentle Hispanic man and a feisty Irish-American woman who interacted with each other and with the audience/camera. We found, however, that the attention of those under 9 tended to wander unless the person on-screen seemed to be speaking directly to them. In a finished version of the CCTV series, the wraparound will be reshot with one personable actor talking directly to viewers. We would have to do further tests to determine whether the host should be male or female, but we think s/he should probably be a minority representative.

In preparation for the CCTV production, we asked our actor/hosts to work with hospitalized children and get a sense of their audience. Although each presented film programs, the woman (who had worked on the project from the very beginning) was more effective on TV. Part of her success was due to her professionalism (both as an educator and an actor) and part of it was due to her personality. But sensitivity was also a significant factor; she neither over- nor under-played her lines because she knew from experience who she was dealing with. One aspect of the series we would not alter is requiring the actor to work in the hospital with pediatric patients of the targeted ages in order to rehearse the role.

Even though we had used them quite successfully in our playroom film programs, we changed our thinking about bilingual introductions after evaluating the CCTV series. Such introductions appealed to adults, especially Spanish-speaking parents, but children were more attentive to and dependent on the actors' demonstrations than their verbal instructions or explanations. To our dismay, the Spanish segments sometimes elicited negative and racist comments on the part of non-Hispanic children. Apparently, they were made uncomfortable and probably felt excluded by a language they did not understand. Because of this, we dropped bilingual introductions from our video programs and do not plan to include them in future CCTV productions. Pairing titles so that one is nonverbal or can be understood from its visual elements seems the best way to meet the needs of children who either do not speak English or for whom English is a second language.

We offered alternative activities for a number of programs in order to determine which would work best. Sometimes both suffered because of this, but usually one was the clear preference. In a revised series we would offer only one activity. The most successful televised activities were those that clearly demonstrated process. Interestingly, the actor who was less artistically competent was more effective in motivating children to do the activities. Functionally, viewers seemed to say, "She's not very good; even I can do better!" They then went on to do what she had done. Her humorously self-deprecating and fairly simple demonstrations encouraged children, whereas the other actor's superior artistic skills apparently intimidated them.

We produced the series on a very tight budget and used only a single camera to record the wraparound. While this presented few problems with the talking-head introductions, it was a serious drawback in the activity demonstrations. In redoing the series, we would therefore use more than one camera so as to demonstrate activities from several perspectives, including an "over the shoulder" angle which would allow viewers to see what was being done from the point of view of the maker. We would also spend more time showing process, and, as we did in our actual production, the demonstrator would speak as if talking aloud while working. Sometimes s/he would directly address the audience.

Our CCTV activity sheets had several design flaws. The most notable were too much visual clutter, too few instructions, and an unwieldy 11″ by 17″ size. Nevertheless, many worked satisfactorily, especially when they were distributed along with the art supplies prior to a program. Besides being available during the televised activity demonstration, they served as reminders and incentives to watch the show.

When we transferred 16mm films to videotape for the CCTV production, we discovered several factors that influenced how well a film would translate from one medium to the other. If color was an essential feature of an animated film, as for example in THE STONECUTTER, the video transfer usually had only limited success because the electronic palette was so different that the film's intense primary and secondary colors were not accurately replicated. Size was also a problem. Small or highly detailed images, such as those in NOVEMBER 1977 or BALTHAZAR THE LION, were rendered illegible due to a combination of screen size and the image breakup caused by the video transmission pattern. Color

and image quality suffered further because television sets were often in need of repair or adjustment. Likewise, complex cinematic sound was ruined by the poor quality of most TV speakers, the worst being bedside speakers that made everything sound tinny.

More than in a playroom screening, televised films required "informative" soundtracks. FELIX GETS THE CAN, a silent cartoon classic from the 1930s, was a significant flop on TV because it lacked comic music to clue viewers to the fact that it was a funny film. Music or significant sound was a requisite for success on TV as both an attention-focus and a noise screen to block out random ward sounds.

Responses to individual films made it clear that certain titles should be eliminated from any subsequent production. In some programs, such as that which included FELIX GETS THE CAN, one of the pair did not work on TV. In others, each film worked with children of different ages but the program as a whole did not successfully keep the attention of the full viewing population. Although quite successful when a series of films were screened outside the hospital in live programs intended for a broad age range, the practice of bracketing the targeted audience (combining a young child's film with one for older children) did not work on television with only two films. On TV each had to reach the entire audience.

We also revised our thinking about the target audience. Since bracketing was unsuccessful, we decided to follow what seemed to be a fairly consistent age division in children's films. Some titles (many from Weston Woods) work best with preschoolers and children up to the age of 6–7, maybe 8. Others generally work best with school age children from ages 6–7 to 10–11. In addition, although a number of programs appealed to children beyond our intended viewing population, there was a fairly clear age range within which children were both capable of and interested in doing the arts activities. Under-sixes generally needed a supervised, group situation in order to successfully complete them, whereas those over 11 (especially boys) often found the activities babyish. Because of this, we identified 6- to 11-year-olds as our target audience for future CCTV programs with related arts activities.

# GENERAL RECOMMENDATIONS

What follows is a brief summary of our findings in which we have generalized from both our playroom and CCTV evaluations. However, insights into why certain titles or programs worked better than others, and a real understanding of the recommendations below can only be obtained by reading the program write-ups and individual film/tape annotations that follow later in this book.

- Carefully consider children's needs, both developmental and environmental, in planning media programs.

- Enlist the support of everyone, from administrators to aides and orderlies, when you begin a media series. Promote it among parents as well as your local press.

- Humanize media! Actively involve staff, volunteers, and visitors in children's programs.

- Set up a regular maintenance program for all media equipment, especially those (such as playroom VCRs) used by a number of different people. Before an emergency occurs, it's a good idea to identify sources for back-up players and TV sets or video monitors.

- Establish a predictable format for your programs. To a fair extent, predictability seems reassuring to hospitalized children.

- Develop a theme for each program and use the various means available (films, introductions, and follow-ups) to reinforce it.

- Avoid making programs too long. Half an hour for either playroom or TV should be the maximum screening length.

- Preview all films. This is fundamental to appropriate programming. And although it is necessary to keep an open mind to avoid adult bias or personal prejudice, do not use a previewed work if it seems unsuitable for pediatric patients. Better no media than to do children harm.

- Choose films that have a resolution children in the hospital can understand. Beware of stories that activate, rather than alleviate patients' fears. Although Snow White eventually awakens, youngsters might focus on how she was "put to sleep"—that is, by deadly poison (for which read anesthesia).

- Select films that foster a sense of hope or that suggest children can successfully cope with the difficulties they must face in the hospital and afterwards.

- Find films that allow children to "see themselves" on-screen. If, for example, your population is largely black, find appropriate African-American titles.

- Choose simply-structured productions. Shun plots with extensive flashbacks, fantasy/dream sequences, or parallel storylines of the meanwhile, back in the jungle... type.

- Avoid works that are too rapidly edited, since pediatric patients find them overwhelming.

- Select works in which the soundtrack is well matched to the visuals and in which actions, not just words, help carry the storyline.

- Avoid films with constant talking, especially if understanding what's happening depends on hearing all the words. Although on-screen dialog may be somewhat easier to follow than voiceover narration, too much of either is problematic, regardless of how good the sound equipment is.

- Be careful of soundtracks in which music and talking are simultaneous, as one can obscure the other.

- Avoid over-loud soundtracks; however, some music or audible sound is helpful. With rare exceptions, films that are too quiet cannot hold children's attention in the disturbingly noisy hospital environment.

- Shun images that might lower the self-esteem of some patients, such as films in which an amputee or a person with a disfiguring scar is depicted as the villain.

- Assure children that everything will work out for the protagonists in dramatic films. Children often identify strongly with such characters, and if they don't survive, what implications does that have for the hospitalized child? It is critical to insure that your statement is true by previewing the films or using MCC's lengthy annotations as a resource.

- Make up appropriate introductions for each film, but be wary of a work that seems to need a long explanation. Perhaps it's not right for this audience or environment.

- Encourage all children to talk about the media they have seen, whether on regular TV or hospital-generated programming. Media is too much a part of the hospital environment to be ignored. Besides, it serves as a nonmedical focus for conversation.

- Encourage children in group viewing situations to talk out loud during screenings. Such verbalizing helps them mentally process what they see/hear/feel.

- Follow playroom screenings with an image/sound skim, a low-pressure, child-centered process for opening a discussion.

- Find some way of making programs participatory—even if it only involves having children rate them.

- Be sure that follow-up activities have some bearing on the films' content or technique—preferably both.

- Thoughtfully structure and limit the activities. Do not overwhelm children with options, but don't be rigid either.

- Explain to those who facilitate them that the goal of the activities is to encourage children's personal responses. There is no "right way" to do them.

- Demonstrate all arts activities. Do not expect children to follow explanations or instructions alone.

- In modeling the arts activities, do not let the demonstrator intimidate children with her/his artistic skills. Not only can art be threatening to children (especially those over 8), but pediatric patients often lose confidence in their own abilities. Just be careful, however, not to infantilize children by doing for them what they can do for themselves.

- Rescreen whatever children want to see again. Having some control over their media programs is therapeutic for hospitalized children.

# REFERENCES

1. Thesi Bergmann and Anna Freud, *Children in the Hospital* (Madison, CT: International Universities Press, 1962).

2. Maureen Gaffney and Gerry Bond Laybourne, *What to Do When the Lights Go On: A Comprehensive Guide to 16mm Films and Related Activities for Children* (Phoenix, AZ: Oryx Press, 1981).

3. The titles we used in the pilot were as follows: THE CASE OF THE ELEVATOR DUCK by Joan Silver; CECILY by Pavla Reznickova; A CHAIRY TALE by Norman McLaren; ELEPHANT by Peter and Jane Chermayeff; HANSEL AND GRETEL, AN APPALACHIAN VERSION by Tom Davenport; IMPASSE by Caroline and Frank Mouris; IRA SLEEPS OVER by Andrew Sugerman; OH BROTHER, MY BROTHER by Carol and Ross Lowell; RED BALL EXPRESS by Steve Segal; SHORELINES by Al Jarnow; SNOW by Geoffrey Jones; and TALEB AND HIS LAMB by Ami Amitai.

4. Bergmann and Freud, *op. cit.*

5. The pilot combinations were: RED BALL EXPRESS with SNOW; IMPASSE with THE CASE OF THE ELEVATOR DUCK; SHORELINES with HANSEL AND GRETEL, AN APPALACHIAN VERSION; IRA SLEEPS OVER with TALEB AND HIS LAMB; ELEPHANT with CECILY; and A CHAIRY TALE with OH BROTHER, MY BROTHER.

6. Richard Lacey, *Seeing with Feeling: Film in the Classroom* (New York: Holt, Rinehart & Winston, 1972).

*Chick Chick Chick.* Courtesy: Churchill Films.

*Solo.* Courtesy: Pyramid Films.

*The Case of the Elevator Duck.* Courtesy: Learning Corporation of America.

# Film/Tape Annotations

by Maureen Gaffney

# TITLES

ANANSI THE SPIDER
ARROW TO THE SUN
BALTHAZAR THE LION
THE BEAR AND THE MOUSE
BEING BY MYSELF
CAPTAIN SILAS
THE CASE OF THE ELEVATOR DUCK
A CHAIRY TALE
CHICK CHICK CHICK
CHICKS AND CHICKENS
THE CREATION OF BIRDS
CURIOUS GEORGE GOES TO THE HOSPITAL
THE FABLE OF HE AND SHE
FELIX GETS THE CAN
THE FROG KING OR FAITHFUL HENRY
GERALD McBOING McBOING
HANDS
HAROLD AND THE PURPLE CRAYON
HAROLD'S FAIRY TALE
HOMMAGE A FRANCOIS COUPERIN
IRA SLEEPS OVER
ISLE OF JOY
JACK AND THE BEANSTALK
KEITH
KUUMBA
L'AGE DOOR
THE LATE GREAT AMERICAN PICNIC
A LITTLE GIRL AND A GUNNY WOLF
LITTLE GRAY NECK
MADELINE
MADELINE AND THE GYPSIES

THE MAGIC PEAR TREE
MARY OF MILE EIGHTEEN
THE MASKMAKER
THE MOLE AND THE EGG
THE MOLE AND THE TELEPHONE
MY BIG BROTHER
NEW FRIENDS
NOVEMBER 1977
OH BROTHER, MY BROTHER
ONE LITTLE KITTEN
PIERRE
PIGS
THE PRINCESS AND THE PEA
A QUEST
ROSIE'S WALK
RUSSIAN ROOSTER
THE SKY IS BLUE
THE SNOWY DAY
SOLO
SOMETHING QUEER AT THE LIBRARY
SOPHIE AND THE SCALES
THE STONECUTTER
A STORY, A STORY
THE STORY OF CHRISTMAS
TALEB AND HIS LAMB
TANGRAM
TCHOU TCHOU
A VISIT FROM SPACE
WHAZZAT?
WHERE THE WILD THINGS ARE
WORM DANCES

# OVERVIEW

The 62 films annotated in this section are far from conventional, run-of-the-mill educational children's films. A few, such as HOMMAGE A FRANCOIS COUPERIN, ISLE OF JOY, and TANGRAM, are not even specifically for children; they are artist-made works and the filmmakers created them as expressions of their personal vision. Although, in many respects, they are an untapped treasure for hospitals, they were not made for hospitalized children and certain ones as well as particular aspects of otherwise pediatric-appropriate films caused problems for the children with whom we tested them in hospitals. Some of the problems were in the films themselves. Others were environmental—particularly when a film was transferred to tape and shown on video/ TV monitors.

As readers will see, however, most worked with pediatric patients. Only a handful were failures. And even the ones that did not work in our programs might have worked with a different age level or a different film partner. If we did not test it, however, we can only report what happened and speculate about how else it might have worked. (For a discussion of what "worked" means, see our criteria for success in the Overview to the next section, Program Descriptions/Evaluations.)

We should, however, warn the reader that in discussing a film, its problematic aspects sometimes loomed out of proportion to its overall impact. Balance was difficult to maintain while probing the issues a problem raised, and, because of the audience, we decided to provide as much information/speculation as possible. We expect the reader will be able to negotiate between possible implications and what generally happened.

Our primary intention for this section was to raise programmers' consciousness about the pediatric audience, while our goal for the next was to foster "the art of programming." While not at cross-purposes, the 2 goals emphasize different aspects of the films. Here, for example, questions of structure and other production decisions (what to show on-screen, the amount and type of sound, and thematic emphasis through repetition) are highlighted and should be a useful framework for evaluating other films for the pediatric population—titles we have not documented. The next section somewhat diminishes the role of the individual film and addresses contextual issues, such as how a pair of films work together, how children respond to them, and how they affect the follow-up activity. While the latter is more practical and advocatory, this section tends to be critical and a bit more analytical.

Our secondary goal for this section was to provide a "preview substitute" for hospital programmers so they could start using media without doing years of research. We are quite aware of the lack of hospital-specific information about the thousands of films for children that are available in the educational market. (The "home video" market is quite a different thing.) And despite our belief that previewing is essential to good programming, we are aware of how difficult this can be in practice—especially to organizations or individuals who do not deal with media on a daily basis. Thus, we hope the following annotations will give readers sufficient information so they know what to expect when and if they decide to use any of the titles discussed.

Before explaining how the annotations are structured (How to Read the Annotations), we should clarify that all ratings, conclusions, and recommendations (including age levels, related readings, etc.) were developed by Maureen Gaffney on the basis of the research write-ups which follow this section.

# HOW TO READ THE ANNOTATIONS

**Title/Credits**

The title is in CAPITAL LETTERS, followed by director's name and (in parenthesis) country of origin and year of production. On the next line is listed: running time rounded to nearest full minute; principal production technique, such as liveaction or animation—and the type of animation when known; use or lack of color; and use/lack of sound beyond narration or dialog.

**Description**

Each film is narratively described in as much detail as seemed relevant to hospitalized children. Some exemplary films are described in detail to facilitate an examination of how and why they work.

**Visual Attributes**

After an indication of what its images look like, there is an estimate of the film's visual density or general crowdedness within the frame. The overall amount of background detail as well as the size and complexity of its images are roughly and intuitively calculated to indicate how much there is to "read" on-screen. High density is of particular concern with very young viewers (for whom it can be overwhelming) as well as when a film is transferred to video.

**Sound**

The main attributes of sound are indicated and then estimated in terms of audio density or general level and intensity of sound. Because they are most problematic, only high and low levels are discussed.

**Video Legibility/Audibility**

If a title was tried on video monitors or TV sets, its clarity in terms of sound and image is noted. If it was only used as a film, this reference is omitted.

**Pace**

Under this heading, the film's overall fastness (quick cuts) or slowness (longer shots) is roughly calculated.

**Structure**

Using designations (such as catalog, dramatic narrative, list, and lyric) from the definition of terms, each film's structure is described/discussed.

## Themes

General and hospital-related themes (cross-referenced in the Index to Film/Tape Themes) are listed along with those that apply only to the film under consideration (which are not cross-referenced).

## Comments

Issues raised during our testing are discussed under this heading. There is also a listing of the programs in which each title was used.

## Suggested Activities

We did not include all the possible activities one could do with each film, but we list the ones most relevant to the film and most likely to succeed with hospitalized children.

## Related Reading

When a film was adapted from a book/story we mention it. Otherwise, we did not list related readings for every title. Rather, we recommended books, stories, or poems when we felt they would expand on or help prepare children for the film experience. We were particularly concerned about preschoolers—especially the chronically ill—who need all the connections they can get. We were also concerned about ethnic balance, about finding other than white Euroethnic references whenever possible. Some suggestions were designed to expand the age range (up or down) for a film or an activity.

## Recommended Age Range in Hospitals

Based on our hospital test results (as well as information from outside the hospital when we did not have a wide enough age range), we estimated the optimal age for each title when used on its own. As the program write-ups verify, however, the age range can fluctuate a great deal depending on what a film is combined with as well as group dynamics (including ethnic and sexual balance), children's conditions, and other contextual factors.

## Hospital Rating

Four stars indicates a superior and hospital-appropriate title. Three stars means the film is good but has a few problems or a limited appeal. Two stars indicates an acceptable film. One means the film is barely acceptable or we are unsure about it. No stars—not recommended.

## Availability

Each film's current distributor as well as prices and formats are listed along with particulars about closed-circuit television rights. Many distributors indicated there would be no additional charge to nonprofit hospitals for CCTV rights if the following conditions were met: if permission to use a film/video on CCTV was obtained in writing from the distributor prior to purchase; if the CCTV system is an in-house system, using hard cable, and operating in one hospital and in one building; and if there was no charge to patients for viewing the CCTV programming. There are exceptions, however, so check each title individually. (Distributors' addresses and phone numbers are in the Selected Resources section.) If not in US distribution, a title may be accessible in either public library or university rental library collections. While we had no idea such works would go out of distribution, the discussion about them may serve as a guide in selecting other works or generate ideas for future productions.

# ANNOTATIONS

## ANANSI THE SPIDER
*by Gerald McDermott* (USA/1969)
7 minutes /cel animation /color

A lively and colorful African folktale about Anansi, the Ashanti trickster-hero, who is seen here in spider form. The film begins with a black spider silhouette swinging, like a pendulum, across the screen as rhythmic African music is heard. The spider freezes in mid-screen and acquires facial features and a headband. The title appears. Anansi spins an elaborate web and a subtitle appears: "A tale from the Ashanti."

Anansi is introduced like a character in a puppet show. "Anansi, he is spider to the Ashanti people," the narrator says; "this is the story of Kwaku Anansi." Then, in a similar manner, each of Anansi's 6 sons is introduced. They all have silhouettes that resemble their father's, but each has a distinctively shaped torso with an emblem that symbolizes both his name and his special skill.

"First son was called See-Trouble; he had the gift of seeing trouble a long way off." He has a triangular body with 4 circles on it.

"Second son was Road-Builder" whose torso is shaped like an *X* on which there is a similarly shaped emblem.

"Thirsty son was River-Drinker," who has a rectangular body with 2 wavy lines across it.

"Next son was Game-Skinner." He has two elongated triangles, like scissor blades, with similar shapes on his torso.

"Another son was Stone-Thrower," who has a round body with a whirling pinwheel on it.

"And last of sons was Cushion; he was very soft." Cushion has a figure-eight with 2 nearly round (Pac Man) shapes in each half of his torso.

Then, as the narrator explains that they were all good sons, the smaller spiders circle around Anansi who sits in the center of a web.

"One time," says the narrator beginning the story proper, "Anansi went a long way from home." Anansi sets off alone across a colorful, abstract landscape that resembles Ashanti fabric designs. Anansi gets lost and falls "into trouble" in a river where he is gobbled up by a sunfish (in the shape of an Ashanti gold weight).

Meanwhile, back home, See-Trouble becomes aware of his father's predicament and cries out,

"Father is in danger!" Immediately, Road-Builder says, "Follow me!" and builds a road for the others. All the spider sons move fast to find Anansi.

When they get to the river an x-ray view shows Anansi in the belly of the fish. See-Trouble says, "Fish has swallowed him!" River-Drinker drains the river bed, leaving the fish on dry land. Game-Skinner opens the fish, leaving only a skeleton. Now free, Anansi does a little dance of celebration to an upbeat tune.

Suddenly, more trouble comes. A falcon swoops down and grabs Anansi in its beak. Stone-Thrower hits the flying bird with a stone. The falcon drops Anansi, and Cushion runs to where his father will land. "Very soft, Anansi came down." Cushion and Anansi touch heads and all the spiders run across a series of hills. "They were very happy that spider family," says the narrator.

The background colors change from warm reds and oranges to cool blues and greens. "All home again that night," the narrator says, "Anansi found a thing in the forest." It is a luminous white globe that is very beautiful and mysterious. Anansi intends to give it to the son who rescued him, but he cannot decide which of them deserves the prize.

Anansi calls out to Nyame, the god of all things, for help. An abstracted human shape is seen in the blue sky. It takes the white light when Anansi asks Nyame to hold the globe until he determines which son to give it to.

As Anansi "discusses" the matter with his sons, they dance around in circles on a web; seemingly they are having a heated debate. "They argued all night," the narrator says.

Nyame sees this and, perhaps tired of waiting, brings the beautiful globe high up in the sky, then disappears. "He keeps it there for all to see. It is still there. It will always be there. It is there tonight." Anansi runs over a hill as the moon shines in the background.

**Visual Attributes:** Delightfully kinesthetic and boldly colored, semi-abstract images that resemble Ashanti block prints or cutouts (although they are actually silk-screened onto clear acetate). Intense figure and background color saturation with rather high visual density.

**Sound:** Periodic male narration in a rich Afro-Caribbean accent with rhythmic African music. Although there is continuous sound, audio density is generally medium or lower because the vocal and music tracks are clearly separated.

**Video Legibility/Audibility:** Generally good legibility despite some disintegration of outlines (due to color fuzziness or trailing after-images) in the first half when red colors dominate. Better than average audibility.

**Pace:** Generally medium.

**Structure:** Narrative. A slightly complex origins tale in 2 parts which is preceded by an effective introduction of the main characters. The first half of the story (concerning Anansi's adventures) makes excellent use of cumulative repetition and has a satisfying, circular closure in that Anansi and his sons return safely home (although there is no visual symbol for home; we are simply told so by the narrator.) The second half of the story (concerning the moon-reward) is not as clearly structured. Not only does it use less action and less repetition than the first half, but also it has an ironic, open ending and thus lacks a totally satisfying closure.

**Themes:** Separation; overcoming danger; returning safely home; familial support; cooperation; rescue; puzzles; the question of who is more deserving; the tale-within-a-tale of how the moon got in the sky.

**Comments:** ANANSI THE SPIDER was very successful with hospitalized children as both a film and a videotape although it has a few aspects worth discussing.

First, the entire film is usually preceded by a didactic 3-minute prologue (neither described above nor included in the overall running time), in which case the story has 2 introductions and runs for 10 minutes. Since the prologue contrasts markedly with the playful film and would have been an information overload, we eliminated it from our hospital programs by running past it before starting the projector/player. (We also do this in nonhospital programs). If you purchase this film/tape, ask the distributor for a version without the prologue.

Second, because the word *moon* is never mentioned in the film, some young children did not understand what globe Anansi found. Some thought it was the sun; some were just confused. Make sure to explain to children—especially those in poor physical/emotional condition and those under 8—that the story has 2 parts and the second half tells how the moon got in the sky. You might also want to explain that globe is another word for ball.

There are several ways to make this delightful film more accessible to either very young or very sick children. One way is to read McDermott's book *Anansi the Spider* before screening the film (which we sometimes do with preschoolers outside of the hospital). Another way is to screen it twice in a row and ask if children have any questions between screenings; children generally enjoy the film even more the second time. Yet another option (which we also recommend with WHAZZAT?) is to show only half of the film the first time you screen it with the very young or very ill. Read the McDermott book to children before you show the film again, then screen it in its entirety. Also encourage children to let you know—even during a screening—if there is anything they don't understand, and be sure to ask if they have any questions after seeing the film or hearing the book.

We used ANANSI THE SPIDER in CCTV Program #1 with THE CREATION OF BIRDS, as well as in Video Programs #9 with MADELINE AND THE GYPSIES and #10 with ISLE OF JOY.

**Suggested Activities:** Collage and design.

**Related Reading:** Preschool and young school age children may enjoy the companion picturebook which was adapted from the film by Gerald McDermott; it is available in paperback.

---

**Recommended Pediatric Age:** 5–12.

**Hospital Rating:** ****

**Availability:**
ANANSI THE SPIDER
Distributed by Films Incorporated/PMI.
16mm film purchase price: $225
¾-inch videotape purchase price: $149
½-inch videotape purchase price: $99
No extra charge for CCTV rights if shown to a viewing population of under 2,400.

---

# ARROW TO THE SUN
*by Gerald McDermott* (USA/1973)
12 minutes / cel animation / color

A practically wordless and mime-like version of a Pueblo legend which makes excellent use of Acoma designs and symbols. As the film begins, a black and gold figure who looks like a *kachina* (a helpful spirit in Pueblo folklore) shoots an arrow toward earth. It touches a young woman and she bears a child who quickly matures and goes to play ball with the village boys. Ostracized and dejected because he has no father, the boy tells his mother he must go to find his sire.

After leaving his pueblo, the young man searches the countryside, encountering 3 animals (lizard, wild fowl, butterfly) and 3 people (farmer, potter, arrow maker). He dances his story for each one but none can help until the arrow maker fashions a special arrow which carries the boy to the sky kingdom.

When the young man announces that he is the sky chief's son, the chief signals that he must endure 4 tests. He successfully passes through 3 *kivas* (Pueblo ceremonial rooms) of pumas, snakes, and bees. However, while in the kiva of lightning, the youth falls to the ground and does not rise. The music stops as the sky chief waits outside, unable to see what is happening. Then, just when he seems defeated, the young man emerges from the last kiva in a dramatic ribbon of light and joins hands with his father.

At his father's request, the young man attaches himself to an arrow and returns to earth bringing with him the sun's creative power. A cornstalk sprouts from the spot where he lands and turns into a corn maiden. Using gestures and flashback images, the young man tells her of his quest.

He and the corn maiden dance then set out for his village. When the couple arrives, everyone—his mother included—joins in a dance of celebration.

**Visual Attributes:** Slightly static, semi-abstract images in warm colors that resemble Pueblo kachinas, pottery, and weaving designs. Intense figure and background color saturation give this a fairly high visual density.

**Sound:** Only 4 brief lines of dialog (in a young man's voice) interrupt this musical. The Native sounding score is effectively rhythmic and varied. Audio density is rather low.

**Pace:** Leisurely.

**Structure:** Narrative—part quest, part origins tale. Although the story effectively uses repetition and variation, it is made complex by the fact that many events accumulate before there is any closure (i.e., the boy is ostracized, sets out on a quest, asks 3 creatures and 3 people if they know who his father is, travels to and arrives at the sky kingdom, endures 4 tests, and then is united with his father). On top of this, closure is short-lived since he immediately sets off again for earth.

**Themes:** Being different; search for identity; self-esteem; separation; overcoming hardship; courage; returning safely home; finding one's place in the world; enriching one's community; origins tale (the origin of corn).

**Comments:** Although ARROW TO THE SUN generally works quite well with children outside of the hospital, it was not a great hit with our test population. The film's accumulating events lacked closure and perhaps too closely mirrored the situation of hospitalized children who, while in the hospital, generally have no closure to their illness. Or perhaps they simply lacked the energy to decode this highly visual and symbolic film.

This does not mean, however, that the film will not work in hospitals. But it would probably work best with preadolescents and older viewers, or those familiar with Southwest culture.

We tried ARROW TO THE SUN in Film Program #13 with THE CASE OF THE ELEVATOR DUCK. We also tried a mini-test of it with SOLO as the second film, which seemed a better match despite the fact that both are so nonverbal. ARROW TO THE SUN worked best when children were encouraged to focus on its design elements.

**Suggested Activities:** Collage and graphic design.

**Related Reading:** Young school age children may enjoy the companion picturebook which was adapted from the film by Gerald McDermott; it is available in paperback.

---

**Recommended Pediatric Age:** 10–14.

**Hospital Rating:** *

**Availability:**
ARROW TO THE SUN
Distributed by Films Incorporated/PMI.
16mm film purchase price: $240
¾-inch videotape purchase price: $149
½-inch videotape purchase price: $99
No extra charge for CCTV rights if shown to a viewing population of under 2,400.

---

## BALTHAZAR THE LION
*by Christa Kozik* (East Germany/1973)
*12 minutes / object animation / color / nonverbal*

This low-key fable begins with a liveaction segment in which an artist paints some small food cartons, such as cereal boxes and egg cartons. His creations then become puppets which enact the droll tale of a voracious circus/zoo lion who eats everything he can sink his teeth into—from the animal keeper's hat to the monkey's musical instruments—until he devours the moon.

Because the world turns dark when the moon disappears, the hand of the artist sets a kerosene lamp in the moon's place. Meanwhile, a scientist in an observatory notes that the moon is missing and alerts the fire department.

When first aid workers arrive at the circus/zoo, they relieve Balthazar's not-too-surprising stomach ache by surgically removing the moon (as well as the other items) and returning it to the sky. After that, the artist who created Balthazar gives him a smaller mouth. As a result, the lion becomes as docile and cooperative as a lamb and accompanies the animal keeper as he makes the rounds to feed the other animals.

**Visual Attributes:** Although there are liveaction segments, the images are mostly somewhat static, three-dimensional box puppets. Except for the scenes with the puppet maker, this has a rather high visual density.

**Sound:** Nonverbal with effects and occasional music. Low audio density.

**Video Legibility/Audibility:** Fair. Because this is rich in visual detail, some information gets lost on the small screen. Because its soundtrack is quiet, it has only fair audibility in the hospital environment.

**Pace:** Leisurely.

**Structure:** Narrative. A meandering tale with many embellishments and a *deus ex machina* resolution. It requires a high level of attention and viewing sophistication.

**Themes:** There are aspects of cooperation (which, unfortunately, are forced on the lion) but the film is more about uncooperative behavior; devouring; don't bite off more than you can chew; rescue; and change and transformation.

**Comments:** We used BALTHAZAR THE LION because of the possibilities it suggests for follow-up activities. However, it was not as successful as we would have liked, in part because it is visually demanding and when shown as a videotape some of its information/impact is lost. It may also have been problematic because it is a didactic tale, a fable. As we discovered in this project, fables (short-hand extractions from a life of experience) do not necessarily tell convincing, child-appropriate stories. More importantly, they do not give hospitalized children the emotional connection with characters they seem to crave.

Of particular note is that school-age children had trouble following the sequence of events when the artist intervenes to make Balthazar's mouth smaller. Perhaps they had trouble following an intervention from outside the cast of characters, but this seems unlikely since it had 2 precedents. Perhaps they were disturbed by the coercion it entailed and, being themselves subject to the coercion of undergoing painful medical procedures, etc., even if for their own good, they simply could not integrate that event into an otherwise frothy story.

We used BALTHAZAR THE LION in CCTV Program #8 with CAPTAIN SILAS.

**Suggested Activities:** Box art, dioramas, assemblage.

---

**Recommended Pediatric Age:** 5–9.

**Hospital Rating:** *

**Availability:**
BALTHAZAR THE LION
Distributed by Wombat Productions.
16mm film purchase price: $250
¾-inch videotape purchase price: $195
½-inch videotape purchase price: $95
No additional charge for CCTV rights.

---

# THE BEAR AND THE MOUSE
*by Michael Rubbo* (Canada/1966)
8 minutes / liveaction / color

This highly verbal adaptation of Aesop's fable about the lion and the mouse is set in North America during colonial fur-trapping days and uses real animals for most of its actors. The film opens with an establishing shot of a woodland pond and introduces a mouse named Mouse. In a quick series of cuts, viewers are introduced to a pair of human hunters who find bear tracks (and later on build some sort of structure); Hawk, who serves as interlocutor and directly addresses other characters (or makes voiceover comments about events); an unseen narrator; and Bear. Following the hunters' building efforts, the hungry Bear catches Mouse but, persuaded by Hawk, lets him go.

Bear soon gets caught in the hunters' sapling cage and Mouse promises to free him with the help of the rest of his family. When the mice swarm all over the trap, the narrator wonders what they can do. As they gnaw at the vines which bind the saplings, Bear wonders what all the chewing is about.

Meanwhile, the hunters are seen walking through the woods. Hawk encourages the mice to keep on chewing then looks left and apparently notices something coming through the woods (which viewers do not see). In a series of cross-cuts, we see mice chewing and hunters walking until Bear pushes the cage open just before the hunters arrive.

The film closes with a scene of frenzied Mouse dancing while, apparently, Bear and Hawk observe the scene as guests of the mice. Hawk comments that he's never seen mice dance like that before, but then he's never seen mice rescue a bear.

**Visual Attributes:** Liveaction with rather low visual density. Since most of the animals were shot quite independently of one another, there is minimal visual integration of the action and very little sense of place.

**Sound:** Continuous male narration in a storyteller's delivery with occasional music. Its high verbal density combined with the narrator's various accents (from Canadian to pseudo-Cockney) sometimes rendered words/meanings unintelligible.

**Pace:** Slow.

**Structure:** List, or more correctly, a would-be narrative that does not cohere. The film's focus is unclear and there is almost no meaningful interaction among characters.

**Themes:** Trapped in a cage or box; reciprocity; small creatures can overcome great obstacles with teamwork; rescue.

**Comments:** Because many young hospitalized preschoolers are literally caged in their cribs at night, THE BEAR AND THE MOUSE seemed to offer interesting therapeutic possibilities. Unfortunately, it did not work very well. Not only is THE BEAR AND THE MOUSE totally dependent on voiceover narration, but the storyteller's character voices are sometimes indistinguishable so it is hard to tell who is supposed to be talking. Besides the fact that the animal actors do not move their mouths when they speak (which bothers children reared on television), the limitations imposed by using real animals means they were photographed individually, for the most part, and are seldom shown interacting in the same shot.

While we have used this film successfully with children outside of the hospital where it acts rather like a puppet show, its wordiness, its dependence on viewer-inference (such as, who is talking to whom and what the humans are doing), its cross-cuts and confusing edits, and its lack of plot-relevant action made this extremely difficult for hospitalized children, especially preschoolers. But the overriding difficulty may have been with the fable format.

Since this was the first fable we tried in the hospital, we conducted a mini-test using a simpler film version of the same fable (Evelyn Lambart's THE LION AND THE MOUSE) with preschool children. That did not work either, so we began to think that perhaps the fable format was too conceptual for hospitalized preschoolers. (For further discussion of fables, see BALTHAZAR THE LION, THE FABLE OF HE AND SHE, PIERRE, and THE STONECUTTER.)

This might do better with young school age children, but its lack of emotion may work against it. We used it in Film Program #2 with ONE LITTLE KITTEN.

**Suggested Activities:** Storytelling and dramatic play.

**Related Reading:** The Aesop fable, "The Lion and the Mouse."

---

**Recommended Pediatric Age:** 6–9.

**Hospital Rating:** *

**Availability:**
THE BEAR AND THE MOUSE
Distributed by Karol Media.
16mm film purchase price: $200
¾-inch videotape purchase price: $150
½-inch videotape purchase price: $150
Probably no extra charge for CCTV rights, but permission must be obtained from the National Film Board of Canada. The prices above are for nonprofit institutions only.

---

# BEING BY MYSELF
*by WGBH-TV* (USA/1975)
6 minutes / liveaction / color

This is the first half of a dual portrait called ALONE IN THE FAMILY (which runs just over 13 minutes in all); the other half is MY BIG BROTHER. Both were produced for the ZOOM TV series.

Preadolescent Lori Morris is part of a large family which owns a seafood restaurant in Maine. Early scenes from this brief portrait show her working as a waitress in the family restaurant and talking about her life by means of a voiceover narration.

Later, when she takes a walk through the small town and sits gazing out at the ocean, she talks about how, in order to get some peace, she likes to get away by herself. "My sister just wants to be a housewife," Lori says, "but I want to travel, live in a log cabin in the woods, just be quiet and peaceful."

Back at the restaurant, she works competently and jokes with a customer about her father's birthday. In the closing scene, Lori, her siblings, and parents gather round a large table to celebrate the paternal birthday. Lori's voiceover tells us that she likes helping her parents because "they work awfully hard for us kids just to make it through the day."

**Visual Attributes:** Liveaction with "normal" image density.

**Sound:** Dialog plus a voiceover narration delivered by the preadolescent female subject. Although the audio density was fairly low, some words were incomprehensible because of the subject's Down East accent and wispy, high-pitched voice.

**Video Legibility/Audibility:** Good legibility but only fair audibility because of the narrator's vocal characteristics.

**Pace:** Medium-slow.

**Structure:** Documentary. An open-ended, slice-of-life portrait with a wide focus.

**Themes:** Siblings; family relationships; preadolescence; female protagonist; competence; small town life.

**Comments:** Because we felt it would be an information overload to show both halves of ALONE IN THE FAMILY at the same time in a program with another film, we used each half separately with the same film on different occasions. This had greater appeal to girls than boys. We tried BEING BY MYSELF in Video Program #20 with OH BROTHER, MY BROTHER and, despite its sketchiness, the film worked fairly well.

**Suggested Activities:** Discussion.

Recommended Pediatric Age: 7–12.

Hospital Rating: **

Availability:
BEING BY MYSELF
(of ALONE IN THE FAMILY)
Distributed by Films Incorporated/PMI.
16mm prints not available.
¾-inch videotape purchase price: $198
½-inch videotape purchase price: $129
Inquire for information about CCTV rights.

## CAPTAIN SILAS

*by Ron McAdow* (USA/1977)
14 minutes / object animation / color

Using a large cast of peanuts and everyday objects such as thread spools, sugar cubes, and popcorn, this film reveals a delightful miniature world in which merchant sailor Silas makes his living by trading trucks for sugar cubes. The film opens with a shot of surf made from blue popcorn. Realistic ocean sounds are heard. Next we see shots of a truck assembly plant (wheels are thread spools) operated by peanut workers. Then we see a wall being constructed with sugar cubes near a seaside cottage with a mailbox that says *Cpt. Silas*.

As a little peanut emerges from the cottage, the narrator introduces us to Captain Silas who lives on Truck Island with his dog (a trout fly). The captain goes into town, enters the bank, and withdraws 4 buttons which he takes to the factory to purchase a truck. Along with his first mate, he drives the truck to a dock where his boat (a wing tip shoe) carries it to the Isle of Sugar. Once there, the captain trades the truck for a load of sugar cubes.

Captain Silas then trades the sugar cubes to a construction company on Truck Island for 8 buttons. After paying his 3 sailors, the Captain has 5 buttons left. He banks 4 and uses the one remaining to buy food.

In the second part of the story, the Captain buys another truck direct from the factory, but as he leaves his first mate "plays some foolish tricks" and sabotages the assembly line. Silas and crew head for the Isle of Sugar but the truck which he intends to trade is damaged en route during a storm; so the Captain junks it, returning with an empty hold and showing a loss in his ledger.

On the return voyage, however, a hungry sea serpent (a red wash cloth) attacks a friendly dolphin (a shaving brush) so the Captain and his sailors harpoon the serpent (with a safety pin) and—after a hair-raising ride—bring it safely into port. There, the local marine circus trades its truck

for the sea serpent, so the Captain and his crew are back in business.

Visual Attributes: Highly kinesthetic three-dimensional objects. Despite a rather high image density, figure and ground are clearly distinguished.

Sound: Minimal male narration delivered in a tongue-in-cheek didactic tone with pseudo-conversational vocalizations and emphatic, jazzy music. Fairly low audio density with clearly separated music and narrative tracks.

Video Legibility/Audibility: Very good.

Pace: Mostly leisurely, except for chase scene in second part.

Structure: Dramatic narrative. A clear story in 2 parts (or chapters) which makes effective use of repetition and variation. There is an introduction, a problem, a climax, and a resolution, followed by a second problem (which, initially, is identical to the first one), a complication, a fortuitous turn of events, a climax, and a resolution.

Themes: Interdependence; the principles of capitalism; making the best of a bad situation.

Comments: A 10-year-old said, "I like little small things like that," after she saw CAPTAIN SILAS and a 12-year-old girl announced, "I got the giggles." Younger children sometimes made references to the hospital situation as when a girl of 5 said that the tag on the washcloth/sea-serpent was "a bandaid." A 3-year-old, who wasn't following the story, enjoyed making noises like the peanut characters in CAPTAIN SILAS.

Although a great success with hospitalized school age viewers, we had some trouble finding the right partner for it. We tried it in Film Program #10 with THE LATE GREAT AMERICAN PICNIC, in CCTV Program #8 with BALTHAZAR THE LION, and in Video Program #24 with CURIOUS GEORGE GOES TO THE HOSPITAL where, because both were long, we only showed half of CAPTAIN SILAS.

Suggested Activities: Box art or dioramas.

Recommended Pediatric Age: 6–13.

Hospital Rating: ****

Availability:
CAPTAIN SILAS
Distributed by Beacon Films.
16mm film purchase price: $320
¾-inch videotape purchase price: $174
½-inch videotape purchase price: $149
Prices are for nonprofit institutions; 16mm price includes ½-inch VHS copy at no additional cost.

# THE CASE OF THE ELEVATOR DUCK
*by Joan Silver* (USA/1974)
17 minutes / liveaction / color

This is a delightful detective story featuring Gilbert, a black urban preadolescent, who solves the problem of what to do with a duck he finds in the elevator of his housing project. The film opens with the image of a black boy (Gilbert) getting dressed in the morning. In a voiceover narration he explains that while some detectives believe in disguises, he thinks "the best thing to do is go natural; that way nobody will suspect you of being a detective." The boy combs his hair and comments that things are a little slow—but that doesn't mean he can take it easy.

The young detective enters an elevator which gets increasingly full of people, all of whom—except for the boy—get out at what is apparently the lobby. The boy pushes the button for his floor, saying to himself, "Think I'll go upstairs and get me some breakfast," when he notices a duck on the elevator. He talks out loud, saying that the duck could get him in bad trouble since "they don't allow no pets in this project." However, when the duck quacks and tries to get out on his floor, he agrees to take the case and hides the duck in his bathroom laundry hamper.

The duck is quickly discovered by Gilbert's mother who worries that they will be evicted for violating project rules, but she allows Gilbert 2 days to find the duck's owner.

Gilbert moves the duck to the bathtub and is busy thinking when his friend comes to the door and asks him to play basketball. Gilbert says he can't because he's "on a case." Later, he walks outside with a duck feather sticking in a makeshift headband—a device he hopes will signal the duck's owner but which is interpreted by younger kids as an invitation to play Cowboys-and-Indians. When a young boy says "Bang bang!," Gilbert plays dead. His friend comes by, dribbling a basketball, looks at Gilbert lying on the ground and says, "Man, you're pitiful." On his way home in the elevator, a little, sad-eyed boy stares at him, but Gilbert makes nothing of it.

A housing policeman, responding to a complaint that there are animals in the apartment, asks if he can take a look around. Gilbert goes to the bathroom to hide the duck in the hamper and sits nervously on it when the man checks the bathroom, but things go smoothly. His mother, however, changes the time limit and says he has to find the duck's owner by the next day or she will take it to the animal shelter. Gilbert says that no one will adopt a full-grown duck; they'll put it to sleep.

On the theory that the duck will be able to find its own way home, Gilbert—dressed only in pajamas—sneaks out of his apartment that night and takes the duck from floor to floor of his building, avoiding the elevator so the housing police won't catch him. After several floors and one close call with the housing police, the duck waddles down a hallway and stops at one particular door. Gilbert rings the bell and hides. The door opens and there stands the sad-eyed boy from the elevator. The duck walks into the apartment and the door closes.

Next morning, however, when Gilbert is doing his usual elevator check, the duck is in the elevator. Frustrated, Gilbert picks it up and heads for the apartment where it went the night before. When the door opens, a young Hispanic woman berates Gilbert for bringing the duck back. She says they cannot keep it or they will be thrown out of the project. Her little brother Julio put the duck on the elevator hoping that someone would adopt it. She asks if Gilbert is trying to break her brother's heart by bringing it back again. "Please," she says, "this is your duck; keep it!" Then she slams the door.

Gilbert feels pretty low for a few moments until he gets an idea. He goes to the lobby and enters what looks like a school. "I brought this duck to the day care center for the kids," Gilbert says, "it belongs to Julio." The teacher calls Julio who chases happily after the duck.

Outside, Julio's sister apologizes to Gilbert. In true detective fashion he accepts it matter-of-factly, saying, "Us detectives run into all kinds of stuff like that." Then Gilbert walks off, probably looking for another case.

**Visual Attributes:** Liveaction (but little real action—mostly talking heads) with "normal" image density.

**Sound:** In addition to music, this is extremely verbal, with both character dialog and a voiceover narration by the boy who plays the lead role. Very high audio density. The young protagonist's black accent and his immature voice made some lines inaudible; in addition, certain information-critical voiceover bridges between scenes were buried by the music which played under the narrator's lines.

**Video Legibility/Audibility:** Very good legibility, but sometimes only fair audibility.

**Pace:** Medium.

**Structure:** Dramatic narrative. A moderately complex story with an introduction, a complication, a false climax, a further complication, a true climax, and a satisfying closure. However, large parts of the storyline are compressed (i.e., quick scene shifts and cuts are used to pack in a lot of information) and plot advancement is done almost entirely with narration and/or dialog.

**Themes:** Creative problem-solving; competence; autonomy; nurturing and tenderness; perseverance; mystery; familial support; understanding parental values; urban life.

**Comments:** Despite its complexity, this charming film was one of the most successful ones we used with our test population, whether urban or rural, all-white or largely black. However, since it is more talk than action and depends on knowledge about the world as well as media experience, THE CASE OF THE ELEVATOR DUCK is usually too difficult for preschool children, even outside the hospital.

The film assumes audience familiarity with basic detective story conventions, although in most respects it is more like a Sherlock Holmes mystery than a police detective mystery in that it relies on the problem-solving skills of its detective protagonist and does not use external clues as focal points for the unfolding of the storyline.

THE CASE OF THE ELEVATOR DUCK also assumes audience knowledge of certain outside references, namely what a housing project is, what a "no pets" rule means, and the fact that some birds have a homing instinct. In addition, it uses narration/dialog and many cuts—rather than observable actions—to get in a lot of information. All this notwithstanding, it has a clear focus and allows itself sufficient time to tell its story.

Its running time makes it essential to pair THE CASE OF THE ELEVATOR DUCK with a very brief partner for a half-hour program. We tried it in Film Program #13 with ARROW TO THE SUN, in CCTV Program #3 with THE SNOWY DAY, and in Video Programs #3 with L'AGE DOOR and #4 with RUSSIAN ROOSTER. It was also one of the films we used in the pilot.

**Suggested Activities:** Storytelling, mystery-solving.

**Related Reading:** Older preschool and school age children may enjoy the storybook by Polly Berrien Berends upon which the film is based; it is available in paperback.

---

Recommended Pediatric Age: 7–13.

Hospital Rating: ****

Availability:
THE CASE OF THE ELEVATOR DUCK
Distributed by Coronet/MTI.
16mm film purchase price: $350
¾-inch videotape purchase price: $275
½-inch videotape purchase price: $275
Probably no extra charge for CCTV rights.

---

# A CHAIRY TALE
*by Norman McLaren* (Canada/1957)
10 minutes / liveaction / b&w / nonverbal

"Once upon a time" read the titles that begin this wordless film, as a man strolls with an open book onto a bare stage. Spotting a straight-back wooden chair, he dusts it with his handkerchief and goes to sit down when the chair pulls away. Again the man tries to sit, but the chair pulls away. After several attempts with similar results, the man pockets his book and suspiciously eyes the chair.

Forced by its behavior into a novel relationship, the man begins to stalk the chair which keeps a careful distance. Slowly, then faster and faster, man chases chair, becoming so engrossed he fails to notice that the chair drops out temporarily to observe the man's frenetic actions. In desperation the man eventually wrestles the chair and forces himself on top, but it bucks like a bronco and throws the man off. Apparently fed up, he then sits on the floor and reads his book.

But now, chair pursues man. Slowly, from offstage, it inches closer and closer. When he fails to notice, the chair bangs its "head" histrionically against the floor. It even lies on its side and peeks to see if the man is watching. But he is not, so the chair moves right under the man's nose and forces the issue.

Perhaps heartened by the chair's persistence, the man decides to try a new tack. He tickles the chair somewhat condescendingly and rocks it like a baby. He entertains it with marches and dances. However, when he tries to sit on the chair, it still backs away. Finally, with exaggerated formality, the man courts the chair and dances a tango with it. But all for naught, since the chair refuses to be a proper seat. Exasperated, the man signals "forget it" and stalks away.

But the chair yanks the man back and presses him to figure out what it wants. Pacing back and forth, the man ponders the situation. Suddenly, he snaps his fingers and smiles with a look of enlightenment. Then, with exaggerated slowness, the man straightens his back and bends his knees to assume the shape of a chair. Delighted, the chair somersaults in mid-air and, as the man dusts off his lap, the chair sits on the man. Satisfied at last, the chair then allows the man to sit on it. "...And they sat happily ever after," read the closing titles.

**Visual Attributes:** Highly kinesthetic black-and-white liveaction with some pixillation (a speeded up motion such as was used in Keystone Cops or Charlie Chaplin films). It has a low image density with a clear separation of figure and ground; a man dressed in white interacts with a white wooden chair against a black backdrop.

**Sound:** East Indian raga music by Ravi Shankar plays continuously and adds important emotional—sometimes almost vocal—coloring. Audio density is medium.

**Video Legibility/Audibility:** Excellent.

**Pace:** Varies from slow to very fast.

**Structure:** Dramatic narrative. A tightly focused drama in 2 acts—the second of which begins when the man loses interest and the chair assumes the role of aggressor—with an effective fairytale-like frame.

**Themes:** Communication; uncooperative behavior; self-assertion; reciprocity; role-reversal; perseverance; don't take things for granted; seeing another's point of view; there's more than one side to an issue; resolving a difference of opinion.

**Comments:** A CHAIRY TALE was a *four-star* success with hospitalized children. This classic work was also the best mime film we used because it has a single, tangible problem which is made clear by the interactions of 2 characters, both of whom are effectively on-screen throughout the entire work. It is noteworthy that there are very few close-ups; the camera generally keeps its distance. (For a discussion of other mime films, see KEITH, THE MASKMAKER, and A QUEST.)

Since we did not plan to do movement activities (a natural follow-up, but not always possible in hospitals), our biggest problem was in finding a good partner. We tried A CHAIRY TALE in Film Program #11 with NEW FRIENDS, in CCTV Program #9 with THE FABLE OF HE AND SHE, and in Video Program #15 with PIERRE. It was also one of our pilot films.

**Suggested Activities:** Storytelling, point-of-view games, puppetry, and mime.

---

**Recommended Pediatric Age:** 3+.

**Hospital Rating:** \*\*\*\*

**Availability:**
A CHAIRY TALE
Distributed by International Film Bureau.
16mm film purchase price: $150
¾-inch videotape purchase price: $150
½-inch videotape purchase price: $150
If there is a charge for CCTV rights, it would be nominal for nonprofit hospitals.

---

# CHICK CHICK CHICK
*by Robert & Michael Brown (USA/1974)*
13 minutes / liveaction / color / nonverbal

During the course of this animal portrait, quiet, close-up shots of eggs hatching in a nest are intercut with faster-paced scenes of hens, chickens, roosters, and other farm animals.

The film begins with a shot of the morning sky and cuts to sleeping chickens while an eerie musical sound is heard. A rooster crows. Hens and chickens open their eyes. A black cat is seen. The rooster crows again. More chicks open their eyes. (Lots of close-ups of their heads.) A bunch of baby chicks emerge from what seems to be a chicken coop with their mother, and banjo picking is heard on the soundtrack.

Cutting back and forth among different animals, the next section of the film shows hens, chicks, and roosters walking and pecking for food. A man's foot is seen in close-up walking toward and opening a gate.

Cut to a shot of a hen sitting on a pile of hay sort of dozing. Camera zooms in and her eyes open. A man's voice calls "Here, chick, chick, chick!" and a hen rises from 3 eggs and goes out the door.

A blurred image comes into focus and reveals an egg, shot in extreme close-up. It has a slight crack in it.

Cut to a shot of a man's hand throwing pellets on the ground. Chickens peck and one hen pecks right into the camera.

Cutting back and forth among different animals, the next section shows chicks walking and giving themselves dust baths. A horse walks by. Two little chicks compete over a beetle; one gobbles it down. There's a long shot of some hens and chicks.

Close-up of the hatching egg, only now the crack is larger and something is breathing inside it.

There is a pan of stalks of corn and the sound of chirping. A baby chick walks into the cow corral.

Close-up pan of the hatching egg with a bigger crack.

Cut to a shot of pigs wallowing in mud. A little chicken lands in the pigsty. A curious pig comes over to smell it. Chick runs quickly away, squawking, and scoots under a fence. A quick succession of shots of chicks and hens, the one little running chick, a cow, a horse, and finally a little chick snuggling safe and sound under a hen's wing.

Close-up of the egg with quite a bit of shell peeled away. The breathing is more evident.

Cut to reflected water with leaves in it. A hoof steps in the water. There is a series of shots of chicken feet, then of chickens drinking, some rather noisily.

Close-up of the hatching egg with a noticeable movement inside the shell.

Cut to a cat and some scurrying chickens. A hawk soars in the sky. A rooster frightens away the cat.

Close-up of the hatching chick which is now almost out of the egg, but it's rather unclear what it is.

The pace increases. There are a series of very quick cross-cuts between chicks on the outside and the hatching chick until the hatchling flaps its wings and peeps.

The pace slows down. There is a cut to the barnyard. It looks like sunset. A truck pulls away, making a cloud of dust. Hens and chicks strut about the yard.

**Visual Attributes:** Sometimes abstracted liveaction images with many close-ups and some artsy out-of-focus shots. Fairly "normal" visual density with an unusual juxtaposition of images.

**Sound:** Nonverbal with realistic, natural sounds and loud, continuous music which changes (depending on whether barnyard or nest is being shown) from lively country sounds of fiddling and banjo picking to the quiet, eerie sound of a bowed saw and/or synthesizer. Audio density is rather high.

**Video Legibility/Audibility:** The close-ups work very well on video monitors; however, because the hatching egg images are unclear (i.e., abstracted from context or explanation), the film has only fair to good legibility. Audibility is fine.

**Pace:** Varies from very slow to fast.

**Structure:** Catalog with a sunrise/sunset frame.

**Themes:** Other than the process of hatching and variations and similarities in chickens, there was no clear-cut theme.

**Comments:** Although this sophisticated study worked moderately well, CHICK CHICK CHICK can be confusing to very young viewers because of the abstraction and the constant intercutting between the slowly hatching eggs and life outside the chicken coop. Also, the eerie music used under the hatching egg images suggests danger, outer space, or "Twilight Zone" stuff to children reared on the conventions of television. We used CHICK CHICK CHICK in Video Program #1 with ROSIE'S WALK.

**Suggested Activities:** By itself this does not really work for arts activities except writing or talking about what was seen. However, when properly paired it can be used to inspire movement and drawing activities.

**Related Reading:** Preschool children might enjoy *The Little Duck*, a photo/picturebook which, in addition to a sweet storyline, shows the life-cycle of a duck from hatching out of an egg to waiting for its own egg/baby to hatch; it is an inexpensive paperback.

Although it doesn't have a very realistic drawing of a newborn chick, *Good Morning, Chick* has a sweet and simple storyline about a young chick's exploration of a farm, complete with cat, rooster, and protective mother hen.

*Egg to Chick* may have more information than most hospitalized preschoolers could handle, but via a sensitive combination of drawings and photographs, it gives an excellent explanation of the development of a chick from an egg.

Most of *Inside an Egg* seems too technical, but pages 42–45 show a series of photographs of a hatching chick and the text explains why it looks so wet and tired.

Reading all or part of one of the above books would be a good prescreening activity and might help young hospitalized preschoolers better understand the film—especially that chickens come from eggs and that they are wet and tired (but not sick) when they first hatch.

---

**Recommended Pediatric Age:** 6–12.

**Hospital Rating:** \*\*\*\*

**Availability:**
CHICK CHICK CHICK
Distributed by Churchill Films.
16mm film purchase price: $240
¾-inch videotape purchase price: $170
½-inch videotape purchase price: $170
No extra charge for CCTV rights unless title is seen in more than one building; then CCTV rights are 10% of title cost, per building. Rights must be renewed annually. Generally, only 16mm prints are available for preview; if you can only preview in video, call to check availability of cassettes.

---

## CHICKS AND CHICKENS
*by Film und Bild* (West Germany/1970)
10 minutes / liveaction / color / nonverbal

This slow-paced look at life on a chicken farm opens with a shot of some eggs. A hen walks into view and sits on the eggs for a while but nothing much happens. Then there is a shot of the eggs beginning to hatch. One little chick pokes its beak out of the shell. Another chick is out all the way and a couple more are working their way out of their eggs. A few chicks walk around. The hen returns to sit on the unhatched eggs while those chicks that have just hatched mill about.

Now the camera shifts to out-of-doors. There are a number of shots of hens and chicks standing and walking about the yard. There is a practice cockfight and a number of birds are seen strutting around. Some take a dirt bath.

A bell rings and all the chicks and hens come out; the mother hen leads her young chicks out a little door. A rooster crows. A baby chick sits on a hen's back.

A dachshund comes by but is chased away by adult birds. Little chicks come out of hiding and mill around until the hen leads them back through the little doorway to their coop.

**Visual Attributes:** Liveaction in muted colors with an almost constant mid-range visual density.

**Sound:** A wordless, musicless film with only the "natural" sounds of chicks, hens, and roosters. Very low audio density.

**Video Legibility/Audibility:** Fair to poor legibility because the images are very small on the video screen; often inaudible and generally too quiet for the noisy hospital environment.

**Pace:** Slow.

**Structure:** An almost unfocused catalog of the daily life of barnyard fowl. Sort of a day in the life of chicks and chickens, but without a clearly chronological frame.

**Themes:** Other than variations and similarities among chickens, there was no clear-cut theme.

**Comments:** This type of low-key catalog works better in a supervised group setting where children can respond to it as a group, labelling and imitating movements. It would also probably work better as a film than a videotape. Although CHICKS AND CHICKENS had some repetition of images, it resulted in oversaturation and boredom on the part of children who saw it on video monitors without the benefit of group dynamics.

Because PIGS presented some problems, we used CHICKS AND CHICKENS as its replacement with ROSIE'S WALK in CCTV Program #2; however, we switched to CHICK, CHICK, CHICK as a partner for ROSIE'S WALK in our video programs.

**Suggested Activities:** By itself this would not generally work for arts activities (with the possible exception of talking about what was seen). However, when properly paired it can be used to inspire movement and drawing activities. A good minimal movement activity would be finger plays (for example, "The Hen and Chickens"—which includes music—on page 18 of *Finger Plays for Nursery and Kindergarten*).

**Related Reading:** See the listings under CHICK CHICK CHICK.

---

**Recommended Pediatric Age:** 2–6.

**Hospital Rating:** *

**Availability:**
CHICKS AND CHICKENS is not currently in US distribution; it may be available in public or university library collections.

---

# THE CREATION OF BIRDS
*by Frederic Back* (Canada/1972)
10 minutes / cutout animation / color / nonverbal

Based on a Native legend about the origin of birds, this tender, slow-moving film makes interesting use of seasonal and animal symbolism. MicMac children play with an old man while adults are busy fishing. A storm-spirit, Howling Wolf, rises like a monster from the water, toppling canoes and blowing the leaves from the trees.

When the old man's wigwam is destroyed, he leads the children into the forest where they find shelter until the wolf returns with ice-cold breath, making the leaves turn color and fall to the ground.

The little group flees to the protection of the evergreens. Howling Wolf huffs and puffs but he cannot blow the leaves or needles from the evergreens, so he departs. The old man directs the children in building a new wigwam.

Howling Wolf goes to where White Bear lives. Soon, the Arctic sky-bear brings winter snow and covers the land with a blanket of white. When the bear departs, children emerge from their shelter. Finding some still-colorful leaves lying under the snow, a girl cries and looks pleadingly upwards.

Gouseclappe (or Glooskap), a human looking sky-god, hears the girl's plea and sends the Sun to drive Howling Wolf and White Bear away. Although the snow melts, the girl remains sad. So Gouseclappe flies down and blows the leaves off the ground, turning them into colorful, chirping birds which fill the trees. The children are happy and leaves once again appear on the trees.

In the concluding segment, trees are shown changing with the seasons—spring, summer, fall, winter, spring, summer, etc.—in a visual round. Credits appear, superimposed over the trees, and the images blur.

**Visual Attributes:** Cartoon cutouts in soft, secondary colors. Visual density tends to be high but characters are generally well separated from their background environment.

**Sound:** Nonverbal with instrumental music which combines a tom-tom rhythm and a lyrical, eminently humable melody. Audio density is somewhat low.

**Video Legibility/Audibility:** Excellent, especially its color. (No doubt because it was originally designed for television.) Its strong melody line was also quite effective.

**Pace:** Leisurely.

**Structure:** Narrative. A slightly meandering origins tale with a number of mood-setting embellishments.

**Themes:** Nurturing and tenderness; delight in nature; familial support; change and transformation; monsters; cycle of seasons; female protagonist; wishes; origin tale (the origin of birds).

**Comments:** THE CREATION OF BIRDS was a true success, despite the fact that in order to follow the storyline children had to pay close attention to the images. Hospitalized viewers found this charming legend highly satisfying and, as we have found in nonhospital screenings, it had a significant and positive impact on children's artwork.

We tried THE CREATION OF BIRDS with various partners: in Film Program #9 with KUUMBA in

CCTV Program #1 with ANANSI THE SPIDER; and in Video Programs #6 with A STORY, A STORY, #7 with THE MAGIC PEAR TREE, and #8 with HOMMAGE A FRANCOIS COUPERIN.

**Suggested Activities:** Collage or drawing.

**Related Reading:** School age children might enjoy the unusual looking picturebook, *How Summer Came to Canada*, another seasonal tale featuring Glooskap which was illustrated with collage images. If the destructive nature of Wolf-Wind is deemphasized, older children might enjoy hearing a shortened and slightly modified version of "How Glooskap Made the Birds" from Cyrus Macmillan's *Glooskap's Country and Other Indian Tales* (Walck); it was anthologized in *Once Upon A Time* edited by Elizabeth H. Gross (Collier).

If you are planning to do seasonal activities involving color, you might want to read children sections of *Hailstones and Halibut Bones: Adventures in Color*; it is available in paperback. Another lovely book on seasons and colors is Myra Cohn Livingston's poetic *A Circle of Seasons*. Volodya Lapin also has an appropriate poem, "Spring Mood," in *Thread One to a Star*.

---

**Recommended Pediatric Age:** 5–13.

**Hospital Rating:** ****

**Availability:**
THE CREATION OF BIRDS
Distributed by AIMS Instructional Media.
16mm film purchase price: $210
¾-inch videotape purchase price: $110
½-inch videotape purchase price: $100
No additional charge for CCTV rights. Also distributed by CBC Enterprises.

---

# CURIOUS GEORGE GOES TO THE HOSPITAL
*by John Matthews* (USA/1982)
15 minutes / puppet animation / color

A little bird flies outside an open window while a monkey sleeps in bed. The bird chirps. Music starts on the soundtrack. The bird chirps again. The monkey wakes, gets out of bed, and waves to the bird. Then he goes to a desk and finds a box labeled "Jigsaw Puzzle." He lifts the box top and, thinking a piece of the puzzle is candy, swallows it.

Just then, the man with the yellow hat comes in and says, "Why George, I see you already opened the box with the jigsaw puzzle. It was supposed to be a surprise for you. Well, let's get to work on it." They set to work on the puzzle. When almost finished, they cannot find one piece. The man looks everywhere but eventually gives up. "Let's go to bed now, George," he says. Blackout.

Next morning at breakfast, George does not feel well. He has a stomach ache and does not want to eat. The man is worried, so he calls Dr. Baker who comes to the house. Dr. Baker looks at George's throat, feels his stomach, and listens to his breathing with a stethoscope. Because he cannot figure out what is wrong, Dr. Baker tells the man to take George to the hospital for x-rays.

At the hospital George drinks some barium and has an x-ray which shows the missing puzzle piece in his stomach. Dr. Baker says he must stay in the hospital for a few days so they can get the piece out.

While waiting outside the admissions office, George sits next to a girl named Betsy who has never been to a hospital before and is quite scared.

After he is formally admitted and gets a name bracelet, a nurse named Carol takes George and the man (with the yellow hat) to the children's ward where George has a bed right next to Betsy. The man stays with George for a while, then leaves, saying he will return in the morning before George goes to the operating room. George cries when the man leaves. Blackout.

In the morning, the man returns and several nurses take George's blood pressure, and give him both a pill to make him sleepy and a shot.

George is wheeled into the operating room where, following a quick look around at the lights and the masked people, he falls asleep.

After his operation, George feels a little sick but the next day, when he is better, he goes to the playroom, puts on a special four-hand puppet show and spins around on the record turntable.

Then, when he is supposed to be resting, the mischievous monkey races a go-cart down the halls and crashes into a food tray, all of which succeeds in making his fellow patients, especially sad Betsy, roar with laughter.

George goes home with the man with the yellow hat and, together, they finish the puzzle because the hospital staff saved the piece George swallowed. The bird appears on the window sill and George waves to it.

**Visual Attributes:** Highly kinesthetic, animated puppets with intricately crafted, three-dimensional sets and props. Image density ranges from low (at the beginning) to rather high (in the hospital), but figures and backgrounds are clearly separated.

**Sound:** Character dialog and female narration with occasional music. Audio density tends to be low.

**Video Legibility/Audibility:** Excellent.

**Pace:** Mostly medium-slow except for turntable and go-cart scenes.

**Structure:** Dramatic narrative. Although the plot has many embellishments, it is well-focused and George is on-screen in almost every shot, which acts as a reinforcing focal point. In addition to an effective opening/closing frame involving George and the bird at home, this film makes strategic use of the blackout—that old stand-by of Hollywood movies—to signal end-of-day for the 2 nights encompassed within the story's time-frame.

**Themes:** Hospitalization; nurturing and tenderness; separation; familial support; puzzles; how ward mates can cheer each other; laughter is the best medicine; flexibility on the part of hospital staff; returning safely home.

**Comments:** CURIOUS GEORGE GOES TO THE HOSPITAL is a wonderful film. Hospitalized children laughed at George's forbidden antics and typically asked to see it again, something we generally do with shorter films but which we did not always plan to do with longer narrative works. At one site, children asked to see the film 5 times in a row—enjoying it more each time. Since this was a recent release and we only got it at the last minute, we did not pair it with another film for an activity nor did we include it in our CCTV programs (although it would have been great for both). We did use it in Video Program #24 with CAPTAIN SILAS.

**Suggested Activities:** Box art and dioramas.

**Related Reading:** Preschool and young school age children may enjoy the picturebook by Margret and H. A. Rey upon which the film is based; it is available in paperback. Young school age children and older preschoolers might enjoy the paperback *Jenny's in the Hospital*, in which a girl of 5–6 breaks her arm and stays overnight in a hospital. Older school age children may enjoy the realistically illustrated paperback about a girl's appendectomy, *Elizabeth Gets Well*.

---

**Recommended Pediatric Age:** 4–10.

**Hospital Rating:** ****

**Availability:**
CURIOUS GEORGE GOES TO THE HOSPITAL
Distributed by Churchill Films.
16mm film purchase price: $355
¾-inch videotape purchase price: $355
½-inch videotape purchase price: $355
No extra charge for CCTV rights unless title is seen in more than one building; then CCTV rights are 10% of title cost, per building. Rights must be renewed annually. Generally, only 16mm prints are available for preview; call about availability of preview videos.

---

# THE FABLE OF HE AND SHE
*by Eli Noyes* (USA/1974)
11 minutes / clay animation / color

This delightful fable about how Hardibars (men) and Mushamels (women) free themselves from sex-role stereotypes opens with some happy-go-lucky vocalizations. As a long shot of an island is shown on-screen, the narrator identifies this as the land of Baramel.

"Wonderful birds and beasts lived there," the narrator continues and, as strange and fabulous creatures appear, he identifies the savage chopachuck (something like a flying octopus), the fierce mushmoo (a type of small pink elephant), and the wild mellowcluck (sort of a snail with a chicken's head).

The narrator explains that Baramel has 2 kinds of people, Hardibars and Mushamels. When he mentions Hardibars, an elongated blue creature with a friendly man's voice says, "Hello! I'm a Hardibar." When he mentions Mushamels, a round salmon-pink creature with a warm, Southern woman's voice says, "Hi there! I'm a Mushamel." As a mixed-age group poses for a snapshot inside a house, the narrator explains that Hardibars and Mushamels live together in families.

A Hardibar explains that Mushamels are too timid to face the fierce mushmoo, which a number of Mushamels affirm. Another male voice explains that Mushamels are too weak to push the mellowcluck off its eggs, and yet another adds that they are too slow to escape the fangs of the speedy chopachuck. A fourth says, "We Hardibars are strong!" Others add, "We will do the hunting." They demonstrate this by overwhelming a chopachuck and carrying it off as a group of Mushamels make admiring *oohs* and *ahs*.

As Hardibars work on a structure, another male voice says that Mushamels are too soft to build houses, and the women say "Right!" A tough-sounding male voice says, "We will build all the houses that need to be built!" The rasp of a saw is stopped when a Hardibar says, "Wait a minute! Hold it! This house, the noise.... Everything is giving me a headache!" One male voice identifies the speaker as He-bar, another adds that he's always complaining. He-bar says, "What I'd really like to do is paint. Couldn't I paint houses instead of building them—make them pretty?"

"He-bar," says the chorus of male voices, "Hardibars do not paint. That is not a Hardibar thing to do!"

A group of Mushamels come on-screen and announce that they will explain about Mushamels. As their words are demonstrated, different women's voices say that Mushamels are best at cooking, watching the babies, and making things pretty and nice. In unison they say, "That's what all Mushamels love to do best."

"Not me!" says one woman's voice as a Mushamel is seen stirring something in a pot. "I'd rather be eaten by a chopachuck than stay all day in a hot kitchen." Different women's voices identify the speaker as She-mel and comment that she is odd—even "peculiar!" Undaunted, She-mel asks why she can't hunt. "She-mel," a woman's voice lectures, "Mushamels cook; they don't hunt!" She-mel replies, "Pooh!"

As another long shot of the island appears, the narrator explains that Baramel has an annual holiday known as Oompah Day. On this day, all Hardibars go to one end of the island and all Mushamels go to the other where they hold contests. Hardibars are seen climbing trees, cutting lumber, and lassoing wild chopachucks. The overall winner is crowned Hardibar of the Year. As he is crowned, the winner flexes his biceps.

Meanwhile, Mushamels have baking, flower growing, and dancing contests. The winner sheds tears of joy as she is crowned Mushamel of the Year.

The long shot of the island is seen again. The narrator explains that, in the midst of the festivities, disaster struck. A bolt of lightning splits the island in half, and Hardibars and Mushamels are separated by a great gulf of water.

When the Mushamels begin to worry about how they will survive, they list the things they cannot do and begin to cry, bemoaning the fact that they will freeze to death. "Hold it everybody," says She-mel, "and stop the crying!" She explains that she does not intend to freeze to death and develops a new way of building a house. Next, she announces that everyone is going hunting and—by singing off-key—the Mushamels drive a wild mushmoo right into the ground.

Meanwhile, the Hardibars are having their own problems. When a group of baby Hardibars won't stop crying, He-bar makes a rocking device which pacifies the children. When the adults realize that they have nothing for dinner, He-bar makes a meal of chopachuck and pompomberry stew in peanut butter sauce which leaves everyone feeling a bit sick. "But little by little," the narrator explains, "their cooking improved."

A long shot of the split island is seen and the narrator says, "Time passed. The Hardibars and Mushamels lived separately on either side of the great gap." A few islanders shout to each other across the water. Suddenly a storm arises, and the narrator explains that a "reversaquake" joined the island together.

Hardibars and Mushamels rush into each other's arms, hugging and kissing. Then the Hardibars announce that things will return to the way they were before; but the Mushamels have other ideas. "Things are going to be different;" they say in unison, "we've learned to do some new things." As the Mushamels demonstrate their new building

technique, it elicits an admiring response from some of the Hardibars.

In turn, the Hardibars cook up a pie of fried mellowcluck with pompom pudding, topped with creamy mushmoo whip. It elicits a positive response from several Mushamels.

As a Mushamel and Hardibar work together raising plants, the narrator explains, "From then on, things were different." In a series of little vignettes, a Hardibar is seen taking care of babies, both Hardibars and Mushamels work together to build a house, and a mixed group sings down a wild chopachuck.

"That year on Oompah Day," the narrator says, "everyone was grateful to He-bar and She-mel for helping them change their ways." So the prize of Hardibar and Mushamel of the Year goes to them. He-bar smiles a toothy grin. She-mel cries huge, happy tears.

Once again, the long shot of the island is seen. The narrator explains that in order to commemorate the names of He-bar and She-mel all Hardibars were called *he* from then on. A group of Hardibars say "he" in unison. "And all Mushamels were called *she*." A group of Mushamels say "she" in unison. Then, as the image of the island is seen again, the narrator concludes: "And so they are still called in Baramel, and a few other places."

To zany vocal sound effects, the sun sets behind the island and the moon rises. The words "the end" appear.

**Visual Attributes:** Abstract figures in a sort of bas-relief playdough animation. Fairly high image density with good separation of figure (via color and shape) from ground.

**Sound:** Character dialog and male narration. Some penny-whistle music but mostly highly inventive, vocally created music and effects. Audio density is medium.

**Video Legibility/Audibility:** Although the bright film colors became somewhat dull in the tape transfer, it was very legible. Excellent audibility.

**Pace:** Medium to medium-fast.

**Structure:** Narrative. A modern fable with a complex structure involving parallel patterns of action and a story which is divided into 4 parts: a prologue, the disaster, the reunion, and an epilogue. Its complexity is somewhat mitigated, at least for older viewers, by the consistent use of a long shot of the island to demarcate the 4 sections, by the voice/shape/color coding of each sex, and by mixing recognizably stereotypic and true-to-life actions/attitudes with the fantastic and symbolic.

**Themes:** Change and transformation; role reversal; social change; making the best of a bad situation; cooperation and teamwork; surviving a disaster with teamwork; pooling resources; jobs should not be sex-determined.

**Comments:** The storyline and details of character and setting are much more developed in THE FABLE OF HE AND SHE than in a traditional fable, so this was better received than other fables, such as THE STONECUTTER. It was, in fact, very successful.

Nonetheless, the sex-role reversal theme is quite sophisticated, even for preadolescents who seem dedicated to establishing their sexual identity within peer-defined limits. At any rate, children did not comment on that message. Hospitalized viewers did understand, however, about cooperating and trying new ideas and they did wonderful clay and playdough artwork.

We tried THE FABLE OF HE AND SHE in Film Program #15 with SOLO; in CCTV Program #9 with A CHAIRY TALE; and in Video Program #23 with SOPHIE AND THE SCALES.

**Suggested Activities:** Clay or playdough sculpture and box art.

**Related Reading:** To emphasize the nonstereotyped sex-role theme, younger children might enjoy discussing *William's Doll* by Charlotte Zolotow which is available in paperback and was also anthologized in *Free to Be... You and Me*. Older children might enjoy "Changing Places" a humorous folktale in which a husband and wife change jobs; the story was adapted by Bernard Garfinkel and has been anthologized in Tomi Ungerer's *Storybook*.

---

**Recommended Pediatric Age:** 7–14.

**Hospital Rating:** \*\*\*\*

**Availability:**
THE FABLE OF HE AND SHE
Distributed by Coronet/MTI.
16mm film purchase price: $250
¾-inch videotape purchase price: $175
½-inch videotape purchase price: $175
Probably no extra charge for CCTV rights.

---

# FELIX GETS THE CAN
*by Otto Messmer* (USA/1924)
7 minutes / line animation / b&w / silent

Felix the Cat is unsuccessfully fishing with worms. When he looks in the river to find out why he is getting no bites, a big fish climbs on the riverbank and eats his bait.

Frustrated and hungry, Felix attempts to steal a fish from a restaurant but gets caught in the act. The irate restaurateur hurls a can that hits Felix on the head. He examines its "Yukon Fisherman" label. Suddenly, the man on the label comes to life and makes exaggerated arm motions as if telling a fish story. A title card appears, saying, "We get 'em that big in Alaska."

Deep in thought, Felix paces as a pair of question marks hover above his head. Inspired, Felix grabs the question marks out of the air and places them on the ground, then whistles to a string of hot dogs hanging in a butcher's window and cracks a whip. They line up before him and turn into sled dogs which pull Felix (on his question mark sled runners) over the hills into the distance.

Felix comes to a dance hall in a snow-covered place. A title card reads: "All through the North they knew the bad man, Dan McStew." When the cat drinks from a bottle, McStew who is standing by the bar shoots at him. Felix, however, dances along the bullets and resumes his quest.

Felix is wading through deep snow when he spies the sign, "To the salmon fisheries." A title card reads: "That year the salmon ran better than ever." Felix sees fish running upstream, literally hopping up-river on their tailfins. Felix tries to swim upstream but is pushed back to where he started. The fish laugh at him.

Felix then spies a ship in the distance. Removing his tail and using it as a telescope, he sees a man in a boat successfully fishing with a net. When a spider drops from a nearby tree, Felix (in a cartoon speech balloon) says, "How quick can you weave me a net?" The spider (in another speech balloon) says, "Watch me!" and quickly weaves a net which Felix is just about to use when a fish pushes him in the water. Unfortunately, Felix becomes entangled in his own net, gets caught in a trawling rig, and is dumped onto a conveyor belt and canned.

A title card reads: "It was Friday in a restaurant back home." A waiter opens a can for an elderly patron who puts his fork into the can and pulls out a long, snake-like object which turns out to be the cat's tail. Felix stands on the table, momentarily assuming the pose of an automobile hood ornament. Then he gives a mischievous wink, plucks the fish from the can label, and swallows it as the customer tips backwards in a faint. Felix gives his stomach a satisfied rub.

**Visual Attributes:** Black-and-white line drawings with minimal background images. Occasional speech balloons and title cards contain printed words. Low image density.

**Sound:** Silent.

**Video Legibility/Audibility:** It had no sound but the images were quite legible.

**Pace:** Medium to medium-fast.

**Structure:** Narrative. A meandering, tongue-in-cheek quest that is amplified by repetition and embellished with visual jokes.

**Themes:** Creative problem-solving; perseverance; puzzles.

**Comments:** FELIX GETS THE CAN is a very demanding work. It not only requires viewers to read the title cards and speech balloons, it is also somewhat dependent on outside references. It helps to know that the Yukon is near (and perhaps synonymous with) Alaska and that salmon are a type of fish. Viewers also need some knowledge about the world in order to get the visual jokes.

Despite all this, FELIX GETS THE CAN might have fared better if we had dubbed in a cartoon music track to let children know that this was a funny work. As a silent cartoon it was not successful. (In a playroom screening this can be "fixed" by playing a piano rag, such as one by Scott Joplin, on an audiocassette player while the film or tape is screened.) We used FELIX GETS THE CAN in CCTV Program #11 with HAROLD'S FAIRY TALE.

**Suggested Activities:** Drawing, cartooning, making flipbooks.

**Related Reading:** For instructions on how to make a flipbook, see pages 24–26 in *The Animation Book* by Kit Laybourne. If you would like to try other paper animation techniques, see pages 18–23 in the same book, or get a copy of *Paper Movie Machines.*

---

**Recommended Pediatric Age:** 6–10.

**Hospital Rating:** **

**Availability:**
FELIX GETS THE CAN
Distributed by the Museum of Modern Art.
16mm film purchase price: $65
¾-inch videotape purchase price: $65
½-inch videotape purchase price: $65
No additional charge for CCTV rights.

---

## THE FROG KING OR FAITHFUL HENRY

*by Tom Davenport (USA/1980)*
15 minutes / liveaction / color

This liveaction version of the Grimm folktale is set in Victorian America and given a slightly tongue-in-cheek treatment. In the opening scene, a spoiled preadolescent girl loses her favorite ball down a well and promises a talking frog that he can sit at her table and sleep in her bed if he retrieves it. When he brings her the ball, however, she callously runs off and leaves him calling after her.

In the next scene, the girl is dining with her father, her sisters, and some guests. There is a loud knock at the door which she answers. Finding the frog, the girl slams the door shut and returns to the table. Gently teasing at first, her father asks who was there. When he learns of her promise, he insists that she invite the frog to dine. In comic counterpoint to the formal setting, the frog sits momentarily on some pillows next to the girl before leaping into her soup bowl and from there all around the table. When the frog announces he is ready to go to bed, her father insists she take him to her room.

Depositing the frog on her dresser, the girl gets ready for and then climbs into bed. The frog immediately demands to be taken into bed. The girl refuses and he threatens to tell her father, whereupon she picks him up and hurls him against the door. To her amazement, a preppie-looking young man hits the floor where the frog should have fallen. She goes to his aid and they talk while the narrator explains that she had broken a spell which turned the young man into a frog and, at her father's wish, the young man becomes the girl's husband.

In the epilogue, a horse-drawn carriage moves down a dirt road while the narrator says that the young man heard a sound which was the breaking of bands around the heart of his servant, Faithful Henry.

**Visual Attributes:** Liveaction with average to low visual density. Except for the epilogue which has practically none, the actions are very clear and there is excellent correlation between what is seen and what is heard.

**Sound:** Occasional male narration but mostly character dialog. Emphatic music which sometimes plays under the narration. Average to low audio density.

**Pace:** Medium-slow.

**Structure:** Dramatic narrative. Like a play with 3 acts and an epilogue, this is an extremely tight, well-focused tale.

**Themes:** Self-assertion; anger; unanticipated consequences; uncooperative behavior; change and transformation; the almost magical transformations of adolescence; conflict with parent; fairness; reneging on a promise; some bad deals work out okay; female protagonist.

**Comments:** We initially tried THE FROG KING OR FAITHFUL HENRY in Film Program #6 because nonhospitalized preschoolers found the film quite amusing. However, it frightened young and low-functioning preschoolers so we did no further testing. This does not mean that it would not work in hospitals, but it would probably work better with school age children and on video monitors (to diminish its visual impact).

When we showed THE FROG KING OR FAITHFUL HENRY following PIERRE, a developmentally delayed 3-year-old became terrified during the dining scene when the frog jumps on the table and a point-of-view shot shows all the diners looking at it. The child said she was afraid that she was going to be eaten, so we stopped the film. She may have been led to expect that, at least in part, by PIERRE in which the little boy *is* eaten by a lion. Nonetheless, when the images of the dining table scene in THE FROG KING OR FAITHFUL HENRY are combined with the hospitalized preschooler's anxiety fantasies concerning mutilation and devouring, such a reaction is understandable. For this reason, we do not recommend this film for preschoolers.

**Suggested Activities:** Creative dramatics, puppetry.

**Related Reading:** Young school age children might enjoy the Grimm tale, "The Frog King or Faithful Henry" in *The Juniper Tree and Other Tales from Grimm.* The same tale is listed as "The Frog Prince" in *The Old-Fashioned Storybook.*

---

**Recommended Pediatric Age:** 8–12.

**Hospital Rating:** *

**Availability:**
THE FROG KING OR FAITHFUL HENRY
Distributed by Tom Davenport Films.
16mm film purchase price: $275
¾-inch videotape purchase price: $150
½-inch videotape purchase price: $60
No additional charge for CCTV rights. Each videocassette contains another short, THE MAKING OF THE FROG KING, at no extra charge.

---

# GERALD McBOING BOING
*by Robert Cannon* (USA/1950)
7 minutes / cel animation / color

A classic cartoon which tells the poignant tale of a handicapped boy who eventually finds a place for himself in the world.

> This is the story of Gerald McCloy and the strange things that happened to this little boy.
> They say it all started when Gerald was 2.
> That's the age kids start talking, at least most of them do.
> But when he started talking, you know what he said?
> He didn't say words...
> He went *boing boing* instead.

So says the narrator, as this film begins. When his father hears Gerald's first sound, he is so alarmed that he calls Dr. Malone, but the doctor says he can't handle the case and leaves Gerald alone with his parents.

Months pass and Gerald gets louder and louder, until one day (when Gerald makes a boom like a big keg of powder) his father says it is time to send him to school. So off he goes as his mother waves goodbye at the door, then Gerald returns because he forgot something and goes off to an old-fashioned schoolhouse. But before long he comes home with a note from the teacher saying that Gerald is hopeless and the school will not accept him.

Gerald tries to make friends with the neighborhood children but they don't want such a different playmate. Some cruelly taunt: "You're name's not McCloy; you're Gerald McBoing Boing, the noise-making boy!"

Depressed, Gerald goes into the bathroom while his father is shaving and inadvertently frightens him. His father sends the boy to his room. Gerald climbs the long dark stairs in a blue mood and decides to run away.

While waiting by a railroad crossing one dark, snowy night, Gerald is approached by a tall, well-dressed man who says,

> Aren't you Gerald McBoing Boing, the boy who makes squeaks?
> I have searched for you for many long weeks.
> I can make you the most famous lad in the nation, for I own the *bing-bong-bung* radio station.

Gerald is hired and when next we see him he is standing in a radio/recording studio making sound effects for a cowboy soap opera as his parents proudly watch. When the show is over, Gerald leaves with his parents and gets in the back of a long limousine as fans crowd the sidewalk. As the vehicle pulls away, the narrator concludes:

> Now Gerald is rich.
> He has friends. He's well fed.
> He doesn't speak words.
> He goes *boing boing* instead.

**Visual Attributes:** Images vary from cartoonish drawings with little background detail to intensely colored scenes that resemble Art Moderne posters of the 1930–40s; Gerald is in almost every image. Fairly high visual density.

**Sound:** A male storyteller delivers both narration and dialog in quickly-paced, rhymed verse which was written by Dr. Seuss. The soundtrack also has occasional music with emphatic and well integrated sound effects. Audio density is medium to medium-high.

**Video Legibility/Audibility:** Very good.

**Pace:** Variable but mostly medium.

**Structure:** Dramatic narrative. Makes effective use of sequential development and repetitive patterns of action, words, and sounds.

**Themes:** Being different; loneliness; separation; running away from home; self-acceptance; social acceptance; reunion with family; handicaps and disabilities; what seems a liability may be a talent; sound-making.

**Comments:** GERALD McBOING BOING was a genuine hit with hospitalized children, and hospital staff considered it thematically important for this population.

Structurally, one of its strong points is that the protagonist is on-screen most of the time which helps focus the film for younger children. We tried it in Film Program #16 with A QUEST and in Video Program #18 with KUUMBA. Although we did not try it on CCTV, it would work very well on such systems.

**Suggested Activities:** Sound-making, storytelling, and painting.

---

**Recommended Pediatric Age:** 6–13.

**Hospital Rating:** ****

**Availability:**
GERALD McBOING BOING
Distributed by Churchill Films.
16mm film purchase price: $175
¾-inch videotape purchase price: $125
½-inch videotape purchase price: $125
No extra charge for CCTV rights unless title is seen in more than one building; then CCTV rights are 10% of title cost, per building. Rights must be renewed annually. Generally, only 16mm prints are available for preview; if you can only preview in video, call to check availability of limited cassettes.

---

# HANDS
*by Karen Johnson* (USA/1970)
3 minutes / animated photos / b&w / nonverbal

A zany celebration of those great performers—human hands. First the thumb, then the index finger, then one, then a pair of hands perform their best tricks (i.e., bending, crossing, clapping, waving, and doing finger plays like "Church and Steeple").

After the initial run-through—each section of which is preceded by a cue-card saying thumb, finger, hand, 2 hands—there is a fast reprise of images followed by an even faster reprise. All is done to the accompaniment of an odd mix of found sounds ranging from applause and a "raspberry" to donkey brays.

**Visual Attributes:** A monochromatic, blue-tinted, black-and-white animation of close-up shots of human hands. Its uniformity of color gives it a fairly high visual density.

**Sound:** Nonverbal with overlapping and often contrapuntal sounds whereby the sound does not match the image. Fairly high audio density.

**Video Legibility/Audibility:** Fairly good.

**Pace:** Varies from slow to frenetic.

**Structure:** A freewheeling and slightly surreal catalog of hand images accompanied by sometimes unrelated sounds.

**Themes:** Variations on the hand with no other clear-cut theme.

**Comments:** There's a lot going on at once in HANDS and that can be confusing and/or overwhelming for some hospitalized children. Also, be careful with works like this if you have any children with epileptic tendencies; flashing or stroboscopic effects (such as this film uses in the last reprise) have been known to induce seizures. Because of this, we do not recommend HANDS for CCTV. We tried it in Video Program #16 with THE PRINCESS AND THE PEA.

**Suggested Activities:** Finger plays and puppetry, especially puppets made by painting directly on children's hands, or puppets which use fingers as legs or arms.

**Related Reading:** Select one of the musical finger games from the chapter "One Finger, One Thumb—Stand Up, Sit Down" in *Elephant Jam* by Sharon, Lois and Bram. Locate one of Sharon, Lois and Bram's outstanding and delightful recordings, *One Elephant, Deux Elephants* or *Smorgasbord*, and play the record/tape as children perform the actions described in this excellent book. Or show children "Isn't It Amazing What a Hand Can Do?" (pages 56–57) in Imogene Forte's helpfully illustrated activity book, *Puppets: Friends at Your Finger Tips*. Or adapt one of the finger plays from *Finger Plays for Nursery and Kindergarten*.

---

**Recommended Pediatric Age:** 6–14.

**Hospital Rating:** ***

**Availability:**
HANDS
Distributed by Karen Johnson.
16mm film purchase price: $45
¾-inch videotape purchase price: $55
½-inch videotape purchase price: $40
No additional charge for CCTV rights.

---

# HAROLD AND THE PURPLE CRAYON
*by David Piel* (USA/1969)
8 minutes / cel animation / color

Harold, an independent-minded toddler, is dressed for bed in his Dr. Dentons when he decides to go for a walk in the moonlight. Because there is no moon he draws one. There isn't anything to walk on either, so Harold draws a long straight path in perspective and sets off with his purple crayon.

When he appears to be getting nowhere on the path, Harold, followed by the moon, takes a shortcut which leads to where he thinks a forest ought to be, so Harold draws one there. Because he doesn't want to get lost in the woods, he draws only one tree—an apple tree—under which he places a toothsome dragon to guard the fruit. He then proceeds to draw himself in and out of adventures with a sailboat and hot air balloon by means of his crayon until he gets tired, at which point he searches for the window of his room.

The search, however, proves fruitless until Harold recalls that his window is always right around the moon. So he draws his window around the crescent which faithfully accompanied him throughout the journey. He then draws his bed, climbs in, pulls up the covers, and falls asleep.

**Visual Attributes:** Minimally colored, almost monochromatic line drawings with little or no background detail; it looks like coloring book artwork and has a low image density.

**Sound:** Male narration with continuous, jazzy music. Medium-high density with good audibility because the narrator's clear voice is not obscured by the music.

**Video Legibility/Audibility:** Excellent.

**Pace:** Leisurely. .

**Structure:** Narrative. An unusual story with a loose, associative-sequential structure which avoids normal cause-and-effect.

**Themes:** Imaginative possibilities of line; creative problem-solving; self-reliance; change and transformation; returning safely home; how much children know about their own environment; the *logic* of early childhood.

**Comments:** As one young child observed enthusiastically during a screening: "That crayon must be magic!" Both HAROLD AND THE PURPLE CRAYON and a follow-up drawing activity were very successful with hospitalized children. The story's associatively connected episodes are given an almost musical coherence by the use of 3 motifs—the crescent moon, the purple crayon, and Harold—which appear in just about every frame and give the film an apparent focus.

As with certain folksongs, the ending is arbitrary and could have occurred at any point. Despite the fact that it does not literally have a circular closure, HAROLD AND THE PURPLE CRAYON has an implied circularity since Harold ends up in bed for the night, which is where he would have been if he had not taken his walk-in-the-moonlight detour.

Although the moose and the porcupine featured in this film do not actually resemble those animals, this posed no real problem because few children know what they look like, and they were not central to the storyline.

When we wanted a replacement for HAROLD'S FAIRY TALE, we used HAROLD AND THE PURPLE CRAYON in Video Program #2 along with A VISIT FROM SPACE. It would also be fine for CCTV.

**Suggested Activities:** Drawing with crayons, coloring, and storytelling.

**Related Reading:** Preschool children might enjoy the picturebook by Crockett Johnson upon which the film is based; it is available from Weston Woods and/or Harper & Row. They might also enjoy the other books by Crockett Johnson, of which *A Picture for Harold's Room* most closely parallels HAROLD AND THE PURPLE CRAYON and would be a good preparation/follow-up to the film.

---

**Recommended Pediatric Age:** 3–7.

**Hospital Rating:** \*\*\*\*

**Availability:**
HAROLD AND THE PURPLE CRAYON
Distributed by Weston Woods.
16mm film purchase price: $195
¾-inch videotape purchase price: $140
½-inch videotape purchase price: $50
Fee structure for CCTV rights is based on the number of buildings in which the title will be viewed times the running time. If title will be shown in only one building, CCTV rights are generally covered in the basic purchase price. ¾-inch videotapes available by special order.

---

# HAROLD'S FAIRY TALE
*by Gene Deitch* (USA/1974)
8 minutes / line animation / color

Dressed in pajamas, the imaginative toddler (from the previous film) goes for a walk, taking along his purple crayon and the moon, and turns the conventions of the fairytale inside-out.

Harold starts off in what is supposed to be an enchanted garden; unfortunately, there is nothing there except a horizon line and the moon, so Harold draws some lines that vaguely suggest a castle. Then he draws a gate, but it is closed so Harold tries to think of another way in.

He draws an odd-looking mouse and a mouse hole, by means of which he enters the building and draws some steps that take him to the throne room. When he finds no throne, he draws a very unconventional-looking chair with a walrus-like king upon it.

By accident, he draws a hole in the wall and climbs down what looks like the letter "A" which turns out to be the hat of an invisible giant witch.

In order to drive her away, Harold draws a bunch of mosquitoes; he gets rid of them with smoke.

The rain which douses the fire to make the smoke also makes the garden bloom with strange-looking flowers, one of which turns out to be a fairy.

Tired from all his activity, Harold sits down on a small rug which turns into a flying carpet. When Harold wants to stop the carpet, he draws the fireplace at home and an easy chair. Next he draws a book and asks his mother (who is not seen) to read him a story.

**Visual Attributes:** Minimally colored, nearly monochromatic line drawings; unfortunately, there are too few images, and they are fragmented or incomplete. In addition, there is almost no action in this sophisticated work. Not only did the fairytale's stock characters (king, witch, fairy) play passive-iconic roles, but they looked too unorthodox to be readily identified. Extremely low image density.

**Sound:** Male narration with continuous music. Medium-high audio density.

**Video Legibility/Audibility:** It has good audibility but, while quite legible, is visually uninteresting.

**Pace:** Very slow.

**Structure:** List. Like HAROLD AND THE PURPLE CRAYON, this unusual work uses an associative structure which lacks regular cause-and-effect relations. Unlike the earlier work, however, this does not cohere. Despite the same motifs, it seems arbitrary and overly capricious.

**Themes:** The imaginative possibilities of lines; change and transformation; self-reliance; returning safely home; fractured fairytales.

**Comments:** Harold is not on-screen as much in this as in HAROLD AND THE PURPLE CRAYON, so HAROLD'S FAIRY TALE does not seem as well-focused. Critical objects such as the castle are only partially drawn, which makes this more of a visual riddle than its predecessor.

Unfortunately, there is also little visual amplification of the narrator's words in this quasi-ironic presentation; viewers hear one thing and see another. In addition, HAROLD'S FAIRY TALE relies on conventions (such as the structure and motifs typical of fairytales) that many hospitalized child viewers, especially minorities or the chronically ill, were not familiar with. Thus, although it was an effective lead-in to drawing activities, the film's imagery and storyline were too conceptual, too unconventional, and too topsy-turvy for hospitalized children. We tried it in Film Program #8 with LITTLE GRAY NECK and in CCTV Program #11 with FELIX GETS THE CAN.

**Suggested Activities:** Drawing, especially with crayons.

**Related Reading:** Preschool children might enjoy the picturebook by Crockett Johnson upon which the film is based; it is currently out of print but is available in many public library collections. The book would probably help children get more out of the film if it were read before the screening.

Five- to seven-year-olds might enjoy *Harold's ABC* which has some parallels to HAROLD'S FAIRY TALE but which is a better inspiration for drawing activities, especially those using letter shapes as a starting point.

---

**Recommended Pediatric Age:** 5–8.

**Hospital Rating:** **

**Availability:**
HAROLD'S FAIRY TALE
Distributed by Weston Woods.
16mm film purchase price: $175
¾-inch videotape purchase price: $175
½-inch videotape purchase price: $175
Fee structure for CCTV rights is based on the number of buildings in which the title will be viewed times the running time. If title will be shown in only one building, CCTV rights are generally covered in the basic purchase price; ¾-inch videotapes available by special order.

---

# HOMMAGE A FRANCOIS COUPERIN
*by Philip Stapp* (USA/1964)
2 minutes / animation / color / nonverbal

Sort of an impressionist/baroque musical, this subtle and exquisite ballet of butterflies and blades of grass is choreographed to a piano/harpsichord study by the French baroque composer Couperin. The film has 2 musical variations of the same piece, one more complex than the other. Echoing the music, the images in "Variation 1" are simple, while those in "Variation 2" are complex with a multiple after-image that correlates to the polyphonic sounds.

**Visual Attributes:** Pastel-colored pointillist animation that suggests Japanese or Chinese nature painting. The image density is somewhat low in the first section and somewhat high in the second section.

**Sound:** Two variations on a theme by Couperin using what sounds like a harpsichord. Medium audio density.

**Video Legibility/Audibility:** Excellent.

**Pace:** Varied.

**Structure:** Lyric. A narrowly focused, mood piece with 2 parts in which the second half is an elaboration on and variation of the first half.

**Themes:** Delight in nature; seasons; springtime or summertime; correlating images to music; design.

**Comments:** The pastoral spring/summer images are well synchronized to the delicate polyphonic score, and HOMMAGE A FRANCOIS COUPERIN was very successful with hospitalized children. We used it in Video Program #8 with THE CREATION OF BIRDS.

**Suggested Activities:** Pastel designs, coloring, painting, and poetry reading or writing—for which you might suggest children use "What Shall I Pack in the Box Marked *Summer*?" or "Three Signs of Spring" as titles for their poems/pictures.

**Related Reading:** Under-sevens might enjoy Leo Lionni's picturebook, *Frederick*, which is available in paperback. This age group might also enjoy Ezra Jack Keat's counting rhyme, *Over in the Meadow*, which has impressionistic collage images of meadow flora and fauna, including turtles, crickets, birds, and fireflies.

School age children might enjoy any of the following poems: Bobbi Katz' "What Shall I Pack in the Box Marked *Summer?*" which is anthologized in *Thread One to a Star*; Federico Garcia Lorca's "Mariposa del Aire" which appears in Spanish only in *Poesia Espanola para Ninos* and in both Spanish and English in the Lorca collection for children called *The Cricket Sings*; David McCord's "Three Signs of Spring" from *Take Sky*; and Charlotte Zolotow's "A Moment in Summer" which originally appeared in her book *River Winding* (Crowell) but is also anthologized in *The Random House Book of Poetry for Children*.

---

**Recommended Pediatric Age:** 3+.

**Hospital Rating:** ****

**Availability:**
HOMMAGE A FRANCOIS COUPERIN
Distributed by International Film Foundation.
16mm film purchase price: $75
¾-inch videotape purchase price: $75
½-inch videotape purchase price: $75
No additional charge for CCTV rights.

---

## IRA SLEEPS OVER
*by Andrew Sugerman (USA/1978)*
17 minutes /liveaction /color

This is the story of how Ira, a white uppermiddle-class suburbanite who appears to be about 6 or 7, prepares for his first sleepover at a next-door neighbor's house. Everything seems great until Ira's older sister asks if he plans to take his teddy bear along. Although he initially says no, a nagging doubt creeps into his mind. So he asks his mother and then his father who both say to take the bear.

But his sister says that his friend Reggie will laugh, so Ira decides not to.

After learning that Reggie plans to tell ghost stories, Ira decides to take his bear. Mother and father are encouraging, but his sister suggests that Reggie will probably ask the bear's name and find Tah Tah babyish. So Ira decides not to take his bear, only to discover that Reggie sleeps with a teddy bear named Foo Foo. Before going to sleep, Ira runs home and gets his bear.

**Visual Attributes:** Liveaction with "normal" image density.

**Sound:** Dialog and music with average audio density.

**Pace:** Medium to medium-slow.

**Structure:** Dramatic narrative with a mildly ironic ending. This story has an almost musical variations-on-a-theme structure with repetitious actions and dialog.

**Themes:** Be yourself; separation; insecurity; friendship; appearances versus needs; siblings; familial support; encountering the unfamiliar; comforting objects.

**Comments:** Because the story is told almost entirely by means of dialog, IRA SLEEPS OVER is more psychological than action-oriented. This lack of action made it too subtle for preschoolers, while the age/problem of the central character made it seem babyish to over-eights. While IRA SLEEPS OVER would be thematically appropriate for hospitalized children in general, it appealed primarily to those 6 to 8—a very narrow age range. We did not program it for CCTV, although it would work very well as a videotape. We tried IRA SLEEPS OVER in Film Program #12 with TALEB AND HIS LAMB and in the pilot.

**Suggested Activities:** Discussion or storytelling.

**Related Reading:** Young school age children might enjoy the picturebook by Bernard Waber upon which the film is based; available in paperback, it has also been anthologized in *Stories for Free Children*. To expand on the theme of a young boy's need for cuddly things, you might share *William's Doll* with under-eights; available in paperback, it was anthologized in *Free To Be...You and Me*.

---

**Recommended Pediatric Age:** 6–8.

**Hospital Rating:** ***

**Availability:**
IRA SLEEPS OVER
Distributed by Phoenix Films & Video.
16mm film purchase price: $350
¾-inch videotape purchase price: $220
½-inch videotape purchase price: $220
No additional charge for CCTV rights.

# ISLE OF JOY
*by Marshall Izen* (USA/1973)
7 minutes /cutout animation /color /nonverbal

Beginning with a black-and-white image of Matisse in a wheelchair, this film progresses through a brief series of lithographic images, but mostly it allows brightly colored, Matisse-like cutouts to dance across the screen to the lilting piano of Debussy's "L'Isle Joyeuse."

Superimposed over the black-and-white image, colored cutouts seem to blossom from Matisse's scissors. They are followed by more cutouts shown against brightly colored, contrasting paper.

Suddenly, the images suggest a marine environment. There are fish, jellyfish, eels, seaweed, mollusks, and starfish, followed by colored squares, more marine life-forms, triangles, wavy lines, and plant-like forms.

Under a warm-weather sky filled with cumulus clouds, a sailboat moves gracefully toward a seashore rimmed with hills.

A lithographic tree sprouts leaves.

A female figure reclines in several poses. She could be either a sunbather or an artist's model.

A black-and-white lithographic line drawing of a female head appears and is surrounded by colorful cutouts of flowers and apples—an image that suggests Eve in the garden of paradise.

A woman dances across the screen. As if hiding, a woman's face appears behind some leaves.

After a series of floral and human images, a human figure transforms itself (Icarus-like) into a bird, then turns back into a human form and dives into a body of water.

Along with marine forms, human figures swim in the water and transform themselves into fish and back again. Many cutout shapes move quickly across the screen, as if caught in a rapidly moving stream.

There are alternating images of dancers, a man and a woman.

A Pan-like figure playing a flute emerges from a lithographic drawing as the music plays a lyrical melody. A female nude, partially hidden among colorful foliage, plays another flute.

A man and woman jeté across the screen. Intercut with the dancers who leap in time to the now pulsating music, colorful images of foliage fragment into smaller leaves.

Surrounded by colorful cutouts of leaves and flowers, the lithographic figures of a man and woman are united in a loving embrace. Suddenly, the entire image starts to spin, keeping time to the dizzying musical finale.

**Visual Attributes:** Boldly colored, Matisse-derived, abstract but recognizable, organic-looking cutouts against contrasting (usually white) backgrounds. This has a variable image density, but it is, on average, somewhat high. The images are choreographed to the soundtrack.

**Sound:** Continuous piano music (Debussy's "L'Isle Joyeuse") with fairly low density.

**Video Legibility/Audibility:** Very good.

**Pace:** Varied.

**Structure:** Lyric. Although this is a highly associative work, musical/visual motifs are repeated throughout and the images generally match the mood/tempo of the music. Water scenes have fluid sounds while the jetes and heartbeats of dancer/lovers have pulsing or rhythmic sounds.

**Themes:** Explorations of color and shape; sensual beauty; delight in nature; love; seasons; summertime; the tropics; a seashore vacation.

**Comments:** As it does in nonhospital programs, ISLE OF JOY had a positive impact on children's artwork. With the right sort of introduction (for an example of which see Video Program #10), it can transport viewers—both children and adults—into a world of esthetic beauty. This was one of our most successful lyrical works for school age children, and would also work successfully with both adolescents and adults. We used ISLE OF JOY in Film Program #14 and CCTV Program #5 with A STORY, A STORY, as well as in Video Program #10 with ANANSI THE SPIDER.

**Suggested Activities:** Design, collage, murals.

**Related Reading:** Children so enjoyed seeing books of Matisse's artwork after viewing the film that we suggest you have one on hand when you show ISLE OF JOY. We found 2 excellent paperbacks, both of which have color plates as well as several photographs of Matisse in his wheelchair (which are helpful in introducing the film). They are *The Cut-Outs of Henri Matisse* and *Henri Matisse: Paper Cut-Outs*.

If you can locate a photo of Matisse in a wheelchair from another source, Braziller has just published a beautiful paperbound edition of *Jazz*. Aside from random thoughts on art (handwritten in French, typeset in English), and an account of its origins during Matisse's debilitating operation, this book contains dozens of exquisite color plates of Matisse's cutouts. Many are double-page spreads.

---

**Recommended Pediatric Age:** 5+.

**Hospital Rating:** ****

**Availability:**
ISLE OF JOY
Distributed by Coronet/MTI.
16mm film purchase price: $180
¾-inch videotape purchase price: $115
½-inch videotape purchase price: $115
No additional charge for CCTV rights.

## JACK AND THE BEANSTALK
*by Lotte Reiniger* (UK/1955)
12 minutes /silhouette animation /color

Based on the popular folktale, this is the story of how a happy-go-lucky young man finds his fortune. When poverty prompts his widowed mother to send Jack to sell their only pig, the boy exchanges it for a bag which, a gnome explains, contains all the riches in the world. Jack's mother discovers only beans in the bag and tosses them out the window.

They quickly sprout and form a vine which reaches to the sky. Jack climbs the beanstalk and finds a giant's castle. The giant's daughter is friendly and hides the boy when her father returns. But soon enough the giant cries, "Fee, fi, fo, fum! I smell the blood of an Englishman!"

Jack grabs the hen who lays the golden eggs, quickly descends, and chops down the beanstalk which falls, along with the giant, to the ground. As Jack and his mother exult in their new prize, the narrator adds that if the hen doesn't wear out, they might really get all the riches in the world.

**Visual Attributes:** Abstracted but highly kinesthetic black silhouette figures of people and animals are animated against brightly colored backgrounds. Medium-high density.

**Sound:** Male narration and character dialog with effective mood-setting music. Although the audio density is medium, it is sometimes hard to understand the British narrator.

**Video Legibility/Audibility:** Generally good. Although there is some disintegration of outlines due to color fuzziness (especially of reds) in videotape, the images are quite legible. Audibility is sometimes only fair, particularly on poor speakers.

**Pace:** Medium-slow.

**Structure:** Dramatic narrative. An action-oriented version of the popular folktale in 2 parts. While the giant's castle segment (part 2) is simplified (i.e., Jack does not go there 3 times, only once), the first part (acquiring the beans), is slightly embellished. The film has effective verbal repetitions and recurring musical motifs.

**Themes:** Autonomy; competence; self-reliance; monsters; overcoming terrors; returning safely home; children may not have adults' knowledge and wisdom but their intuitions can be correct.

**Comments:** JACK AND THE BEANSTALK was a great success with hospitalized children, and the conquering of the giant/monster seemed especially therapeutic. However, because children can get "stuck" on small details, it helps to warn those familiar with the storyline that in this version Jack sets off with a pig, instead of a cow. We tried JACK AND THE BEANSTALK in Video Program #14 with

TANGRAM, but it would also work on CCTV and as a film.

**Suggested Activities:** Collage and shadow-puppetry.

**Related Reading:** Six- to nine-year-olds might enjoy the version of "Jack and the Beanstalk" in *The Old-Fashioned Storybook* by Schwartz and Archibald. Over-nine's might enjoy the picturebook version of *Jack and the Beanstalk* by Tony Ross which is very tongue-in-cheek, but don't read it before screening the film or the movie may appear too babyish. As a follow-up activity resource, you might show children "Shadow, Shadow on the Wall" (pages 16–17) in Imogene Forte's helpful book, *Puppets: Friends at Your Fingertips.*

---

**Recommended Pediatric Age:** 6–14.

**Hospital Rating:** \*\*\*\*

**Availability:**
JACK AND THE BEANSTALK
Distributed by Museum of Modern Art.
16mm film prints are not available.
¾-inch videotape purchase price: $125
½-inch videotape purchase price: $125
No additional charge for CCTV rights.

---

## KEITH
*by Frank Moynihan* (USA/1973)
10 minutes /liveaction /color /nonverbal

This is a simple recording of a street act by mime Keith Berger in front of New York City's Plaza Hotel. The performance is framed by sequences in which a pensive young man in a suit is transformed into and back from a mime. His transformation via white-face make-up and a black leotard is accomplished through time-lapse photography.

The performance itself begins when a statue comes to life as a robot. After walking around the edge of a fountain (with movements very like the "moon walk" popularized by Michael Jackson), the mechanical man becomes trapped in an invisible box which gets smaller and smaller, nearly crushing him, until he cuts a narrow slit in one wall and manages to dive through the opening.

**Visual Attributes:** Liveaction; medium to high image density.

**Sound:** Constant piano music underscores the action. Low audio density.

**Video Legibility/Audibility:** Good audibility with sometimes poor legibility.

**Pace:** Slow.

**Structure:** Narrative. A simple mime drama, framed by dream-like transition scenes from/to a young man in a park.

**Themes:** Trapped in a box; self-reliance; escaping an oppressive situation; dreams and daydreams.

**Comments:** Because Keith's performance was shot outdoors in low light conditions with many people and buildings in view, it can be difficult to distinguish performer from background. Some images, especially long shots like the one which begins the actual performance, are barely legible on video monitors. (Compare this to the write-ups of A CHAIRY TALE, THE MASKMAKER, and A QUEST, the other mime films we used.)

The film seemed too down for this audience and children did not pick up on the imprisonment/escape theme (although that might be helped with an introduction). Apparently somewhat disturbed by it, a 10-year-old girl noted that the man in KEITH "never smiles." We paired it with A QUEST in CCTV Program #6.

**Suggested Activities:** Mime and mask-making.

---

**Recommended Pediatric Age:** None.

**Hospital Rating:** 0

**Availability:**
KEITH
Distributed by Billy Budd Films.
16mm film purchase price: $150
¾-inch videotape purchase price: $150
½-inch videotape purchase price: $150
No additional charge for CCTV rights.

---

# KUUMBA
*by Bob Bloomberg & Jane Aaron* (USA/1978)
8 minutes /cutout animation /color

A delightful and fairly contemporary West Indian tale which explains the origin of the steel drum. The film opens with an introduction explaining that in Swahili, an East African language, creativity is called *kuumba*. "Creative people enrich their community with new ideas," says the narrator as the imagery changes to a bird's-eye-view of the Caribbean.

"Off the coast of South America, on the island of Trinidad," the narrator explains, "we have a most delightful custom." After a simulated zoom in to the island, the screen fills with a mask which dances for a moment and is then removed to reveal a smiling black woman. "Every year, a few weeks before Easter," the narrator continues, "the whole country comes to a halt so that we can celebrate Mardi Gras, or carnival as we call it." There is a quick montage of steaming pies, a girl in an angel

costume, a man playing a flute, and another man playing a guitar as a pleasant Caribbean melody plays on the soundtrack.

The story proper begins with a scene of a black boy rhythmically tapping an inverted wooden tub and wooden slats arranged like a xylophone with some sticks and a carpenter's hammer. Off-screen, a woman asks, "Simon, what is that?"

"I'm making a new instrument for carnival, Ma," he replies.

"Another instrument?" his mother asks somewhat wearily as she removes his drum. "Well, this one will have to get along without my wash basin."

Just then a man calls from off-screen, "Who's got my hammer?" Simon's eyes open wide; he mutters, "Uh-oh!" as hands remove hammer and xylophone. A bearded man apologizes, explaining that he needs the hammer and wood to finish his float for carnival, then adds, "It starts tomorrow, you know."

The boy remains sitting until his mother calls out, telling him not to forget to put some wood on the fire. The last of his elaborate instrument vanishes as Simon gathers the twigs for kindling. "Oh well," he muses philosophically, "it wasn't the right sound anyway."

In the kitchen Simon lifts the lid of a saucepan which is heating on top of the stove. The pot top burns his fingers and he drops it, making a ringing sound. Simon's eyes grow wide as he considers the sound.

The next scene shows Simon's mother and another woman hanging costumes on a clothesline. "Poor Simon," his mother says, "I'm afraid he won't have an instrument to play." The smaller woman (who may be his older sister) explains that Simon is looking for a special sound.

Meanwhile, the boy is in the kitchen, banging on glasses, dishes, cups, pots, and pans. The man teases him by saying that he can't take the kitchen to carnival. One of the women adds that they need the pots and pans for "the crab and callaloo."

"Oh well," sighs Simon, "that wasn't it either."

Peeking into the kitchen, the man asks what special sound the boy is seeking. "I don't know for sure, Dad," Simon answers, "but I'll know it when I hear it." His mother (or sister) comments that she hopes Simon hears it soon because it is getting dark.

Simon walks around outside, running a stick along a picket fence. Then he takes out a comb and blows on his make-shift kazoo. Next he blows into some bottles, some of which are partially filled with water. Lastly, he taps on some rocks, but one turns out to be a turtle which gets up and walks away.

A storm is approaching so Simon heads indoors where he stares listlessly out a window. Simon holds out his hand to catch a few raindrops. One hits a metal barrel beneath the window, making an interesting sound. Simon's eyes reflect images of raindrops and seem to pop out of his head. He goes outside and moves the barrel. Soon he is hammering the top and a lilting sound is heard as the sky turns dark.

The pale color of the sky reveals that it is morning. Simon's mother opens her window shutters and says, "Listen!" His father asks, "What is that?" And his sister replies, "It's Simon."

The boy appears in the yard with a sawed-off oil drum suspended from his neck. There are funny markings on the surface of the drum. "This is it! This is it!", he cries excitedly as he hits the drum. "I made it from the old oil drum in the yard."

"Simon, it's just beautiful," says his sister who runs to get a closer look at the instrument.

"Let me carve 2 sticks for your drum," says his father who joins them in the yard.

"And I'll make a strap so you can carry it," says his sister. "And I've got the perfect costume for you," adds his mother.

As each one speaks, their contribution appears magically. Then, as costumed revelers similarly surround him, dancing and making music, the narrator concludes by saying: "Simon's creation, the steel drum, has become the national instrument of Trinidad. The sound is enjoyed all over the world and no carnival would be complete without it."

**Visual Attributes:** Pastel-colored, cutout images with minimal background detail. (They are somewhat primitive looking since they were made by children and young adults.) Medium-low image density.

**Sound:** High density and word-dependent opening/closing with a male narration and music playing simultaneously. Nearly continuous character dialog in West Indian (Jamaican) accents with occasional but highly engaging Caribbean music. Mostly medium sound density with good audibility except for the too-fast introduction and some muffled words by the women.

**Video Legibility/Audibility:** Good.

**Pace:** Varied, but mostly medium.

**Structure:** Dramatic narrative. A clear and well-structured story with effective amplification of the problem (by means of repeating phrases and repetitive patterns of action) and a satisfying resolution. The 2 introductions, defining *kuumba*, and setting the stage in Trinidad, go too fast and may be confusing, but once the focus shifts to Simon the story structure is very clear.

**Themes:** Creative problem-solving; familial support; perseverance; carnival; holiday celebrations; costumes; sound-making; music; the experimental method; enriching one's community.

**Comments:** Aside from offering a warm and positive portrayal of a black family, KUUMBA accurately captures aspects of the experimental urges of middle childhood. It has always been well-received outside of the hospital, as it was with our test population.

Although it is highly verbal and sometimes uses a sophisticated animation technique (in which parts—hands and/or heads—-instead of the whole body are used to represent secondary characters such as the father), Simon's dilemma is easily understood. Moreover, he appears on-screen for most of the story proper which helps focus viewers.

We originally tried using KUUMBA as a stimulus to collage, but (like A LITTLE GIRL AND A GUNNY WOLF which uses children's painted artwork) its images do not look like cutouts. It works better as a lead-in to music-making. After seeing KUUMBA in our CCTV program, a boy asked if we were going to make drums like in the film. He was very excited at the prospect and was genuinely disappointed when he learned that we were only going to draw a detective mystery. We took his idea seriously and tried it with music in our video programming.

KUUMBA had several partners: in Film Program #9, THE CREATION OF BIRDS; in CCTV Program #13, SOMETHING QUEER AT THE LIBRARY; and in Video Program #18, GERALD McBOING BOING.

**Suggested Activities:** Music-making, sound-making, and storytelling.

---

**Recommended Pediatric Age:** 6–12.

**Hospital Rating:** ****

**Availability:**
KUUMBA
Distributed by Beacon Films.
16mm film purchase price: $160
¾-inch videotape purchase price: $174
½-inch videotape purchase price: $149
Probably no extra charge for CCTV rights. Prices are for nonprofit institutions only and 16mm price includes a ½-inch VHS copy.

---

## L'AGE DOOR
*by George Griffin* (USA/1975)
2 minutes /line animation /color /nonverbal

The title appears, framed in a square which opens like a cube to reveal a human form approaching from a great distance, working its way through a series of doors or box-sides that open one into the other. At points, there are images that resemble hallways and 2 legs sneak across a hall from one door to another.

Eventually the man stands in front of a cube, looking puzzled. He climbs on top, slips into the box, and now the doors/box-sides open in all directions, hinged on the left, right, top, or bottom.

A huge head emerges like a jack-in-the-box and a huge hand pursues the man who suddenly seems very small. He crawls underneath the cube....

Suddenly, emerging from a very wide, square-shaped door, the man stands in front of it, then picks it up as if it were an oversized painting. As he places it between him and the viewer, the sound of a door slam is heard.

**Visual Attributes:** Monochromatic dark brown line drawings against a white ground. Very low image density.

**Sound:** Silent except for a door slam at the end.

**Video Legibility/Audibility:** The images were sometimes illegible on video monitors, and the lack of sound did not work in the hospital environment.

**Pace:** Medium-fast.

**Structure:** Lyric. This associative and existential work can be confusing for children, because there is neither a clear-cut problem nor a clear-cut ending.

**Themes:** Puzzles; perseverance.

**Comments:** We thought L'AGE DOOR would work as a mood setting piece in a mystery program. However, it was just too far out and existential for hospitalized children, who seem to need a more clearly defined closure. We tried it in Video Program #3 with THE CASE OF THE ELEVATOR DUCK.

**Suggested Activities:** Puzzles, drawing, flipbooks.

---

**Recommended Pediatric Age:** None.

**Hospital Rating:** 0

**Availability:**
L'AGE DOOR
Distributed by the Museum of Modern Art.
16mm film purchase price: $40
¾-inch videotape purchase price: $40
½-inch videotape purchase price: $40
No additional charge for CCTV rights.

---

# THE LATE GREAT AMERICAN PICNIC
*by Dan Bailey* (USA/1978)
7 minutes /liveaction /color /nonverbal

In a droll commentary on contemporary American fast foods and billboard ads, real people mobilize some unusual puppets—a collection of billboard personalities and products—and set the scene for a picnic in the great outdoors.

Opening titles read: "You are invited to a picnic at Cat Hollow." So, apparently, is the Marlboro Man who saunters over the crest of a hill, supported by a pair of denimed legs and sneakered feet. He is joined by other billboard images in their real and various billboard sizes.

A sleek black limousine pulls up and the Black Velvet Whiskey woman (Cheryl Tiegs) emerges and reclines on the picnic blanket. An oversized pretzel joins her and 2 puppeteers give her a huge cigarette, then carelessly drop it on the grass. Fortunately, Smokey the Bear rushes over and stomps the butt out.

A chorus line of Coke bottles dance on a hilltop with an even larger-sized bottle of Pepsi as the star of their little revue. The hillside gradually becomes littered with everything from a Stroh's beer can, led in on a lasso by the Marlboro Man, to an oversized taco which is dropped from a passing cardboard jetliner.

Real people (wearing bluejeans, white tee-shirts, and white Lone Ranger-style masks) choreograph their oversized puppets so that the usually static images have appropriate movements: the horse lopes, the snowman rolls, the Black Velvet lady glides, and Smokey dashes in to save the day.

The film closes with a long shot of the entire scene just after the Marlboro Man saunters by as if checking to see what came of the picnic.

**Visual Attributes:** Liveaction with medium image density.

**Sound:** A jazzy vocal (humming, whistling) and instrumental (guitar) country soundtrack with cartoon musical effects. Fairly low audio density.

**Pace:** Leisurely.

**Structure:** Catalog with an invitation/introduction and a circular structure framed by the Marlboro Man.

**Themes:** Variations on a concept; billboard advertisements; pop art.

**Comments:** The lack of both storyline and emotional theme may have contributed to THE LATE GREAT AMERICAN PICNIC's difficulty with hospitalized children, although the film might work with teenagers. We tried it in Film Program #10 with CAPTAIN SILAS, a combination we have used quite successfully outside of the hospital. However, because THE LATE GREAT AMERICAN PICNIC did not really work with our targeted age group, we did not try it in either CCTV or video programs.

**Suggested Activities:** Box art and/or collage using magazine advertisements.

---

**Recommended Pediatric Age:** None.

**Hospital Rating:** 0

**Availability:**
THE LATE GREAT AMERICAN PICNIC is not currently in US distribution; it may be available in public or university library collections.

---

# A LITTLE GIRL AND A GUNNY WOLF
*by Steve & Marion Klein* (USA/1971)
6 minutes /cutout animation /color

A delightful black variation on, and a less threatening version of "Little Red Riding Hood." "This is the story of a little girl who goes pitter-patter, pitter-patter through the forest," begins a child narrator, "and the big bad gunny wolf who goes honka-cha, honka-cha after the little girl."

Another child (speaking less clearly than the first) continues the narration: "Once upon a time there was a little girl that lived with her mother on the edge of the forest."

Her mother always told her, says another child, never to go in the forest. "Because in that forest," continues a fourth child, "lives the big bad gunny wolf."

But one day, when she is all alone, the girl ventures into the woods to pick pretty flowers for her mother. Pitter-patter, pitter-patter, pitter-patter, she walks to pick some white flowers. She is just about ready to go home when she sees some yellow flowers and walks pitter-patter, pitter-patter, pitter-patter to pick them. Then, deep in the forest, she spots some lovely orange flowers and picks them too.

She is almost ready to go home when— "Boo!"—out from behind a tree (a chorus speaks) jumps the big bad gunny wolf. The girl starts to run, pitter-patter, pitter-patter. But the big bad gunny wolf runs after her (again a chorus) "honka-cha, honka-cha, honka-cha."

When he catches her, the wolf says, "Why for you move?" The little girl says she doesn't know. Then, because she is afraid and doesn't know what else to do she sings a silly song (delivered by another chorus): "Walkee, walkee, walkee, walkee, walkee, walkee, walkee, walkee, walkee, walkee."

Since her song puts the gunny wolf to sleep, the little girl runs pitter-patter, pitter-patter, pitter-patter away. But the rustle and the crunch of the leaves wake the wolf and he runs honka-cha, honka-cha, honka-cha after her.

When he catches up with her he asks angrily, "Little girl, why for you move?" Again, she says she doesn't know and begins to sing her silly song. Just as before, the wolf falls asleep.

This time, the little girl runs as fast as she can through the forest. She runs so fast, however, that she drops her white flowers and her orange flowers and her yellow flowers. "But she ran, and she ran, and she ran, as fast as she can—uuh-ah, uuh-ah, uuh-ah."

She went all the way home. And guess who was standing at the door waiting for her? A chorus answers, "Her mother!" who asks where she has been. The little girl starts to cry and says a few unintelligible lines, ending with a promise never to do it again.

"And you know what?" asks the umpteenth narrator. "She'll never go in the forest again!"

The film ends with still photos of the black kindergarten children who narrated and made the artwork for this unusual work, which is explained by a woman's voiceover as children sing in the background.

**Visual Attributes:** Animated cutouts of kindergarteners' brightly colored and slightly abstract paintings. Rather high image density.

**Sound:** Almost totally word-dependent. Serial and choral narration by black children with music only at the beginning and end. Somewhat high sound density with fairly good audibility. Despite the usual child-narrator problems of breathiness and too-rapid line readings, the formulaic plot and the appealing repetitive phrases helped children follow the storyline.

**Pace:** Medium.

**Structure:** Dramatic narrative with an effective introduction of the 2 main characters and a circular closure. This film makes good use of repetition, both verbally and visually.

**Themes:** Female protagonist; running away from home; separation; monsters; overcoming terrors; silly songs; returning safely home.

**Comments:** Although it generally appealed to all hospitalized preschoolers, A LITTLE GIRL AND A GUNNY WOLF had special appeal for black viewers. Nonetheless, both its soundtrack and imagery can be unclear, so children need a thorough preparation to get full measure from this delightful production. Either give them a summary of the story or read them *The Gunniwolf* before a screening. It is also a good idea to let children see the film more than once if they want to do so.

We tried A LITTLE GIRL AND A GUNNY WOLF in Film Program #3 with THE SKY IS BLUE and would have liked to try it on CCTV but could not obtain permission. Based on testing other films, however, A LITTLE GIRL AND A GUNNY WOLF would probably not work well on CCTV or video monitors because its images would be blurry and its soundtrack (which is essential to comprehension) would be muffled on TV/video speakers.

**Suggested Activities:** Painting, storytelling, choral speaking.

**Related Reading:** Preschoolers and young school age children might enjoy *The Gunniwolf*, a picturebook by Wilhelmina Harper, from which the film was adapted.

Recommended Pediatric Age: 3–8.

Hospital Rating: ***

Availability:
A LITTLE GIRL AND A GUNNY WOLF
Distributed by AIMS Instructional Media.
16mm film purchase price: $130
¾-inch videotape purchase price: $110
½-inch videotape purchase price: $100
No additional charge for CCTV rights.

Suggested Activities: Drawing, painting, storytelling.

Recommended Pediatric Age: 3–9.

Hospital Rating: ****

Availability:
LITTLE GRAY NECK is not currently in US distribution; it may be available in public or university library collections.

## LITTLE GRAY NECK
*by L. Amalrik* (USSR/1947)
18 minutes /cel animation /color

A melodramatic tale about a young goose who gets left behind when her flock migrates south for the winter. Wounded while saving a rabbit from the evil fox and too weak to catch up with her mother (who thinks she is dead), the gosling settles in for the winter.

Cheered and fed by some friendly rabbits, Little Gray Neck's wing mends bit by bit while the fox becomes suspicious about why she didn't leave with the other geese. The fox almost gets her when the river freezes solid, but the rabbits divert him.

Later, when her wing has healed completely and the river begins to thaw, Little Gray Neck pretends it is still broken and lures the fox from ice floe to ice floe until he drowns, at which point her flock returns and the gosling is happily reunited with her mother and siblings.

Visual Attributes: Disney-like cartoon images in muted colors. Somewhat low image density.

Sound: Character dialog and male narration with an orchestral music track. Medium audio density.

Pace: Varied but generally slow.

Structure: Dramatic narrative.

Themes: Abandonment; separation; female protagonist; monsters; competence; brains outwit brawn; cooperation and teamwork; reciprocity; friendship; self-reliance; overcoming terrors; survival; seasons; reunion with family.

Comments: LITTLE GRAY NECK was one of the most potentially scary preschool films we tried, but it was a great success in a supervised playroom situation when lots of during-film interaction and verbalization were encouraged. We tried it in Film Program #8 with HAROLD'S FAIRY TALE (although HAROLD AND THE PURPLE CRAYON would work better). We did not try LITTLE GRAY NECK on CCTV because of the possibility that it might be frightening for unaccompanied preschoolers and young school age children.

## MADELINE
*by Robert Cannon* (USA/1952)
7 minutes /cel animation /color

This animated film introduces us to the old house in Paris where 12 little girls live "in 2 straight lines" with Miss Clavel. Although she is the smallest, Madeline is the most liberated; she is unafraid of mice and tigers in the zoo.

One night, however, Madeline wakes up crying with pain. A doctor is called and Madeline is rushed to the hospital to have her appendix removed.

Ten days later, Miss Clavel and her girls visit the hospital and are surprised at Madeline's presents and the scar that she proudly shows them. When Miss Clavel returns home with the other girls, they become envious of Madeline and want their appendixes removed.

Visual Attributes: Stylized cartoon images—at times resembling Dufy landscapes—with minuscule people and poor separation of figure from ground. High image density.

Sound: A storyteller's narration in rhymed verse with emphatic music. Rather high sound density with fair to poor audibility because the female narrator speaks quickly in a whispery, high-pitched voice with a French accent.

Video Legibility/Audibility: Poor.

Pace: Varied.

Structure: Narrative. A 3-part story without focus or closure. The first part concerns the daily regime of the 12 girls and identifies Madeline as somewhat different from the rest. The second deals with Madeline's appendicitis and hospitalization. The third leaves Madeline in the hospital and switches the focus to the other girls' response to Madeline's illness.

Themes: Hospitalization; abandonment; separation; female protagonist.

Comments: It should be noted that "the old house in Paris" is described simply as that—not as a boarding school—so it could be seen as an orphanage or foster home (which might be distressing to hospitalized children).

Generally, MADELINE was too complex and unfocused for our hospital test population who, unlike the school groups with whom we previously tested it, were generally unfamiliar with the book. The soundtrack was another hindrance because children could not understand what the narrator was saying, even on 16mm sound systems.

On top of this, staff at one hospital asked us not to test the film there since the book had caused a child to become quite depressed. Neither the book nor the film reassures children that Madeline goes home, which is a major issue for hospital patients since many fear they have been or will be abandoned.

We had an interesting commentary on the film from a child at one of the sites where we showed it in a CCTV program. A girl of 8 had an emergency appendectomy and saw MADELINE 4 days after her operation. She was visibly confused and upset during the part where Madeline's schoolmates want to go to the hospital to have an operation. "They want to go to the hospital too?" she asked in a disbelieving tone. And she wanted to know why there were no doctors or nurses in the hospital. Next day, she talked about when Madeline showed her schoolmates her scar. Although called a scar in the film, this 8-year-old knew it as a suture line around a wound, and that difference bothered her a lot. She ended the discussion by saying: "Really being in the hospital isn't like that, and it made me feel bad about my own operation."

By and large, MADELINE seems more appropriate for the siblings of hospitalized children or for children who are not hospitalized. (For contrast, see CURIOUS GEORGE GOES TO THE HOSPITAL which, so far, has proved more popular with hospitalized children than with children in nonhospital settings.)

Because of time pressures, we had not yet tried the film when we planned the CCTV pilot. Thus, MADELINE was included in CCTV Program #4 along with THE SKY IS BLUE. The CCTV testing bears out the negative results of a mini-test we did with the film.

This should be shown only to children who are already familiar with the book, which means it should be shown on an individual or small-group basis, not on CCTV. It usually works best with girls.

**Suggested Activities:** Painting and drawing.

**Related Reading:** Children, especially girls, who are already familiar with the book by Ludwig Bemelmans upon which the film was based will probably enjoy the book in the hospital; it is available in paperback. Five- to ten-year-olds might enjoy the realistically illustrated paperback, *Elizabeth Gets Well*. It is also about an appendectomy and sibling envy, but is both more accurate and more reassuring, since the girl goes home.

---

**Recommended Pediatric Age:** 7–10.

**Hospital Rating:** *

**Availability:**
MADELINE
Distributed by Churchill Films.
16mm film purchase price: $165
¾-inch videotape purchase price: $115
½-inch videotape purchase price: $115
No extra charge for CCTV rights unless title is seen in more than one building; then CCTV rights are 10% of title cost, per building. Rights must be renewed annually. Generally, only 16mm prints are available for preview; call about availability of preview videos.

---

## MADELINE AND THE GYPSIES
*by Vaclav Bedrich* (Czechoslovakia/1959)
7 minutes /animation /color

An appealingly colorful but very wordy chapter in the continuing adventures of Madeline. Pepito, the son of the Spanish Ambassador, invites his neighbors to the Gypsy carnival and circus where, at least for a while, everyone has a great time. Unfortunately, when rain forces Miss Clavel and her charges to flee for home, she realizes that Madeline is missing.

Meanwhile, Madeline and Pepito, who got stuck on the Ferris wheel, are put up by the Gypsy Mama and travel with the carnival troupe to their next site. There they learn some circus skills such as tightrope walking and balancing on horseback.

Eventually they drop Miss Clavel a postcard and, with the rest of her girls, she rushes "to the scene of the disaster." At that very moment the Gypsy Mama looks into her crystal ball and sees Miss Clavel coming, so she dresses Madeline and Pepito in a lion costume to hide them. The would-be lion is, however, released from its cage by an elephant and wanders through the countryside until it meets a hunter. Realizing it might get shot, the lion manque returns to the circus where Miss Clavel et al. have just arrived.

Although the Gypsy Mama and the Strong Man cry, Madeline heads for home where the 12 girls sit down to dinner. "The best part of a voyage by plane, by ship, or train," concludes the narrator, "is when the trip is over and you're home again!"

**Visual Attributes:** Gaily colored and slightly static cartoon images with wonderful circus scenes. It has a rather high image density, but a better separation of figure/ground than MADELINE.

**Sound:** A rapid female storyteller's narration of rhymed verse with continuous music. Unlike her predecessor, this narrator does not have a French accent. Fairly high audio density.

**Video Legibility/Audibility:** Fairly good.

**Pace:** Medium-fast.

**Structure:** Dramatic narrative. A complex story with parallel courses of action: in Paris this went on; meanwhile, back at the carnival, that went on. It has a better focus than MADELINE and a more effective closure because Madeline does go home (albeit to her group living situation). However, Pepito's fate is unresolved: his character vanishes once the group heads home.

**Themes:** Abandonment; separation; circus and carnival; abduction and rescue; running away from home; returning safely home.

**Comments:** MADELINE AND THE GYPSIES uses a contrapuntal audio-visual technique, whereby what is seen does not always match what is said. This can be very confusing to children who are not in tiptop physical condition and have many conflicting emotional issues weighing on their minds. The film also presents a negative stereotype of Gypsies (and we had a few in our population).

In relation to the kidnap theme, MADELINE AND THE GYPSIES leaves certain questions unanswered. What was the disaster and what were its consequences? Why did the Gypsy Mama want to hide Madeline and Pepito when she knew Miss Clavel was coming? Finally, what happened to Pepito after he boarded the train?

Because this seemed better structured than MADELINE and featured a female protagonist, we tried it with ANANSI THE SPIDER in Video Program #9, but it would be better as a film.

**Suggested Activities:** Painting.

**Related Reading:** Preschoolers and young school age children might enjoy the picturebook by Ludwig Bemelmans upon which the film is based; it is available in paperback.

---

**Recommended Pediatric Age: 4–7.**

**Hospital Rating: ✳✳**

**Availability:**
MADELINE AND THE GYPSIES
Distributed by Films Incorporated/PMI.
16mm film purchase price: $170
No video. No CCTV rights available.

---

# THE MAGIC PEAR TREE
*by Wango Weng & Alfred Wallace* (USA/1970)
5 minutes /shadow-puppet animation /color

Based on a Chinese folktale, this is the story of what happens when a selfish fruit peddler refuses to give even a withered pear to a poor old farmer on a very hot day. As the men argue, a crowd gathers and eventually someone buys the old man a pear. He eats it and plants one seed which magically grows into a tree full of ripe pears. Some boys pick and share them with everyone in the crowd.

When all the pears are gone, the old farmer cuts the tree down and goes on his way. Just then, the stingy peddler notices that all his pears are gone. A bystander exclaims, "You got exactly what you deserve for how you treated the old man."

**Visual Attributes:** Somewhat static, monochromatic rod/shadow puppets, dressed in Chinese imperial costumes which resemble traditional papercuts. There is no background imagery. Visual density is low.

**Sound:** Male storyteller's narration with continuous, traditional style Chinese music. Rather high audio density.

**Video Legibility/Audibility:** Good legibility. Fairly good audibility.

**Pace:** Slow.

**Structure:** Dramatic narrative. A very clear and moralizing tale, told almost entirely in dialog, which allowed children to anticipate the turn of events.

**Themes:** Sharing; selfishness; fairness; magic; retribution.

**Comments:** If hospitalized children are prepared for this film's unusual appearance, they will probably respond quite favorably because the retribution theme in THE MAGIC PEAR TREE so well reflects the middle-aged child's sense of justice. We tried it with THE CREATION OF BIRDS in Video Program #7.

**Suggested Activities:** Papercuts and shadowpuppets.

**Related Reading:** Older school age children and adolescents might enjoy *Chinese Papercuts: Their Story and How to Make and Use Them* which is available in paperback and includes a listing of over 30 places around the US where Chinese papercuts are sold. It also has a few pages (73-75) on shadow puppets.

Younger children might enjoy making the simple cookie cutter shadow-puppets illustrated on pages 14-15 in Imogene Forte's excellent activity book, *Puppets: Friends at Your Finger Tips.*

Recommended Pediatric Age: 7–12.

Hospital Rating: ****

Availability:
THE MAGIC PEAR TREE
Distributed by A. Wallace Estate.
16mm film purchase price: $150
¾-inch videotape purchase price: $150
½-inch videotape purchase price: $150
No additional charge for CCTV rights.

## MARY OF MILE EIGHTEEN
*by Svend-Erik Eriksen* (Canada/1981)
11 minutes /mixed animation /color

One winter night in rural Northwest Canada, Mary Fehr sees the shimmering northern lights from her bedroom window. Mary is convinced that because of the lights, the next day will bring something special. But the next day is quite ordinary until, on the way home from school, her father's truck goes off the road.

While waiting for it to be fixed, Mary is approached by a puppy. She asks if she can keep it, but her father notes that the little dog is part-wolf and, reminding her that the family keeps only those animals which work or provide food, says no. Sadly, Mary takes the little wolf into the woods, leaves it there, and wistfully goes about her after-school chores.

Just before dinner the pup appears at the house and Mary is again told that she cannot keep it. So she brings it to a neighbor's farm, returns home, and goes to bed without eating. Later that night, however, the little pup, who has returned again, warns the family when a coyote enters the henhouse. When Mr. Fehr discovers this, he thinks that the little wolf might just earn his keep, so he brings the pup to Mary's bed and tells her she can keep it.

Visual Attributes: Static representational images with some cutout animation. Clear separation of figure from ground. Low image density.

Sound: Female narration and character dialog with occasional music. Fairly low audio density.

Video Legibility/Audibility: Good.

Pace: Very slow.

Structure: Dramatic narrative. A low-key but solidly structured story with several slice-of-life embellishments.

Themes: Wishes; conflict with parent; rural farm life; family relationships; winter; seasons; boy-gets-dog variation; female protagonist; competence; understanding parental values.

Comments: Although not a blockbuster success, this tender and low-key film did work with hospitalized children, especially girls. The 3 appearances of the wolf pup have an almost folktale pattern, and the classic parent-child conflict surrounding the dog builds to a satisfying, wish-fulfilling conclusion.

The brief opening vocalization sounded scary or weird to some children; because of this, it might be best if the opening segment (when the northern lights are on-screen) is played at a lower volume than the rest of the film.

We used MARY OF MILE EIGHTEEN in CCTV Program #10 with NOVEMBER 1977. Since the latter was not very successful on CCTV with hospitalized children, we would recommend another partner for MARY OF MILE EIGHTEEN. This would work better in the playroom in either film or video.

Suggested Activities: Discussion or storytelling.

Related Reading: Young school age children might enjoy the picturebook by Ann Blades upon which the film is based.

Recommended Pediatric Age: 8–12.

Hospital Rating: ***

Availability:
MARY OF MILE EIGHTEEN
Distributed by Karol Media.
16mm film purchase price: $275
¾-inch videotape purchase price: $250
½-inch videotape purchase price: $250
Probably no extra charge for CCTV rights, but permission must be obtained from the National Film Board of Canada. The prices above are for nonprofit institutions only.

## THE MASKMAKER
*by John Barnes* (USA/1975)
7 minutes /liveaction /color /nonverbal

In this mime performance by Marcel Marceau, a man in white leotards and white make-up sits atop a cube on an empty stage. He seems to be making something with his hands. After a while, he puts "it" in front of his face which turns his expression from pensive to happy. When he removes what was apparently a mask, his face looks somewhat sad.

He puts on another invisible mask and becomes a forbidding looking person. He removes that and puts on another whereby he becomes a juggler. With the next, he becomes a smiling musician. With another, he becomes a haughty flamenco dancer and has a little trouble getting the mask off.

The man puts on a series of masks, each of which evokes a change in his personality, until he comes to a laughing face. When he first tries to remove it, however, the laughing mask will not budge. While his unchanging face continues laughing, he keeps trying to remove the mask until his body seems exhausted. He gets more and more desperate. Finally, with one last tug, he removes the mask and looks relieved.

**Visual Attributes:** Liveaction mime performance with only one man on an empty stage. Clear separation of figure from ground. Low image density.

**Sound:** Because we bypassed the self-defeating spoken introduction, this was a nonverbal film. Dulcimer and/or guitar music was the only sound. Low audio density.

**Video Legibility/Audibility:** Good, except when artsy close-ups and edits destroy the physical tension created by the performer.

**Pace:** Slow.

**Structure:** Dramatic narrative. A fairly sophisticated cumulative story which is effectively amplified by repetitive patterns of action.

**Themes:** Be yourself; appearances versus needs; hiding behind a mask.

**Comments:** THE MASKMAKER worked better than either KEITH or A QUEST for hospitalized children, but because it lacks interaction between characters (as in the highly successful A CHAIRY TALE), it is a bit abstract. Nonetheless, this mime film seemed particularly appropriate for preadolescents and teenagers.

The running time listed above does not include the didactic 3-minute introduction Marceau gives prior to his performance. We recommend that you bypass the introduction (which turns off nonhospitalized children and would doubtless put hospitalized children to sleep), and make up your own introduction. We tried this in Video Program #19 with WHERE THE WILD THINGS ARE.

**Suggested Activities:** Mask-making, mime, discussion.

---

**Recommended Pediatric Age:** 8–16.

**Hospital Rating:** ***

**Availability:**
THE MASKMAKER
Distributed by Encyclopedia Britannica.
16mm film purchase price: $175
¾-inch videotape purchase price: $185
½-inch videotape purchase price: $175
No extra charge for CCTV rights, but hospital must pay an additional 30% of purchase price for each copy it makes of any EBE title.

---

# THE MOLE AND THE EGG
*by Zdenek Miler* (Czechoslovakia/1975)
6 minutes /cel animation /color /nonverbal

As if making an entrance from the wings of a stage, Mole (a sexless animal *everychild*) appears on-screen carrying an egg. S/he puts it down and points to the egg, after which the title appears. The egg sprouts feet and runs off-screen, followed by Mole.

A hen sits contentedly until a disturbance underground frightens her away from the egg she is hatching. Mole burrows up beside the egg and wonders who it belongs to. S/he takes the egg to a mouse, a rabbit, and a dog but they don't know whose it is.

Soon Mole and the egg come to a conveyor belt full of other eggs. After rolling the egg onto the belt, Mole and egg enter a factory where they are picked up by an automated arm and dropped in a bin with broken eggs. Apparently as a result, Mole's egg develops a crack. Undaunted, Mole gets him/herself and the egg back on the conveyor belt.

When a chick emerges from the cracked egg, Mole and Chick laugh delightedly. Suddenly, the little creatures are nearly decapitated by a mechanized saw and tossed into a huge bowl full of eggs and flour. Mole and Chick climb up the shaft of a huge beater, but they are almost carried into the oven when they get stuck in some gooey dough.

Although they get off just in time, Chick hops back on the conveyor belt to eat the baked goods emerging from the oven and gets packaged with some biscuits. When Mole goes to rescue Chick, s/he is also packed in the box, but they wiggle so much that their package falls and breaks open, whereupon they head for home.

With a biscuit under one arm, Mole returns with the Chick to the mouse, the rabbit, and the dog. Each, in turn, directs them to the now crying hen who was seen in the beginning. When hen and Chick are happily united, Mole crumbles the biscuit and they contentedly peck at it.

**Visual Attributes:** Highly kinesthetic cartoon images with medium to low density. The easily recognizable characters are clearly distinguished from the background.

**Sound:** Emphatic vocalizations (without words) and colorful cartoon music and cartoon effects. Somewhat low audio density.

**Video Legibility/Audibility:** Very good.

**Pace:** Medium-slow.

**Structure:** Dramatic narrative. A well-constructed journey-quest for very young children that begins with a structurally sound "theatrical" introduction of the 2 main characters. Not only does the story have a highly satisfying closure, but it makes effective use of a mirror-image frame when Mole asks the same 3 animals, at journey's beginning/end, who the egg/chick belongs to.

**Themes:** Abandonment; separation; nurturing and tenderness; change and transformation; friendship; perseverance; reunion with family; puzzles; whose baby is this?

**Comments:** THE MOLE AND THE EGG was very successful with hospitalized preschool children. The only real problem was that young viewers did not always understand what was happening in the factory and anxiously anticipated negative results for which the film (unlike LITTLE GRAY NECK and TCHOU TCHOU) provided no catharsis. Because of this we only recommend it for preschoolers in adult-supervised programs.

Often if a film shows a young child or animal without its mother or father, preschool children ask where its mommy is. Even outside the hospital we tell children that, after the film ends, Mole goes home to her/his parents. Because of hospitalized children's fear of abandonment, we recommend that something similar be said to compensate for the fact that Mole is not shown with his/her mother. We used THE MOLE AND THE EGG with TCHOU TCHOU in Film Program #5.

**Suggested Activities:** Puppetry, especially objects-as-puppets.

**Related Reading:** Preschoolers might enjoy any of the following books as preparation for the film. *Little Chicken* and *Good Morning, Chick* are illustrated, clothbound picturebooks that deal with the adventures of a young chick and indicate that the chick came from an egg. (Although loose, there are some structural parallels to the adventures that Mole and Chick undergo in the film; we found no books to explain the factory machines.)

*Jessie the Chicken* uses photographs and drawings to explain basic facts about chickens; the second and third pages would be sufficient to let young preschoolers know that chicks come from eggs. (This book, however, would not be effective with CHICK, CHICK, CHICK because the newly hatched chick is dry and fluffy, not wet and tired looking as it is in the film.)

---

**Recommended Pediatric Age:** 3–7.

**Hospital Rating:** \*\*\*

**Availability:**
THE MOLE AND THE EGG
Distributed by Phoenix Films & Video.
16mm film purchase price: $160
¾-inch videotape purchase price: $115
½-inch videotape purchase price: $115
No additional charge for CCTV rights.

---

# THE MOLE AND THE TELEPHONE
*by Zdenek Miler* (Czechoslovakia/1974)
7 minutes /cel animation /color /nonverbal

In the further adventures of this sexless *everychild*, Mole pushes an old-fashioned telephone to the center of the screen and stands next to it. When the telephone rings, Mole runs away and the title appears. There is a fade to the opening scene of the story proper.

Mole is busily digging in what looks like a suburban garden. S/he hears a ringing sound and wonders what it could be. After a bit of digging, s/he unearths a wire, then with a bit more effort a ringing telephone. Mole lifts the receiver like a barbell but gets scared by the sound of the dial tone, drops it, and hides behind the body of the phone.

Curiosity soon outweighs fear, so Mole comes back and plays with the dial until the words "Allo, allo" are heard from the mouthpiece, at which point s/he runs away.

Since Mole cannot resist a new experience, s/he returns. S/he rides the receiver's cradle like a rocking horse and treats the phone like playground/gymnastic equipment, until it rings, whereupon Mole leaps to the ground.

When the receiver makes a barking sound, s/he takes off, only to return with a bone for the "dog." Before long, however, the receiver begins to meow noisily. After trying a few other approaches, Mole quiets it by dousing it with water. But this causes the receiver to shiver and cough, so Mole wraps it in a muffler and brings it a pillow.

When the receiver makes baby cries, Mole picks it up and rocks it tenderly. As the sky turns dark, Mole yawns and lies down beside his/her new friend. Unfortunately, it starts to snore. When other means have failed to quiet it, Mole comes up with a new idea. S/he turns the telephone dial and a lullaby plays on the receiver. Mole then snuggles beside the "baby" and goes to sleep.

**Visual Attributes:** Highly kinesthetic cartoon images with medium-low visual density. Easily recognizable character is distinguished from minimal background.

**Sound:** Nonverbal with continuous orchestral music punctuated by vocal and cartoon sound effects. The sighs, groans, and quizzical vocalizations which Mole and the telephone receiver make are especially effective. Medium audio density.

**Video Legibility/Audibility:** Very good.

**Pace:** Medium.

**Structure:** Dramatic narrative. A simple story with an effectively repetitive and episodic format: introduction, problem to be solved, false climax one, false climax 2, false climax 3, and so on to its final and slightly ironic conclusion. The introductory curtain call in which Mole and telephone appear prior to the title helps very young viewers stay with the film's opening scene; together with the title, it gives them something to anticipate.

**Themes:** Encountering the unfamiliar; puzzles; nurturing; creative problem-solving; taking a new look at a common artifact; sound-making; a playful exploration of point of view; the experimental or scientific method of early childhood.

**Comments:** The use of everyday sounds and recognizable actions makes THE MOLE AND THE TELEPHONE a particularly effective riddle for young children. In focusing on universal childhood urges and basic (if somewhat symbolized) human experiences, this is perhaps the most accessible of all the Mole films/tapes. It may also be the best structured. It is certainly the most comprehensible and successful one in the series that we have tested, both in and out of hospitals. (Interestingly, it is very similar both conceptually and structurally to A CHAIRY TALE.)

Although cause-and-effect in THE MOLE AND THE EGG has some basis in reality and Mole models a fundamental scientific method, the film is also reminiscent of the fanciful transformations in folk lullabies such as *Hush Little Baby*.

> Hush little baby, don't say a word,
> Mama's gonna buy you a mocking bird.
> If that mocking bird won't sing,
> Mama's gonna buy you a diamond ring.
> If that diamond ring turns brass,
> Mama's gonna buy you a looking glass.
> Etcetera.

Its only problem is that the telephone is old-fashioned and European looking. Be sure to warn children about this. We tried THE MOLE AND THE TELEPHONE as a replacement for THE MOLE AND THE EGG in Video Program #17 with TCHOU TCHOU. It would also work on CCTV and as a film.

**Suggested Activities:** Using objects-as-puppets and playing point-of-view games.

---

**Recommended Pediatric Age: 3–8.**

**Hospital Rating: \*\*\*\***

**Availability:**
THE MOLE AND THE TELEPHONE
Distributed by Phoenix Films & Video.
16mm film purchase price: $175
¾-inch videotape purchase price: $120
½-inch videotape purchase price: $120
No additional charge for CCTV rights.

---

# MY BIG BROTHER
*by WGBH-TV* (USA/1975)
6 minutes /liveaction /color

This is the second half of a double portrait called ALONE IN THE FAMILY (which runs for just over 13 minutes in all); the other half is BEING BY MYSELF. Both were originally produced for the ZOOM public television series.

The film was shot primarily in Harlem (New York City) and opens as a black boy sticks his head out a window on a fire escape and shouts across an alley or air shaft for his friend to meet him in the street for a game. Then, as the boy pulls his head inside, the camera shows his apartment. In a voiceover narration, the boy says that his name is Dexter Maxwell and he has lived alone with his mother for 4 years in their four-room apartment.

The next scene shows preadolescent Dexter and his friends playing stoop ball in the street. After that, Dexter is seen going into a subway to accompany his mother to work on Wall Street (which is at the other end of Manhattan Island, quite a ride from Harlem). The attraction of riding the subway is expressed when he says, "I look at Chinese people because they're interesting to me, and probably I'm interesting to them....I just keep peeking around at different kinds of people, the way they look, the way they talk."

In another scene, Dexter and his mother are walking along a street while the boy's voiceover tells us that lack of father and brother prompted him to ask for a Big Brother, something he learned about from television.

Dexter and a man walk down a busy street, while his voiceover explains that most of his friends got white big brothers while his is black—which is just fine because he lives nearby. As they look over street vendors' wares, Dexter confides that he converted his big brother into an avid movie fan.

Rhythmic music comes up on the soundtrack as the scene shifts to a dance class with about 20 boys and girls, including Dexter. As the youngsters dance, Dexter explains that dancing demands some of the same skills as sports. The film ends with a shot of the dancers' animated faces.

**Visual Attributes:** Liveaction with "normal" visual density.

**Sound:** Some dialog, but mainly protagonist/subject voiceover narration. Generally low sound density with good audibility except when the boy does not enunciate clearly.

**Video Legibility/Audibility:** Generally good.

**Pace:** Medium.

**Structure:** Documentary. A fairly unfocused, slice-of-life portrait, more like a list than anything else.

**Themes:** Family relationships; wishes; siblings; preadolescence; loneliness; urban life.

**Comments:** Because we felt it would be an information overload to show both halves of ALONE IN THE FAMILY with another film, we used each half separately with the same film on different occasions. We tried MY BIG BROTHER in Video Program #21 along with OH BROTHER, MY BROTHER; this was a variation of Video Program #20.

**Suggested Activities:** Discussion and making family portraits.

---

**Recommended Pediatric Age:** 6–10.

**Hospital Rating:** ***

**Availability:**
MY BIG BROTHER
(of ALONE IN THE FAMILY)
See BEING BY MYSELF since both titles are included in the prices listed there.

---

# NEW FRIENDS
*by Dirk Wales* (USA/1981)
12 minutes /animation /color

This is the story of a mallard who gets left behind when his flock heads south for the winter. While trying to catch up with them, the duck gets lost and lands in New York City. Initially, it is a very cold, hostile environment, but eventually he makes friends with an unusual assortment of street-smart animals.

Rex, a frog who lives in the sewer system, takes him on an underground tour of "the sights," but Howard is not happy about the creatures he sees swimming around their raft so he decides to live elsewhere. After some tough pigeons drive him away from their neighborhood, the mallard meets a mouse named Albert who invites him to share a garbage pile with him and some other mice.

When the garbage is collected next day, duck and mice homestead an abandoned theater and, with all their friends, put on a variety show which includes dancing cockroaches, barking dogs, and acrobatic squirrels. A wrecking ball brings their idyllic commune to an end; however, since the weather has warmed up, sleeping outside is not so unpleasant as before.

Mallard, mice, and frog visit the city's famous landmarks, and his friends are given an aerial tour by the duck. Just as the tour ends, some ducks fly by. The mallard announces that they are his group and departs. His dejected friends comment that nothing lasts forever, especially in New York. Just then, the mallard returns and the frog asks if he has come to say goodbye. He says he already has, to the ducks. Frog and mice are delighted that the mallard has chosen to stay with them.

**Visual Attributes:** Water-color looking images with low image density.

**Sound:** Character dialog with jazzy music that plays continuously when there is no talking. Fairly low sound density with good audibility.

**Pace:** Medium-slow.

**Structure:** Narrative. Although in some respects this could be considered a dramatic narrative, it seems more like a quest than anything else (and, because of this, causes viewers some of the same problems as ARROW TO THE SUN).

**Themes:** Abandonment; separation; loneliness; friendship; survival; seasons; urban life.

**Comments:** Unfortunately, NEW FRIENDS' quest-like search for a place to live has no real closure until the end, and that may not be the most satisfying closure for hospitalized children. More than anything else, most patients want to get back with their own families. The film's story may also have been a bit too ironic, and its colors may have been too washed-out to counteract the generally bleak hospital environment. Thus, while not a failure, NEW FRIENDS was also not a real success. We tried it in Film Program #11 with A CHAIRY TALE.

**Suggested Activities:** Drawing and discussion.

**Related Reading:** Young school age children may enjoy the picturebook, *Howard*, by James Stevenson, upon which the film is based.

---

**Recommended Pediatric Age:** 9–12.

**Hospital Rating:** *

**Availability:**
NEW FRIENDS
Distributed by Made-to-Order Library.
16mm film purchase price: $250
¾-inch videotape purchase price: $250
½-inch videotape purchase price: $250
No additional charge for CCTV rights.

---

# NOVEMBER 1977
*by Susan Rubin* (USA/1978)
3 minutes /line animation /color /nonverbal

Using a delightful, personal shorthand of images and sounds, the filmmaker catalogs November's events from autumn weather—a kite in the wind, a pumpkin, gray skies, clouds, rain, a falling leaf—to her own birthday. Eleven pears and a Thanksgiving turkey serve as icons for a month rich in pleasures and disappointments, romance and solitude.

Three things happen simultaneously in this film. First, small childlike drawings of each day are animated in a square on the left side of the frame, while (second) numbers from 1 to 30 register chronologically in a box at the bottom center of the frame. Third, as each day's main event is recorded, a freeze-frame image of it is recorded on the calendar-grid of a month which occupies the right side of the frame.

**Visual Attributes:** Abstract, child-like line drawings are incorporated into a complex visual structure using still images, words/letters, and moving pictures. Rather high visual density.

**Sound:** Effects only—no music. Low audio density.

**Video Legibility/Audibility:** Poor. The 3 areas of visual focus (large frame, calendar grid, date) were nearly illegible on video monitors, so children could not follow this nonverbal and musicless film.

**Pace:** Medium-fast.

**Structure:** Catalog. A highly unusual and chronologically structured work featuring a calendar-diary.

**Themes:** Although it was vague, there was some reference to memories and diaries.

**Comments:** NOVEMBER 1977 is a wonderful and challenging film, but on video monitors it looked like hieroglyphics. In addition, there was too much going on at once, so hospitalized children did not know where to look. If you use it, show it as a film. We tried it in CCTV Program #10 with MARY OF MILE EIGHTEEN.

**Suggested Activities:** Keeping diaries and making calendars. If you can locate some good art postcards or book illustrations, older children might like to make a visual calendar or *Book of Days* such as illuminators did in medieval manuscripts. Suggest that they focus on pleasant, amusing, or personally significant events in the past.

Help them structure and frame the scope of the activity by limiting their efforts to one picture for each unit of a clearly defined time-period, such as their 3 best vacations/trips, the 4 best parties/celebrations they ever went to, or what the first day of each school year has been like since first grade. It is probably a good idea to limit the number of pictures to 4 unless the children are in exceptionally good condition.

---

**Recommended Pediatric Age:** 9–14.

**Hospital Rating:** **

**Availability:**
NOVEMBER 1977
Distributed by Susan Rubin Films.
16mm film purchase price: $190
¾-inch videotape purchase price: $150
½-inch videotape purchase price: $100
No additional charge for CCTV rights.

---

# OH BROTHER, MY BROTHER
*by Carol & Ross Lowell* (USA/1979)
14 minutes /liveaction /color

As this film begins, 6-year-old Josh looks wistfully at family photographs and explains how, now that Evan is 2, his younger brother doesn't kiss him anymore. Meanwhile, Evan plays gleefully on an indoor swing in the bedroom the boys share. Pulled by urges to both compete and participate, Josh joins Evan on the swing.

Both boys play outdoors on a clear autumn day. Within a short time, they move from pleasure to tears and back as the older boy knocks the younger one down and then makes him laugh with a repertoire of silly faces. Later, they roll and tumble in the leaves as their mother rakes nearby until Evan rambunctiously hits Josh in the face. The older boy runs crying to get comforted by his mother, followed jealously by the younger boy who also wants to be held. In a voiceover Josh says: "Sometimes I wish I didn't have a brother."

Indoors, the boys have a mid-staircase discussion about love during which Evan announces that he loves only Mommy. Josh tries to educate by example: "I love Mommy, Daddy, and you; I can love lots of people." When this tack fails, he pretends to be a baby. Tenderly, Evan strokes his forehead and chants, "My baby, my baby...." as Josh drinks from the younger boy's bottle.

Josh is busily constructing the World Trade Center with wooden blocks. Evan wants to help but Josh says he's too young. Evan successfully adds a block but then knocks the structure down in a fit of pique when he mistakenly thinks Josh called him "yucky" instead of lucky.

Later, Josh is playing alone in the bathtub. Dressed for bed in Dr. Dentons, Evan climbs upstairs looking for his brother. He enters the bathroom and, to squeals of forbidden pleasure, climbs fully clothed into the tub.

Lights are out and both boys are in bed. Josh is sound asleep, but Evan is awake, playing with his baby doll. He calls to Josh and, when he gets no response, climbs onto his brother's bed. In a tender and ironic moment, Evan delivers the long sought kiss and says, "Good night, Jossie."

**Visual Attributes:** Liveaction with "normal" image density.

**Sound:** Mostly child dialog but some voiceover narration by the older boy; occasional flute and/or piano music. Medium audio density.

**Video Legibility/Audibility:** Generally very good, but audibility is sometimes only fair because the children's voices can be hard to hear on poor speakers.

**Pace:** Medium.

**Structure:** Dramatic narrative. A well-structured, slice-of-life portrait of brothers which uses the motif of seeking a kiss as a unifying device. Although in some respects this is a documentary (or docudrama, if you like, since parts were clearly staged) it has a strong dramatic quality, is nicely amplified by repetition, and has a highly satisfying—if slightly ironic—closure.

**Themes:** Love; memories; self-assertion; siblings; nurturing and tenderness; interdependence; reciprocity; uncooperative behavior; family relationships; the complexity of early childhood.

**Comments:** The irony of OH BROTHER, MY BROTHER's ending was the most effective use of irony of any of the films/tapes we tested in hospitals. Its success is no doubt due in part to effective structure and repetition, but it may also be due to the fact that this type of irony is fairly normal in human interactions, even among young children.

We were a little afraid that this might prove a painful reminder of families from whom children were separated; however, hospitalized children enjoyed it immensely. We tried OH BROTHER, MY BROTHER with 2 different documentary vignettes, BEING BY MYSELF and MY BIG BROTHER, for Video Programs #20 and #21. It was also one of the films we used in the pilot.

**Suggested Activities:** Discussion and drawing family portraits.

**Related Reading:** Preschoolers might enjoy *Peter's Chair*, the sweet story of how a young black boy reconciles his jealousy of a new baby sister; it is available in paperback. Under-sevens might also enjoy *William's Doll*, which focuses on a boy's need to have a doll for a love-object; it is available in paperback and was anthologized in *Free To Be... You and Me*.

As an antidote to the film's sweetness, under-sevens might enjoy *Big Brother*, a picturebook in which a younger sister comes to terms with her older brother's teasing. Over-sevens might enjoy poems which express some of the other "pain-in-the-neck" aspects of having younger siblings. Two such poems, "Lil' Bro'" by Karama Fufuka, and "My Brother" by Marci Ridlon, are on page 136 of *The Random House Book of Poetry for Children*.

---

**Recommended Pediatric Age:** 4+.

**Hospital Rating:** ****

**Availability:**
OH BROTHER, MY BROTHER
Distributed by Pyramid Film & Video.
16mm film purchase price: $325
¾-inch videotape purchase price: $195
½-inch videotape purchase price: $95
No additional charge for CCTV rights.

---

# ONE LITTLE KITTEN
*by Tana Hoban* (USA/1980)
3 minutes /liveaction /color /nonverbal

Like photos on a decorative wall calendar, this film catalogs the activities of one little kitten. A flowered straw hat lies on the grass; a kitten crawls out from under the brim and scratches its ear.

The kitten explores the underside of a red wagon. It sits inside a tire swing then leaps down.

It crawls out from a rolled up yellow rug.

The kitten plays among the rungs of a cane-backed chair that has a ball of twine on it, then runs away.

It peeks from inside a brown paper bag, crawls out and looks around.

The little cat tries climbing out of a cardboard box and knocks it over.

Next, it plays with a pair of blue sneakers.

The little creature snuggles with its mother who grooms it.

Finally, the kitten is sound asleep. Sneakers are seen in the background.

**Visual Attributes:** Liveaction. Fairly low image density with consistant focus on kitten.

**Sound:** Musical duet of clarinet and flute; rather low sound density.

**Pace:** Medium.

**Structure:** Catalog. A very basic animal study with neither plot nor chronological structure.

**Themes:** While there was, in some respects, no real theme, the film has aspects of variations on a concept and the typical places to find a kitten.

**Comments:** This sweet, consoling film was especially effective for low-functioning preschoolers, but children had to be warned that the big cat was its mother and that she was only grooming or kissing the kitten. We tried ONE LITTLE KITTEN in Film Program #2 with THE BEAR AND THE MOUSE.

**Suggested Activities:** Minimal movement activities, such as finger plays (for an example of which see "Mrs. Pussy's Dinner," which includes music, on page 58 of *Finger Plays for Nursery and Kindergarten*).

**Related Reading:** Young preschoolers might enjoy Tana Hoban's poetic, black-and-white photo/picturebook, *One Little Kitten*, or the inexpensive paperbound picturebook, *Kittens Are Like That*. Slightly older preschoolers, especially urban or black children, might enjoy the open-ended story in Ezra Jack Keat's picturebook, *Hi, Cat!*, which is available in paperback.

Young school age children might enjoy Eleanor Farjeon's poems, "A Kitten" from her book, *Poems for Children*, and "Cats" which was anthologized in *The Random House Book of Poetry for Children*.

**Recommended Pediatric Age:** 2–6.

**Hospital Rating:** ****

**Availability:**
ONE LITTLE KITTEN
Distributed by Films Incorporated/PMI.
16mm film purchase price: $190
¾-inch videotape purchase price: $149
½-inch videotape purchase price: $99
No additional charge for CCTV rights if
shown to a viewing population of under 2,400.

# PIERRE

*by Maurice Sendak* (USA/1976)
6 minutes /line animation /color /song

In this delightful send-up of cautionary tales, Carole King sings about a preschool boy whose response to everything is: "I don't care!" The film opens on an urban scene with some children on a stoop. A young woman sings about a boy named Pierre and says that his story has a "suitable moral."

A young boy, dressed in pajamas, is fooling around in bed—doing somersaults and such—when a woman (who looks rather old-fashioned and grandmotherly but is identified as his mother) enters the room and greets him. "Good morning darling boy, you are my only joy." Pierre frowns and says, "I don't care!"

At the kitchen table, the boy sits resistantly with arms crossed while his mother asks if he wants some cream of wheat. Then she asks him not to sit backwards on the chair, or to pour syrup on his hair. To all her requests, Pierre responds, "I don't care!"

Pierre inverts the cereal bowl and puts it on his head, wraps the table cloth around him like a cape, and holds a broom like a spear. His mother, dressed in a coat and hat, says he is acting like a clown, then asks the boy if he would rather come to town or stay at home. To both comments and questions, Pierre says, "I don't care!" So his mother walks off and leaves him.

Pierre cartwheels over to a folding chair and does a headstand on its seat. A man (his father), dressed in a coat and hat, enters and tells the boy to get off his head or he will have to go to bed. Trying a bit of logic, the man observes that the boy's head is where his feet should be and that if he stays that way they'll never get to town. Then switching to bribery, the man says that if the boy will only say "I care" he could fold the folding chair. Pierre responds the same way to threat, to logic, and to bribe: "I don't care!" So his mother and father walk off together. "They didn't take him anywhere."

Pierre walks backwards and bumps into a lion who asks if he is ready to die and Pierre says, "I

don't care!" Then as the lion elaborates on what will happen if he eats the boy, Pierre lounges against the beast and responds to every comment with "I don't care!"

The lion wants to know if that is all he has to say and then asks if it is okay to eat him. Pierre replies with typical nonchalance. The boy even leaps into the mouth of the lion who promptly belches.

All at once, Pierre's parents arrive and see the lion, who is looking ill, lying in Pierre's bed. His mother pulls the lion's beard, his father hits the lion on the head with the folding chair, and when they ask "Where is Pierre?" the lion opens its mouth and Pierre's voice, somewhat diminished, says, "I don't care!"

The father points to the lion's stomach and says that Pierre must be in there, whereupon both parents pick up the bed and run off-screen.

A doctor stands on an examining table and shakes the lion upside down. When the lion roars, Pierre falls to the floor, rubs his eyes, scratches his head, and laughs "because he wasn't dead." His parents walk on-screen and ask if he's okay, but he spins around and says he's fine and asks to be taken home.

The lion boots the table (along with the doctor) off-screen and comments that if Pierre would care to go, he would take the boy home. To everyone's surprise Pierre says, "Indeed, I care!" So as his parents hop on the lion's back, Pierre balances on the beast's head.

The singer/narrator informs us that the lion "took them home to rest and stayed on as a weekend guest." Then, when the word "care" appears on-screen, Pierre dances on the letters and knocks each one out of sight with a little broom as the narrator concludes: "The moral of Pierre is CARE!"

**Visual Attributes:** Simple and somewhat static line drawings against a white background. Low image density.

**Sound:** A song in rhymed verse with an appealing, rhythmic melody. While the stanzas are sung by a woman, the chorus or refrain is sung by a child. Because it is a song, some words may be difficult to understand, but this does not interfere with overall comprehension. Fairly high audio density.

**Video Legibility/Audibility:** Generally very good perhaps because, like THE CREATION OF BIRDS, this was designed for television.

**Pace:** Medium.

**Structure:** Narrative. A simple, episodic story with predictable and recurring patterns of action. Verbally it has a strongly rhythmic pattern of questions with a simple refrain which remains unchanged until the very end.

**Themes:** Self-assertion; abandonment; separation; devouring; uncooperative behavior; visiting a doctor; reunion with family; a variation on "Little Red Riding Hood"; the almost magical transformations of early childhood.

**Comments:** By the time we were planning the programs which included PIERRE, we knew that fables would be difficult for hospitalized children. We considered PIERRE an anti-fable and somehow failed to consider that, even as a send-up of cautionary tales, it uses the fable format. (For more about fables, see BALTHAZAR THE LION, THE BEAR AND THE MOUSE, THE FABLE OF HE AND SHE, and THE STONECUTTER.)

Moreover, because as adults we realized that Pierre's parents do not emotionally desert their child, we also failed to recognize that this story literally involves parental (or grandparental) abandonment. The responses of some children corrected these oversights.

A few hospitalized children did not find PIERRE an unmitigated pleasure, and they are the ones who made us examine our own assumptions about it. The film raised important issues for them and served as a therapeutic stimulus for working out personal problems. One of the issues it may have touched on—something that many young hospitalized children fear—is that illness and hospitalization are punishments for not being good. Because of this, we do not recommend PIERRE for screening in anything but an adult-supervised situation; thus, it would not be appropriate for CCTV programming.

Despite all, PIERRE was generally quite a hit. Being able to say no—if only through fantasy—was an important aspect of the film, and the vicarious pleasure most children derived from Pierre's refusal to cooperate was noted by hospital staff as one of its strong points. Like other short shorts, PIERRE benefits from being seen more than once. We paired it with THE FROG KING OR FAITHFUL HENRY for Film Program #6 and with A CHAIRY TALE in Video Program #15.

**Suggested Activities:** Puppetry and dramatic play.

**Related Reading:** Preschoolers might enjoy the picturebook by Maurice Sendak upon which the film is based. Children might also enjoy listening to the record/audiocassette of *Really Rosie* by Carole King, or the audiocassette version of the Broadway musical (which starred children). However, "The Ballad of Chicken Soup," with its discussion of death and kidnapping, may not be appropriate for all hospitalized children; use the recordings selectively. (As with MADELINE, children who were familiar with the television or ½-inch version of REALLY ROSIE or knew the record before they entered the hospital will likely have no problems with this material.)

It might be fun to let children make a sandwich size, paper bag puppet of Pierre or the lion as they sing along or act out the story. Let them follow the simple instructions for a paper bag puppet on page 17 in Imogene Forte's activity book, *Puppets: Friends at Your Finger Tips* or use the activity sheet that accompanies Video Program #15.

---

**Recommended Pediatric Age:** 3–8.

**Hospital Rating:** ****

**Availability:**
PIERRE
Distributed by Weston Woods.
16mm film purchase price: $175
¾-inch videotape purchase price: $130
½-inch videotape purchase price: $90
Fee structure for CCTV rights is based on the number of buildings in which the title will be viewed times the running time. If title will be shown in only one building, CCTV rights are generally covered in the basic purchase price; ¾-inch videotapes available by special order.

---

# PIGS
*by Carroll Ballard* (USA/1967)
11 minutes /liveaction /color /nonverbal

This highly cinematic animal study begins with shots of dawn on a farm. Then, using close-ups and shots from different angles, parts of pigs' bodies (back, head, snout, ear, eye) are intercut with images of small birds, perhaps sparrows. All of this is backlit or shot under low light conditions, so the images are dark.

There is a series of shots of pigs rising to their feet inside a barn. When some piglets are shown out of doors and running away from the camera, the title appears. There is a cut to piglets running toward the camera, followed by a number of shots of suckling pigs.

Another long shot of the farm. A human approaches a feeding trough and pigs, both adults and babies, eat—chomping, gnashing, and slopping their feed as enhanced sounds of pig grunts are heard on the soundtrack.

There is a catalog of other animals: a cow, a black-faced sheep, a sheepdog, a cat, some geese, a horse, and another cow. This is followed by a catalog of the farmer carrying hay from the barn on a pitchfork, closing a corral gate, walking over a furrowed field to a tractor and plow.

A number of shots of full-grown pigs in the barnyard, in a meadow, and in a field with geese follow. Then a montage of pigs in a muddy yard, followed by several shots of pigs scratching themselves, especially their rumps with variously shaped tails, using hooves, trees, fences, etc.

A catalog of young pigs cavorting and rough-housing is followed by close-ups of different pigs' ears and snouts. Then there are images of pigs covered with mud.

A long shot of a pig in front of a building with fields in the background is followed by images of sleeping pigs. There is another long shot of the farm with some wildflowers in the foreground, then a close-up of the flowers (poppies), followed by a fade to sleeping pigs. Cut to butterflies flitting through poppies as a sow and some piglets walk/ run through the field.

**Visual Attributes:** Sometimes abstracted liveaction with a somewhat high image density.

**Sound:** Only natural sounds and an electric/acoustic country-sounding guitar which is sometimes disconcerting. Low audio density.

**Pace:** Varied.

**Structure:** Catalog. PIGS falls somewhere in between the simplicity of CHICKS AND CHICKENS and the complexity of CHICK CHICK CHICK; however, it is more like the latter in its abstraction of images (i.e., showing only parts of the animals' bodies) and catalog-within-a-catalog structure.

**Themes:** Although there was no real theme per se, there was a suggestion of the variations and similarities in animals.

**Comments:** PIGS might have worked better with a young school age audience than with preschoolers. Its dark, back-lit images created an ominous mood at the beginning of the film, a mood that did not change for certain viewers as the film progressed. Since very few hospitalized children actually knew what a pig looked like, the film's artistic but puzzle-like approach to the animal only confused very young viewers. The presence of adults often helped but, because of this, we decided not to use it on CCTV. We did use PIGS in Film Program #1 with ROSIE'S WALK.

**Suggested Activities:** By itself this does not really work for arts activities except for writing or talking about what was seen. However, when properly paired, it can be used to inspire movement and drawing activities.

**Related Reading:** As a preparation for the film, young children might benefit from looking at Ozzie Sweet's fine black-and-white photographs in *The Book of the Pig;* older children might also enjoy hearing/reading the informative text by Jack Denton Scott. (Unfortunately, this excellent book seems to be out of print, but may be available in public library collections.) *Curly the Piglet* tells the story of how the runt of a litter is cared for by 2 siblings who live on a farm.

---

**Recommended Pediatric Age:** 7–10.

**Hospital Rating:** **

**Availability:**
PIGS
Distributed by Churchill Films.
16mm film purchase price: $210
¾-inch videotape purchase price: $145
½-inch videotape purchase price: $145
No extra charge for CCTV rights unless title is seen in more than one building; then CCTV rights are 10% of title cost, per building. Rights must be renewed annually. Generally, only 16mm prints are available for preview; call to check availability of preview cassettes.

---

## THE PRINCESS AND THE PEA
*by Scott Hill* (USA/1982)
10 minutes /puppet animation /color

A narrator begins with the familiar "once upon a time" as a despondent prince sits at dinner with his parents. He is sad because he has been unable to find a real princess.

A storm arises and a solitary figure approaches the castle. A young woman, who claims to be a princess from afar lost in the storm, is admitted to the royal drawing room. The prince engages her in conversation while his mother (who looks like a Carol Burnett take-off of an aging vamp) prepares a twenty-mattress test in the guest bedroom.

Everyone except Princess Jana is at breakfast the next day and things are a bit tense until she arrives. When the queen asks how she slept, Jana says "Dreadfully!" As the prince beams triumphantly, the butler whispers to the maid that only a real princess could be that sensitive, sensitive enough to feel a pea under 20 mattresses.

As prince and princess ride horses and watch the stars through a telescope, the narrator explains that now the prince was very happy because he had finally found a real princess. The film ends as the butler dusts off the pea which sits, carefully preserved, on a red velvet pillow.

**Visual Attributes:** Static, semi-representational puppets with well-crafted three-dimensional sets and props. Numerous close-ups and a clear differentiation between figure and ground. Medium image density.

**Sound:** A brief opening/closing male narration but mostly character dialog with occasional chamber music. Rather low sound density.

**Video Legibility/Audibility:** Quite good.

**Pace:** Leisurely.

**Structure:** Dramatic narrative. Although fairly straightforward, the basic Andersen plot is embellished with many small details and psychologically revealing interactions that make it somewhat sophisticated and even tongue-in-cheek.

**Themes:** Loneliness; family relationships; romance; true love will win out; sometimes young people see what their parents cannot; female protagonist; adolescence; fractured fairytales.

**Comments:** This delightful and somewhat liberated version of a dry and enigmatic tale is an excellent example of how some stories can be vastly improved when translated to film.

Before a screening it helps to warn viewers that sometimes they will be able to see the marionette's strings or support rods.

We tried THE PRINCESS AND THE PEA with HANDS in Video Program #16. It would also work in film and on CCTV.

**Suggested Activities:** Box art and puppetry.

**Related Reading:** Because it will probably be a disappointment (the movie is so much better), we do not advise reading the Hans Christian Andersen fairytale as a follow-up activity, but it might work as preparation for under-tens. Illustrator Paul Galdone has a fairly faithful version of *The Princess and the Pea* which would probably appeal to children 6–9.

Six- to nine-year-olds might also enjoy Jane Yolen's anti-stereotypical *Sleeping Ugly* in which she reworks the story of "Sleeping Beauty"; it is available in paperback.

Over-eights might enjoy any of the following stories: "Atalanta," a gentle, nonsexist fairytale by Betty Miles from *Free To Be...You and Me;* "Petronella," a brassy, liberated fairytale by Jay Williams which is anthologized in *Storybook* but was originally published as a book; and "The Princess Who Stood on Her Own Two Feet," a sophisticated, feminist fairytale by Jeanne Desy in *Stories for Free Children.*

---

**Recommended Pediatric Age:** 7–14.

**Hospital Rating:** ★★★★

**Availability:**
THE PRINCESS AND THE PEA
Distributed by Hill-Gatu Productions.
16mm film purchase price: $225
¾-inch videotape purchase price: $175
½-inch videotape purchase price: $175
No additional charge for CCTV rights.

---

# A QUEST
*by Dan Bailey* (USA/1980)
8 minutes / liveaction / color / nonverbal

Set in a lush green landscape, this mime-pageant uses lettered banners like cue-cards to let viewers know what is happening. It tells the story of a knightly quest featuring actor/mimes as well as enormous parade-type puppets.

A white knight prances over a grassy hill. His horse, a papier-mache construction worn around the actor's waist, is humorously set off by shorts and sneakers. Suddenly, the white knight comes face to face with a knight similarly outfitted in black and red. Two colorfully costumed peasants appear in the foreground with a banner that reads "Conflict." The knights charge and after a few sallies and a few misses, they have a "Reconciliation." Now friends, they ride off together in "Harmony."

Behind them a great multi-colored puppet, resembling a Chinese dragon and carried by numerous people, appears as the peasants hold up a banner reading "Peril." Together the knights slay the dragon—"Success"—and fall asleep.

Meanwhile, an even bigger dragon approaches and the peasants hold up a sign saying "Impending Doom." The knights have almost had it when "An Ally" (in the form of a colossal rod puppet dressed like a queen) makes swaying movements that apparently cast a spell on the dragon. "Victory!"

There is dancing and celebration by everyone, including the dragons who join the triumphal procession of "Celebration."

**Visual Attributes:** Liveaction with sometimes poor differentiation between figure and ground. Low image density.

**Sound:** Nonverbal with medieval instrumental music. Low density.

**Video Legibility/Audibility:** Sound was fine but its reduced images were sometimes illegible.

**Pace:** Varied but mostly medium-slow.

**Structure:** Narrative. An episodic quest in pageant form.

**Themes:** There was no clear-cut theme except that pageants and pageantry are enjoyable.

**Comments:** Although A QUEST uses banners with words to describe the protagonists' feelings and identify plot elements, it is not always clear who is who and what is what. Thus, it is a good idea to review the entire chain of events before screening it with children in poor or fair condition. With children in good or excellent condition, it would be helpful to review the storyline up to the point of "Success" and let the ending be discussed afterwards.

A QUEST did not work well with school age viewers, but it was quite successful in playroom programs with preschool groups for whom mask-making and parades have more appeal. The biggest problem the film poses for preschoolers is the cue-card banners, but they can be read/explained by adults before and during the screening. You might also want to explain that a quest is a type of trip or journey which old-fashioned armored knights took to find adventure and meet new people.

We tried this with GERALD McBOING BOING in Film Program #16 and with KEITH in CCTV Program #6.

**Suggested Activities:** Pageants, parades, puppetry, and mask-making.

**Related Reading:** Although it does not deal with quests per se, Tomie de Paola's *The Knight and the Dragon* is a humorous and largely nonverbal picturebook about a reluctant dragon and an equally reluctant knight-errant which older preschoolers and young school age children might enjoy.

---

**Recommended Pediatric Age: 4–8.**

**Hospital Rating: ***

**Availability:**
A QUEST is not currently in US distribution; it may be available in public or university library collections.

---

## ROSIE'S WALK
*by Gene Deitch* (USA/1970)
5 minutes /cel animation /color

A barnyard hen takes an afternoon constitutional "across the yard, around the pond, over the haystack, past the mill, through the fence, under the beehives...," and gets back home in time for dinner. While she strolls around the farm, Rosie fortuitously avoids the predatory maneuvers of a comically inept fox.

The film starts when, as if calling out a square dance, the narrator says, "And now, Rosie's Walk." Fiddle music begins and a series of stills show a barn, a goat near a haystack, a wagon near some beehives, and another image of the barn showing the whole farm in the background.

A close-up of Rosie in her hen-house is followed by a medium-long shot of Rosie walking down the hen-house ramp while a fox hides underneath.

As Rosie crosses the yard, the fox leaps to attack her but misses and lands on a rake, the handle of which knocks the creature on the snout and becomes wedged between its teeth. Rosie walks on. The fox slumps on the rake, but Rosie doesn't seem to notice.

When Rosie circles the pond, the fox follows, leaps, and misses, taking a dive into the water. Rosie keeps on walking. The fox makes bubbling noises in the pond, but Rosie doesn't seem to notice.

Observed by a tethered goat, Rosie, followed by the fox, climbs the haystack. In another effort, the predator pounces and misses once again. Rosie travels on. The haystack falls apart, burying the fox except for its head and tail. Rosie still doesn't seem to notice and the goat just stares in silence. When the unflappable hen walks past the mill, she trips the rope suspending a huge sack of flour. The flour pours onto the leaping fox and foils another attempt to catch her, which Rosie doesn't seem to notice.

The little hen slips through an opening as the fox makes a high-jump over the fence, only to land in a cart which starts to roll downhill. And, as Rosie passes effortlessly underneath them, wagon and fox crash into a row of beehives. With her usual nonchalance, Rosie marches on while the fox disappears over a hill, pursued by an angry cloud of bees.

Rosie climbs the ramp to her little house, as the narrator concludes, "in time for dinner." The film ends with a partial review of her journey in stills (some of which were also seen in the preview): a long shot of the farm, a close-up of the barn, the beehives, another view of the barn, and another long shot of the farm.

**Visual Attributes:** Slightly static, stylized cartoon images that resemble Pennsylvania Dutch designs. Fairly low image density.

**Sound:** Occasional male narration over a rousing fiddle rendition of "Turkey in the Straw." Rather high sound density.

**Video Legibility/Audibility:** Very good.

**Pace:** Slow, except for the quick review.

**Structure:** Narrative. A simple, cumulative story that is nicely amplified by repetitive patterns of action. This also has a circular closure, in that Rosie starts out from and ends up in the same place.

**Themes:** Avoiding disaster; female protagonist; returning safely home.

**Comments:** Although the images in ROSIE'S WALK are fairly static, the camera actually seems to dance, stepping in for close-ups—first of the hen going past a landmark, then of the fox following in her footsteps—and stepping out for long shots of Rosie continuing her journey as the fox is detained. All the while, Rosie's consistently calm demeanor, the narrator's dead-pan delivery, the 1-2-3 camera rhythm, and the upbeat music serve to de-emphasize the danger in this slow-motion slapstick comedy. Once the pattern became evident, children had a great time anticipating what would happen.

Not surprisingly, ROSIE'S WALK was a great success and children often enjoyed it even more the second time we screened it, which we recommend doing. The only difficulty it presents for young hospitalized children occurs because the fox is never mentioned or identified by the narrator. Unless the fox is introduced as a character beforehand and unless children understand that foxes (like cats) chase birds (hens are birds), they may miss the film's droll humor. You might also want to explain that this is not a nice fox; it may justify its being chased by the child-terrifying bees.

A three-year-old watching ROSIE'S WALK thought the fox was "like my cat at home." Although he had probably never seen a fox, he got clues from the film and interpreted them correctly. On the other hand, a chronically ill three-year-old who lived at the hospital, did not know which of the animals on-screen was the fox.

The one structural flaw is that the preview is not the same as the review, and that neither shows the essential actions with their corresponding landmarks: across/yard; around/pond; over/haystack; past/mill; through/fence; and under/beehives. Also, the opening music may be a bit loud (especially for those sitting near the speaker, if it is shown as a film), so we suggest lowering the volume until the story proper begins.

We programmed ROSIE'S WALK in Film Program #1 with PIGS, in CCTV Program #2 with CHICKS AND CHICKENS, and in Video Program #1 with CHICK CHICK CHICK.

**Suggested Activities:** Drawing, journey/movement games, map-making, and mural-making.

**Related Reading:** Preschoolers might enjoy the picturebook by Pat Hutchins upon which the film is based; it is available in paperback from Weston Woods and/or Collier.

---

**Recommended Pediatric Age:** 2–8.

**Hospital Rating:** \*\*\*\*

**Availability:**
ROSIE'S WALK
Distributed by Weston Woods.
16mm film purchase price: $125
¾-inch videotape purchase price: $95
½-inch videotape purchase price: $50
Fee structure for CCTV rights is based on the number of buildings in which the title will be viewed times the running time. If title will be shown in only one building, CCTV rights are generally covered in the basic purchase price; ¾-inch videos available by special order.

---

# RUSSIAN ROOSTER
*by Steve Segal* (USA/1975)
3 minutes /cameraless animation /color /nonverbal

With an amusing mix of airplane and swimming metaphors, this film demonstrates that not only does practice make perfect—well, *almost* perfect—but also that the underdog sometimes comes out on top. It begins as hand-printed titles and musical credits move from right to left against a white ground. Footprints of birds, followed by blue, green, and orange bands of color, appear on-screen in time to the music.

Suddenly a funny looking chicken flops into view as it makes a bad landing. Emphasizing its ineptitude, the bird stumbles along the ground. Nonetheless, it keeps moving and, after reversing directions, starts to run. Once the bird has built up speed, it flaps its wings and attempts a take-off, but, ooops, it doesn't make it! The bird's eyes cross and its head spins in classic cartoon *goof-up* language, but the bird keeps trying.

Finally airborne, it faces the camera and makes a combined grimace/grin that is surprisingly toothy, does the Australian crawl as if swimming through the air, then rolls over on its back and kicks its feet, making it clear that despite all that went before flying is a piece of cake. Another series of colored bands appear on-screen and, making the toothiest smile imaginable, the self-satisfied bird does a series of barrel rolls, swivels its head, and does the breast stroke.

There is a simulated close-up of people's feet, then some images of 3 men with rifles who march in time to the music. Their necks stretch up and down—rubbernecking—as they look above their heads in all directions.

The bird now passes through a number of colored bands, then flies over and under a series of colored squares. A dotted line that looks like sky writing emanates from behind it, making a circle, a loop, and a straight line.

The bird flies through sections of red, yellow, green, purple, and orange, heading away from the viewer until it is just a squiggle in the distance.

Suddenly, the bird is back as large as life, wiggling and stretching to the music. The hunters shoot at it to no apparent end. A tree appears, from which the men suspend a cage-like trap.

A trumpet sounds. Colors fly like bullets from the hunters' guns. There are more close-ups of their feet. They switch directions. The bird circles the tree. The men shoot in one direction and then another. The bird snips the rope with its beak, the cage lands on the men, trapping the hunters, and the music comes to a finale.

**Visual Attributes:** Simplified but slightly primitive and cartoonish line drawings against a white background without details. Varied image density.

**Sound:** An energized orchestral version of Rimsky-Korsakov's overture to "Le Coq d'Or." Fairly high sound density.

**Video Legibility/Audibility:** Very good.

**Pace:** Medium to fast.

**Structure:** Dramatic narrative. This is a fairly sophisticated story in 2 parts with embellishments of abstract color. While the bird's first problem is to master flying, this only becomes clear as the film proceeds. Closure of the first part is therefore rather subtle and may be missed by very young viewers. The problem of avoiding the hunters in the second part is much more obvious, as is the closure.

**Themes:** Competence; avoiding disaster; role reversal; retribution.

**Comments:** Hospitalized children enjoyed this film, but it needs an introduction. It helps to warn children that RUSSIAN ROOSTER is a very short cartoon about a funny looking chicken who, when the film begins, is not very good at flying. Later, 3 hunters want to catch it, but the chicken is smarter than s/he looks.

Because it is short and somewhat fast, and because the colored bands may confuse some viewers if they see it only once, it helps children's comprehension and enjoyment to screen the film more than once.

RUSSIAN ROOSTER is a good programmer (i.e., a short film that can help set or change a mood when combined with a longer film) so we used it in Video Program #4 with THE CASE OF THE ELEVATOR DUCK and in Video Program #5 with SOLO. It would also work as a film and on CCTV.

**Suggested Activities:** Drawing, making flipbooks, and making up stories to musical compositions.

---

**Recommended Pediatric Age:** 4+.

**Hospital Rating:** ****

**Availability:**
RUSSIAN ROOSTER
Distributed by Coronet/MTI.
16mm film purchase price: $100
¾-inch videotape purchase price: $65
½-inch videotape purchase price: $65
No additional charge for CCTV rights.

---

## THE SKY IS BLUE
*by Ritchard Raxlen* (Canada/1969)
5 minutes /cutout animation /color /nonverbal

Using naive and child-like cutout images, this film relates the saga of a boy who goes up, up, up into the starry atmosphere and then down, down, down to earth and home again. Just after the title appears, the sound of wind is heard over piano notes and 3 daisies bend in unison, then clouds float across the screen and a butterfly comes into view. A spotted dog wags its tail, runs uphill, and rolls over excitedly as a boy with a kite follows behind. Dog greets boy with a little bark and the boy pats the animal's head. When the boy releases the kite, he is pulled up into the sky.

As the boy smiles and waves, the kite pulls him up into the clouds. Suddenly, a large bird approaches and squawks. The boy opens his mouth in surprise. When the bird departs without event, he resumes smiling.

An airplane passes by and the boy's mouth opens to a big "O." Although rocked a bit by the plane's draft, nothing more serious happens and, once again, the boy smiles.

As kite and boy continue to ascend, a hot-air balloon with a gondola barely misses them. They pass unharmed through a brief electrical storm, until they reach the stars.

Violin music is heard as the unwitting astronaut passes a planet. Unfortunately, exhaust from a rocket/space ship loosens his grip on the kite string. He shouts "Help!" and, fortunately, lands on the planet.

Unfortunately, he is attacked by a red crab-like monster with large pincers. Fortunately, just as the monster is about to grab him, the boy is rescued. A flying saucer arrives and zaps the monster with a ray gun. The space ship opens and a friendly bear-like creature invites the boy inside. Just before they take off, the boy's kite comes into view so they grab it and begin their descent from the stars.

When the flying saucer lands on a cloud, a smiling blond angel stands nearby. The boy swaps his kite for the angel's halo, but after some playing around, boy and kite return to the waiting spaceship. They travel downward through the clouds, past an electrical storm, and alight in the water near a deserted island.

The boy hops to land and the little space creature dives about in the water before taking off. The boy waves goodbye.

To an upbeat piano rag, the boy flags down and goes aboard a cruise ship. When the liner approaches land, he hops off, still carrying his kite, and waves goodbye.

As the opening musical theme is heard again, the kite pulls the boy along the ground until he comes to a house. The spotted dog comes out and whimpers. The boy pats the dog and, with kite in tow, they enter the house.

Lights in the windows dim as nighttime stars form an arc over the boy's house.

**Visual Attributes:** Sparse child-like cutouts against a blue background. Low image density.

**Sound:** Mostly piano with occasional violin music and effects. Generally low sound density.

**Video Legibility/Audibility:** Very good.

**Pace:** Slow.

**Structure:** Narrative. A simple, episodic story in which a series of problems (beginning with simply avoiding trouble and ending with trying to get home) are solved. The film makes effective use of repetitive actions and images such as mirroring the electric storm on the way down. Its only embellishment, and one which causes minor confusions, is the scene with the angel. Although the house is not shown in the beginning, the film has an implied circular closure because the boy ends up at home which is where, one assumes, he started from.

**Themes:** Rescue from a series of mishaps; returning safely home; what goes up must come down.

**Comments:** The simple journey-adventure of THE SKY IS BLUE was a great success as a lead-in to collage activities. Some children did not recognize the kite and others did not know what a kite was, so that should be explained before screening this work, as should the fact that one of the creatures the boy encounters is an angel with a halo (since some children did not recognize that image either).

We tried it in Film Program #3 with A LITTLE GIRL AND A GUNNY WOLF, in CCTV Program #4 with MADELINE, and in Video Programs #12 with THE SNOWY DAY and #13 with TANGRAM.

**Suggested Activities:** Collage and *fortunately/unfortunately* storytelling games. The latter is a circle game whereby children invent a story in which the main character gets into and out of scrapes until the story reaches a satisfactory closure. Encourage each child to take a turn by moving around the circle from right to left (or left to right). The first one to speak (perhaps an adult) gives a brief description of the main character and mentions some neutral but highly physical activity s/he is engaged in. The second person continues to describe the character's activities, beginning with *"Fortunately..."* The third person introduces a problem by saying, *"Unfortunately..."* The fourth person finds a way out of the predicament, starting off with *"Fortunately...."*

Children should alternate between good news and bad news until the story has gone around the circle one or more times, depending on their involvement and age. Make sure to end the story on a happy note.

To help structure the activity for very young children it might help to say the appropriate word before each one takes a turn, and to explain that *"fortunately"* means good things happen, while *"unfortunately"* means something bad happens.

**Related Reading:** To prepare very young children for the film, or to give young school age children some ideas for structuring the storytelling game, you might want to read them Remy Charlip's picturebook, *Fortunately* which has been retitled and printed in paperback as *What Good Luck! What Bad Luck!*

---

**Recommended Pediatric Age:** 2–7.

**Hospital Rating:** \*\*\*\*

**Availability:**
THE SKY IS BLUE
Distributed by Karol Media.
16mm film purchase price: $150
¾-inch videotape purchase price: $150
½-inch videotape purchase price: $150
Probably no extra charge for CCTV rights, but permission must be obtained from the National Film Board of Canada. The prices above are for nonprofit institutions only.

---

## THE SNOWY DAY
*by Mal Wittman* (USA/1964)
6 minutes /iconographic animation /color

A lyrical, slow-moving tale about Peter, a black preschool child, and his day in the city snow. The film opens with the screen divided diagonally—white below, blue above. A red figure slides down the wavy line separating the colors. A guitar strum is heard on the soundtrack and a few snowflakes fall. The title appears as both it and the name of the author are read by the narrator.

From inside, a young boy looks out a window as the narrator says: "One winter morning, Peter woke up and looked out the window. Snow had fallen during the night. It covered everything as far as he could see."

All dressed in red, a black child stands outside looking at high-piled snow. "After breakfast," the narrator explains, "he put on his snowsuit and ran outside."

Peter experiments with the wonderful white snow, walking first like a duck with toes pointed out, then like a pigeon with toes pointed in.

He drags his feet to make tracks, then uses a stick to add a third track to the parallel tracks made by his feet.

He uses the stick to hit a tree and knocks down some snow.

He watches big kids having a snowball fight. He wishes he could join them but realizes that he isn't old enough yet.

So he builds a snowman.

Then, lying on his back and moving his arms up and down and his legs in and out, he makes angel silhouettes.

He climbs a great pile of snow, pretending to be a mountain climber, then slides down the side.

He makes a snowball and puts it in his pocket to save.

He goes inside and, while his mother helps him undress, he tells her what he did in the snow.

He sits in a bubble-bath with a yellow duck and a sailboat and thinks about the day's events.

Before going to bed, he looks in his coat pocket, but it is empty. The snowball is gone.

Sadly, Peter goes to sleep.

He dreams of a bright yellow sun which melts the snow.

The next morning, however, when he looks out his window, the snow is still there and new flakes are falling. After breakfast, Peter goes outside with a child from across the hall. Together, he and his friend walk between 2 huge mounds of snow.

**Visual Attributes:** Fairly abstract, and static images; once in a while it is hard to tell figure from ground. Low image density.

**Sound:** Occasional female narration (storyteller style) with intermittent guitar music. Low audio density.

**Video Legibility/Audibility:** Generally good legibility with some fuzziness or outline disintegration of red colors in videotape. Generally good audibility except when the wards were very noisy.

**Pace:** Very slow.

**Structure:** Narrative. This simple, episodic, slice-of-life narrative uses realistic and mundane events in a chronological time-frame beginning in the morning of one day and ending on the morning of the next. Since its iconographic animation technique involves minimal motion and each image is quite separate from the other (in a manner that mimics the picturebook from which it was adapted), it is more like a narrative poem than a dramatic narrative.

**Themes:** Delight in nature; urban life; seasons; winter; familial support; early childhood; even good things are better when they are shared.

**Comments:** THE SNOWY DAY was delightfully relaxing and reassuring, and especially appropriate for winter programs in our hospital sites with urban preschoolers, the greatest majority of whom were black. It also works with children up to age 8 if they are in poor or fair condition. Its quietness and meditative pace seem appropriate for capturing the wonders of a snowy day. The only real problem may be that it has too low a sound level for use in a noisy playroom or for CCTV programming at times when the hospital is not quiet.

Although based on a book made via collage, this film does not inspire collages. It works very well, however, in combination with other, more direct collage inspirations. We tried THE SNOWY DAY in Film Program #4 with TANGRAM, in CCTV Program #3 with THE CASE OF THE ELEVATOR DUCK, and in Video Programs #11 with THE STORY OF CHRISTMAS and #12 with THE SKY IS BLUE.

**Suggested Activities:** Graphic design and painting.

**Related Reading:** Preschoolers might enjoy the picturebook by Ezra Jack Keats upon which the film was based; it is available in paperback from Weston Woods and/or Penguin.

With young school age children, you might try one or more of the following poems: "Cynthia in the Snow" by Gwendolyn Brooks from *Bronzeville Boys and Girls*, which also appears in *Listen, Children, Listen;* "First Snow" by Marie Louise Allen which is anthologized in both *Poems Children Will Sit Still For* and *The Random House Book of Poetry for Children;* "Snowy Morning" by Lilian Moore from *I Thought I Heard the City* and *Thread One to a Star;* and "Snow Country" by Dave Etter which is also included in *Thread One to a Star.*

---

**Recommended Pediatric Age:** 3–7.

**Hospital Rating:** ****

**Availability:**
THE SNOWY DAY
Distributed by Weston Woods.
16mm film purchase price: $175
¾-inch videotape purchase price: $130
½-inch videotape purchase price: $50
Fee structure for CCTV rights is based on the number of buildings in which the title will be viewed times the running time. If title will be shown in only one building, CCTV rights are generally covered in the basic purchase price; ¾-inch videotapes available by special order.

---

# SOLO
*by Mike Hoover* (USA/1972)
15 minutes /liveaction /color /nonverbal

A genuine cliff-hanger as well as something of a metaphor for solving insurmountable problems, this is the story of one man's ascent up a mountain. In the early morning light, a man walks through a misty forest as a *Swingles Singers'* vocalization comes up on the soundtrack. The credits roll over shots of snow formations and a waterfall.

The man climbs through a crevasse and starts to ascend a wall of rock. When he reaches an overhang, he pulls out rock-climbing gear. Whistling, he carefully places the pitons to hold his rope and hammers them into the rock. There are numerous close-ups of his face and hands as he works.

The camera pans up the mountain, following a rope to the man. He is about to place a hook in a crevice when he spots a tiny frog. He scoops it out and strokes it gently, then wraps it in a piece of paper which he puts in his shirt pocket.

From a distance, the camera shows a steep face of rock. A human voice echoes as something swings back and forth along the cliff. The camera zooms in to show that it is the man, swinging almost weightlessly at the end of his rope. As the music switches to a dance melody, the man swings back and forth and seems to be having a good time. One shot reveals blood on his hand, but otherwise everything is upbeat.

Later, after he has inched up the face of a mountain, the camera pulls back to reveal how high he has climbed.

When he reaches another obstructing overhang, more equipment comes into play. Dangling precariously from foot slings and trying to make it over the lip of the precipice—as only natural sounds are heard on the soundtrack—a piton falls and is heard bouncing from rock to rock. Suddenly, his foot sling gives way, and the climber smashes against the mountain. He loses his red cap and some equipment. He spins helplessly for a few moments. He even gets a bloody nose which he wipes, matter-of-factly, with his hand.

He puts out a leg to stop himself from spinning and pulls himself back up. As music resumes on the soundtrack, the climber finds his cap in a crevice and puts it on. There is a fade to black.

A series of shots from different angles show the climber inching his way up a crevasse. As music builds, there is a shot of a snow-covered mountain peak with a little figure moving along it which, in close-up, turns out to be the climber. The camera pulls back to reveal that the man is on a jagged peak surrounded by clouds. He is close, but he has not yet reached the top.

The man moves upward through crumbled glacial snow. Using a pick and spikes on his boots, he climbs a wall of ice.

Now the climber is above the snow. Although obviously cold, he removes his gloves to get a better grip of the last obstacle: a rocky overhang which he mounts using only his hands, arms, and legs.

As wind comes up on the soundtrack, the camera observes him from above, standing somewhat precariously on the mountain top with arms outstretched in triumph.

All at once, he is running downhill, leaping and rolling head-over-heels down a snow-covered section of the mountain as upbeat music is heard on the soundtrack.

Like a spider, he slips down a rope in the crevasse he climbed on the way up.

He reaches tree-growth level and, coming to a stream, splashes through the water and sits on a rock. Removing his backpack, the man pulls out a piece of paper and carefully puts it in the water.

The little frog swims out of the "envelope" and rests momentarily on the man's hand. He nudges it gently and the frog swims off. The film ends with a shot of the mountain as wind blows on the soundtrack.

**Visual Attributes:** Liveaction with somewhat below average image density.

**Sound:** Mood-setting instrumental music with choral scat-type singing and emphasized natural sound effects. Rather low audio density.

**Video Legibility/Audibility:** Excellent.

**Pace:** Varied, but mostly medium.

**Structure:** Dramatic narrative. Although this was made to suggest a documentary, it is an episodic story with one major problem to be solved by one character. The only embellishment—one which hospitalized children particularly appreciated—is the picking up and freeing of the frog.

**Themes:** Autonomy; courage; delight in nature; survival; nurturing and tenderness; competence; overcoming obstacles; overcoming hardship; overcoming injury; don't give up until you reach your goal.

**Comments:** To our surprise and delight, SOLO was one of the most successful films we used with older viewers. It is a compelling drama and has an effective illustrative musical score. However, because of its tension-producing and realistic qualities, we were leery of using SOLO without adults present so we did not use it on CCTV. We programmed it with THE FABLE OF HE AND SHE in Film Program #15 and in Video Program #5 with RUSSIAN ROOSTER.

**Suggested Activities:** Discussion and storytelling.

---

**Recommended Pediatric Age:** 8+.

**Hospital Rating:** ****

**Availability:**
SOLO
Distributed by Pyramid Film & Video.
16mm film purchase price: $350
¾-inch videotape purchase price: $195
½-inch videotape purchase price: $95
No additional charge for CCTV rights.

---

# SOMETHING QUEER AT THE LIBRARY
*by Nell Cox* (USA/1978)
10 minutes /liveaction /color

When Jill and Gwen discover that someone has vandalized the books they borrowed from the library, they attempt to find the culprit while simultaneously training a reluctant basset hound for a dog show competition. The film opens with a shot of 2 preadolescent girls walking to the checkout desk at a public library. As they talk, viewers learn (if they can hear the rapid dialog) that there is a dog show only a week away and one of the girls intends to show her basset hound, Fletcher.

A black male librarian says: "You know these books are oversized; they're not supposed to go out of the library, but I'll let you take them for one week. Okay?"

The girls promise to be careful. As they leave the building with the librarian, they see a basset hound. "That's Fletcher," one of the girls notes, and we learn from their conversation that the dog has never been in a dog show before.

In front of a house, the girls are attempting to train the dog but are getting nowhere fast. When they give up on "fetch," they retreat to a shaded porch to look up other tricks.

"We probably should have started to train Fletcher sooner."

"Yeah, like 1948."

"Oh, my goodness. Look!"

The camera reveals that some pictures have been cut out of their books. Afraid that Mr. Hobart will think they did it, they resolve to "catch the creep who did it" all by themselves. So they look through the books for clues. All they find is a dark fingerprint and a funny looking drawing.

"If we don't find the culprit ourselves, we'll probably have to pay for the books."

In their classroom they pass notes with a replica of the drawing on it, hoping someone will recognize it.

In another scene the 2 girls assess Fletcher's looks.

In a school corridor, they approach a girl. One of the pair says, "When you taught your dog to do tricks, did you get any books out of the library— the public library?" When she says she used the school library, the detectives look crestfallen.

Meanwhile, the girls continue to train Fletcher but his response is not encouraging.

Later on, after concluding that the fingerprint came from chocolate and after figuring out that all the pictures removed from the books were of one breed of dog, they go to the library to learn more about Lhasa apsos.

When the big day arrives, the girls take Fletcher and a bag with yoghurt and strawberries to the dog show. They split up and one goes looking for the Lhasa apsos in hopes of finding the book vandal. Pam, who is hanging out there, explains that she loves Lhasa apsos but her parents won't let her have a dog. The young sleuth confronts her: "Is that why you cut those pictures out of the library books?" Things culminate in a chase scene in which Jill and Gwen trap Pam in a tree where she confesses.

After Fletcher wins a prize for best markings, the 3 girls are in the library where the same man (Mr. Hobart) seen at the beginning works out a

deal with Pam so that she can repay the library for the damage she did.

**Visual Attributes:** Liveaction with a very high image density.

**Sound:** Almost continuous dialog, spoken very fast by preadolescent girls, with very little music. Very high audio density with few visual correlations.

**Video Legibility/Audibility:** Poor.

**Pace:** Too fast.

**Structure:** Dramatic narrative. A complex and confusing episodic story with a dual focus: training a dog for competition and finding the book vandal. Although it does have a circular closure (beginning/ending in the library), the storyline is too compressed and too unfocused to be clear.

**Themes:** Female protagonist; creative problem-solving; mystery; preadolescence; two heads are better than one; retribution.

**Comments:** This only works with children in good condition and it works best with girls. While similar in some respects to THE CASE OF THE ELEVATOR DUCK, especially in relying on viewer familiarity with detective story conventions, SOMETHING QUEER AT THE LIBRARY was not nearly as successful.

SOMETHING QUEER AT THE LIBRARY apparently tried to do too much for hospitalized children. Some critical information was given only visually (such as the discovery that the books had been cut up) and, when the film was transferred to videotape and shown on small screens, this information was lost.

In addition, the film was entirely dependent on dialog, most of which took place among preadolescents and suffered from the usual child-actor problems of lack of clarity and too rapid line readings. When the film was shown on video monitors, the soundtrack was even more difficult to hear. But when shown in the noisy context of a hospital, it was often inaudible. (When we showed it on CCTV, a girl of 6, straining to hear the soundtrack through a small bedside speaker, complained that doing so made her head hurt. A boy of 9 remarked: "I hear, but I don't know what they're saying.")

However, the greatest drawback for hospitalized children may have been the film's pace and structure, and the mere presence of a circular closure could not offset its complex, confusing presentation. First of all, there was no real introduction of its main characters, Jill and Gwen; the film begins in "fast forward" without orienting viewers to who, what, where, when. Second, the film has a confusing, dual focus with a lot of unessential embroidery (such as the jokes between the girls). Third, the storyline is compressed: too much information is packed into 10 minutes. Fourth, there is little elucidating action; the entire storyline (except the chase scene) is advanced via dialog and there are no evident cause-effect relations. Fifth, the camera does not help focus viewers: too much of the film is composed of medium or medium-long shots. And sixth, scenes are truncated and transitions between scenes are too fast; although there are at least four different locations, many scenes (such as those that take place in school) have neither set-ups nor closures.

It is noteworthy that the film is fairly faithful to the book, which has many of the same structural flaws. However, since children can read the book at their own pace and it is part of a series with conventions that readers become familiar with, the book seems to work better than the film. We tried SOMETHING QUEER AT THE LIBRARY with KUUMBA in CCTV Program #13.

**Suggested Activities:** Discussion, mystery storytelling.

**Related Reading:** Girls 7–10 would probably enjoy Elizabeth Levy's picturebook mystery series, *Something Queer is Going On, Something Queer on Vacation, Something Queer at the Haunted School, Something Queer at the Ball Park, Something Queer at the Lemonade Stand,* and *Something Queer at the Library* (from which the film was adapted); the series is available in paperback. Those who are familiar with the books will certainly get more out of the film if you decide to use it. A similar (but more globe-trotting) series for boys would be the TinTin comics by Herge which are available in both French and English.

---

**Recommended Pediatric Age:** 7–10.

**Hospital Rating:** **

**Availability:**
SOMETHING QUEER AT THE LIBRARY
Distributed by Churchill Films.
16mm film purchase price: $225
¾-inch videotape purchase price: $160
½-inch videotape purchase price: $160
No extra charge for CCTV rights unless title is seen in more than one building; then CCTV rights are 10% of title cost, per building. Rights must be renewed annually. Generally, only 16mm prints are available for preview; if you can only preview in video, call to check availability of limited cassettes.

---

# SOPHIE AND THE SCALES
*by Julian Pappe* (France/1974)
10 minutes /pixillated liveaction /color /nonverbal

A wish-fulfilling fantasy about how a mild-mannered girl gets back at an abusive piano teacher. The film opens with a tranquil family scene in a parlor. When the grandfather clock chimes, the girl gets up from her reading, puts on a straw boater, picks up her schoolbag, kisses mother, father, and dog goodbye twice each (identifying this as a European production), and descends a set of stairs.

It is dark outside; the moon is in the sky. The girl seems timid and hides behind a tree when she hears a dog bark. She waits nervously by a railroad crossing until a train passes.

She comes to a building and climbs another set of stairs. Inside, a strange-looking woman demonstrates piano scales while a parrot makes funny, mocking sounds. After some hesitation, the girl sits down to play. When she hits a wrong note, the teacher overreacts and demonstrates how to do it. Following this, Sophie plays the scales and makes another mistake. The teacher gets upset and threatens Sophie who hides until she is dragged back to the piano.

Sophie plays the scales again. When she hits a wrong note, she cowers. The teacher grabs the girl and throws her around. Sophie hides under a chair while the parrot makes a non-stop stream of raucous but unintelligible comments.

The teacher becomes so overwrought that she tears the piano score to shreds. Then, while the woman gesticulates to portraits of musicians on the wall, Sophie correctly plays the lesson with her feet.

The teacher recovers, offers Sophie candy, puts out a new score, and cleans up while Sophie wolfs down one candy after another. The woman plays something a bit more complicated than scales and calls for Sophie to repeat it.

Sophie curtseys, reads the score, and scratches her head. The teacher plays the piece again. Sophie looks puzzled. Finally, she sits down at the piano and plays the piece rather well for a while. When Sophie hits a wrong note, however, she slides under the piano as the woman chases her.

Again, Sophie attempts the more complicated piece. Inevitably, she hits a wrong note. This time the teacher climbs over the piano toward the girl while Sophie holds her off with a chair, as animal trainers do lions. The woman gets more overwrought than before and collapses.

Sophie plays the piece correctly—with the piano stool—and the woman revives. Then, while the teacher demonstrates another piece, Sophie devours more candy. The woman puts a portrait of Chopin on the piano and plays, neglecting her student, while Sophie unravels a partially completed sweater.

When the teacher comes out of her reverie, she notices what Sophie has done, chases her around the room once again, and beats her up in a slapstick and highly pixillated scene. Finally, the teacher opens the door and throws Sophie out.

In a sort of trance, the woman returns to the piano and plays to the portrait of Chopin. Unobserved, Sophie returns and mimics the woman behind her back. Then she goes on the offensive and slams the keyboard cover on the teacher's hands and spins the woman in the air like television wrestlers do.

Mock-wickedly rubbing her hands, Sophie goes out the door, waves goodbye, picks up her hat and bag, and heads home. Once again, she passes the moon in the sky, waits at the railroad crossing, and hides from the barking dogs. She pauses pensively before she gets to her house, but she mounts the stairs.

In the parlor, everything is as it was before. Mother is still knitting; father is still reading the newspaper; the dog is sitting attentively on a stool. She kisses them all—twice—and picks up her doll as the sound of Chopin-esque music comes up on the soundtrack.

**Visual Attributes:** Liveaction images animated in a pixillated style so that characters appear very puppet-like, which is emphasized by costumes (such as yarn wigs) and distinctly fake props and sets. Fairly low image density.

**Sound:** Almost continuous, well-integrated piano music with some cartoonish effects. Rather low audio density.

**Video Legibility/Audibility:** Good.

**Pace:** Mostly slow, except for a few very fast scenes at the dramatic climax.

**Structure:** Dramatic narrative. A simple story with effective repetition and a circular closure.

**Themes:** Self-esteem; escaping an oppressive situation; anger; uncooperative behavior; female protagonist; keeping secrets; abuse; Jekyll-Hyde behavior; music lessons; retribution; wish-fulfilling fantasy.

**Comments:** SOPHIE AND THE SCALES was a successful and therapeutic film but, unless children are warned that this is about taking piano lessons from a nasty teacher, some may find it confusing. We tried SOPHIE AND THE SCALES in Video Program #23 with THE FABLE OF HE AND SHE but it would also work as a film.

**Suggested Activities:** Box art, puppetry, storytelling, and creative dramatics.

---

**Recommended Pediatric Age:** 6–14.

**Hospital Rating:** ****

**Availability:**
SOPHIE AND THE SCALES is not currently in US distribution; it may be available in public or university library collections.

---

# THE STONECUTTER
*by Gerald McDermott* (USA/1965)
6 minutes /cel animation /color

To the accompaniment of a koto, the camera pans down a mountainous landscape suggested by vividly colored silhouettes. It pauses on the silhouette of a man, dressed in a kimono, who is chipping stone with a chisel and hammer.

"Tasaku was a stonecutter," the narrator says. "He asked for nothing more than to work each day, and this pleased the spirit who lived in the mountains." Thus begins the tale of a stonecutter's undoing when he becomes discontent to be himself.

After observing a royal procession, Tasaku becomes envious and wishes aloud for the prince's wealth. "The spirit who lived in the mountains heard him and, that night, transformed the stonecutter into a prince." As background colors change from rich brown to royal blue, a pair of giant arms and hands reach down from the sky, turning Tasaku's silhouetted hut into a tall Japanese palace.

Tasaku appears in a multi-layered kimono and a tall hat. "Tasaku was overjoyed. Every afternoon he'd walk in his garden." But, when he discovers that the sun has the power to burn his precious flowers, he realizes that the sun is more powerful than a prince and becomes envious. "He implored the mountain spirit to change him into the sun." As music tempo increases, giant arms and hands reach down and transform the man in a kimono into a mask-like sun. All the while, Tasaku and the background go through several changes of color.

"Tasaku became the sun and was happy for a time." He especially enjoys scorching the crops, which wither, turn dark, and fall from their branches, until he discovers that clouds are more powerful than the sun.

At his request, the giant hands transform Tasaku into clouds. "He made storms and flooded the land." However, he soon discovers that the mountain is more powerful than the clouds. "Make me into the mountain," he demands. The spirit transforms Tasaku as before, then departs.

Images in the film have now come almost full-circle. As in the beginning, viewers see the outline of a mountain. This time, however, Tasaku *is* the mountain. The sound of a stone chisel is heard and the narrator says that, deep inside, Tasaku trembled. Then, as the camera pans down the landscape, it reveals a stonecutter—a stranger—chipping away at the mountain that Tasaku has become.

**Visual Attributes:** Abstract, Matisse-like shapes in bold, intense colors; it is not always possible to distinguish figure from ground. Rather high image density.

**Sound:** Sparse male narration with almost continuous Japanese koto music. Medium to low audio density.

**Video Legibility/Audibility:** Good audibility but poor legibility due to color saturation and abstract imagery. Also, colors became somewhat muddy in the tape transfer.

**Pace:** Slow.

**Structure:** Dramatic narrative with a subtle ironic ending. The storyline is simply structured and has a repetitive, spiral format. It is not a circle because, while the opening/closing images are almost identical, there is a difference in who/what Tasaku is.

**Themes:** Be yourself; self-esteem; self-acceptance; magic; role-reversal; change and transformation; wishes granted; unanticipated consequences; color.

**Comments:** Before getting into a lengthy analysis of how and why this worked in the hospital, I should explain that THE STONECUTTER is a beautiful and highly unusual film which we have used quite successfully in other contexts. But, because it uses images (such as men in kimonos) that are both unfamiliar and abstract, because it is more pageant than drama, and because the compressed story has no amplifying action, THE STONECUTTER was too difficult for hospitalized children to follow despite the fact that the storyline is simple and repetitive. (To contrast this with other treatments of abstraction, see CHICK CHICK CHICK, ISLE OF JOY, PIGS, RUSSIAN ROOSTER, THE SNOWY DAY, TANGRAM, and WORM DANCES.)

Its biggest drawback, however, may have been its lack of emotion. The stonecutter is not a character viewers can easily identify with. Not only does Tasaku lack a face [which need not be a hindrance to identification (see, for example, JACK AND THE BEANSTALK)], but he loses both his identifiable form and his humanity to become abstract forces of nature which, at least in the context of this moral tale, do not evoke an emotional response. Moreover, the stonecutter that chips away at Tasaku-as-mountain looks exactly like Tasaku-as-stonecutter, something even viewers outside of the hospital find confusing. Finally, all else aside, hospitalized children may have had trouble identifying with Tasaku's power trip of unprovoked and wanton destruction (which is quite unlike the uncooperative behavior in A CHAIRY TALE and the retribution in SOPHIE AND THE SCALES).

We are led to conclude that the satirical didacticism typical of a traditional fable does not give hospitalized children the emotional support they need, and thus fails to engage their interest. (For further discussion of fables, see BALTHAZAR THE LION, THE BEAR AND THE MOUSE, THE FABLE OF HE AND SHE, and PIERRE.)

On top of all this, THE STONECUTTER is so much about color—and depends so much on seeing the images clearly—that it loses a great deal when transferred to videotape. (However, even in respect to its colors the film can be confusing; everything,

from backgrounds to the main character, changes color in an almost random fashion.)

Thus, while usually an excellent stimulus for collage in other institutional sites, THE STONECUTTER did not succeed as an art motivator in the hospital, even with children in top physical/emotional condition. This could have been due, at least in part, to the fact that the film needs very good screening conditions in order to be appreciated, and that is something rarely possible in a hospital during daylight hours.

Although we did not try it, the film itself might do better—as sometimes happens in other institutional contexts—if children become familiar with the book before the screening. It might also do better with preadolescents and adolescents. Like ARROW TO THE SUN, it may simply be too demanding for young hospitalized children. We tried THE STONECUTTER in a mini-test as a film and programmed it with TANGRAM in CCTV Program #7. It works best as a film.

**Suggested Activities:** Silk-screen printing and tissue paper collage.

**Related Reading:** School age children might enjoy the picturebook by Gerald McDermott which was adapted from the film; it is available in paperback from Weston Woods and/or Penguin.

---

**Recommended Pediatric Age:** 9–12.

**Hospital Rating:** **

**Availability:**
THE STONECUTTER
Distributed by Weston Woods.
16mm film purchase price: $175
¾-inch videotape purchase price: $130
½-inch videotape purchase price: $50
Fee structure for CCTV rights is based on the number of buildings in which the title will be viewed times the running time. If title will be shown in only one building, CCTV rights are generally covered in the basic purchase price; ¾-inch videotapes available by special order.

---

# A STORY, A STORY
*by Gene Deitch* (USA/1973)
10 minutes /cel animation /color

An African folktale about how Ananse the Spider (here in human form) bought stories from the Sky God for the people of earth. The gum doll (tar baby) episode is classic.

Following a series of 3 still images—a leopard, a hornet's nest, an Ashanti fertility doll—the narrator says the title as the words, "A Story, A Story" appear on-screen. This is followed by another series of stills: a skinny old man with a wispy beard, a fleshy man sitting on a throne, a woman dancing near a flowering tree (all of whom are black), some wasps, a gourd, and a pudgy hand with many rings resting on a brass box.

Minimal animation begins as the story starts, and the camera pans a traditional-looking African village. The narrator says that what is about to be said is not necessarily true; it is just a story, nothing more. The camera stops on a skinny old man who is surrounded by a group of children. The narrator explains that once there were no stories on earth because they all belonged to Nyame, the Sky God. The camera pans to an image of a fleshy man with his hand firmly on a bright box.

The story proper begins with Ananse climbing a web-ladder up to the sky. "Ananse, the Spider-man, wanted to buy the Sky God's stories, so he spun a web up to the sky."

Nyame laughs when he hears what Ananse wants and tells him: "The price of my stories is that you bring me *Osebo*, the leopard of the terrible teeth, *Mmboro*, the hornet who stings like fire, and *Mmoatia*, the fairy whom men never see." When Ananse agrees to his terms, the Sky God asks how such a weak and small old man can pay his price.

Ananse climbs down from the sky kingdom and runs through the jungle until he encounters the leopard who says Ananse has arrived just in time to be his lunch. But the wily spiderman proposes that they first play a binding-binding game, a ruse to which the cat agrees. In a short time, Ananse binds the creature with vine creepers and leaves him hanging from a tree. He says, "Now, Osebo, you are ready to meet the Sky God," as the music builds to a small crescendo then fades.

Next, a large banana leaf and a calabash are shown as still images. Then Ananse walks with the leaf over his shoulder and the calabash in his hand until he comes to the nest of Mmboro the hornet. Sprinkling water from the calabash, the spiderman creates the impression that it is raining and suggests that the hornets fly into the calabash so that rain will not tatter their wings. When they have all entered, Ananse puts a stopper in the mouth of the gourd and says, "Now, Mmboro, you are ready to meet the Sky God."

As he places the gourd on the leopard's stomach, percussion instruments reach a crescendo and Ananse does a little dance.

There is a montage of jungle foliage and the image of a hand holding a moon-faced Ashanti fertility doll. The narrator explains that Ananse carved a doll and covered it all over with a sticky latex gum, then he filled a bowl with pounded yams and placed doll and bowl at the foot of the flamboyant tree where fairies like to dance. (The narrator says that Ananse carves a little doll holding a bowl, but the image is of a separate doll and bowl.) The spiderman hides behind a bush and waits.

Shortly, a woman in traditional dress comes dancing along the path and sees the yams. "Gum baby, may I eat some of your yams?" she asks. (The narrator calls her a fairy.)

Ananse tugs on a string attached to the doll which seems to nod its head. The fairy finishes all the yams and says, "Thank you, gum baby." The doll does not respond so the fairy threatens to slap the doll's "crying place" unless it answers. Since it does not, she hits the doll in the mouth. Her hand sticks to its face, and the fairy threatens to slap the doll again if it does not release her. When she slaps the doll a second time, her other hand sticks fast. Furious, she pushes against the doll with her bare feet which also stick. Suddenly, Ananse comes out of hiding (we see only his feet) and says, "Now you are ready to meet the Sky God, Mmoatia."

There is an image of a spider web being woven while a number of percussion instruments reach a small crescendo. Osebo, Mmboro and Mmoatia are bound inside a web which Ananse hauls up to the sky.

The spiderman appears before Nyame and presents the "price" for the Sky God's stories. Nyame commands all in his court to sing the praises of Ananse. As the image of the story box appears, Nyame says that from that day forward his stories belong to Ananse and shall be called "spider stories."

Ananse climbs down to his village with the box, and the film ends with an image of the box from which all sorts of African silhouettes (mostly animals and people) emerge. "And when he opened the box," the narrator says, "all the stories scattered to the corners of the world." He then concludes with a traditional storyteller's coda.

> This is my story . . . . If it be sweet, or if it be not sweet, take some elsewhere and let some come back to me.

**Visual Attributes:** Somewhat static, stylized images that resemble block prints or cutouts; generally white background with minimal details. Fairly low image density.

**Sound:** Almost continuous narration by a man with a rich, Afro-Caribbean accent—basically a storyteller's delivery in which the narrator says everyone's lines; emphatic, African-sounding percussion music. Medium audio density.

**Video Legibility/Audibility:** Excellent audibility with generally good legibility (despite muddy skin tones).

**Pace:** Medium-slow.

**Structure:** Dramatic narrative. A fairly straightforward origins tale involving 3 tasks which makes effective use of recurring patterns of action and is framed by an explanation about the origin of stories; however, this film is quite dependent on words and the flow of events is a bit disjointed because it so closely follows the book from which it was adapted.

**Themes:** Competence; brains can outwit brawn; creative problem-solving; returning safely home; origin tales (the origin of stories).

**Comments:** A STORY, A STORY was a great success with hospitalized children, particularly older boys who admired the spiderman's cleverness.

While the inconsistent apples-and-oranges mix of stills (leopard-hornets-doll) that opens the film (which should have been either leopard-hornets-fairy or vines-calabash-doll) may not have undermined the film, it didn't help. The main problem with A STORY, A STORY for children both in hospitals and outside is that the fairy Mmoatia does not look like a stereotypical fairy. Make sure to warn young children about this.

We tried A STORY, A STORY in both Film Program #14 and in CCTV Program #5 with ISLE OF JOY (an excellent partner), and in Video Program #6 with THE CREATION OF BIRDS.

**Suggested Activities:** Collage and storytelling.

**Related Reading:** Under-nines might enjoy the picturebook by Gail E. Haley upon which the film is based; it is available in paperback from Weston Woods or from Atheneum.

---

**Recommended Pediatric Age:** 6–14.

**Hospital Rating:** \*\*\*\*

**Availability:**
A STORY, A STORY
Distributed by Weston Woods.
16mm film purchase price: $235
¾-inch videotape purchase price: $170
½-inch videotape purchase price: $50
Fee structure for CCTV rights is based on the number of buildings in which the title will be viewed times the running time. If title will be shown in only one building, CCTV rights are generally covered in the basic purchase price; ¾-inch videotapes available by special order.

---

# THE STORY OF CHRISTMAS
*by Evelyn Lambart* (Canada/1974)
8 minutes /cutout animation /color /nonverbal

Jointed, medieval-looking figures present a wordless nativity pageant based on the traditional story of the birth of Jesus. A tunic-clad angel accepts a branch of lilies from the disembodied hand of God and gives it to a peasant woman who is picking fruit from a tree. The passage of time is suggested as white flowers turn red and snowflakes fall.

Now dressed in a cape and riding on a donkey, the woman is accompanied by a bearded man who knocks on one, then another doorway. A man who answers the second knock directs the weary-looking couple to a nearby stable.

As a bright star shines above, an angel pauses on the stable roof then flies to talk with some shepherds. Overcoming their initial apprehension, three shepherds set off, apparently in the direction of the stable.

A star is seen by three kingly men, each of whom picks up a small treasure chest or goblet, and one after another they go in search of the star. When their paths converge, the kings travel together.

Soon, shepherds and magi arrive at the stable to pay homage to a baby who lies kicking his feet on a bed of straw. The camera pulls back to reveal a small village spread beneath a bright star.

**Visual Attributes:** Jointed, cutout figures move against a black ground. Somewhat low image density. Stock figures such as the angels were hard to identify because they were not costumed in stereotypical ways.

**Sound:** Medieval instrumental music. Low audio density.

**Video Legibility/Audibility:** Fair.

**Pace:** Slow.

**Structure:** Narrative. A loosely connected series of incidents based on the traditional story of the birth of Jesus. More pageant than drama, the film's format is confusing, particularly for young children or those unfamiliar with the story, because it lacks normal cause-and-effect relationships and events are not well-integrated.

**Themes:** Although there was no clear-cut theme, it has aspects of pageantry, the origin of Christmas, and holiday celebrations.

**Comments:** Since the filmmaker presumes audience familiarity with the sequence of events and the cast of characters, make sure children are familiar with the story before they see this film.

THE STORY OF CHRISTMAS (like THE STONECUTTER) suffers from having no characters which whom hospitalized children can identify, although it might do better in church-run hospitals than it did in our test sites. Also like THE STONECUTTER, it is highly dependent on the beauty and color of its images, thus it works better as a film than as a videotape. We tried it with THE SNOWY DAY in Video Program #11.

**Suggested Activities:** Collage or puppetry.

**Related Reading:** To offset the Euroethnic-looking whiteness of this film, children—especially children of color—might enjoy Langston Hughes' poem, "Carol of the Brown King" which has been anthologized in *Listen, Children, Listen.*

## TALEB AND HIS LAMB
*by Ami Amitai* (Israel/1975)
16 minutes /liveaction /color

Based on a Bedouin folktale, this film focuses on the dilemma his love for a lamb causes a young shepherd. It opens with a shot of a woman walking across a barren landscape. "In the dry Negev desert," the narrator begins, "fathers tell their sons this story." The title appears with no images under it, as if it were the title page of a book.

As singing is heard on the soundtrack, the camera pans across a green landscape and zooms in on a herd of sheep. The narrator explains that herding is boy's work, and there is a montage of shots of a boy and a long-eared lamb. Taleb (apparently the boy on-screen) was given a lamb by his father, the narrator explains, and the 2 became inseparable. "But this joy could not last, for shepherds raise male lambs to be sold for slaughter; and, although Taleb knew this, he turned his thoughts only to love...."

There are several shots of a Bedouin tent. Two men visit another man inside the tent and drink some coffee.

Singing is heard on the soundtrack and Taleb moves his flock toward the tent as the sun sets.

"Only later that evening did Taleb learn of his father's plans," says the narrator over Bedouin dialog, "and he begged him to spare the lamb." Inside the tent while his family gathers for a meal, Taleb—clutching his beloved lamb—is entreating his father. The woman (his mother) stops pounding the food to intercede for the boy, but to no avail. His father will not change his mind. Taleb bows his head.

After a montage of early morning shots, Taleb's father moves in front of the tent with a group of lambs. His mother, who is sweeping, says something to her husband before he loads the sheep into a small truck and drives off.

Later, when Taleb gets up, his mother says nothing about the lamb, "so Taleb hoped that his father had changed his mind." However, en route to school via donkey, Taleb stops to see his beloved pet and finds the lamb is gone. He picks up the lamb's bell and angrily tosses it to the ground.

"Even though this is not done among the Bedouins," Taleb decides to defy his father. Instead of going to school, he heads for a highway and hitchhikes.

A montage of the marketplace. Taleb walks through the crowd as the narrator says, "When Taleb arrived at the marketplace, he made his way to the sheep market—and soon enough he saw his lamb."

After another montage of people and activities in the sheep market, Taleb approaches his lamb in the truck. He grabs it and runs away as a heart-beat percussion is heard on the soundtrack. "He knew he was stealing from his own father, but he loved his lamb with all his heart and could not let it go for slaughter." The boy runs with his lamb into the wilderness. In a deserted place, he settles tenderly with the lamb and goes to sleep.

Meanwhile, back home, his father and mother have a quarrel in Bedouin. "I am going to find that thief and teach him a lesson," the narrator says in English.

A series of shots of Taleb surviving in the wilderness. He finds a water hole. He makes a fire with some flint and twigs to keep away predators.

The next morning, boy and lamb awake, as happy singing is heard on the soundtrack. Taleb finds an edible plant and the lamb eats some grass.

Meanwhile, the boy's father sets out from the tent on horseback.

More shots of Taleb and his lamb in the desert.

The father encounters a shepherd in the desert.

The camera pans the *wadis* (rocky valley) where Taleb and the lamb now seek shelter. Taleb discovers a cave and kills a quail-like bird which he roasts over a fire.

"On the third day," as Taleb is drawing water from a well, someone sees him. He grabs his lamb and hides.

Not long after that, apparently, the man who saw him encounters Taleb's father.

Cut to Taleb running.

Cut to Taleb's father on horseback.

Taleb is hiding in a cave when his father approaches. The camera shows alternating close-ups of boy and man. Finally, as the man talks to the boy in Bedouin, the narrator translates: "'Come here, defiant son,' ordered Hassan, 'give me the lamb!'"

Taleb gives the lamb to his father who puts it in front of him on the saddle. The boy follows, walking behind the horse. The narrator concludes by saying that although Hassan was proud of his son's courage, he sold the lamb, for he thought that would make his son grow wise and strong.

Just then, the frame freezes and the narrator says, "But it is also told that Hassan saw into his son's heart and gave him the lamb to begin his own flock."

Action resumes. There is a close-up of Taleb smiling—mounted behind his father. As they ride away together, the narrator says: "The fathers end this tale by saying, 'The way this tale should end is for you to decide, for true wisdom is born of hard but just decisions.'"

**Visual Attributes:** Liveaction with fairly high image density.

**Sound:** Almost constant male storyteller's narration in English, plus intermittent Bedouin dialog and indigenous-sounding singing and percussion music. Not only does the English narrator frequently talk over the Bedouin dialog, but at times there is singing under both, which results in 3 simultaneous vocalizations. High sound density with sometimes poor audibility.

**Pace:** Varied.

**Structure:** Dramatic narrative. A fairly complex story which uses parallel action and a storyteller's frame involving both an introduction and a double, lady-or-tiger ending.

**Themes:** Self-assertion; courage; fairness; conflict with parent; preadolescence; understanding parental values; nurturing and tenderness; competence; running away from home; survival; retribution; boy-gets-dog variation; lady-or-tiger ending.

**Comments:** This did not go over too well with younger children, but it did work with those 9–12, perhaps because TALEB AND HIS LAMB is a fairly complex and demanding film.

We were hoping children would be encouraged by Taleb's bravery and competence (as nonhospitalized children are), but generally that did not happen. Thematically, TALEB AND HIS LAMB had little appeal for under-nines. Perhaps they could not get beyond the literal, realistic looking running away to see this as a rite of passage to autonomy and independent decision making. Perhaps also, the stern patriarch who ignores the pleas of both wife and son—the parent who never shows a tender, caring emotion—is antithetical to the needs of pediatric patients. (For other parent-child conflicts, see THE CASE OF THE ELEVATOR DUCK and MARY OF MILE EIGHTEEN.)

Structurally, the film may be too complex for all but preadolescents in fairly good condition. Although Taleb is clearly introduced, his father and his mother are not and, since this is an unconventional-looking family, some children remain confused about who is who for quite a while. Then once the drama starts to unfold, the filmmaker cuts back and forth between Taleb and his father, a technique which in itself can confuse young viewers. Finally, because the dual endings are not clearly distinguished and are almost entirely narrator-dependent, the second, more appealing one frequently goes unnoticed. The freeze frame seems to be at fault, for at that point many viewers believe the film has ended. Even in nonhospital sites many children do not hear the second ending because they stop paying attention when the action stops (even though it resumes again briefly) and

many have strong emotional reactions to the first ending's unfairness. For this reason, children must be warned about the dual ending. The film also needs a good sound system.

Because of its narrow range of appeal and its complex sound and visual techniques, we did not use TALEB AND HIS LAMB in either our CCTV or video programs. We used it in Film Program #12 with IRA SLEEPS OVER (not a homogeneous pairing) and in the pilot.

**Suggested Activities:** Discussion.

---

**Recommended Pediatric Age:** 8–14.

**Hospital Rating:** \*\*\*

**Availability:**
TALEB AND HIS LAMB
Distributed by Barr Films.
16mm film purchase price: $345
¾-inch videotape purchase price: $345
½-inch videotape purchase price: $345
CCTV rights cost an additional 50% of film price for the life of the film.

---

# TANGRAM
*by Alan Slasor* (USA/1975)
3 minutes /cutout animation /color /nonverbal

Using geometric shapes from the ostensibly Chinese puzzle called a tangram, this lyrical film illustrates and celebrates various silhouette shapes which gracefully move in time to music. A yellow-green square is centered against a royal blue background as a delicate flute and piano composition begins. At first, the square is solid. Then lines appear, outlining the 7 pieces of the tangram: a square, a rhomboid, and 5 triangles. The overall square breaks up and the 7 pieces float around the screen, coming together again in the shape of a square, but this time it is not solid: there is an opening through which the blue background shows.

The square dissolves and the pieces reform themselves as a solid triangle—angle up, like a pyramid. The original triangle dissolves and is reformed with an opening in it.

The triangle dissolves and the 7 tangram shapes form a parallelogram—initially solid but then with an opening.

The parallelogram dissolves and reforms in a spiral or pinwheel shape which spins, dissolves, and reforms itself as... A lobster or crayfish which moves around the edge of the screen and dissolves into...

A snail that inches across the bottom of the screen, looks around, and dissolves into...

A fish which swims around the screen, moving its fins, and dissolves into a sunfish-type fish which leaps up toward the top of the screen where it dissolves. The tangram pieces fall to screen-bottom where they assume the shape of...

A seated frog that opens its mouth, hops, and becomes... A flying bird that becomes...

A rabbit that moves its ears, wiggles its tail, and hops across the screen, only to dissolve into...

An upright cat which moves its head up and down as if cleaning itself, then changes position a few times, and turns into...

A horse that lowers its head, rears on its hind legs, and canters across the screen.

There is a reprise of the animals—from snail and frog to rabbit, bird, cat, and horse—and out of the dissolve which follows the horse, a person in pants and a flattened conical hat walks quickly across the screen, does a few somersaults, then leaps in opposite directions across the screen (or perhaps it is 2 people). In a concluding somersault, the person spins in the center of the screen and re-forms the square which began the film as the music reaches a finale.

**Visual Attributes:** Simple yellow-green, geometric cutouts (silhouettes) move against a blue background, and each animal moves in a characteristic manner which offers clues to what the image represents. Although color saturation is high, the images are easy to read because the figure/ground colors do not change. Fairly low image density.

**Sound:** Highly effective lyrical music with a flute and piano. Low audio density.

**Video Legibility/Audibility:** Excellent.

**Pace:** Mostly medium-slow.

**Structure:** Lyric. This well-focused film effectively uses both repetition and variation in a dance of simple silhouettes. It has a perfect circular closure, beginning and ending with a single square.

**Themes:** Variations on a concept; tangrams; an exploration of geometric shapes; change and transformation; design; puzzles.

**Comments:** This exemplary lyric worked, on different levels, with the broadest age range of any film we tested with hospitalized children. However, it absolutely requires more than one screening as well as an introduction (for examples of which see the programs we used it in). Children must also be warned that TANGRAM has no story, no words, and is very short. We used it in Film Program #4 with THE SNOWY DAY, in CCTV Program #7 with THE STONECUTTER, and in Video Programs #13 with THE SKY IS BLUE and #14 with JACK AND THE BEANSTALK.

**Suggested Activities:** Design, collage, and solving tangram puzzles. Many educational toy stores have tangram kits; Galt Toys has a particularly nice puzzle and booklet (in English, French, Italian, German, and Dutch) by Ravensburger Games.

**Related Reading:** To prepare them for the screening and the guessing-game or puzzle-like aspects of TANGRAM, preschoolers might benefit from Tana Hoban's photo/picturebooks, *Circles, Triangles and Squares* or *Shapes and Things*.

As a follow-up, children over 8 might enjoy trying to solve tangram puzzles, an excellent solitary activity for bedridden youngsters. Dover publishes several books: *The Eighth Book of Tan: 700 Tangrams; Tangrams: 330 Puzzles;* and *Tangrams ABC Kit* and *The Fun with Tangrams Kit*, both by Susan Johnston and both with puzzle templates. There are two other books with puzzle pieces: *Tangram: The Ancient Chinese Shapes Game* and *Tangrams: Picture-Making Puzzle Game.*

---

**Recommended Pediatric Age:** 2+.

**Hospital Rating:** ****

**Availability:**
TANGRAM
Distributed by Pyramid Film & Video.
16mm film purchase price: $110
¾-inch videotape purchase price: $110
½-inch videotape purchase price: $110
No additional charge for CCTV rights.

---

## TCHOU TCHOU

*by Co Hoedeman* (Canada/1972)
15 minutes /object animation /color /nonverbal

In this slow-moving but dramatic fantasy, a boy and a girl who are either playmates or siblings outwit and tame a fearful dragon. The film opens with the image of a colorful block-built environment and some unusual, echoing sounds. Then to an amusing percussion, an insect and a lady bug (each painted on wooden cubes) crawl by. The title appears over train-like sounds.

A bird twitters, and a boy walks into view. Like everything in the environment, he is made of painted wooden blocks—in this case, 3 cubes stacked on top of one another. He picks up a ball, tosses it in the air, and balances it on his head. A girl (also made of 3 cubes) comes into view and the boy greets her. They play hopscotch as lyrical organ music is heard.

After a while, ominous echoing sound effects interrupt the children's play. A block-dragon appears, roaring in the distance and slithering toward them.

The ladybug scampers away and the children quickly build a small fortress. While they hide, the dragon moves around their playground—roaring, knocking things down, and making a mess. Then it leaves.

The children clean up. They rebuild their playground and resume playing as lyrical music is heard on the soundtrack. The girl goes down a slide. The boy balances on a ball. They play together on a see-saw.

Suddenly, with a roar and the same ominous sound effects as before, the dragon reappears. The boy angrily throws blocks at it from above, but this only makes the dragon furious. It knocks everything down, leaving the place in a shambles.

After the dragon has gone, the boy is visible but the girl is nowhere to be seen. He pokes through the rubble and eventually finds her, lying on the ground. An "uh-oh" sound is suggested by a musical instrument and the boy seems worried, but then the girl opens her eyes, straightens herself out, and helps him clean up the place, after which the children erect a sign outside the playground with a picture of a dragon and an arrow that suggests "Dragons go that way."

Before long, the dragon returns, but now its theme music is less threatening. Perhaps intrigued by the image of itself, it dances around the sign then heads in the direction indicated.

Watching from their hideout, the children are pleased with their handiwork. The dragon encounters another sign (which pops up like a mushroom) and obligingly goes in the direction indicated by the arrow, which amuses the children. However, on the third such encounter, the effect diminishes; the dragon knocks the sign down and moves in another direction.

Lights dim and night falls. Then, as a loud snoring is suggested on the soundtrack, the children sneak about, carrying large wheels into a dark place and moving blocks around.

The result of their effort becomes evident the next morning. When the dragon wakes up, instead of making its usual roar, it sounds like a steam whistle. And instead of slithering, the dragon moves in a streamlined manner. The children have transformed the creature into an amusement park choo-choo train. Happily, girl and boy hop on board—as do the bird, ladybug, and insect. All have a pleasant ride as upbeat music plays on the soundtrack.

**Visual Attributes:** Semi-abstract puppets made from painted cubes and rectangles that resemble children's blocks; occasionally it is hard to distinguish figures from ground, but generally the images are legible. Rather high visual density.

**Sound:** Unusual and dramatic sound effects with intermittent lyrical music which provides critical information to young children about the course of events. Somewhat low audio density.

**Video Legibility/Audibility:** Good.

**Pace:** Leisurely.

**Structure:** Dramatic narrative. Although it has numerous small embellishments, this is a fairly straightforward story with 3 repetitively patterned episodes.

As a result of their encounters with the dragon, the children take an increasingly active role. The first 2 times the dragon appears they simply hide in a shelter; the third time they develop the signs and then, while it sleeps, they go to the dragon and transform it into a playmate.

**Themes:** Creative problem-solving; friendship; monsters; overcoming terrors; change and transformation; converting an enemy into a friend.

**Comments:** TCHOU TCHOU was a great success in playroom screenings where children were encouraged (with adults demonstrating) to *boo* when the dragon appeared and cheer when it went away. Not only did this keep young children actively involved during this long, wordless film, but it gave them a clue to its structure and offset the potentially scary dragon music/effects.

Preschoolers must be warned that TCHOU TCHOU is a scary film. Because of its potential scariness—largely due to the soundtrack—we do not recommend this for unsupervised screenings and did not use it in our CCTV programs. We used it in Film Program #5 with THE MOLE AND THE EGG as well as in Video Program #17 with THE MOLE AND THE TELEPHONE.

**Suggested Activities:** Puppetry, objects-as-puppets, block play, dramatic play, and dictating stories or captions for pictures the children draw.

**Related Reading:** This story has interesting parallels to *The Dragon's Tears*, a picture-play in 16 panels; out of print, it may be available in public libraries. Somewhat related is *The Knight and the Dragon*, a droll picturebook with a "reluctant dragon" theme by Tomie de Paola which is available in paperback. Low-functioning children might better understand the film if they are familiar with either book (or a synopsis of the film's storyline) before seeing it.

As a follow-up, make and/or try dramatic play with the dragon-type hand-puppets in Forte's book, *Puppets: Friends at Your Finger Tips*. See lizard on page 20, snake on pages 36-37, or alligator/crocodile on page 63.

---

**Recommended Pediatric Age:** 3–10.

**Hospital Rating:** ****

**Availability:**
TCHOU TCHOU
Distributed by Encyclopedia Britannica.
16mm film purchase price: $265
¾-inch videotape purchase price: $220
½-inch videotape purchase price: $210
No extra charge for CCTV rights, but hospital must pay an additional 30% of purchase price for each copy it makes of any EBE title.

# A VISIT FROM SPACE
*by Zlatko Grgic* (Yugoslavia/1965)
11 minutes /animation /color

"For this story we need," begins the narrator, and as he lists them, images corresponding to his words appear in a dozen boxes which line up in several rows on-screen, "a town, a tree, lots of apples, a little girl, a basket, a little bench, a chair, a ladder, a kite, a miraculous flying machine, 2 even more wonderful creatures, and, finally, a mother. And now the story can start!" From here until the very end, this film is essentially nonverbal, and each time one of the above items appears for the first time, it is framed momentarily as if on a card, then the frame fades, and the object is integrated into the scene.

The story proper begins as a little girl (introduced in the opening line-up) tries unsuccessfully to get at some apples on a tree. To get closer, she pulls a bench with a chair on it up to the tree, puts a ladder on top of the chair, and piles more things on top of that—including a kite and a suitcase. Now, however, the pile is too high and a passing butterfly knocks the precarious assemblage down.

Undaunted, the girl ties the kite to a basket and climbs in. By this means she gets within reach of the fruit and picks 2 apples—one with each hand. While trying to decide which to eat, a flying saucer goes by and severs the kite string.

As the background color changes, the flying saucer lands nearby, out of sight of tree or girl. Huge eyes protrude from the saucer and look around, then the saucer opens like a clam, revealing 2 pairs of little eyes inside. Two small, pale creatures with large heads emerge from the spaceship only to be frightened by the kite which lunges uncontrollably. They pull out a gun but are afraid to use it. When one finally pulls the trigger, a cork attached to a string pops out.

The unruly kite seems to be chasing them and lands on one of the little creatures. Frightened, the other one hops back in the flying saucer which zooms away.

When the girl comes over the hill looking for her kite, she finds it lying on the ground. She picks it up and accidentally steps on the little space creature. In a classic slapstick comedy routine, they frighten and bump into each other until the girl offers the creature an apple. It, however, is unsure what to make of the fruit until the girl demonstrates by biting into hers. In a burst of enthusiasm, the creature then gobbles its apple—as well as the girl's—which leaves her momentarily nonplussed.

Next the girl tries to determine what the creature is. As she gestures, the image of a frog appears around the little extraterrestrial. The girl apparently wants to know if it is a frog. The creature shakes its head no. Similarly, the girl asks if it is a kangaroo, and she gets another negative response.

When the girl insists on a response, the creature points to the sky and the camera zooms in to a planet with lines suggesting Martian canals. So the girl conjures up the image of a space ship.

Now, reversing roles, the little creature uses sign language to ask if the girl is a kite. She says, "nyeh" or some such negative response and signals for the creature to follow her. She skips off toward the tree and the creature imitates her movements as a pleasant melody is heard on the soundtrack.

The background color changes back to green (as before) and the new friends are seen eating lots of apples. Suddenly, a voice calls out, like a mother calling her child to come home. The girl says "mama" while the words *mama, mutti,* and *mommy* appear in the air above her. Plaintively, the space child utters "mama" and, looking toward the sky, begins to cry.

Determined to help, the girl resorts to her apple tree strategy and stacks objects so the little creature can get closer to the sky. First she puts the bench in place, then the chair, then the ladder, then bellows, record player, horn, hat, and jack-in-the-box. A butterfly passes by, but this time, instead of toppling her tower, it stabilizes the structure.

After filling the basket with apples, the girl works the bellows to make the kite rise. The extraterrestrial leaps into the basket which, pulled by the kite, heads toward Mars. The visitor from space says "mama" and waves goodbye to the girl, who then runs home.

Initially the windows of her house are dark, but as lights come on, signalling nightfall, the narrator says: "Children, when the day is over and the stars begin to peep, look up at the sky. Look very carefully. There among those little worlds, you can see a star and a trail leading to the star." A trail of apple cores leads to Mars, and the narrator concludes by saying, "He landed successfully."

The words "the end" appear on-screen in five languages.

**Visual Attributes:** Child-like cartoon images with little or no background imagery. Rather low visual density.

**Sound:** Mostly nonverbal with an opening/closing commentary by a male narrator; cartoon vocal and sound effects with evocative programmatic or illustrative orchestral music. Low audio density.

**Video Legibility/Audibility:** Good audibility and legibility although there was some fuzziness or disintegration of outlines in videotape when the background color changed to red.

**Pace:** Slow.

**Structure:** Dramatic narrative. A story in 3 parts, each of which has a different problem for the girl to solve (i.e., getting to the apples, getting acquainted with the extraterrestrial, getting her friend home) and each of which is successfully closed before the next segment begins.

The story as a whole is effectively framed with an introductory/concluding commentary by a narrator. The prologue is more like a stage manager's prop and character list than a traditional storyteller's opening, but it works very well as a visual/aural introduction.

**Themes:** Abandonment; separation; being different; female protagonist; friendship; returning safely home; extraterrestrials; cross-cultural communication; early childhood; problem-solving.

**Comments:** This sweet and reassuring film was highly successful with hospitalized preschoolers, at least in part because it was so well structured. Aside from using effective repetition and incorporating basic childhood urges into the storyline (climbing to get something desireable, meeting someone new, wanting to go home to mother), the fact that each of the 3 problems/parts was satisfactorily closed before the next one began made A VISIT FROM SPACE especially appropriate for preschool viewers. The film also worked with older children, sometimes as old as ten.

We used A VISIT FROM SPACE with HAROLD AND THE PURPLE CRAYON in our Video Program #2, but it would also work as a film and on CCTV.

**Suggested Activities:** Storytelling and drawing.

---

**Recommended Pediatric Age:** 3–9

**Hospital Rating:** ****

**Availability:**
A VISIT FROM SPACE
Distributed by Charles Samu.
16mm film purchase price: $200
¾-inch videotape purchase price: $100
½-inch videotape purchase price: $100
No additional charge for CCTV rights.

---

# WHAZZAT?

*by Art Pierson, Jr.* (USA/1975)
10 minutes /clay animation /color /nonverbal

Based in part on the Arab/Indian folktale, "Six Blind Men and the Elephant," the first half of this classic film establishes how 6 little clay blobs solve their problems through teamwork. In the latter half, the little creatures encounter a mysterious animal. By sharing their impressions with each other, they come to a consensus about what it is.

Exuberantly, like a circus lion bursting through a paper covered hoop, a variegated ball breaks through a sheet of white paper and rolls across the screen. Six colored segments peel away from the ball and transform into lively, anthropomorphic clay creatures.

They slither, roll, and inch along while chattering excitedly in a nonverbal, bird-like language. All at once, a menacing gray mass surrounds them. One of the creatures, a lavender slowpoke, gets too close and is engulfed, only to be rescued by the others who then stack up like a totem pole and arc over the imprisoning gray mass to freedom.

Merging, separating, rolling, and crawling, the creatures continue on their journey as music provides appropriate cues. Suddenly, an earth-splitting tremor occurs. The creatures peer into a fissure which widens and forms a deep cavern. They briefly debate how to proceed. Then Blue elongates, forming a bridge and they all cross the rift, all except for Lavender. Timorously, the little creature sets out across the make-shift bridge but, when half-way across, Blue loses hold of one side. Both creatures hang precipitously from the cliff until their companions pull them to safety and a happy reunion.

The group heads on but now the light changes and, as thunderous sounds are heard, the ground shakes. Inquisitive, the creatures take turns investigating the source of the noise.

Yellow approaches and touches the unknown thing with a hand-like appendage. Returning to the rest of the group, Yellow gestures as the image of a brick wall appears behind him/her.

Next, Blue approaches the thing and coils around part of it. Blue returns to the group and makes gestures while the image of a tree momentarily appears behind her/him.

Red, Orange, and Green set out together but each encounters a different part/aspect of the unfamiliar thing. When they return to the others, they take turns describing it—with gesture and image—as a rope, a spear, and a snake.

Having gathered their data, the creatures deliberate and discuss what they experienced until the information finally makes sense. With great excitement, the six companions exclaim in unison: "ELEPHANT!"—the only word in this film.

Now that its identity is resolved, the creatures approach the friendly beast and roll up its trunk—all, that is, but Lavender who trails behind as usual. Gently, the elephant picks the slowpoke up with its trunk and deposits the little creature on its head among its family/friends.

Joining together again in ball formation, the creatures roll to the tip of its trunk as the elephant trumpets in delight.

**Visual Attributes:** Mostly abstract, biomorphic playdough images with no background details. Generally low image density.

**Sound:** Although this has one word, it is basically nonverbal with pseudo-conversational vocalizations and effective, illustrative music. Medium audio density.

**Video Legibility/Audibility:** Generally good, although the bright film colors became somewhat dull in the transfer to videotape (but this may be correctable).

**Pace:** Varies but mostly medium.

**Structure:** Dramatic narrative. A well-structured story in 2 acts with a circular frame in which the characters start/end as a ball. The pattern of cooperation established among the creatures in the first 2 episodes (act one), effectively sets up the more complex pattern of interaction used to solve the problem in act two. However, the second act is fairly sophisticated and can be confusing for very young children.

**Themes:** Cooperation and teamwork; change and transformation; creative problem-solving; familial support and/or friendship; overcoming obstacles with teamwork; nurturing and tenderness; interdependence; communication; different points of view; there's more than one side to an issue; the experimental method; resolving a difference of opinion; many heads are better than one; encountering the unfamiliar; pooling resources.

**Comments:** WHAZZAT? was extremely successful and only fell short of perfect reception because some young viewers had trouble following the second act, but generally that did not diminish their enthusiasm for this classic short. It has so many things going for it—bright colors, free movement of the little clay blobs, lively illustrative music, the appealing characterization of the Lavender baby, the theme of working together, and the visual metaphor (the ball) of reunion with family/friends—that we strongly recommend using it, even with very young or low-functioning preschoolers.

The best way to use WHAZZAT? with such a population would be to screen the film twice, a few hours or a day apart, with the same individuals or groups. Initially, only screen act one. Between screenings read children one of the many versions of "The Blind Men and the Elephant," then screen the film in its entirety. We used it in Film Program #7, in CCTV Program #12, and in Video Program #22 with WORM DANCES, a perfect partner.

**Suggested Activities:** Clay and playdough sculpture. You can also use this as a focus for group activities of any sort.

**Related Reading:** To prepare preschoolers for the second part of the film, you might want to read *What Do You See?*, a poetic and minimally verbal picturebook which deals with the theme of different perspectives. And/or they might enjoy the wordless photo/picture puzzlebooks *Look Again* and *Take Another Look*.

Young school age children might enjoy the 2 brief and riddle-like versions of "The Blind Men and the Elephant" on page 54 in *Noodles, Nitwits and Numbskulls* which is available in many public library collections.

---

**Recommended Pediatric Age:** 3–13.

**Hospital Rating:** ****

**Availability:**
WHAZZAT?
Distributed by Encyclopedia Britannica.
16mm film purchase price: $250
¾-inch videotape purchase price: $260
½-inch videotape purchase price: $250
No extra charge for CCTV rights, but hospital must pay an additional 30% of purchase price for each copy it makes of any EBE title.

## WHERE THE WILD THINGS ARE
*by Gene Deitch* (USA/1973)
8 minutes /animation /color

As Big Band radio music is mixed with other sounds, the film opens with a preview montage of still images: a moon, a sailboat, and some monsters. A pulsing heart-beat sound gets louder as the camera pulls back from the image of an arm with a clawed hand. Then there is an image of a child in a white cat-like costume hammering a rope of sheets to a wall. There is another still of the child chasing a little dog with a fork.

The story proper begins from a fade to black and opens on the still image of the same child. The image itself occupies the center of the screen and is framed in black.

The narrator begins the story. "The night Max wore his wolf suit and made mischief of one kind and another, his mother called him 'Wild Thing' and Max said, 'I'll eat you up!' so he was sent to bed without eating anything." The narrator delivers the lines without haste and, as he does, successive images of the child expand to fill the screen. During this time the child begins to move, at first jumping up and down, then chasing a dog.

Max's mother is not shown but, suddenly, the boy is in his bedroom which remains framed in black until the room transforms. As the narrator explains that a forest began to grow in Max's room, an eerie, "Twilight Zone" pulsing is heard and the walls of his room become overgrown with vegetation. When the room seems to have become a forest, there is a zoom in to the moon. When the camera zooms out, Max is in a ship, sailing across a body of water.

As the sound of wind is heard underneath his voice, the narrator says, "And he sailed off through night and day and in and out of weeks." Max passes a sea-serpent and approaches land, the place where the wild things are.

Several huge monsters jump up and down on the shore, leaving holographic or stroboscopic afterimages, while they "...roared their terrible roars and gnashed their terrible teeth and rolled their terrible eyes and showed their terrible claws...."

Their monstrous activity continues until Max tells them to be still and tames them with the trick of staring into all their eyes without blinking. The wild things are impressed—even frightened—and, calling Max the most wild thing of all, make him king.

Regally seated on a mound, wearing a crown and holding a scepter, Max cries out, "Let the wild rumpus start!" Music, absent since Max stilled the beasts, resumes—along with a pounding sound and a strange grating noise—and both Max and the monsters leap about leaving the same after-images as before.

When Max says "Now stop!" the music track runs at a slower speed and the action similarly slows down. Max sends the wild things to bed without supper and they are seen snoozing in the forest as Max sits pensively in a royal tent. He is lonely and wants to be where someone loves him "best of all."

Max gives up being king of the wild things and sets off in his boat for home. The wild things cry out from shore, "Oh please don't go—we'll eat you up—we love you so!" But Max says no and waves goodbye as the wild things repeat their blurry, monstrous dance and the narrator repeats the line about their terrible roars, etc.

As his boat heads for home, strange and discordant music is heard. The sound changes to the more mellow radio music when Max's fantasy world dissolves to his own room where, on the table in the corner, he finds supper waiting—"...and it was still hot." The strange music resumes under the closing credits.

**Visual Attributes:** Alternately static and stroboscopic images drawn with many cross-hatched lines; foregrounds and backgrounds as well as the grotesque creatures are quite detailed; colors are muted and generally dark. Rather high image density.

**Sound:** Occasional male narration in a storyteller's delivery with a combination of music and found or fabricated sounds. The extremely unusual music track (which sometimes plays 1940s radio music and/or vocalizations at the wrong speed) includes pounding (what a bad headache might sound like), screeching animals, and the grinding of automobile engine gears. High audio density.

**Video Legibility/Audibility:** Fair.

**Pace:** Varies from slow to fast.

**Structure:** Dramatic narrative. A journey-adventure with effective repetition and variation (the monsters repeat what Max said to his mother). If the opening images can be considered a prologue, the journey is framed by the same beginning/ending location which gives it a circular closure; Max starts and finishes in his own bedroom.

**Themes:** Anger; monsters; dreams and daydreams; devouring; early childhood; uncooperative behavior; resolution of a problem through fantasy; returning safely home.

**Comments:** The film's over-use of both visual and sound effects has transformed a therapeutic fantasy into a "Twilight Zone" experience and—for better or worse—diminished the story's impact. Nonetheless, when tested outside the hospital, children as old as fifth graders said that except for its blurry images they liked the movie better than the book. Because of this, and because it touches on important themes, we decided to try WHERE THE WILD THINGS ARE in the hospital where it was quite successful in a supervised playroom situation.

With certain ethnic groups, the fact that the opening stills are framed in black may present problems or suggest things that were not intended by the filmmaker.

We tried it with THE MASKMAKER in Video Program #19.

**Suggested Activities:** Puppetry and mask-making.

**Related Reading:** Preschoolers and young school age children might enjoy the picturebook by Maurice Sendak upon which the film is based; it is available in paperback from Weston Woods and/or Harper & Row.

So that this can become a vehicle for discussion or artwork, you might want to share Harry Behn's poem, "Growing Up," with older children to help them put their young childhood fears in perspective; the poem has been anthologized in *The Random House Book of Poetry for Children.*

---

**Recommended Pediatric Age:** 5–9.

**Hospital Rating:** ***

**Availability:**
WHERE THE WILD THINGS ARE
Distributed by Weston Woods.
16mm film purchase price: $195
¾-inch videotape purchase price: $140
½-inch videotape purchase price: $50
Fee structure for CCTV rights is based on the number of buildings in which the title will be viewed times the running time. If title will be shown in only one building, the CCTV rights are generally covered in the basic purchase price; ¾ - inch videotapes available by special order.

---

# WORM DANCES
*by Eli Noyes* (USA/1980)
3 minutes /clay animation /color /nonverbal

A primal, bas-relief musical in which one playdough shape turns into another. Lots of delightful wiggling to a carefree vocal and hand-clapping soundtrack.

Little red, wormy creatures emerge from what looks like brown earth. They return to the holes from which they came, then emerge once again and dance around before returning to the earth.

Brown images in different shapes and sizes move across the screen. Beige-colored clay fills the screen and its surface is manipulated. Various cake-icing textures, from flat to ripples and swirls, appear and are erased by the magic of animation.

Against a green background, yellow worms chase brown worms while red ones dance in and out of little holes in the ground.

As if on an assembly line, 7 mustard-yellow blobs move along a pathway then leap onto some brown hot-dog shaped things which line up in a neat row.

Little green plants sprout. White balls merge with red balls and form a flower.

Brown worms emerge from and return to sand-yellow earth.

In a bird's-eye-view of a landscape, a white road cuts among green trees. Oblong blobs (the roofs of vehicles?) pass along the road.

Little white balls emerge from a beige background, flatten out, roll up, and return to the ground.

Now, in a stereotypical "frontal" landscape, birds fly over some mountains as the sun shines in the sky. A cloud passes and drops a blanket of snow on the mountain tops.

The word "end" appears in red playdough letters.

**Visual Attributes:** Abstract biomorphic shapes in a bas-relief playdough animation. Despite intense color saturation there is a clear separation of figure from ground. Medium image density.

**Sound:** Rhythmic hand-taps and vocalizations such as humming and whistling. Fairly low audio density.

**Video Legibility/Audibility:** Excellent.

**Pace:** Medium-fast.

**Structure:** Lyric. A playful and associative exploration of clay shapes with some repetition.

**Themes:** Variations on a concept; exploring the design possibilities of clay or playdough; change and transformation.

**Comments:** This delightful musical was phenomenally successful. Its whimsy and upbeat rhythm made it one of our *four-star* hospital hits. But, because it is so brief, WORM DANCES needs to be screened more than once, which children love.

This is an amazing inspiration for clay and playdough activities. Even outside of the hospital WORM DANCES (as well as WHAZZAT?) motivates children to work for longer periods of time, doing more innovative shaping than if they had not seen it. In the hospital, this sort of motivation can be essential to children's persevering in an activity. Moreover, it helps ease the tension of working in the presence of unfamiliar children.

We tried this with WHAZZAT? (a perfect partner) in Film Program #7, in CCTV Program #12, and in Video Program #22.

**Suggested Activities:** Clay and playdough sculpture.

---

**Recommended Pediatric Age:** 2–14.

**Hospital Rating:** ****

**Availability:**
WORM DANCES
Distributed by Noyes & Laybourne.
16mm film purchase price: $150
¾-inch videotape purchase price: $150
½-inch videotape purchase price: $150
No additional charge for CCTV rights.

*A Chairy Tale.* Courtesy: International Film Bureau.

*Pierre.* Courtesy: Weston Woods.

*Harold and the Purple Crayon.* Courtesy: Weston Woods.

*A Visit from Space.* Courtesy: International Film Programs.

# Program Descriptions/
# Evaluations

# OVERVIEW

Before discussing the different types of programs, we should define the criteria by which they were evaluated and the basis on which we determined whether or not each film, the combination and sequence of films, and the follow-up activity "worked."

Our criteria for determining the success of a film or tape were that it must (1) be pertinent to the needs of hospitalized children, (2) be comprehensible to them, (3) hold their interest, and (4) motivate a positive or at least therapeutic response, either verbal or artistic. Our Child Life consultants helped us determine whether or not a film had therapeutic applications. The positive responses were self-evident.

Our criteria for determining a successful combination of films were that both must (1) balance each other in terms of appearance, pace, narrative-versus-nonnarrative, etc., (2) thematically reinforce each other, and (3) help motivate the follow-up activity. In addition, the first one had to set up but not overshadow the second one.

Our criteria for determining the success of an activity were that it must (1) appeal to the pediatric population, (2) be possible for them to do, and (3) facilitate the expression of their responses to the films. Implicit in the latter is that it have some real relationship to the films, not be simple busy work.

But the criteria underlying all—the individual titles, the pairings, and the activities—were that programs, both in the playroom and on closed-circuit television, had to foster meaningful human interaction and help make children feel better.

Our evaluations are fairly stringent, partly because we felt it was important to be careful and partly because having witnessed the wonder of successful *four-star* programs in the hospital it was hard to settle for almost right. We also felt it was essential to mention any problems we encountered in order to inform our readers as fully as possible. Thus, there are instances when a fairly successful program is described in less than glowing terms.

We apologize for this if it seems misleading, but we expect the reader will be able to separate significant problems from minor ones.

Program write-ups are listed in chronological order of development, with film first. They include participatory film programs designed for the playroom, for closed-circuit television, and for videocassettes in the playroom. Generally, all CCTV or video programs would work as film programs and, except when there is information to the contrary, video programs could also be used as closed-circuit television programs.

To facilitate the reader's ability to decide whether or not to try a particular activity, the write-up for each program contains a chart which lists: Activity, Materials, Dexterity, and Age Level. Following each is relevant information about the general type of activity, the ages it worked best with, and the materials as well as the dexterity required to execute it. In considering the dexterity rating, readers should keep in mind that most activities will be somewhat difficult for children with IVs due to the physical limitations imposed by the intravenous apparatus.

Although the film and CCTV write-ups often refer to introductions, few were documented. But the video introductions (to both the tapes and the activities) were documented in full as models. Hospital staff and others who work in nonprofit organizations (excepting those involved in media production or distribution) may freely reproduce these video introductions for staff or volunteers to use in face-to-face programs with children. However, they cannot to be used on television or in prerecorded programs of any sort without the explicit permission of the Media Center for Children.

The activity sheets found in the video programs can be duplicated. For use in face-to-face programs and with the same stipulations as for the video introductions, hospital staff and others in nonprofit organizations may make as many copies of the video activity sheets as they want.

# PLAYROOM FILM PROGRAMS

## by Maureen Gaffney and Anne Munzer Bourne

Using insights derived from both our pilot and our work outside of the hospital, we developed 30 playroom film programs. Half the programs were for preschoolers (roughly children 3–6) and half were for school age children (7–12), but children above/below our target ages attended screenings.

From January to April of 1983, we evaluated the playroom film programs at 3 sites in New York City: Bellevue Hospital, New York Hospital, and St. Luke's/Roosevelt Medical Center. Only 16 programs are documented in this section, however, and they are listed in the order they were done. (The remaining ones were for planning purposes and the results were inconclusive.) With the exception of Program #15, which was only tested at 2 sites, the others were tried at all 3 sites.

### PRESCHOOL PROGRAMS

#1. Films about barnyard animals—a story and an observational study—with drawing as the follow-up. (1/83)

#2. Films about animals—one an observation of a domestic animal, the other a story involving wild animals—with painting/dramatic play as the follow-up. (1/83)

#3. Cutout animations that feature adventurous youngsters—one black, the other white—with collage as the follow-up. (2/83)

#4. Cutout animations—a catalog of shapes and a story about an urban black boy—with collage as the follow-up. (2/83)

#5. Dramas about how friends help one another overcome threatening situations, with block play as the follow-up. (2/83)

#6. Stories about human-animal relationships—one between a boy and a lion, the other a girl and a frog—with puppet-making as the follow-up. (2/83)

#7. Clay animations—a catalog of shapes and a story—with clay sculpture as the follow-up. (3/83)

#8. Animated adventure stories—about a brave female and a clever male—with drawing as the follow-up. (3/83)

### SCHOOL AGE PROGRAMS

#9. Folktales made from cutouts—one Native American, the other West Indian—with collage as the follow-up. (1/83)

#10. Films that use common three-dimensional objects in unusual ways, with box art as the follow-up. (1/83)

#11. Stories about adapting to new and unusual situations, with drawing/storytelling as the follow-up. (2/83)

#12. Stories about separation from beloved animals, with collage storytelling as the follow-up. (2/83)

#13. Stories about capable young men—a mythical Native American and a contemporary African-American—with collage/storytelling as the follow-up. (2/83)

#14. Animations—one using abstract cutouts derived from Matisse, the other representational images based on African folk art—with collage as the follow-up. (2/83)

#15. Stories—one realistic, one symbolic—of how people overcome difficulties, with clay sculpture as the follow-up. (3/83)

#16. Films that feature unusual looking or sounding characters, with mask-making as the follow-up. (3/83)

# Playroom Film Program #1

| | |
|---|---|
| **Activity:** | Drawing. |
| **Materials:** | Paper, felt-tip markers, crayons. |
| **Dexterity:** | Minimal. |
| **Age Level:** | Preschool. |

## ROSIE'S WALK
(5 minutes/animation/narration)

A barnyard hen takes her afternoon constitutional across the yard, around the pond, over the haystack, past the mill, through the fence, under the beehives, and gets back home in time for dinner. As she strolls around the farm, Rosie fortuitously avoids the predatory maneuvers of a comically inept fox. Based on the book by Pat Hutchins and set to the tune of "Turkey in the Straw," this simple and nearly slow-motion slapstick is both droll and delightful.

## PIGS
(11 minutes/liveaction/nonverbal)

A highly cinematic catalog of pigs on a farm. This sophisticated study begins with break of day and shows pigs (from little sucklings to huge sows and hogs) as they root, suck, scratch, wallow, tail-wag, walk, run, and sleep. In addition to cataloging various types of pig activities, the camera also shows the diverse shapes of pigs' ears, snouts, eyes, and tails.

## Evaluation of the First Film

We tested this with 11 children, ages 3–10, but most were 3–6. ROSIE'S WALK has a clear storyline which ends as the hen returns safely home, an appropriate theme for hospitalized children. However, since many young and/or disadvantaged children were unaware that foxes chase hens, and did not even know that the other animal in the film was a fox, it is imperative to mention the fox before screening it with preschoolers. To describe the fox as "silly" helps set an appropriate tone for this nonthreatening and low-key journey/adventure.

Children derived enjoyment from watching the hen avoid the fox and from labeling what they saw. Some even identified with aspects of the film, projecting issues that applied to their own hospitalization. A 3-year-old with a leg problem mentioned that the chicken was "walking bad."

In several instances we showed the film more than once and children got more from it each time. A Child Life specialist explained, "We ended up showing ROSIE'S WALK a number of times and kids got into tracing Rosie's walk—almost telling the story along with the film—and better understanding the fox's disasters each time, anticipating and waiting for them to happen." ROSIE'S WALK is a *four-star* film, appropriate in subject and mood for hospitalized children. It set a reassuring tone which contributed to the success of PIGS.

## Evaluation of the Second Film

The first screening of PIGS was not as successful as subsequent sessions, which were preceded by a thorough explanation of pigs and how they live. Such information produced more positive results, and children with no previous information about pigs were better able to appreciate this animal catalog. Many had questions and wanted more information about pigs.

Despite its improved reception, PIGS has several aspects which make it difficult for hospitalized preschoolers. The backlit morning images are too dark for children to see clearly, particularly in daytime film screening conditions. As a result, some children became nervous and anxious about what was happening. Also, close-ups of pig noses, ears, and tails confused children who were not familiar with the whole animal. Those abstract, puzzle-like qualities and an overabundance of cuts make PIGS too demanding for preschoolers who are not in tip-top condition (although it might be appropriate for school age children). Thus we decided to replace it with another catalog featuring a more familiar animal, such as a chicken. (See CCTV Program #2 and Playroom Video Program #1.) We also decided to avoid dark, dimly lit images since they seem to create a threatening mood.

## Evaluation of the Activity

Although their artwork had little or no relationship to the films, preschoolers (even at the site of the first screening) enjoyed the whole experience immensely. They opened up in a way that amazed Child Life staff and became very trusting and communicative during the activity session. In fact, hospital staff said their artwork was both highly personalized and more controlled than it had been the day before. One boy, admitted to the hospital for emergency surgery, drew monsters, super-heros, and snacks because, as he explained, food was on his mind. "One of the things I don't like about this hospital," he stated, "is that they don't give you snacks."

Originally, we included painting as an option along with drawing, but few children wanted to use poster paints—some because they did not want to get dirty. Apparently, quite a number of hospitalized children fastidiously try to avoid making a mess, even the limited mess of poster paints. Such children preferred to draw.

# Playroom Film Program #2

| | |
|---|---|
| **Activity:** | Painting or dramatic play. |
| **Materials:** | Paper, felt-tip markers, brushes, and paint. |
| **Dexterity:** | Minimal. |
| **Age Level:** | Preschool. |

## ONE LITTLE KITTEN
(3 minutes/liveaction/nonverbal)

Like a calendar which features an adorable kitten in a dozen typical situations, this film shows the same young feline in a series of locations and activities, from playing among the rungs of a wooden chair and hiding in a cardboard box to being groomed by its mother. A sweet and very basic animal catalog with neither plot nor chronological structure. Although its images are not identical to those in the film, author/filmmaker Tana Hoban has a conceptually similar book of the same title.

## THE BEAR AND THE MOUSE
(8 minutes/liveaction/narration)

A North American adaptation, set in colonial fur-trapping days, of the Aesop fable, "The Lion and the Mouse." Real animals with human character voices (using British/Canadian accents) enact this drama of how small creatures can sometimes help even great big ones, such as bears.

## Evaluation of the First Film

We tested this with 12 children, ages 2–13, but most were 3–6. While ONE LITTLE KITTEN was not sufficiently stimulating or interesting to children over 6, the very young loved this pleasantly slow and nonthreatening catalog. Preschoolers enjoyed labeling what they saw, and some even mentioned their pets at home. An abuse victim kept saying throughout: "I want to talk to the kitty."

Since the film includes a segment with the kitten and its mother, it is important to mention the mother cat in the introduction and to talk a bit about how mother cats lick their kittens to clean them. Without such an introduction, some preschoolers negatively misinterpreted the big cat's actions.

## Evaluation of the Second Film

THE BEAR AND THE MOUSE was too complicated for the majority of preschoolers who viewed it. The story is not only poorly structured, but the narrator's various accents made it difficult for children to understand what he was saying. Also, using real animals with human voiceovers confused many young children; they seemed unable to sort out the discrepancy between make-believe animal voices and real animal images. This may have been especially difficult since, developmentally, this age group is sorting out real from make-believe. What little success the film had came when we turned off the sound and narrated the story ourselves.

Although its treatment was not appropriate for their age level, the theme of entrapment is appropriate for hospitalized preschoolers since many are literally locked in their cribs when no adults are around to supervise them. This would be an appropriate focus for dramatic play, an activity that was spontaneously and successfully done in response to THE BEAR AND THE MOUSE at one of our sites (see below).

THE BEAR AND THE MOUSE works best with children 5 and older, especially boys, but it needs a thorough introduction involving a run-through of the plot, embellished with dramatic actions. Because it requires so much "assistance" and because it works with a different age level than the first film, we decided to find a more appropriate partner for ONE LITTLE KITTEN.

## Evaluation of the Activity

Neither painting nor making up a story about animals (the activities we originally proposed) were successful follow-ups to the films. For one thing, they were too unstructured; for another, they did not relate to both films. ONE LITTLE KITTEN was not conducive to storytelling, and the liveaction images in THE BEAR AND THE MOUSE were not conducive to drawing/painting. Those who attempted these activities lost interest fairly quickly.

Most children simply experimented with paint, but at one site 3 very mobile boys, all roommates, painted for a while and then got involved in dramatic play. In talking with the youngest (who was 2½) about his picture of someone in a cage, it became clear that he had many unresolved fears about the bear. We asked if he would like to act out the process of being trapped in a cage and then released. He did, so his roommates (who were each 3 years old) joined in. Everyone crawled under a large table (the cage) and took turns being locked up and released. Upon being released, the trapped person got hugs—lots of hugs—from everyone else. The 3 boys, who made up the entire group for that screening, enacted the simple scenario again and again and thoroughly enjoyed its reassuring and tender actions.

Reinforcing the basic story events through actions seemed much more appropriate to THE BEAR AND THE MOUSE than our proposed activity. It may be essential with very young preschoolers.

# Playroom Film Program #3

| | |
|---|---|
| **Activity:** | Collage. |
| **Materials:** | Construction paper, pre-cut shapes, scissors, and glue-sticks. |
| **Dexterity:** | Average, except for those with IVs. |
| **Age Level:** | Preschool. |

## A LITTLE GIRL AND A GUNNY WOLF
(6 minutes/cutout animation/choral narration)

Adapted from Wilhelmina Harper's book, *The Gunniwolf*, this delightful variation on the story of "Little Red Riding Hood" features the artwork and choral narration of a kindergarten class. The little black girl who ventures into the woods to pick pretty flowers outwits a mean old gunny wolf by singing him to sleep with nonsense songs and gets home safe and sound.

## THE SKY IS BLUE
(5 minutes/cutout animation/nonverbal)

Using naive and child-like cutout images, this is the saga of a young man whose kite takes him up, up, up into the starry heavens and then down, down, down to earth and home. Although he has several close calls on his journey, everything works out fine in the end.

## Evaluation of the First Film

We tested this with 14 children, ages 2–11, but most were 3–5. A LITTLE GIRL AND A GUNNY WOLF got the children's full attention. Although the very youngest had difficulty following the storyline, they enjoyed the film's bright colors and repetitive elements. Black children in particular liked the fact that a black child is the protagonist and that black children made the film.

Despite occasionally being hard to hear, everyone enjoyed the choral narration. The repetitive phrases are a real hook for preschoolers. If the choruses are told to children beforehand, they enjoy saying them along with the narrators.

Before screening the film, however, it is important to emphasize that the girl returns safely home. And it helps to let children practice saying the repetitive phrases. One way to do both would be to read the book upon which the film is based. Otherwise, try saying something like this.

> This is a story about a little girl who goes to pick some flowers in the woods; she walks with a *pitter-pat, pitter-pat, pitter-pat* sound. (Ask children if they can repeat it.) In the woods, the little girl meets a mean old gunny wolf; he runs with a *honka-cha, honka-cha, honka-cha* sound. (Ask children to repeat that.) The clever little girl sings the wolf to sleep with a silly song: *"Walkee, walkee, walkee..."* (Try that.) In the end, she returns home to her mother, safe and sound.

## Evaluation of the Second Film

THE SKY IS BLUE is a simple, slow-paced adventure that children 3 and older easily followed, enthusiastically labeling what they saw and anticipating upcoming events. It requires a minimal introduction but we discovered that it was important to show a kite (three-dimensional if possible) before the screening since many children had no idea what a kite was or did. One thought the film's protagonist was using a helicopter to go up and down. It is also advisable to emphasize that, although the boy goes up, he does come safely down.

## Evaluation of the Activity

A Child Life specialist summed up the program this way: "The films set a nice tone for the group activity, which was calm as well as focused and was sustained for a relatively long time. This was impressive, especially considering the children's ages!" Colorful collages were enthusiastically attempted by all and the activity was a great success despite the fact that children's collages did not relate to A LITTLE GIRL AND A GUNNY WOLF (perhaps because its images look more like paintings than cutouts). Interestingly, references to THE SKY IS BLUE showed up in most children's collages. Not only were its images much simpler than those in the first film, they looked like cutouts.

It helped to have pre-cut shapes for very young children, but older preschoolers enjoyed cutting their own.

# Playroom Film Program #4

| | |
|---|---|
| **Activity:** | Collage. |
| **Materials:** | Construction and tissue paper, pre-cut shapes, scissors, glue-sticks. |
| **Dexterity:** | Average, except for those with IVs. |
| **Age Level:** | Preschool. |

## TANGRAM
(3 minutes/cutout animation/nonverbal)

A delightful musical puzzle. Using 7 angular pieces from the Chinese puzzle called a tangram (which includes a square, a rhomboid, and 5 triangles), this lyrical film illustrates various silhouette shapes, from fish and snail to cat and horse. Each appears briefly on-screen, moves in a characteristic way, then transforms into another shape.

## THE SNOWY DAY
(6 minutes/iconographic animation/narration)

A lyrical, slow-moving sketch of a black preschooler's day of fun and exploration in the city snow. Peter spends the first day alone but the next day, when he wakes to discover that the snow is still there, he sets out with a friend with whom he can share his experiences.

## Evaluation of the First Film

We tested this with 14 children, ages 3–8, but most were 3–6. TANGRAM worked extremely well when introduced by the combination of a brief story and a simple demonstration arranging pieces of a tangram into basic shapes and a few animal silhouettes. This combination served as a "hook" to involve children both emotionally and intellectually in the film. It also suggested, on a level they could understand, what the film was about; if expressed straight out, its esthetic purpose would have been of scant interest to preschoolers.

We told children that once upon a time a tile-maker accidentally dropped a square tile (modeled with a ceramic bathroom tile) which broke into 7 pieces. (We showed them a tangram, which can be made using the template that accompanies Playroom Video Program #13.) The tile-maker wanted to fix it but when she tried to put the pieces back into a square, other shapes appeared. We made an arrangement (not square) and asked children if it was a square. "If not, what is it?" This process was repeated a few times before the film began.

It is important to warn children that the film has no words, no story, and is very short. And encourage them to label aloud the different shapes they see. During the film we asked viewers if the first shapes that appeared on-screen (some of which are triangles and squares with holes in them) were squares. After a while we asked them what the shapes looked like. When the tangram returns to a square at film's end, we sometimes said, "The tile-maker did it; she got the tile back into a square."

Young children derived great satisfaction from identifying the film's silhouettes and they appeared quite lighthearted after seeing it. But both the film and its audience benefit from a repeat screening; children love to see TANGRAM again and are more enthused and verbal the second time around. It is also a perfect lead-in to collage, and the combination of visual introduction, the labeling/guessing game, and the film itself promotes a playful curiosity about the possibilities of arranging and combining shapes.

Prior to the second screening and as a preliminary exercise in combining shapes, we gave each child a tangram to manipulate as s/he watched. Children enjoyed this a great deal. Just make sure the tangrams are not too large for small hands to manage; a width of between 4 and 5 inches is fine.

## Evaluation of the Second Film

THE SNOWY DAY is a low-key narrative about a preschooler's day in the snow. Its slow pace and the gentle quality of the female narrator's voice set a reassuring tone. Children's faces and bodies relaxed and appeared calm during the screening. Young boys, black boys in particular, identified with the film's protagonist: "That's not Peter in the story, that's me," said a 3-year-old burn patient (who was induced to take a painful bath on the strength of Peter's taking a bath in the film).

A perfect mood piece, THE SNOWY DAY is appropriate for the age and developmental levels of preschoolers. All related to the situation and wanted to tell stories of their own snow experiences, something that may have been helped by the fact that we showed it, coincidentally, a day or so after a major snowstorm.

Although THE SNOWY DAY can sometimes inspire collage, the artwork of patients in our test population related more to TANGRAM, which was more compelling, both visually and kinesthetically. In addition, TANGRAM had been reinforced by our introduction as well as the use of tangram shapes in the activity. It might have helped to include pre-cut organic or biomorphic shapes that would relate more to THE SNOWY DAY.

## Evaluation of the Activity

This film combination was very effective and produced a *four-star* program. TANGRAM piqued children's interest in manipulating shapes while THE SNOWY DAY presented comforting and mundane images (playing in the snow, taking a bath) in a highly graphic manner. Children could not wait to begin making collages and the activity was highly charged; pre-cut shapes made it accessible to children as young as 3. As testimony of their involvement, many worked on their collages for half an hour or longer. Children also verbalized a great deal while they worked. One 3-year-old made a running commentary as he completed several rather complex collages, explaining generally: "Gonna cut a triangle..., an ice-cream cone; this is a pie—a yellow pie." Participants exhibited universal feelings of satisfaction following the activity, but the best reaction came from a child of 5. Upon completing her first collage, the child remarked: "I didn't know I could do this before!"

# Playroom Film Program #5

| | |
|---|---|
| **Activity:** | Block play. |
| **Materials:** | Blocks, plastic or wooden eggs. |
| **Dexterity:** | Minimal. |
| **Age Level:** | Preschool. |

## THE MOLE AND THE EGG
(6 minutes/cel animation/nonverbal)

Mole, an *everychild* character featured in a number of cartoons, finds an egg and wonders whose baby it is. While searching for its parents, Mole and Egg (which hatches during the course of their journey) travel through a mechanized bakery and packaging factory. All is happily resolved in the end when the Chick is reunited with its mother.

## TCHOU TCHOU
(15 minutes/object animation/nonverbal)

A slow-moving but dramatic fantasy made entirely from children's colored wooden blocks. A boy and a girl (either playmates or siblings) amuse themselves in a playground until a block-dragon threatens their security. The child characters build a fort in self-defense, but the dragon knocks down the walls. In the end, however, the children outwit the dragon and tame it, even making it part of their play by turning it into a choo-choo train.

## Evaluation of the First Film

We tested this with 11 children, ages 3–6. THE MOLE AND THE EGG was very well-received by hospitalized preschoolers. Despite a slight drop in energy during the factory scene (which was confusing), they were quite absorbed by the film. They giggled to the soundtrack (which consists of child-like sounds and pseudo-dialog) and enthusiastically labeled and/or explained to each other what was happening.

A few children became extremely tense during the cookie factory scene, so an introductory explanation of it is essential. Without one, children anticipated the worst outcome since they did not know what was going on. It is important to tell them that, perhaps contrary to experiences in their life, machines (not people) make cookies in the factory shown in the film.

We also found it effective to provide children with concrete aids to hold during the screening. Plastic or wooden eggs and a stuffed-animal mole helped children personalize the film experience. (A dozen plastic eggs are manufactured by a number of companies, including Child Guidance; we found wooden eggs of various sizes at craft supply stores.)

THE MOLE AND THE EGG was thematically appropriate and worked well with the second film. Its nurturing theme and the reunion of the egg/chick with its mother was highly engaging. At that point in the film, a mother at one screening was moved to hug her child. And Child Life staff from several hospitals felt they could use the film in a therapeutic manner.

## Evaluation of the Second Film

Totally engaging despite its length, TCHOU TCHOU is an appropriate and powerful film when used in a supervised group setting. As a counterbalance to its intensity, however, it needs to be paired with a more gentle film such as THE MOLE AND THE EGG.

Although somewhat frightening at times, young viewers in our test groups derived pleasure from being scared, which served as a therapeutic tension-release. It is essential, however, to warn children that TCHOU TCHOU is both scary and has a happy ending.

In our introduction, we encouraged children to *boo* when the dragon appears, and cheer when it goes away. We also found it helpful to describe the dragon as somewhat "silly" and not nearly as fearful as its music suggests. (In this respect, we found that it helped to reduce the volume because the dragon's signature music is the most alarming aspect of the film; booing when the dragon appears also counteracts the music.)

Children verbalized throughout, identifying with the girl and boy protagonists. A Child Life specialist said: "Children responded by identifying all familiar objects, and the process of booing the dragon and cheering the kids in the film enabled them to become involved in the story—which helped make this a very successful film."

Because of TCHOU TCHOU's scariness, it should be screened only in groups, and children 3 or under should be accompanied by an adult. Thus it is not recommended for closed-circuit TV.

## Evaluation of the Activity

Block play was a huge success. Most children enthusiastically reenacted the danger and escape scenes from TCHOU TCHOU and played symbolically with blocks in new and creative ways. A few decorated and played with wooden eggs, an activity which related more to THE MOLE AND THE EGG but which also proved successful.

The structured responses (boos, cheers) that we engaged in during the screening were very effective in encouraging children to act out afterwards. Some children hid behind things in the playroom (a piano at one site) and took turns being the dragon, but mostly children acted out the dragon scene with blocks. One bedridden 4-year-old played for over an hour and was still going strong when we had to stop.

In their follow-ups children relished the opportunity to make their own worlds with places to hide and retreat for safety, an aspect of the activity which was of particular significance in the hospital setting. This was a *four-star* program and most groups had such a good time playing with blocks afterwards that they did not want to stop and go back to their rooms for lunch.

# Playroom Film Program #6

| | |
|---|---|
| **Activity:** | Puppet-making. |
| **Materials:** | Paper sandwich bags, construction paper, felt-tip markers, crayons, scissors, and glue-sticks. |
| **Dexterity:** | Average, except for those with IVs. |
| **Age Level:** | Preschool. |

## PIERRE
(6 minutes/line animation/song)

In this delightful musical send-up of cautionary tales (based on the picturebook by Maurice Sendak), Carole King sings about a preschool boy who says "I don't care!" to everything. Pierre refuses to cooperate or to be neat. He is so laissez-faire that he doesn't care to go out with his parents, and he doesn't even care when he gets swallowed by a lion. His parents, however, do care and they rush him to the doctor who shakes the boy out from the lion's mouth, alive and better than ever. After that, of course, Pierre learns to care, and the lion becomes his friend.

## THE FROG KING OR FAITHFUL HENRY
(15 minutes/liveaction/dialog & narration)

A liveaction version of the Grimm folktale which is set in Victorian America and is given a humorous, tongue-in-cheek treatment. Unlike certain versions of the tale, the girl/princess in this film throws the frog against a wall instead of meekly kissing the annoying little beast.

## Evaluation of the First Film

We tested this with 13 children, ages 3–8. PIERRE was highly successful with the majority of the hospital audience. Although very young preschoolers did not necessarily follow the sequence of events, they enjoyed the music, the rhymes, and the simple line drawings. PIERRE was also terrific to show twice! During the first screening, children worked to figure out the story; during the second, they relaxed, hummed along, and frequently joined in the "I don't care" chorus.

We introduced the film with handmade, sandwich bag puppets of Pierre and the lion. This device was very effective. Not only did it help children personalize the film, their dialog with the puppets gave them a sense of involvement in and perhaps control over the story's events. It also provided an appropriate transition to the activity.

Most children did not understand the film's ostensible moral (to care), but that did not seem to matter. As a Child Life specialist observed: "It's good for children to express some sort of defiance when they're in the hospital. They have to comply with their treatment, but it's very healthy if some part of them can say 'I don't care!'" This became evident in the follow-up activity when children repeatedly got involved in dramatic play with puppets, drawing directly from the "I don't care" aspect of PIERRE. Therapeutically, it was beneficial for them to be able to say *no*, if only vicariously.

## Evaluation of the Second Film

THE FROG KING OR FAITHFUL HENRY is difficult to evaluate. It does not seem appropriate for hospitalized preschoolers because they did not understand the story and misinterpreted some of the events/images. A few hid their faces at various times during the film. Most demonstrated tension and anxiety, and their fears were probably left unresolved because they did not understand the ending. Despite the fact that a number of girls found the princess appealing (we used a paper bag princess to introduce the film), many children saw the frog as a monster. For others, the film's point-of-view shots emphasize the vulnerability of the frog, with whom they may have identified.

In general, this film seems to suggest frightening topics, and it was not clear how preschoolers were internalizing them. Most could not answer our basic questions, but observation made it clear that THE FROG KING OR FAITHFUL HENRY was more scary and confusing than tension releasing. Thus while we have little real information, we have serious reservations about this film for hospitalized preschoolers (although it might work with older children). We plan to find a more suitable partner for PIERRE.

## Evaluation of the Activity

Puppetry worked quite well. Children enjoyed making puppets from sandwich bags and really extended themselves in dramatic play. Interestingly, puppets were drawn from both films. Boys either made Pierres or frogs and girls made princesses.

The activity worked best when we demonstrated how to make the puppets and encouraged children to copy our models, which were very basic and not so well-made as to be beyond preschoolers' abilities. Children enjoyed being able to see samples of what they were to make, as well as a modeling of the process. They then did their own variations and added their own details.

# Playroom Film Program #7

| | |
|---|---|
| **Activity:** | Clay or playdough sculpture. |
| **Materials:** | Modeling clay, porcelain clay, or playdough. |
| **Dexterity:** | Minimal to average. |
| **Age Level:** | Preschool. |

## WORM DANCES
(3 minutes/clay animation/nonverbal)

An upbeat scat and percussion musical in which one primal playdough shape turns into another. The colorful, eye-pleasing transformations and delightful wiggling to a carefree soundtrack make this film a perfect lead-in to clay or playdough activities. (This was repeated after WHAZZAT?)

## WHAZZAT?
(10 minutes/clay animation/nonverbal)

Six lively clay creatures change shape and move about, helping each other explore their environment. When the friends discover an unknown creature (in the section based on the Arab/Indian tale about the blind men and the elephant), they each describe it nonverbally from a different point of view. After 5 of them have depicted what they know about it, the group pools its resources and figures out what the creature is. In unison, all shout "ELEPHANT," the only word in this joyful classic.

## Evaluation of the First Film

We tested this with 14 children, ages 3–10, but most were 3–8. Preschoolers thoroughly enjoyed the whimsical, playful movements and sounds in WORM DANCES. The filmmaker's singing was particularly infectious, as a 5-year-old confirmed: "I like it when he says 'doo-doo-dah!'"

WORM DANCES works marvelously when shown twice. Children seemed to enjoy the second screening even more than the first. To a marked degree, many joined in with the scat vocals during the second screening. It was a tremendous success—a *four-star* hit—as was the entire program.

## Evaluation of the Second Film

Although young preschoolers could not always follow the entire course of events in WHAZZAT?, they were generally engaged and amused by it. Viewers delighted in the cliff-hanging scenes in the first part of the film, thoroughly enjoying the tension and release. They also derived pleasure from watching the clay creatures move, join together, and divide. (It should be noted that the creatures are of indeterminate sex; one child referred to them as female.)

There were several instances when children made statements about the film that seemed to be directly related to themselves. We found it interesting that many identified with the purple/lavender slowpoke who kept getting left behind, but who was eventually reunited with the rest of the group (or family).

Structurally, the film becomes confusing to preschoolers during the encounter with the elephant. It might be effective to screen the film twice, perhaps on separate occasions. During the first screening, stop the film before the section involving the elephant. The second time, show the entire film after explaining in an introduction that the little creatures are going to find an elephant. It might also be helpful to precede the second screening by reading a simple version of "The Blind Men and the Elephant."

## Evaluation of the Activity

It was an easy transition from the films to the activity. Preschoolers were highly motivated and energized. They seemed to like the control they had with clay and appeared more assertive than in some other activities. Several even asked to come back again in the afternoon (since our preschool programs took place in the morning) and play some more with the clay, which they did. And despite the fact that we were screening other films for the school age group, those who came back kept on working from the ideas in WORM DANCES. A few even sang scat as they worked!

One boy, whose hands were bound due to burns, directed an adult to construct little creatures and then squashed them with his chin (which seemed a very constructive way for him to act out his anger and frustration).

The combination of films was an extremely effective lead-in to clay/playdough activities and elicited more depth and enthusiasm than is usual with clay play. In addition, many children used elements from both films in their art, which is a sign that the pairing works. This was a *four-star* playroom program that we transferred to television (CCTV Program #12) as well as video (Playroom Video Program #22).

# Playroom Film Program #8

| | |
|---|---|
| **Activity:** | Drawing with a magic crayon. |
| **Materials:** | White paper and crayons. |
| **Dexterity:** | Minimal. |
| **Age Level:** | Preschool. |

## LITTLE GRAY NECK
(18 minutes/cel animation/dialog & narration)

A gripping Disney-like cartoon about a young gosling who is inadvertently left behind by her family when the geese migrate south for the winter. Not only does the little goose survive with the help of some friendly rabbits, she also manages to outwit the treacherous, predatory fox and save the rabbits. In the end, she is happily reunited with her mother and siblings.

## HAROLD'S FAIRY TALE
(8 minutes/line animation/narration)

Simple line drawings, adapted from Crockett Johnson's book, tell the further adventures of Harold. Dressed in his pajamas, the imaginative preschooler goes for a walk with the moon and his purple crayon and turns the conventions of the fairytale inside out. Along the way he defeats a giant witch and lifts the evil spell from a barren garden.

## Evaluation of the First Film

We tested this with 11 children, ages 2–9, but most were 3–6. LITTLE GRAY NECK was highly successful with children 3 and up. As one Child Life specialist noted: "LITTLE GRAY NECK was a lovely, tender film which appeals to quite a wide age range. Three-year-olds were as involved as 7-year-olds." Thematically appropriate in that it deals with separation from and reunion with family, this long melodrama offers both tender, nurturing episodes and exciting—even scary—scenes.

It is essential, however, to give the film a careful introduction. Children must be warned that there are scenes with a mean and hungry fox. Further explain that, while those scenes may be a bit scary, the little goose is very clever and tricks the fox by pretending to have a broken wing, so everything works out all right in the end.

Because it is such a powerful film, LITTLE GRAY NECK must be paired with a lighter work to create a balanced program. Also, it is too strong for young patients to watch alone; thus we did not use it and do not recommend it on TV.

Although the second film worked on some levels, we sensed a genuine letdown after one that a 6-year-old characterized as action-packed. A few children even asked to see LITTLE GRAY NECK again (which we accommodated). And despite the fact that the drawing activity related more directly to the second film, many children drew ducks or geese and named their characters after those in LITTLE GRAY NECK.

## Evaluation of the Second Film

HAROLD'S FAIRY TALE worked well enough in the context of this program but it proved somewhat problematic. It has minimal action and depends on a great many conventions (such standard fairytale components as castles, fairies, and witches) but depicts them in such an unusual way that they were unrecognizable to hospitalized viewers. Children were, moreover, greatly confused by the film's conceptual and extremely word-dependent storyline.

The major strength of HAROLD'S FAIRY TALE was that it worked as a lead-in to the drawing activity, particularly when we gave children crayons to hold during the screening. It might have worked better if children had been familiar with the character of Harold either from reading *Harold and the Purple Crayon* or *Harold's Fairy Tale*, or from seeing HAROLD AND THE PURPLE CRAYON. (The latter would have worked better both conceptually and structurally for this population and would make a better partner for LITTLE GRAY NECK.)

## Evaluation of the Activity

Handing out purple crayons, or a child's favorite color, before the screening was an effective focusing device for youngsters as they watched the film. And despite its simplicity, drawing was both calming and energizing; children were highly motivated to do it. Some even imitated the monochromatic color scheme from HAROLD'S FAIRY TALE in their artwork. One child was persuaded to leave the playroom to get a painful shot, but he returned—still holding a crayon—eager to finish his picture.

# Playroom Film Program #9

| | |
|---|---|
| **Activity:** | Collage. |
| **Materials:** | Construction paper, pencils, crayons, scissors, glue-sticks. |
| **Dexterity:** | Average, except for those with IVs. |
| **Age Level:** | School age. |

## THE CREATION OF BIRDS
(10 minutes/cutout animation/nonverbal)

A wordless MicMac legend about the origin of birds, this tender, slow-moving film about the seasons makes effective use of animal symbolism, respectively, the Howling Autumn Wolf and the Winter Snow Bear, and features a female protagonist.

## KUUMBA
(8 minutes/cutout animation/dialog & narration)

A contemporary origins tale from Trinidad which explains how an ingenious boy invented the steel drum the night before the parade and carnival celebrations held in conjunction with Mardi Gras. The film makes excellent use of sound and Caribbean music and gives a positive image of the black family. Although somewhat primitive-looking, the child-made artwork is appealing.

## Evaluation of the First Film

We tested this with 24 children, ages 5–15. THE CREATION OF BIRDS is mildly challenging and children enjoyed watching the film. Its child-like animation is generally nonthreatening and a number of youngsters mentioned that they liked the technique.

We found it interesting that, because of the discovery element involved in interpreting the film's nonverbal storyline, children internalized it on their own levels and none appeared frightened by the wolf. Many made personalized references to what was happening and apparently experienced control over the story, a needed and beneficial feeling for hospitalized children. In addition, the film had a satisfying emotional element—surviving hard times—that our Child Life consultants agreed children really related to. All in all, THE CREATION OF BIRDS left groups centered, energized, and contented. But it set a pretty high standard for the next film.

## Evaluation of the Second Film

KUUMBA was successful but seemed a bit of a letdown after such a moving first film. Its catchy music, however, ends the program on an upbeat note, a good place to begin the arts activity. KUUMBA's one real drawback has to do with how it opens and closes. Its introduction is generally lost on pediatric patients. And as soon as Simon invents his special instrument, most stop paying attention and thus miss the last few minutes of the film. However, because the rhythm of the closing music keeps some engaged, it might be effective to start the activity as the dance number and credits roll by, using the film's soundtrack as background music. It might be a nice idea to play some records/tapes of steel band music while children do their artwork.

KUUMBA worked particularly well with black children who identified with its Afro-Caribbean music and competent black characters. A few children were from the Dominican Republic and other West Indian islands. Both they and others wanted to discuss their own experiences with steel drums.

Despite KUUMBA's being somewhat outshined by THE CREATION OF BIRDS, the program worked and could be used quite successfully as is. Nonetheless, we decided to experiment with finding each film another and more evenly matched partner.

## Evaluation of the Activity

In our introduction, we compared the films, saying that one was about creation by magic and the other was about creation by experimentation—about using your own ideas to meet your needs. After the screening, children were instructed to make a collage (a picture or a design, either real or make-believe) of something they would like to create.

Generally, children's collages related directly to THE CREATION OF BIRDS. Many used images of the wolf, leaves, birds, and, in particular, trees in their artwork. One of the activity's strengths was that children could make it as simple or as complex as they wanted. One boy cut out a wonderful bird whose wings he wanted to flap and for which he needed brads. A child of 7, who initially had trouble making leaves on a tree just the way he wanted them, worked for an entire week perfecting a collage based on the tree-leaf-bird motif from THE CREATION OF BIRDS.

Overall, despite a minor imbalance in the films, this proved to be a *four-star* program and a very successful activity. As one girl enthusiastically remarked: "It was like a pajama party!"

# Playroom Film Program #10

| | |
|---|---|
| **Activity:** | Making box art. |
| **Materials:** | Shoe boxes, styrofoam packing peanuts, wooden clothespins, pipe cleaners, felt scraps, tongue depressors or popsicle sticks, stickers, cardboard or heavy paper, old greeting cards, wallpaper and carpet samples, magazines with lots of pictures, small manufacturing scrap material and other junk, construction paper, pencils, markers, scissors, masking and/or cellophane tape, and glue (nontoxic, quick-drying). |
| **Dexterity:** | Considerable; difficult with IVs. |
| **Age Level:** | School age. |

## THE LATE GREAT AMERICAN PICNIC
(7 minutes/liveaction/nonverbal)

In this country musical, real people mobilize some unusual oversized puppets—a collection of billboard advertisement cutouts which include the Marlboro man, the Black Velvet Whiskey woman, Smokey the Bear, and fast-food products from Coke and Pepsi to Big Macs—and set the scene for a picnic in the great outdoors. More of a tableau than anything else, this film could be a tongue-in-cheek comment on the modern American diet or pop art or both.

## CAPTAIN SILAS
(14 minutes/object animation/narration)

Making imaginative use of a large cast of peanuts and household objects such as blue-tinted popcorn (the sea), a shaving brush (dolphin), and a wing tip shoe (boat), this droll film presents a delightful miniature world in which merchant-sailor Silas makes his living by trading trucks (made from thread spools) for sugar cubes (the principal building material used on Truck Island).

### Evaluation of the First Film

We tested this with 15 children, ages 9–16. By and large, the zany billboard picnic in THE LATE GREAT AMERICAN PICNIC did not appeal to hospitalized children. Their only real enthusiasm was for the way the giant billboard characters were moved. A number of children focused on the food, which could be either a problem or an opportunity to address the problem, since many hospitalized children are on special or restricted diets. Not only did our test groups find the film unfunny (although children outside the hospital think it quite amusing), THE LATE GREAT AMERICAN PICNIC did not hold their interest. This may have been due to its lack of story

or an appropriate introduction. In either case, we decided to replace it.

### Evaluation of the Second Film

Children were intrigued with the inventive use of familiar objects in CAPTAIN SILAS and liked how the peanut characters "used all the stuff we use." There was much spontaneous talking and interpreting as children's imaginations ran free. The film's only drawback was a slight lull in the story during the sea storm, at which point children's attention often drifted. Excluding that brief interlude, patients were captivated and amused. They all followed the storyline and looked gratified as the film ended. Most importantly, they could not wait to create their own imaginary worlds.

### Evaluation of the Activity

The box art activity (gluing styrofoam peanuts, pipe cleaners, construction paper, and found objects into a shoe box which served as a stage) was a spectacular follow-up to CAPTAIN SILAS. But, since few children could identify the billboards in THE LATE GREAT AMERICAN PICNIC, they did not incorporate billboards into their boxes. None used magazine ads.

A group context works very well for this activity because it allows children to get ideas and solutions to mounting problems from each other. It also supports their energy levels. Although highly rewarding, this is a complex activity and requires more than half an hour. Some children, for the most part those 10–12 and significantly more boys than girls, became so engrossed in their boxes that they were still working on them an hour later.

As you can tell from the list of materials, it takes a while to collect all the supplies for this activity. We kept boxes, labeled according to type, and collected the materials over a period of weeks or months. We asked many people for small supplies and odds-and-ends. We begged from our friends, local wallpaper and carpet stores, and any businesses that did a lot of shipping/receiving (including hospital gift shops) or that had small parts left over after their product was manufactured or assembled. We picked up empty (adult sized) shoe boxes in large batches from shoe stores in our neighborhood. We would telephone a few weeks prior to the program and ask the store manager to save boxes and tops. Even the people in huge and seemingly impersonal Manhattan stores were glad to help us, especially when we told them what it was for.

If the activity is to run smoothly, it is important to have the objects well organized visually before children come to select them and to limit the number of objects they can take initially. To forestall hoarding and to prevent children from being overwhelmed, we allowed them to take only 10 objects at first; when they had used that batch, they could take 5 more each time they needed new supplies. To help children focus, we put the materials on a table that was separate from the area they were working in. We also used the shoe box tops as trays—both to hold children's own supplies and to separate small objects on the materials table. (And we saved them for use again later in Playroom Film Programs #13 and #15.)

It is very helpful to show children a model before they begin. The idea that the box is to be used as a stage viewed from the side needs to be reinforced with a visual aid.

# Playroom Film Program #11

| | |
|---|---|
| **Activity:** | Drawing. |
| **Materials:** | Paper and colored pencils. |
| **Dexterity:** | Minimal. |
| **Age Level:** | School age. |

## A CHAIRY TALE
(10 minutes/liveaction/nonverbal)

This humorous and sometimes slapstick, black-and-white mime-drama about reciprocation is enacted by a man and an animated chair. Ravi Shankar did the compelling raga-like score for this classic film in which, after learning that not all chairs can be taken for granted, a man practices the golden rule.

## NEW FRIENDS
(12 minutes/animation/dialog)

Based on the book, *Howard*, by James Stevenson, this is the whimsical story of a mallard who, while en route south for the winter, gets lost and lands in New York City where he eventually makes friends with an unusual assortment of street smart animals. Despite his initial aversion to the city, the duck grows so attached to his new friends—and to the Big Apple itself—that he decides to stay there.

## Evaluation of the First Film

We tested this with 11 children, ages 9-16. A CHAIRY TALE was extraordinarily successful with children from a wide range of ethnic backgrounds. Viewers anticipated the protagonists' struggles and were fascinated by the film's technique—principally by how the chair was "animated." After an enjoyable and amusing ten minutes, A CHAIRY TALE left children centered and content. "Whenever I see a film like that," a 9-year-old remarked, "I like to laugh."

Since the chair's humanity intrigued everyone, only the very ill or the very young will need to be told what viewers can otherwise discover for themselves. "It was a lot like humans," another child of 9 observed, "the way they acted it out."

## Evaluation of the Second Film

NEW FRIENDS had a special appeal for New Yorkers, but children's reactions were difficult to interpret. As with THE CASE OF THE ELEVATOR DUCK and other highly narrated films, there was little verbalizing during the screening. And lack of response indicated that most children did not understand the film's subtle humor. In addition, its pale watercolor-look may have been too subdued for projection in less than ideal viewing situations.

Although the story deals with separation and survival, it sidesteps the issue of reunion when the duck chooses to stay with his new friends, rather than rejoin his group/family. Thus, despite an apparently hospital-appropriate theme, NEW FRIENDS has potential problems regarding separation anxiety. In part because it is set in winter (and we showed it in winter), hospital staff thought the film brought up feelings of being cold as well as lonely.

All in all, although the theme of abandonment did appear in children's artwork, it was difficult to tell whether or not the film's effect was constructive. Because NEW FRIENDS did not seem well-matched for A CHAIRY TALE (which worked fabulously) we decided to pair each with another, more appropriate partner. If used, NEW FRIENDS requires an introduction explaining that ducks usually go south for the winter, since many children were unaware of this.

## Evaluation of the Activity

Although the program managed to make children in the various groups comfortable, their artwork was generally uninspired and few related to the films. An Arabic girl who spoke no English drew a flock of ducks flying home; another girl drew a chair, which hospital staff said was the best drawing she had ever done and the only one she ever completed.

Basically, this combination of films did not create the sort of synergy which energizes children's artwork, but the activity itself may have been a problem. Drawing—for older children in particular—was either too uninteresting or too threatening (if they felt they were bad artists) or both. Older children require more structure and more novelty in their activities than younger children do, and plain old drawing provides neither.

# Playroom Film Program #12

| | |
|---|---|
| **Activity:** | Collage/storytelling. |
| **Materials:** | Paper, picture magazines with animals, scissors, glue-sticks. |
| **Dexterity:** | Average, except for those with IVs. |
| **Age Level:** | School age. |

## IRA SLEEPS OVER
(17 minutes/liveaction/dialog)

Adapted from Bernard Waber's book, this is the story of 6-year-old Ira's first sleepover. Anxious about whether or not to bring his teddy bear, Ira has numerous discussions about it with his parents and his older sister. Finally, fearful of his friend's ridicule, Ira leaves the bear at home, only to discover that his friend Reggie sleeps with a stuffed animal.

## TALEB AND HIS LAMB
(16 minutes/liveaction/narration)

Based on a Bedouin folktale, this gripping drama focuses on the dilemma of a young shepherd who loves his pet lamb and will not allow his father to sell it at the market. Taleb kidnaps the lamb and runs away with it, surviving for several days in the desert. Eventually, however, his father finds the boy and his lamb and the tale offers viewers a choice of endings: in one the boy is punished for disobeying his father; in the other he is rewarded for his bravery.

## Evaluation of the First Film

We tested this with 14 children, ages 6–16, but most were 6–11. IRA SLEEPS OVER elicited mixed responses, in part because of the nature of the problem being addressed, and in part because its white, suburban, middle-class characters, setting, and values made it difficult for urban, minority children to identify with.

The film did appeal to a narrow age range (6–8) for whom it raised issues about separation and generated meaningful discussions about sibling relationships and children's own stuffed animals. As one Child Life specialist remarked: "Despite the film's stilted, suburban, middle-class aspects, its deeper message affected young school age children and they related to it."

Older children, however, were bored and pairing it with TALEB AND HIS LAMB did not work. Those who might have appreciated TALEB AND HIS LAMB were so turned off by IRA SLEEPS OVER that they literally left the room. IRA SLEEPS OVER would work in a program for young school age children (6–8), if paired with a film more appropriate for that age.

## Evaluation of the Second Film

TALEB AND HIS LAMB is a sophisticated and engaging film which is thematically appropriate for preadolescents and works best with viewers over 8. Unfortunately, most over-eights walked out during or just after the screening of IRA SLEEPS OVER. Those who did stay were engaged by TALEB AND HIS LAMB and were eager to discuss it afterwards, particularly the issues it raises about parents, children's rights, and authority.

TALEB AND HIS LAMB requires an introduction that warns children about its dual ending; otherwise they become confused about the story's resolution. Not too surprisingly, the majority of children preferred the ending where the father spares the lamb to start a flock for Taleb and were relieved that his "daddy took him home." TALEB AND HIS LAMB needs another partner, since it seemed successful despite this odd coupling.

## Evaluation of the Activity

Our suggestion to cut out animals from magazines and create a story did not interest most children. Part of the problem was that we lost so many older children (because of IRA SLEEPS OVER) and younger children did not want to attempt storytelling. TALEB AND HIS LAMB was inspirational to those who tried it but, overall, the activity lacked vitality. It seems to suffer from some of the same problems as the activity in Playroom Film Program #11. Both the program and the activity must be redesigned.

# Playroom Film Program #13

| | |
|---|---|
| **Activity:** | Collage/storytelling. |
| **Materials:** | Shoe box tops, picture magazines, scissors, glue. |
| **Dexterity:** | Average, except for those with IVs. |
| **Age Level:** | School age. |

## ARROW TO THE SUN
(12 minutes/cel animation/minimal dialog)

In this nearly wordless, mime-like film, a Pueblo legend unfolds (also available as a picturebook by Gerald McDermott). When a boy, born rather miraculously, matures he is rejected by his peers in the village and goes on a quest to find his divine father. The young man finds his father in the heavens, but he must prove himself by enduring 4 tests. After successfully completing the task, father and son are reunited briefly and then the young man returns to his village on earth, bringing with him the fertilizing powers of the sun.

## THE CASE OF THE ELEVATOR DUCK
(17 minutes/liveaction/dialog & narration)

Based on the book by Polly Berrien Berends, this is a delightful detective story about Gilbert, a black urban preadolescent, who solves the case of what to do with a duck he finds in the elevator of his "no pets" housing project.

## Evaluation of the First Film

We tested this with 8 children, ages 7–17, but most were 10–13. ARROW TO THE SUN needs a careful introduction because our hospitalized viewers had no experience with the Pueblo symbols it featured. For this reason, we not only told a synopsis of the story, we also showed and discussed important images from the book: the *kachina*-like characters, the pueblo villages, the *kivas*, and the corn maiden. Without such a preparation, children found the film too abstract and could not follow the storyline.

Despite this, ARROW TO THE SUN received a mixed review. It seemed to work for those 12–14, but not universally. Many children found the ending anticlimactic and unclear. During the screening, viewers were quieter than usual and did not respond to our prompts, despite the fact that some were obviously following and correctly interpreting the story.

ARROW TO THE SUN was not an entirely effective partner for the second film. It was too drawn out and the storytelling activity related more to the latter. However, ARROW TO THE SUN might have potential for use in hospitals if properly introduced and followed with a more graphic activity such as printmaking or block printing, and if combined with a shorter partner.

## Evaluation of the Second Film

THE CASE OF THE ELEVATOR DUCK is a *four-star* film. Accessible and pleasing to a wide age range, most children thoroughly enjoyed the film's low-key humor and capable protagonist. While it had a special appeal for black and urban children, all of our test groups were energized by and absorbed in this story of a young detective and enthusiastically created their own detective stories afterwards. As one Child Life consultant observed: "THE CASE OF THE ELEVATOR DUCK was real; its situation, the language, everything was believable."

One purported amnesiac—a child of about 8 or 9 who had been found wandering the city streets and who claimed he could remember nothing about his life or his parents—summarized THE CASE OF THE ELEVATOR DUCK before we screened the film; apparently, he had seen it in school. The boy, who insisted he could not even remember his own name, recalled the entire story in great detail. This clued hospital staff to the possibility that, while the child undoubtedly had serious problems, amnesia might not be one of them. Hospital staff were also surprised when the boy drew his story, which included a person, because that was the first time he had drawn a person since entering the hospital.

## Evaluation of the Activity

We asked children to cut out pictures from magazines and glue them inside shoe box tops to tell a visual detective story. We did not ask them to write anything down, which often seemed threatening. Rather, children were encouraged to explain what was happening verbally. Somehow, the process of cutting out pictures to tell a story (instead of drawing), being allowed to explain things vocally (instead of in writing), and working within an unusual and three-dimensional framework made this a successful activity. But it worked best when it was highly structured. Without such structure, older children were too self-conscious to attempt the activity.

Aside from giving children more guidance and focus, this story-collage may have worked better than the one in Playroom Film Program #12 because the films were better suited for the activity. If nothing else, ARROW TO THE SUN was visually compelling and THE CASE OF THE ELEVATOR DUCK was both energizing and inspirational.

# Playroom Film Program #14

| | |
|---|---|
| **Activity:** | Collage. |
| **Materials:** | Construction and origami paper, markers, pencils, scissors, and glue-sticks. |
| **Dexterity:** | Average, except for those with IVs. |
| **Age Level:** | School age. |

## ISLE OF JOY
(7 minutes/cutout animation/nonverbal)

An enchanting Debussy-Matisse musical film! Beginning with the image of Matisse in a wheelchair (scissors in hand), this lyrical celebration of beauty moves quickly through a series of lithographic images until it gets to vividly colored cutouts derived from the work of Matisse. For the rest of the film, cutouts of flowers and gardens, sailboats and sunbathers, swimmers and fish, lovers and birds dance across the screen to the gentle strains of Debussy's "L'Isle Joyeuse" played on a piano.

## A STORY, A STORY
(10 minutes/cel animation/narration)

An African folktale about the origin of stories which features the wily trickster-hero, Ananse the Spiderman. This film is based on a picturebook by Gail E. Haley and tells how Ananse (here in human form) accomplishes 3 tasks: capturing Osebo, the leopard of the terrible teeth; trapping Mmboro, the hornet who stings like fire; and catching Mmoatia, the fairy whom men never see. He does this, and brings the creatures to the sky god Nyame in order to buy Nyame's box of stories for the people of earth.

## Evaluation of the First Film

We tested this with 12 children, ages 6–16, but most were 8–16. ISLE OF JOY was introduced by a combination of storytelling and showing children a picture of Matisse in a wheelchair (available in several of the books about him) as well as some postcard reproductions (from museums) of his cutouts. The benefit of postcards is that children can handle them easily and unlike a book more than one person at a time can see them.

Our verbal introduction gave children enough information about the film to both involve them and suggest why the filmmaker made it. Without a "hook" to grab them emotionally, children might be disinclined to give the film a chance. Without an inkling of its purpose (in suggesting which we made liberal use of "poetic license") older children often respond negatively to nonnarrative works.

> The film you are about to see was made from cutout images that resemble the work of an artist named Henri Matisse. The story of how he came to make his cutouts is interesting.

> Matisse was a painter most of his life, but when he grew old he became very ill. (Show picture of Matisse.) While recovering, he decided to make art that would heal or help him get better. He decided to decorate the walls of his room, but he was confined to a wheelchair and painting the wall was difficult. He solved the problem by cutting shapes out of colored paper and gluing them on the walls. (Pass out postcards.)

> Our film is based on those cutouts, but it has neither words nor a story. It's like a dance—maybe more like a dream—of joy and beauty. As you watch it, why not call out what you see. Let's look at the ISLE OF JOY.

Children noticeably relaxed and enjoyed the film's colorful images as they floated across the screen. Intrigued, many wanted to see it again, and the film worked particularly well with more than one viewing. Children also enjoyed looking at the book and postcards of Matisse's artwork, especially after they had seen the film. In considering what Matisse accomplished despite his disability, a 7-year-old said, "He's amazing!"

The film is visually engaging and children enjoyed discovering familiar shapes on the screen, but it's greatest strength is that it sets a tranquil mood and inspires creative artwork. A teenage viewer said the film was about "having nothing to worry about." It is a wonderful "island retreat" for sick children!

## Evaluation of the Second Film

A STORY, A STORY is a complex and highly verbal narrative and children need a thorough introduction to its characters. We found it helpful to use illustrations from the book (from which the film was adapted) to introduce the characters and give a synopsis of the plot. The story itself was most successful with older children. But although younger ones had some difficulty following the course of events, they enjoyed the film's upbeat, rhythmic music and appealing images.

In programming terms, A STORY, A STORY balanced the first film effectively. Its narrated story and representational images offset the abstract images and associative structure of ISLE OF JOY. Interestingly, as one child remarked, the colorful images that escape from the box at the end of A STORY, A STORY are similar to those in ISLE OF JOY. Their screening order was important, too, in that a nonnarrative film usually suffers by comparison when it follows a story; but when it goes first, the lyric as well as the story benefits.

Children appeared satisfied and energized when A STORY, A STORY ended. And, despite the fact that in some situations we screened ISLE OF JOY again before starting the collage activity, a number of children in those screenings used elements from A STORY, A STORY in their artwork. Others used images derived from ISLE OF JOY.

## Evaluation of the Activity

We suggested that children cut out shapes and glue them onto paper to make a collage. Although we encouraged them to make their shapes without drawing, many were uncomfortable with that so they used markers and/or pencils to outline their shapes before cutting them. A few children resisted—exhibiting the classic "moment of terror" that grips almost everyone when given an unfamiliar art assignment. They protested, saying: "I can't cut like Matisse!" or "I'm not a good artist!" But after encouragement and the reassurance that we did not expect it to be prize-winning art (just a fun thing to do) they got over their fears and did impressive collages.

This was a *four-star* program that we transferred to television (CCTV Program #5).

# Playroom Film Program #15

| | |
|---|---|
| **Activity:** | Bas-relief sculpting with playdough. |
| **Materials:** | Clay or playdough, shoe box tops, and instruments such as plastic forks, tongue depressors, and pencils for manipulating and marking the clay. |
| **Dexterity:** | Average, except for those with IVs. |
| **Age Level:** | School age and young adolescent. |

## SOLO
(15 minutes/liveaction/nonverbal)

A genuine cliff-hanger, as well as something of a metaphor for solving insurmountable problems, this well-shot dramatic story (with the look of a documentary) shows how one man makes a successful solo ascent of a rugged mountain. In a rocky crevice along the way, he finds a small tree frog. The climber carries the amphibian with him as he goes up, and releases it in a stream on the way down.

## THE FABLE OF HE AND SHE
(11 minutes/clay animation/dialog & narration)

A delightful tale in which inhabitants (Hardibars and Mushamels) of the imaginary island of Baramel change their attitudes about sex-defined job roles as a result of a natural disaster. The unusual names (chopachucks, mushmoos, pompomberries, reverse-a-quake), the imaginative bas-relief playdough animation, and the amusing storyline give this film universal appeal.

## Evaluation of the First Film

We tested this with 17 children, ages 6–17, but most were 7–13. SOLO was a remarkable success! Thematically, it seems highly appropriate for hospitalized children because it is about a character who faces a difficult obstacle and overcomes it. The film's gripping drama (which looks like a documentary) is nicely balanced with a tension-release ending. Despite its toughness, SOLO also has soft touches, notably, the brief but poignant interaction with a frog, for whom children demonstrated concern. Patients thoroughly enjoyed its pace, the suspense of the climb, and its satisfying closure. "SOLO was quite therapeutic for kids who were struggling with serious physical problems," observed a Child Life specialist at one of our sites. "Although they didn't say a lot, I thought they identified with the climber's struggle of working to conquer something hard and meeting with success."

Because the film looks so realistic, children need to be forewarned that it's a story (without words). They should also be told that, although it may be a bit scary at times, the film has a happy ending.

We thought SOLO might be too powerful for under-sevens and did not test it with that audience. For this reason we also decided not to use it on TV since anyone could watch it that way. However, the film appeals to all viewers over 7 and is a wonderful stimulus for discussions, especially for boys 10 and older; many teens talked spontaneously among themselves during the screening. Although not directly related to the arts activity, SOLO worked well in this particular program.

## Evaluation of the Second Film

THE FABLE OF HE AND SHE delighted and amused hospitalized children. It was also an effective follow-up to SOLO—light and comical after such a gripping drama. THE FABLE OF HE AND SHE worked best for children 9–13, but all ages appreciated it for different reasons and on different levels. Under-nines liked its whimsical tone and animation style, while over-nines enjoyed its storyline and imaginative vocabulary. Children generally appeared energized and satisfied after seeing THE FABLE OF HE AND SHE. Interestingly, although it involves a change in attitudes about sex-defined job roles, very few children commented on the film's role-reversal theme. However, one 11-year-old noted: "Things change; men have to learn to cook." Most children did mention sharing work and learning new ways of cooperating.

## Evaluation of the Activity

Using the shoe box tops as pans or containers worked very well for the sculpture activity. It not only gave children a frame for their sculpture (which we encouraged them to do in the bas-relief mode of THE FABLE OF HE AND SHE), it also gave them a spatial context within which to work. After the usual and temporary hesitation, children really enjoyed themselves. One 11-year-old remarked that she liked working with clay better than painting, pasting, or cutting.

THE FABLE OF HE AND SHE was a perfect lead-in to the clay/playdough activity. Many older children lifted ideas and images directly from the film, while younger ones did a more personal experimentation. Everyone, however, participated in the activity with a high level of enthusiasm. The films and the activity were accessible and appealing to school age children as well as teenagers, largely because they could be interpreted on different levels and adapted to different developmental needs. A *four-star* program!

# Playroom Film Program #16

| | |
|---|---|
| **Activity:** | Mask-making. |
| **Materials:** | Paper plates, tongue depressors, tissue paper, masking tape, crayons, markers, pencils, scissors, a stapler, glue-sticks. |
| **Dexterity:** | Average, except for those with IVs. |
| **Age Level:** | School age. |

## A QUEST
(8 minutes/liveaction/nonverbal)

Set in a lush green landscape and featuring actor/mimes as well as multiperson dragons and huge parade-puppets, this elaborate and sometimes silly pageant tells the "medieval" saga of a knightly quest. During the performance, actors use cue-banners (which read: conflict, reconciliation, impending doom, victory, and celebration) to let viewers know what is happening.

## GERALD McBOING BOING
(7 minutes/cel animation/narration)

A classic cartoon, narrated in verse (written by Dr. Seuss), this is the sometimes poignant tale of a handicapped boy who eventually finds a place for himself in the world. From the day he uttered his first sound, Gerald McCloy was unable to talk; he could only go "beep-beep" or "boing-boing." Because of this, he is rejected by his neighbors, his peers, and his local school. Gerald's handicap becomes an asset, however, when he is hired by a radio station to make sound effects.

## Evaluation of the First Film

We tested this with 10 children, ages 6–16, but most were 10–13. Although the one genuine point of interest was the film's puppetry technique, school age children did not appear engaged during A QUEST and it was impossible to stimulate any discussion afterwards. A number of our consultants commented that the film's humor seemed too subtle or sophisticated for the majority of children; however, when we tried A QUEST in a mini-test with preschoolers, it worked much better.

Despite these results, we tried A QUEST on CCTV (Program #6). Due to time pressure, we did not fully document our playroom findings before we developed the TV programs. But we were also optimistic that a different partner and an introduction stressing its silliness would make it work.

## Evaluation of the Second Film

GERALD McBOING BOING was terrific for our test population. Its theme involving a child who succeeds in life despite a noticeable handicap is quite appropriate for pediatric patients. All ages seemed to find it moving and they giggled and laughed throughout. Even children who were too young to follow the storyline enjoyed listening to the narrated verse and the protagonist's special noises.

While older children otherwise had no trouble understanding the course of events, some of the pleasure in this story was missed by those unfamiliar with old-fashioned radio sound effects. Quite a few did not follow what was happening in the radio show scene. It is therefore important to explain about the sound effects, either before or after the screening. After may be better because then such an explanation does not give away the ending.

## Evaluation of the Activity

GERALD McBOING BOING was the stronger film, but the mask-making activity was directly linked to A QUEST. As a result, it was not successful and the program failed to motivate school age children. A majority did not even attempt to make a mask. The principal exception was a Guatemalan girl who spoke no English. She actually made a couple of masks, but that may have had more to do with the fact that masked performances are part of the Guatemalan folk culture than with the films. A combination of sound- and puppet-making might have worked better as a follow-up to this pairing.

*The Creation of Birds.* Courtesy: Société
Radio-Canada.

*Rosie's Walk.* Courtesy: Weston Woods.

*Mole and the Telephone.* Courtesy: Phoenix Films.

# CCTV PROGRAMS

## by Maureen Gaffney, Mary Ann Renz Bonarti, and Gil Coyle

Using the playroom film programs as our model, we designed 13 experimental closed-circuit television programs, roughly intended for children 5–10. To help motivate viewers in their rooms to do the follow-ups, we developed and distributed activity sheets for each program. So that we could get some idea of how far up or down each program would go, we observed and interviewed children above and below the 5–10 target age. In addition, we tried most programs with small groups in the playroom both because bedside monitors at one site were too small and because we wanted to compare the reactions of solitary viewers to those in a group.

The material aspect of the arts activities would be considerably diminished by having children do them in their own rooms instead of the well-supplied playroom, so we made a number of TV activities fairly conceptual. Sometimes it worked, sometimes it did not. Success often reflected how well we structured it and how clearly the actors demonstrated it on television.

CCTV programs were televised and evaluated at a number of sites in 1983. They were tested in May and June at Children's Hospital/National Medical Center in Washington, DC, Downstate Medical Center in Brooklyn, NY, and St. Luke's/Roosevelt Medical Center in New York City. In August they were tested at Eastern Maine Medical Center in Bangor. Unlike the playroom film programs, they are not listed in the order of their testing.

## Conditions for Using Films on CCTV

Although this should be checked in each case with the appropriate distributor, generally the films discussed in this section can be used on closed-circuit television in hospitals when and if the following conditions are met:

- Permission to use a film or tape on CCTV is obtained in writing from the distributor prior to purchase. The letter should mention the title and give some details about the type of programming it will be part of and the number of beds it will reach.

- The CCTV system is an in-house system, using hard cable and operating in one hospital and in one building only. Should a system cover more than one building, discuss the particulars with the distributor to clear use of the title.

- There is no charge to patients for viewing the CCTV programming. This may mean not charging rental fees for TV sets in order to get educational rates, which are cheaper than those for which a fee is charged.

# PROGRAM TITLES/DESCRIPTIONS

**#1. Tales of How**
Unusual-looking origins tales—a Native American account of how birds were created, and an African suggestion for how the moon got in the sky, are followed by a board game which incorporates elements from both tales.

**#2. Fine Feathered Friends**
A look at chickens—a nonnarrative study on the one hand and a simple story on the other—is followed by a board game based on the story.

**#3. City Adventures**
Stories about black urban boys—one animated, the other liveaction—are followed by a drawing activity.

**#4. And That's the Good News**
Animated adventures—one about a boy, the other about a girl, and one with words, the other without—are followed by a drawing activity.

**#5. Tropical Murals**
Animations set in the tropics—a nonnarrative celebration of Matisse's cutouts and an African folktale about the origin of stories—are followed by a collage/mural activity.

**#6. Masks and Puppets**
Liveaction pantomimes—one with a single mime in white-face, the other with costumed actors and parade dragon puppets—are followed by a mask-making activity.

**#7. Curious Puzzles**
Unusual animations which appear to be made from cutouts—one a wordless exploration of the Chinese tangram, the other a Japanese folktale—are followed by a puzzle-solving activity.

**#8. Unusual Creatures**
Imaginatively animated stories—one featuring animals made from small boxes, the other featuring peanut people and household objects—are followed by a box art activity.

**#9. An Unusual Twist**
Stories about characters who adapt to unfamiliar situations—one a wordless liveaction, the other a clay animation with words—are followed by a playdough activity.

**#10. Memories and Wishes**
Two gentle works—a calendar of memories and the story of a wish come true—are followed by a structured drawing activity.

**#11. Drawing Tall Tales**
Transformational cartoons—one about an inventive kid with a magic crayon, the other about a resourceful cat—are followed by a structured drawing activity.

**#12. A Touch of Fun**
Delightful clay animations—a wordless exploration of playdough's possibilities and a story of friendship and communication—are followed by a clay activity.

**#13. Working It Out**
Stories about good problem solvers—a black boy who invents a musical instrument, and white girls who clear up a mystery—are followed by a drawing activity.

# CCTV Program #1

| | |
|---|---|
| **Activity:** | Playing/coloring a board game. |
| **Materials:** | Activity sheets, markers, styrofoam or paper cups, and pennies or other coins. |
| **Dexterity:** | Minimal. |
| **Age Level:** | 7–13. |

## THE CREATION OF BIRDS
(10 minutes/cutout animation/nonverbal)

A wordless MicMac legend about the origin of birds, this tender, slow-moving film about the seasons makes effective use of animal symbolism, respectively the Howling Autumn Wolf and the Winter Snow Bear, and features a female protagonist.

## ANANSI THE SPIDER
(7 minutes/cel animation/narration)

A lively and colorful Ashanti folktale. In the first section, Anansi (in spider form) is rescued from trouble by his 6 resourceful sons. The second half of the tale explains how the moon came to be in the sky.

## Evaluation of the Program

We recorded the responses of 36 viewers at 4 sites; their age range was 2–13, but most were 5–13. Overall this highly successful program produced an interesting sexual polarity among older children: boys 10–13 preferred ANANSI THE SPIDER; girls of the same ages preferred THE CREATION OF BIRDS.

Of the pair, ANANSI THE SPIDER seemed the greater success on TV. Visually it was very strong, even on small monitors. Its sound was also compelling and many, especially black children said they liked the music as well as its "designs." But it can suffer from bad audio equipment because of the narrator's deep, accented voice.

The symbolism in THE CREATION OF BIRDS presented some problems because few children paid close attention to the wraparound in which it was explained. (As we learned only later, one of the problems may have been how we described—or failed to describe—the animals. Howling Wind Wolf appears initially as a sort of water monster, so many children did not recognize it as a wolf.)

Surprisingly, given their general lack of attention to introductions, children closely watched the segment in which the board game was explained. Board games seem to have high appeal.

## Evaluation of the Activity

Viewers were instructed to find a friend and make some markers, one per person, from small bits of folded paper, pieces of clay or playdough, buttons, or whatever they could find. They were also directed to find a paper cup and a few pennies. The actors on-screen showed viewers how to shake the cup and throw the coins. *Heads* counted as one, *tails* as 2. The person with the highest initial score went first.

To play the game, markers were placed at the starting place (where the MicMac girl and Anansi are) and moved around the board counterclockwise. Coins (scored as above) determined how many places each marker moved during a play. If a marker landed on an area with a cul-de-sac (where fish, wolf, bear, and so on waited), the player had to visit with them and forfeit his/her next turn.

The winner was the player whose marker got home or arrived back at the starting point first. However, if a marker approached home base and the player's throw did not land it there exactly, s/he had to go around the board again.

As a result of our evaluations, we concluded that the game board needed revision. It needed more white space, both to make coloring easier and to more clearly define the spaces in which the markers are to move. Children also asked us to print instructions on the activity sheet so they could play the game with their families.

The 11½″ x 17″ sheet (reproduced in miniature on the following page) was a good size for a game board, but we decided to reduce it to 8½″ x 11″ so it would more easily reproduce and better fit on children's bed-trays.

## Suitability of the Activity

Our intention in developing a circular board game was to visually reinforce the idea of going safely home after a series of adventures. In this respect, the game was quite successful. It was also an excellent undertaking for children to do in their rooms. Older viewers, who had a more developed sense of how to play such a game, followed the actors' instructions quite well. Children 7–10, particularly girls, enjoyed coloring the game board. Boys 9–13 actually played the game, which became a pleasant source of self-generated interaction among them in their rooms.

## Comments about the Wraparound

Aside from explaining about the animal symbols in introducing THE CREATION OF BIRDS, it might help to highlight the change of seasons. Using a globe to locate the geographic areas (Canada, Ghana) where the tales originated did not work at all. For ANANSI THE SPIDER it might be helpful to draw and label all the characters—Nyame as well as Anansi and his sons—on the activity sheet so viewers can pick them out as they appear on-screen.

Activity Sheet for CCTV Program #1

Activity Sheet for CCTV Program #2

# CCTV Program #2

| | |
|---|---|
| **Activity:** | Playing/coloring a board game. |
| **Materials:** | Activity sheets, crayons, styrofoam or paper cups, and pennies or other coins. |
| **Dexterity:** | Minimal. |
| **Age Level:** | 6–8. |

## CHICKS AND CHICKENS
(10 minutes/liveaction/nonverbal)

In this slow-paced look at life on a chicken farm, hens incubate a clutch of eggs and hatch a brood of chicks. The hens protect their babies and show them how to find food. When a dachshund approaches, adult birds repel the intruder. Once the danger is gone, the baby chicks come out of hiding.

## ROSIE'S WALK
(5 minutes/cel animation/narration)

A barnyard hen takes her afternoon constitutional across the yard, around the pond, over the haystack, past the mill, through the fence, under the beehives, and gets back home in time for dinner. As she strolls around the farm, Rosie fortuitously avoids the predatory maneuvers of a comically inept fox. Based on the book by Pat Hutchins and set to the tune of "Turkey in the Straw," this simple and nearly slow-motion slapstick is both droll and delightful.

## Evaluation of the Program

We recorded the responses of 27 viewers at 4 sites; their age range was 2–18, but most were 2–8. Response to the program was mixed. ROSIE'S WALK was successful with those 2–11, but CHICKS AND CHICKENS was a problem for almost everyone except a preschool group that saw the program in a playroom.

While it had recurrent actions, events in CHICKS AND CHICKENS were not made clearer by repetition. In this case, less might have been more. The film was loosely structured at best. Not only did it seem overlong, but certain cuts made little or no sense. In addition, the soundtrack was not effective for hospital monitors. Besides being inaudible at times, its natural sounds did not provide enough cues to focus children's attention or generate an appropriate mood. Even the one dramatic event involving a dachshund failed to elicit much response. As a whole, this low-key catalog neither holds together

nor reads well on television monitors. It was a total blur on very small monitors. We decided to try another title with ROSIE'S WALK in subsequent testing. (See Video Program #1.)

ROSIE'S WALK, on the other hand, was highly effective. The storyline was clear, and its strong musical soundtrack and simple images worked quite well on television.

## Evaluation of the Activity

Although this was a simpler board game than the one for CCTV Program #1, certain instructions were the same. For example, viewers were told to get a friend and make or find markers using folded pieces of paper, bits of clay, small blocks, etc. They were also directed to locate a paper or styrofoam cup and put from one to 3 coins in it. Viewers were shown how to shake the cup and throw the coins. *Heads* counted as one, *tails* as 2. Based on their score, players calculated the number of spaces they could move.

The object of the game was simply to start out from Rosie's house and, going clockwise around the board, get back home safe and sound. To begin, each player threw the coins. The person with the highest score went first and players took turns. Coins, scored as above, determined how many places each marker moved during a play. There were no penalties as there were in the game for Program #1, the lack of which—in combination with young films—made it unappealing to older children.

The player whose marker arrived home first won. However, if a player did not get the exact number of points needed to land precisely on home base, s/he had to wait until the next round and keep trying until the correct number came up.

Our tests indicated that children enjoyed the activity sheet (reproduced in miniature on the previous page) and used it on various levels. However, because this was a simple game, it did not have as wide an appeal as that in the first program.

As we learned with the earlier game board, children wanted more white space as well as instructions printed on the activity sheet. While it was an appropriate size for a game board, our 11½″ x 17″ sheet was too large for bed-trays and was not the standard size for photocopy or offset reproduction. Thus, we decided to eliminate the border (which did not appeal to children) and redesign the game on a standard 8½″ x 11″ page.

## Suitability of the Activity

As with the previous board game, our intention in developing this activity was to visually reinforce the idea of going safely home. In this respect, it was highly successful. It was also an excellent project for viewers to do in their rooms. In a sexual preference pattern similar to the one that emerged with CCTV Program #1, girls 6–8 enjoyed coloring the game board, while boys of the same ages preferred to play the game. Coloring was all that preschoolers could manage, but they enjoyed doing that; the game itself was too difficult for them.

The game works best with children 6–8. Even though it does not reach our entire target population, we may leave it as is and consider this a program for viewers of that narrower age range.

## Comments about the Wraparound

CHICKS AND CHICKENS might have worked better if we had prepared viewers for the eggs' hatching. The most important aspect to emphasize in ROSIE'S WALK is the fox, since it is never mentioned by the narrator; the wraparound must both set up the drama and prepare children for its humor.

In introducing the activity, the plain game board was hard to see on television. However, it was quite visible after it had been colored, and children imitated the colored sheet on-screen. Interestingly, viewers over 8 reacted to the humor between our male and female hosts, but not to the rules of the game. Under-sixes understood neither; the humor was too sophisticated and the rules needed repetition.

# CCTV Program #3

| | |
|---|---|
| **Activity:** | Drawing or making a collage. |
| **Materials:** | Activity sheets, construction paper, crayons, pencils, scissors, and glue-sticks. |
| **Dexterity:** | Minimal to average. |
| **Age Level:** | 6–12. |

## THE SNOWY DAY
(6 minutes/iconographic animation/narration)

A lyrical, slow-moving sketch of a black preschooler's day of fun and exploration in the city snow. Peter spends the first day alone but the next day, when he wakes to discover that the snow is still there, he sets out with a friend with whom he can share his experiences.

## THE CASE OF THE ELEVATOR DUCK
(17 minutes/liveaction/dialog & narration)

Based on the book by Polly Berrien Berends, this is a delightful detective story about Gilbert, a black urban preadolescent, who solves the case of what to do with a duck he finds in the elevator of his "no pets" housing project.

## Evaluation of the Program

We recorded the responses of 17 viewers at 3 sites; their age range was 3–13, but most were 6–8. In this program we tried to bracket our targeted audience by combining a film for the younger part of that age range (THE SNOWY DAY) with one for the older age range (THE CASE OF THE ELEVATOR DUCK). It did not work.

THE SNOWY DAY is extremely slow, has a sweet and gentle tone, and features a preschool protagonist. It is best for children 2–5 and only works with those 6–8 who are in poor condition. Older viewers were bored by it, which did not help the second film. However, those who knew the book on which THE SNOWY DAY is based were thrilled to see it on TV; interestingly, they were mostly 6–8.

THE CASE OF THE ELEVATOR DUCK uses a fairly sophisticated narrative convention (the detective story), has a lot of talking, and features a preadolescent hero. It had great appeal for viewers over 6. (Although not the targeted audience, children 3–6 had a hard time following the storyline, particularly the part where Gilbert and the duck go down the stairs to find the duck's home.)

As is, the program works for viewers up to 8 in less than good condition. If we want to reach children 5–10, we need a better partner for THE CASE OF THE ELEVATOR DUCK. THE SNOWY DAY should be used only in preschool and early primary programs.

## Evaluation of the Activity

It was suggested that viewers create a scene on the activity sheet, which was a blank sheet with a border of silhouetted city images. They were given the option of drawing or using collage materials. By and large, children enjoyed doing a follow-up to this program, but they did not use the ideas suggested in the wraparound. Part of the problem may have been our instructions and modeling; the task should have been more focused and we should have chosen one activity—not two—and demonstrated it at length. Also, if we want to do drawing as a follow-up to THE CASE OF THE ELEVATOR DUCK, we must choose an animated film with strong visuals since children have a hard time using liveaction works as a basis for drawing.

## Suitability of the Activity

Drawing or collage were fine for children 6–12 to do in their rooms. With a lot of adult help, under-sixes enjoyed making collages, many of which showed snow scenes. For the most part, children over 6 drew remembered images from the films.

## Comments about the Wraparound

In addition to preparing viewers for THE SNOWY DAY's quietness, we might also want to show the book, or artwork from the book, if we want to talk about how its collage images were made from torn and cut paper. We should also devote more time on-camera to demonstrating how to make a collage if we want children to do it as a follow-up. The most effective thing is to demonstrate the process. We must *show*—not tell!

Aside from defining a housing project and a "no pets" rule, it is helpful to tell children that THE CASE OF THE ELEVATOR DUCK is a detective story.

Activity Sheet for CCTV Program #3

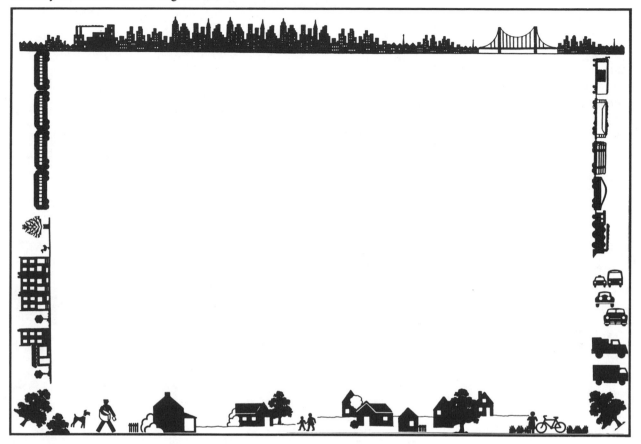

Activity Sheet for CCTV Program #4

# CCTV Program #4

| | |
|---|---|
| **Activity:** | Drawing related bad/good events. |
| **Materials:** | Activity sheets, crayons, pencils. |
| **Dexterity:** | Minimal. |
| **Age Level:** | None appropriate. |

**THE SKY IS BLUE**

(5 minutes/cutout animation/nonverbal)

Using naive and child-like cutout images, this is the saga of a young man whose kite takes him up, up, up into the starry heavens and then down, down, down to earth and home. Although he has several close calls on his journey, everything works out fine in the end. (This was repeated after MADELINE.)

**MADELINE**

(7 minutes/cel animation/narration)

Based on the picturebook by Ludwig Bemelmans, this film tells the story (in rhymed verse) of the semi-liberated Parisian schoolgirl Madeline, and her emergency visit to the hospital to have her appendix removed. (Unfortunately, she is not shown leaving the hospital.)

## Evaluation of the Program

We recorded the responses of 15 viewers at 2 sites; their age range was 2–15, but most were 3–12. This program proved more successful with viewers younger than our target audience and must be rethought.

THE SKY IS BLUE was great for children 2–5 who were compelled by its simple storyline and clear images. In many cases, it fostered a mood that allowed viewers to relate well both to the actors on-screen and to the follow-up. Showing it twice worked very well for preschoolers who enjoyed coloring in the activity sheet or drawing (with help) things they had seen in the film. Unfortunately, children over 6 found it babyish and were especially turned off when they had to see it twice. (Although it would not have helped with older viewers, we later learned that it was best to repeat such works immediately, rather than showing them after the second film.)

MADELINE worked best for girls 7–12 but was too difficult for under-sevens to follow. A 9-year-old girl who had read *Madeline* enjoyed it tremendously, as is generally true when children are familiar with the book from which a film is adapted.

Aside from structural flaws and the problem with Madeline's not leaving the hospital, MADELINE suffered a lot in the transfer to video; its colors became muddy and the size reduction made its images illegible at times. On the other hand, THE SKY IS BLUE was fine on all monitors.

## Evaluation of the Activity

In developing the follow-up, we wanted to reinforce the idea that, despite some bad news, the characters in the films end up okay (the good news). It was suggested that viewers draw pictures for a very simple story in 2 parts: one with bad news and the other with good news. Those headings, in that order, were printed on the activity sheet. (This was a nonverbal variation of the *fortunately/unfortunately* activity described in the annotation for THE SKY IS BLUE.) Although preschoolers generally enjoyed it, drawing and storytelling seemed threatening and/or uninteresting to most children over 6 outside of the supportive playroom environment.

## Suitability of the Activity

It did not work for any age group. Not only was the task vague and unfocused, but the films did not generate sufficient energy for the activity. The activity sheet itself also lacked structure.

## Comments about the Wraparound

If we want children to use the bad news/good news concept in their artwork, we have to make the idea very clear. We should also ask some thought-provoking, open-ended questions.

# CCTV Program #5

| | |
|---|---|
| **Activity:** | Making a collage mural. |
| **Materials:** | Construction paper, scissors, glue-sticks, possibly butcher paper. |
| **Dexterity:** | Average, except for those with IVs. |
| **Age Level:** | 5–15. |

## ISLE OF JOY

(7 minutes/cutout animation/nonverbal)

An enchanting music video! Beginning with the image of a man in a wheelchair, this lyrical celebration of beauty moves through a series of lithographic images to vividly colored cutouts derived from the work of Matisse. Flowers and gardens, sailboats and sunbathers, swimmers and fish, lovers and birds dance across the screen to the gentle strains of Debussy's "L'Isle Joyeuse."

## A STORY, A STORY

(10 minutes/cel animation/narration)

An African folktale about the origin of stories. Ananse the Spiderman (in human form) accomplishes 3 tasks: capturing Osebo, the leopard of the terrible teeth; trapping Mmboro, the hornet who stings like fire; and catching Mmoatia, the fairy whom men never see. He brings the creatures to the sky god Nyame to buy his box of stories.

## Evaluation of the Program

We recorded the responses of 38 viewers at 4 sites; their age range was 4–17, but most were 5–12. Overall response to this program was very favorable, with no observable differences between those in their own rooms and those in playrooms.

The colorful and highly kinesthetic imagery of ISLE OF JOY appealed to all children, with the exception of some boys 10–13 who saw it on a black-and-white monitor.

Because it is a narrative, A STORY, A STORY was the stated preference of most viewers, although girls 11–15 preferred ISLE OF JOY. Children under 7 had some trouble following its rather verbal narrative, but A STORY, A STORY worked particularly well with boys over 7, and with black children of all ages. As a 9-year-old said, she liked A STORY, A STORY "because it's about my people."

Both films were quite legible on small monitors, except for the series of objects that emerge from the box at the end of A STORY, A STORY—images that were important inspirations in film screenings (see Playroom Film Program #14). The music in both was highly effective.

## Evaluation of the Activity

Our intention was to encourage children to decorate their rooms with self-made and hopefully self-healing art. It was suggested that viewers make a mural using cutout images modeled after those from either film. Although we developed an activity sheet for this program, (what we call a *blank with a border*) we did not use it on television. Instead we showed a large sheet of butcher paper filled with cutout images when we learned that our minimal activity sheet did not work outside the playroom.

Children responded well to the collage idea and used elements from both films. Interestingly, many made abstract designs similar to the images in ISLE OF JOY. (This corroborates what we have learned outside the hospital: although children say they prefer stories, they often do better art in response to highly visual, artistic films.)

Both program and follow-up were effective with a deaf boy who could not read lips and a girl with a brain tumor whose motor functions were poor. Although the boy had attended a number of screenings, he largely acted out and never got involved in activities. After moving pleasurably in rhythm to the imagery of both films, he made a fine collage without any trouble. In a playroom situation, the girl made an abstract design. Since she was acutely aware of her lack of coordination, successfully creating a collage gave her a real sense of accomplishment.

## Suitability of the Activity

This was an excellent own-room undertaking that worked on different levels with all ages. Of our target population, however, children 5–7 in poor condition needed encouragement to do the activity; a group screening in the playroom may be advisable for children of that age/condition.

## Comments about the Wraparound

When introducing ISLE OF JOY, first talk about Matisse to personalize him, then show his designs that resemble images from the film. Also, make a cutout before the screening in order to show the process that is implicit in the film. The introduction to A STORY, A STORY was too talky; children lost interest because the visual aspect was minimal. Perhaps it would help to show pictures of the characters (blown up from the book) as their names are mentioned. In setting up the activity, model both cutting and tearing, since children with IVs might find tearing paper easier than cutting.

# CCTV Program #6

| | |
|---|---|
| **Activity:** | Mask-making. |
| **Materials:** | Activity sheets, crayons, scissors, construction and tissue paper, yarn, a stapler, paper plates, tongue depressors, masking tape, and glue. |
| **Dexterity:** | Considerable; difficult with an IV. |
| **Age Level:** | 10–11. |

## KEITH
(10 minutes/liveaction/nonverbal)

A simple recording of a street mime performance by Keith Berger in which a statue turns into a mechanical man who gets all boxed-in and then escapes. The performance is framed by sequences in which the mime is transformed from, and in the end returns to, a pensive young man in street clothes. His transformation to a mime in white-face and black leotards is accomplished via time-lapse photography.

## A QUEST
(8 minutes/liveaction/nonverbal)

Set in a lush green landscape and featuring actor/mimes as well as multiperson dragons and huge parade-puppets, this elaborate and sometimes silly pageant tells the "medieval" saga of a knightly quest. During the performance, actors use cue-banners (which read: conflict, reconciliation, impending doom, victory, and celebration) to let viewers know what is happening.

## Evaluation of the Program

We recorded the responses of 21 viewers at 3 sites; their age range was 3–17, but most were 4–9. While there was a great deal of interest in the program's subject, the program itself was only partially successful.

Because foreground images in KEITH did not stand out clearly from the background, the film was difficult to read on TV monitors. In addition, its unusual structure made it hard for children to anticipate what was going to happen, and no one understood that the action on-screen involved imprisonment and escape. These factors, combined with its slow pace, made KEITH ineffective on TV and a poor lead-in to the second film.

A QUEST was brighter and funnier, but it was only moderately successful. Although they could understand it, viewers over 8 did not find the film compelling. When watching in their own rooms, younger children missed too much; they either could not read or did not know what the words meant. The best reception for A QUEST occurred in group screenings with children 4–8.

Despite their drawbacks, each film appealed to some viewers. However, they did not work together and the program as well as the follow-up worked best in a group situation. Thus we cannot recommend this as a model for CCTV.

## Evaluation of the Activity

It was suggested that viewers make a mask using either the activity sheet or a paper plate. The sheet (which is greatly reduced on the following page) was not successful because the character was unidentifiable and did not relate to either film, the mask's proportions were wrong for children's faces, and it lacked instructions. The best masks were made from paper plates which were devised as hand-held masks; a tongue depressor was inserted in the lower portion to provide a handle.

## Suitability of the Activity

Although the film's low motivation levels may have had something to do with it, mask-making was not stimulating enough for older children except in a group situation, and it was too difficult for younger ones to do without adult assistance. It was, however, quite successful with those 4–8 in a playroom setting. At one site, children of that age who watched the program in a playroom made scary masks and then paraded through the halls to frighten the nurses.

## Comments about the Wraparound

The introduction to KEITH should demonstrate how mime make-up is applied as well as give some explanation of the imprisonment/escape theme. The introduction to A QUEST should preview and show the words that appear on the banners during the film—something audiovisual to make that aspect less difficult for younger viewers.

More demonstration of the mask-making technique would have been better in terms of the follow-up. And in using the activity sheet, children should be advised to color their masks before cutting them out.

Activity Sheet for CCTV Program #6

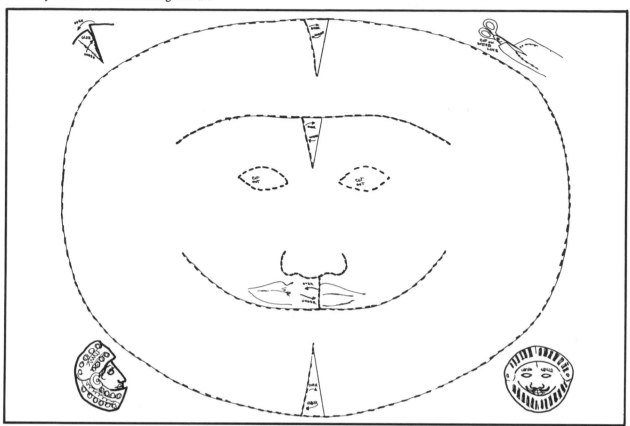

Activity Sheet for CCTV Program #7

# CCTV Program #7

| | |
|---|---|
| **Activity:** | Making/solving tangram puzzles. |
| **Materials:** | Activity sheets, construction paper, pencils, rulers, scissors, glue-sticks. |
| **Dexterity:** | Average, except for those with IVs. |
| **Age Level:** | 6–16. |

## TANGRAM
(3 minutes/cutout animation/nonverbal)

A delightful music video puzzle. Using 7 angular pieces from the Chinese puzzle called a tangram (which includes a square, a rhomboid, and 5 triangles), this lyrical film illustrates various silhouette shapes, from fish and snail to cat and horse. Each appears briefly on-screen, moves in a characteristic way, then transforms into another shape. (This was repeated after THE STONECUTTER.)

## THE STONECUTTER
(6 minutes/cel animation/narration)

This is an ancient Japanese fable with abstract images that resemble Matisse cutouts and seem to be made from layers of bright-colored tissue paper. The story (which is also available as a picturebook by Gerald McDermott) concerns Tasaku, a dissatisfied stonecutter, who asks the Mountain Spirit to change him into a prince, and then into the sun, and so on until he comes full circle—almost. The *be yourself* point is subtly made.

## Evaluation of the Program

We recorded the responses of 26 viewers at 3 sites; their age range was 3–17, but most were 6–11. This program got a mixed review. TANGRAM was highly successful with all ages, while, except for a positive response from 3 children, THE STONECUTTER was not. Because its images are abstract and rather static, THE STONECUTTER was visually difficult to follow on TV; but if children focused primarily on the narration, its visuals became distracting. This, combined with the constant ward interruptions and poor audio on many monitors, made it nearly impossible for viewers to stay involved with THE STONECUTTER.

Interestingly, a number of children saw this program more than once and were quite responsive and involved the second time. Following her second viewing, a girl of 11 did a tissue paper collage (one of the options in the wraparound) which was dif-

ferent from her first viewing when she worked with tangrams. Since she was one of the few children who opted for the collage activity, we have not included further discussion of it. That she was motivated, however, to do a different activity following her second viewing raises interesting questions about our decision to focus on only one activity in future productions.

## Evaluation of the Activity

Children were given a tangram template and directed to cut out and arrange it in the shape of an animal or person and then glue it onto a large paper of contrasting color. Unfortunately, our original tangram proportions were unmanageably large and children had to glue together 2 sheets of construction paper to form a base for their completed tangrams. Also, the plain black shapes (without diagrams) on the activity sheet were frustrating to most youngsters, as was the fact that its images were not identical to the ones they had seen in the film.

Due to the strength of TANGRAM, the activity worked very well once we modified the size of the tangram template. Children of all ages enjoyed making tangrams, although those under 5 as well as those in traction or with IVs needed a lot of help with cutting.

## Suitability of the Activity

Making tangrams worked best with children 6–16 in good condition and was an excellent project for viewers to do in their rooms.

## Comments about the Wraparound

The introduction to TANGRAM was acceptable, but it would be better to manipulate the tangram pieces on-screen using some of the shapes from the film, rather than simply showing completed silhouettes. Also, it would have been better to screen TANGRAM twice in a row, rather than after the second film.

THE STONECUTTER's introduction was too long and complex. It should be a rule of thumb that if a film requires either a very complex or a very lengthy verbal introduction, it should not be shown on TV to hospitalized children.

# CCTV Program #8

| | |
|---|---|
| **Activity:** | Making box art. |
| **Materials:** | Shoe boxes, styrofoam packing peanuts, pipe cleaners, wooden thread spools, wooden clothespins, felt scraps, patterned paper, cardboard, construction paper, markers, scissors, and glue. |
| **Dexterity:** | Considerable; difficult with an IV. |
| **Age Level:** | 5–9. |

## BALTHAZAR THE LION
(12 minutes/object animation/nonverbal)

As the film begins, an artist paints some small cartons and then uses them as puppets to tell the droll tale of a voracious circus/zoo lion who eats the moon. Not surprisingly, the moon is more than Balthazar can handle, so emergency medics relieve his stomach ache by removing the moon and returning it to the sky. After that, the artist makes the lion's mouth smaller and Balthazar becomes as docile as a kitten.

## CAPTAIN SILAS
(14 minutes/object animation/narration)

Making imaginative use of a large cast of peanuts and household objects such as blue-tinted popcorn (the sea), a shaving brush (dolphin), and a wing tip shoe (boat), this droll film presents a delightful miniature world in which merchant-sailor Silas makes his living by trading trucks (made from thread spools) for sugar cubes (the principal building material used on Truck Island).

## Evaluation of the Program

We recorded the responses of 29 viewers at 3 sites; their age range was 3–17, but most were 4–11. As a whole this program was very successful and, despite the length of both films, children 5–9 thoroughly enjoyed it. Watching the program and doing the follow-up required a fair amount of energy on the part of children. Consequently, we do not recommend screening this back-to-back with another long or demanding TV show. The one place this program did not work was at Downstate; the 7″ monitors there so reduced the films' images that it was impossible to see details, and both were highly detailed.

Of the pair, most viewers (boys in particular) preferred CAPTAIN SILAS. Its action and simple narrative generally carried it even when audio reception was poor, and children exhibited a great deal of interest in its animation technique. BALTHAZAR THE LION was problematic in some respects (for details see its annotation).

## Evaluation of the Activity

Children were given shoe boxes and a lot of small odds and ends to make a three-dimensional world-in-miniature. Box art was an amazing success with all who tried it, but it had greatest appeal for children 5–9. This may have had something to do with the titles in this program (particularly BALTHAZAR THE LION), because making box art usually appeals to children as old as 11–12 outside the hospital.

Pediatric patients in traction or with IVs uniformly had difficulty doing this activity. Such children can be helped considerably if boxes and glue cups are taped onto their bed-trays so they cannot fall off or tip over.

## Suitability of the Activity

The greatest difficulty with doing box art in viewers' rooms was getting materials to them. Another problem involved the way in which glue is typically distributed in hospitals, namely, in one-ounce medication cups that are almost inevitably knocked over. Despite its success, we thus recommend that this activity be done in the playroom, with the obvious exception of children in isolation or those who are otherwise confined to their rooms.

## Comments about the Wraparound

The introduction to the activity, particularly the process of making the pipe-cleaner monkey, was extremely effective in motivating children. But if we want to emphasize the type of box art shown in BALTHAZAR THE LION, we should demonstrate how boxes can be combined or otherwise altered to make an animal.

# CCTV Program #9

| | |
|---|---|
| **Activity:** | Modeling playdough. |
| **Materials:** | Playdough. |
| **Dexterity:** | Minimal to average. |
| **Age Level:** | 5–12. |

## A CHAIRY TALE
(10 minutes/liveaction/nonverbal)

This humorous and sometimes slapstick, black-and-white mime drama about reciprocation is enacted by a man and an animated chair. Ravi Shankar did the compelling raga-like score for this classic film in which, after learning that not all chairs can be taken for granted, a man practices the golden rule.

## THE FABLE OF HE AND SHE
(11 minutes/clay animation/dialog & narration)

A delightful tale in which the inhabitants (Hardibars and Mushamels) of the imaginary island of Baramel change their attitudes about sex-defined job roles as a result of a natural disaster. The unusual names (chopachucks, mushmoos, pompomberries, reverse-a-quake), the imaginative bas-relief playdough animation, and the amusing storyline give this film universal appeal.

## Evaluation of the Program

We recorded the responses of 25 viewers at 3 sites; their age range was 3–17, but most were 3–11. This program was highly successful. "It made me forget the pain in my feet!" As one child's comment indicates, it helped pediatric patients get out of themselves, or at least relocate their energies to a pleasurable experience.

The films balance each other quite marvelously and the program as a whole seemed perfectly suited for our target audience. Both were appropriate for TV and worked well on all sizes and types of monitor. A CHAIRY TALE was great for all ages, including preschoolers. THE FABLE OF HE AND SHE worked best with viewers 6–11.

A number of children saw this program twice, and they thoroughly enjoyed the program as well as the follow-up each time. For instance, an Asian girl of 10 made a playdough dumpling and a little cooking pot after the first screening. After her second viewing, she made a reverse-a-burger, a hot dog, a doughnut, and a bird.

## Evaluation of the Activity

Playdough worked extremely well as a follow-up. Each of the actors demonstrated a different approach to working with playdough, but one (an imitation of the bas-relief animation technique in THE FABLE OF HE AND SHE) was not attempted by anyone. The other (making unusual foods, which was a thematic borrowing from THE FABLE OF HE AND SHE, and serving them in unusual ways, which was a thematic borrowing from A CHAIRY TALE) was imitated by a number of children. While most opted for making unusual foods, the range of fabricated objects was extremely wide, including mushamels, chopachucks, and things from children's own imaginations.

## Suitability of the Activity

This was an excellent undertaking for children in their rooms. It succeeded with a wide range of ages and physical conditions, even those in traction. The optimum age range was 5–10 or even 12, but younger children also enjoyed it—in their own rooms as well as in the playroom—if they were in a small group.

## Comments about the Wraparound

The demonstration of making unusual foods (especially the reverse-a-burger that had the bun in the middle and the meat on the outside) was one of our most successful activity introductions because the process was shown step-by-step and the concept was clear and simple.

In redoing this, the introduction to THE FABLE OF HE AND SHE might mention that something unusual happens. The idea of new ways of doing things was very effective and many children picked up on that in their responses to the film.

# CCTV Program #10

| Activity: | Drawing a picture series. |
|---|---|
| Materials: | Activity sheets, pencils, markers, and crayons. |
| Dexterity: | Minimal to average. |
| Age Level: | 8–12. |

## NOVEMBER 1977
(3 minutes/line animation/nonverbal)

Using a personal shorthand of images and sounds, the filmmaker draws a movie of her experiences and, by placing a snapshot-like still of each day in a calendar-grid, preserves a memory of all the days in the month of November 1977. Although conceptually sophisticated, the film's child-like images are quite simple. Viewers will recognize pumpkins, clouds, rain, cats, birds, a Thanksgiving turkey, and other familiar icons, as well as an indication that one day is/was the filmmaker's birthday. (This was repeated after MARY OF MILE EIGHTEEN.)

## MARY OF MILE EIGHTEEN
(11 minutes/mixed animation/dialog & narration)

A classic dog story, only here a girl gets the much-desired pet. Based on the book by Ann Blades, this slow-moving film tells the story of a Mennonite farm girl who lives with her family in northern Canada. When Mary sees the northern lights shimmering in the sky, she imagines that something special will happen the next day, and it does, in a touching if not entirely predictable way.

### Evaluation of the Program

We recorded the responses of 11 viewers at 3 sites; their age range was 3–12, but most were 6–10. Children generally demonstrated considerable interest in this program's theme. Wishing for good things to happen or enjoying memories of happy times seems an appealing focus for hospitalized children. Unfortunately, the films did not work together. MARY OF MILE EIGHTEEN is a heart-warming story, but its slow pace and almost somber music gave it a rather downbeat mood and it needs an upbeat (but not too upbeat) partner to offset this. While children, particularly girls, enjoyed it, MARY

OF MILE EIGHTEEN did not generate much energy for the activity.

NOVEMBER 1977 suffered considerably from being transferred to videotape. It was so reduced as to be barely legible; on the tiny Downstate monitors it was literally eye-straining. Repeating NOVEMBER 1977 helped neither it nor the program.

Girls 8–12 and boys 10–12 generally did best with both the program and the follow-up, but the latter needs serious revamping. For the most part, the films were too low-key to pique interest in or generate energy for an arts activity.

### Evaluation of the Activity

It was suggested that viewers draw a series of 8 pictures in the boxes on the activity sheet. The pictures, which correspond to the calendar grid in NOVEMBER 1977, were to represent a visual diary of special memories or special wishes. The idea was intriguing to many children, but the task was too unstructured and the sheet was unstimulating. For some, particularly those under 7, the squares were too small. Children who did this most successfully worked in small groups and had a lot of adult encouragement. But even those who were most enthusiastic about the activity ran out of ideas; 4 pictures might have been enough.

### Suitability of the Activity

This worked best in the playroom with girls 8–12 and boys 10–12. It seems to require the stimulation of others.

### Comments about the Wraparound

For introducing MARY OF MILE EIGHTEEN we need a legible picture of the northern lights. The idea of a diary was appealing and children were very interested in it, but we cannot expect them to execute a visual diary (of wishes or "memory snapshots") if we do not model and better structure the activity. Problems with the size and number of the squares aside, inadequate demonstration could be the reason children did not use the activity sheets appropriately.

Activity Sheet for CCTV Program #10

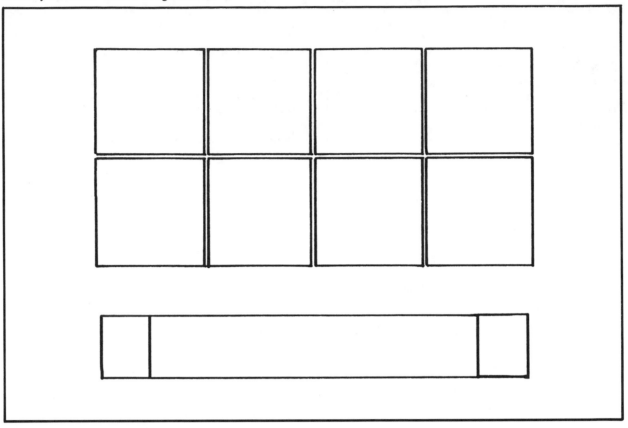

Activity Sheet for CCTV Program #11

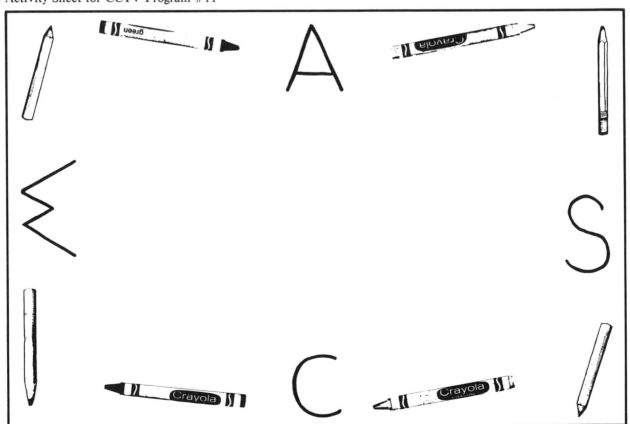

# CCTV Program #11

| | |
|---|---|
| **Activity:** | Drawing and altering basic shapes. |
| **Materials:** | Activity sheets, crayons, markers, and pencils. |
| **Dexterity:** | Minimal. |
| **Age Level:** | 5–10. |

## HAROLD'S FAIRY TALE
(8 minutes/line animation/narration)

Simple line drawings, adapted from the artwork of Crockett Johnson's book upon which this film is based, tell the further adventures of Harold. Dressed in his pajamas, the imaginative preschooler goes for a walk with the moon and his purple crayon and turns the conventions of the fairytale inside out. Along the way he defeats a giant witch and lifts the evil spell from a barren garden.

## FELIX GETS THE CAN
(7 minutes/line animation/silent)

In this black-and-white cartoon classic, a resourceful cat goes to great lengths to get a dinner of Alaskan salmon, including converting question marks into sled runners and enlisting some hot dog links from a butcher shop as a sled dog team. Title cards appear intermittently.

## Evaluation of the Program

We recorded the responses of 25 viewers at 3 sites; their age range was 3–17, but most were 3–9. Both films transferred well to video and both read well on small monitors, but while it appealed to children 5–10, the program had some serious problems. HAROLD'S FAIRY TALE was too uneventful, too slow, and the protagonist was too young for school age viewers. The lack of sound in FELIX GETS THE CAN was a real liability on TV.

Despite all, the program worked rather well in the playroom. Not only were children's levels of energy and attention higher, but the group process helped the drawing follow-up.

## Evaluation of the Activity

The activity was more successful than the films. Actors in the wraparound transformed letters from the alphabet into different things, much the way Harold transforms the letter *A* into the hat and head of a giant witch. The activity sheet, another blank with a border, had images of crayons and pencils around the sides, along with the letters *A, C, S,* and *W*. It was suggested that viewers transform those letters into other things and then outline their own shapes, changing them into whatever they liked.

This sort of structured drawing worked quite well with youngsters 3–16. Interestingly, children seemed to put more energy into and got more out of watching the activity demonstration than in watching the films. They universally enjoyed the activity sheet, and, although they liked drawing with crayons, they especially enjoyed felt-tip markers.

## Suitability of the Activity

Children of all ages used the sheets creatively, and while preschoolers did better in group situations, our target population found this an entertaining project to do in their rooms. Those over 7 made pictures out of letters, while those under 5 mostly colored in the border and experimented with colors. Children 5–9 drew pictures or images from both films and used the activity sheet letters as well.

## Comments about the Wraparound

We used a gigantic five-foot pencil (from Think Big in New York City) as an introduction to HAROLD'S FAIRY TALE which we characterized as a do-it-yourself story, a draw-it-yourself adventure. Although a giant purple crayon would have been better, the pencil was both amusing and effective as a lead-in to the screening and the activity. Changing letters into shapes for the introduction to FELIX GETS THE CAN was highly visual and very effective. Viewers 7–10 particularly enjoyed that part of the follow-up.

It is noteworthy that the activity sheet for this program was the only one, aside from the board games, that succeeded visually on the television screen. Moreover, when we handed the sheets out prior to the program (which we learned was considerably more effective than distributing them afterwards), children got excited when they recognized the activity sheet on TV.

# CCTV Program #12

| | |
|---|---|
| **Activity:** | Modeling playdough. |
| **Materials:** | Playdough. |
| **Dexterity:** | Minimal to average. |
| **Age Level:** | 5–11. |

## WORM DANCES
(3 minutes/clay animation/nonverbal)

An upbeat scat and percussion music video in which one primal playdough shape turns into another. The colorful, eye-pleasing transformations and delightful wiggling to a carefree soundtrack make this film a perfect lead-in to clay or playdough activities. (This was repeated after WHAZZAT?)

## WHAZZAT?
(10 minutes/clay animation/nonverbal)

Six lively clay creatures change shape and move about, helping each other explore their environment. When the friends discover an unknown creature (in the section based on the Arab/Indian tale about the blind men and the elephant), they each describe it nonverbally from a different point of view. After several have depicted what they know about it, the group pools its resources and figures out what the creature is. In unison, all shout "ELEPHANT," the only word in this joyful classic.

## Evaluation of the Program

We recorded the responses of 31 viewers at 3 sites; their age range was 2–16, but most were 3–12. The program was a hit with all ages, but it worked best with children 5–10. WORM DANCES was successful all across the board. It not only had no problems, it often worked even better the second time.

WHAZZAT? suffered somewhat in the video transfer, both in terms of color and legibility, so it was not as effective as in film (see Playroom Film Program #7). We hope the problem was simply due to a poor copying job and that, with color balancing, other video transfers will be better.

Despite this legibility problem, the program as a whole was extremely successful. One of its appeals is that both films are nonverbal so there was no language problem for viewers with a poor command of English. Other strong points were the upbeat mood of both films, and the delightful possibilities the animation in each suggests for working with playdough or clay. This was also a wonderful program/activity for parents to share with their children.

One 10-year-old child who watched in his room said that he felt good during the entire program. A child of 5 whose right hand was in an IV splint went to the playroom and asked for more playdough after working for a while in his room. A 9-year-old girl in isolation, who was in terrible pain during the screening, worked with playdough for 2 whole days and produced an amazing trayful of small but highly imaginative sculptures.

The program worked for both solitary viewing and group screenings, but the highest activity motivation occurred in group situations. One particularly successful group screening with preschoolers included mothers who worked with their children. At another highly successful group screening, we gave children 3–8 some playdough to manipulate before they saw the program, and then we showed the program twice in a row.

## Evaluation of the Activity

Children largely experimented with the creative possibilities of playdough. They were highly motivated and inspired by the films, especially by WORM DANCES. Interestingly, the activity worked well for those with IVs as well as those in traction.

Our activity sheet offered the option of a drawing follow-up, but playdough was such a natural that, except for a few children who asked for crayons, coloring was negligible.

## Suitability of the Activity

Excellent for viewers 5–11 to do in their own rooms. Children 4 and younger seemed to need a small-group setting.

## Comments about the Wraparound

Viewers got a lot of energy from the films and were eager to start working with playdough. Perhaps we should begin the wraparound by working with playdough and not have a follow-up demonstration at all so that none of their enthusiasm dissipates. Clearly we should focus only on playdough.

Activity Sheet for CCTV Program #12

YOU CAN

DRAW ANIMALS

OR FORM THEM IN CLAY

BY STARTING WITH A BASIC SHAPE

AND ADDING DETAILS — EYES,

    EARS, LEGS, FEATHERS, ETC.

Activity Sheet for CCTV Program #13

# CCTV Program #13

| | |
|---|---|
| **Activity:** | Drawing a detective mystery. |
| **Materials:** | Activity sheets, crayons, markers, and pencils. |
| **Dexterity:** | Minimal to average. |
| **Age Level:** | 7–10. |

## KUUMBA
(8 minutes/cutout animation/dialog & narration)

A contemporary origins tale from Trinidad which explains how an ingenious boy invented the steel drum the night before the parade and carnival celebrations held in conjunction with Mardi Gras. The film makes excellent use of Caribbean music and, although somewhat primitive-looking, the child-made artwork is appealing.

## SOMETHING QUEER AT THE LIBRARY
(10 minutes/liveaction/dialog)

When Jill and Gwen decide to train Fletcher, a basset hound quite set in his ways, for an upcoming dog show, they go to the public library to do some research. Later, they discover that someone has cut all the pictures of Lhasa apsos from the books they borrowed. Their attempts to find the culprit, and save their own necks, result in some amusing slapstick.

## Evaluation of the Program

We recorded the responses of 28 viewers at 3 sites; their age range was 3–15, but most were 6–10. This combination of titles got a mixed review. KUUMBA was fine for all ages and worked well in all hospitals despite the various technical problems we encountered with TV monitors. Music is a very strong aspect of the film, and many children mentioned it and/or moved to it.

SOMETHING QUEER AT THE LIBRARY was a letdown after KUUMBA. For the most part, it is too choppy and too dialog-dependent. It absolutely failed on Downstate's small monitors and in rooms with faulty equipment. However, under optimal screening conditions, the program works well with children 7–10 (particularly girls) in good condition.

## Evaluation of the Activity

One of the actors in the wraparound used the program activity sheet to make up a comic-strip story about a girl who solves "The Case of the Missing Cookies." She explained that in her house cookies (paralleling the chocolate candy in SOMETHING QUEER AT THE LIBRARY) are always missing; she thought that if she did a detective story she might figure out who the culprit was.

The actor showed viewers a series of drawings. The first was the empty cookie jar. The second, and first clue, shows fingerprints on the cookie jar. (Fingerprints were another clue in SOMETHING QUEER AT THE LIBRARY). The third was a trail of cookie crumbs leading to her next-door neighbor's house. The fourth was a picture of her neighbor with cookie crumbs on her hands. The actor then suggested that viewers make up their own detective mystery. Of all the children observed, however, only a few imitated the story from the wraparound: 3 girls (ages 8, 9, and 12) and a boy of 10. Apparently, they were more motivated by the wraparound than by the films.

Since it was too unstructured, our activity sheet (another blank with a border) was not helpful. Two boys thought there was a mystery to be solved within the border, which would have been a great idea, but was not the case. Some children were disappointed because the sheet had nothing to do with KUUMBA. Others complained that the basset hound did not look like the one in SOMETHING QUEER AT THE LIBRARY. When a border has pictures, children want them to relate directly and often quite literally to the films.

## Suitability of the Activity

The idea of making up a detective mystery was very exciting to viewers 7–10, but they did not know how to execute it. Not only must we find a better film combination, we must develop a better way to present the activity so children can make up their own stories without too much adult assistance. (THE CASE OF THE ELEVATOR DUCK would be a suitable replacement for SOMETHING QUEER AT THE LIBRARY, especially in hospitals with a sizable black population.)

## Comments about the Wraparound

The introduction to SOMETHING QUEER AT THE LIBRARY, with its long-winded explanation of Lhasa apsos, was completely lost on viewers, and the problem-solving connection between the films was somewhat overshadowed by the detective story idea. Ideally, we should incorporate something from each film in the activity.

Our demonstration of the detective story was a step in the right direction, but if we want to attract older children we must not use crayons, which they regard as babyish. Above all we must provide a clear structure and spell out the steps essential to a detective story. Give viewers a simple breakdown, such as: (1) detective discovers the crime but there is no evidence of who did it; (2) detective finds a clue—the first evidence; (3) detective finds another clue; (4) using both clues and a little brainwork, detective figures out who did it; (5) case closed.

*The Sky Is Blue.* Courtesy: Films Incorporated.

*Tangram.* Courtesy: Pyramid Films.

*Tangram.* Courtesy: Pyramid Films.

*Jack and the Beanstalk.* Courtesy: Primrose Productions.

# PLAYROOM VIDEO PROGRAMS

## by Maureen Gaffney and Mary Ann Renz Bonarti

After documenting the results from our CCTV and playroom film programs, we planned 24 playroom video programs that incorporated all we had learned. Some were designed for preschool children, some for school age children. In addition, we designed others that worked with all or parts of both age groups. As in our earlier programs, children above and below the target age were included in most screenings.

Note that the age level indicated at the start of each program refers to the activity. Age levels for the pairing of tapes are listed under the program evaluation, as are age levels for each videotape in that program. However, the overall age levels for each tape are listed in the annotations section.

Video playroom programs were evaluated at 5 sites from January through April 1984. Sites included Bellevue Hospital, Downstate Medical Center, New York Hospital, St. Luke's/Roosevelt Medical Center, and Westchester County Medical Center. Program numbering bears no relationship to the overall order in which they were tested; however, if the same title is used several times, the order in which it is listed reflects the order in which it was tested.

Because the programs in this section represent the sum of what we learned in the course of the project, we documented our introductions to the tapes as well as the activities. We hope these "scripts" will serve as models for hospital programmers to follow and improve on. Nonprofit organizations (excepting those involved in media production or distribution) may reproduce them for staff or volunteers to use in face-to-face programs with children. However, these introductions cannot be used on television or in prerecorded programs of any sort without prior permission in writing from the Media Center for Children.

One word of warning: do not follow the introductions too rigidly in a playroom situation. They are merely guidelines. Sometimes we could not ask all the follow-up questions. Sometimes other things came up spontaneously. In addition, we always asked children to rate the videotapes. This was part of our evaluation process but also, as we learned long ago, something children in or out of the hospital enjoyed doing.

The activity sheets found in this section were designed to be copy masters and may be duplicated without limit under the same terms described for the "scripts" above. For information about conditions under which the tapes discussed herein may be used on hospitals' closed-circuit television systems, see the Preface.

# ACTIVITY/TITLE LISTING

Unlike our previous write-ups, we have listed below only the type of activity and the videotape titles for each program. This was done to emphasize how variously tapes can be used. It will be most informative to read all the write-ups for a title in the order listed. Subsequent programs were often—but not always—improvements on earlier ones.

#1. **Coloring/Playing a Board Game**
CHICK CHICK CHICK
ROSIE'S WALK

#2. **Drawing with a Magic Crayon**
HAROLD AND THE PURPLE CRAYON
A VISIT FROM SPACE

#3. **Drawing a Mystery Story**
L'AGE DOOR
THE CASE OF THE ELEVATOR DUCK

#4. **Drawing a Mystery Story**
RUSSIAN ROOSTER
THE CASE OF THE ELEVATOR DUCK

#5. **Drawing**
RUSSIAN ROOSTER
SOLO

#6. **Making a Collage**
THE CREATION OF BIRDS
A STORY, A STORY

#7. **Making a Magic Tree Collage**
THE CREATION OF BIRDS
THE MAGIC PEAR TREE

#8. **Making a Seasonal Collage**
HOMMAGE A FRANCOIS COUPERIN
THE CREATION OF BIRDS

#9. **Making a Collage**
MADELINE AND THE GYPSIES
ANANSI THE SPIDER

#10. **Making a Mural Collage**
ISLE OF JOY
ANANSI THE SPIDER

#11. **Making a Christmas Collage**
THE STORY OF CHRISTMAS
THE SNOWY DAY

#12. **Making a Collage**
THE SNOWY DAY
THE SKY IS BLUE

#13. **Making a Collage**
TANGRAM
THE SKY IS BLUE

#14. **Making Shadow Puppets or Tangrams**
TANGRAM
JACK AND THE BEANSTALK

#15. **Making Paper Bag Puppets**
PIERRE
A CHAIRY TALE

#16. **Making Finger Puppets**
HANDS
THE PRINCESS AND THE PEA

#17. **Making an Egg-carton Dragon**
THE MOLE AND THE TELEPHONE
TCHOU TCHOU

#18. **Making Musical Instruments**
KUUMBA
GERALD McBOING BOING

#19. **Mask-making**
THE MASKMAKER
WHERE THE WILD THINGS ARE

#20. **Drawing a Special Place**
BEING BY MYSELF
OH BROTHER, MY BROTHER

#21. **Drawing a Family Portrait**
MY BIG BROTHER
OH BROTHER, MY BROTHER

#22. **Modeling Playdough**
WORM DANCES
WHAZZAT?

#23. **Sculpting Playdough**
SOPHIE AND THE SCALES
THE FABLE OF HE AND SHE

#24. **Making Box Art**
CAPTAIN SILAS
CURIOUS GEORGE GOES TO THE HOSPITAL

# Playroom Video Program #1

| | |
|---|---|
| **Activity:** | Coloring/playing a board game. |
| **Materials:** | Activity sheets, crayons, markers, coins, paper or styrofoam cups. |
| **Dexterity:** | Minimal. |
| **Age Level:** | 6–8. |

## CHICK CHICK CHICK

(13 minutes/liveaction/nonverbal)

A highly stylized catalog with numerous close-ups of chickens, hens, and roosters. Scenes of an egg that slowly hatches during the course of this animal study are intercut with scenes of barnyard life outside the chicken coop.

## ROSIE'S WALK

(5 minutes/cel animation/narration)

A barnyard hen takes her afternoon constitutional across the yard, around the pond, over the haystack, past the mill, through the fence, under the beehives, and gets back home in time for dinner. As she strolls around the farm, Rosie fortuitously avoids the predatory maneuvers of a comically inept fox. Based on the book by Pat Hutchins and set to the tune of "Turkey in the Straw," this simple and nearly slow-motion slapstick is both droll and delightful.

## Introduction to the First Tape

"Both videotapes are about hens and chickens. Do you know where chickens come from? How are they born?" (Be sure to discuss hatching.) "Where do chickens live? What do they eat?"

"In the first tape a chicken is hatching from an egg while other baby chicks play, and eat, and do chicken things. One catches and eats a big bug because bugs taste good to chickens. During the tape you will also see other farm animals. You can tell us out loud what they are because this videotape has no words and no story. It is called CHICK CHICK CHICK."

Play the tape and do an image/sound skim: "What do you remember best from that video? Does anything you saw or heard stick out in your mind?" If you can, ask how the tape made children feel. "Was there anything you didn't understand? Do you have any questions or comments about the tape?"

## Introduction to the Second Tape

"The next videotape is also about a chicken. It is called ROSIE'S WALK and tells the story of a grown-up chicken named Rosie. Rosie the hen loves to walk around her farm. One day, as you will see, she is followed by a very hungry fox who hopes to eat her. But don't worry; the fox is rather silly and Rosie the hen gets home safe and sound. It's okay to talk out loud as you watch ROSIE'S WALK."

Play the tape and do an image/sound skim: "What do you remember best from that video? Does anything you saw or heard stick out in your mind?" If you can, ask how the tape made children feel. "Was there anything you didn't understand? Do you have any questions or comments about the tape?"

## Introduction to the Activity

"Here is a game you can play. (Hold up activity sheet.) "It is based on the walk that Rosie took. This path is like a map of Rosie's walk. Little markers will move around it. If you like, you can color it in. Here is one that I started." (Demonstrate.)

"When you have finished coloring the sheet, you can play the game. You can also play the game without coloring it beforehand.

1. This is a game for anywhere from 2 to 4 players. Each player should pick out a marker and each marker should be different. Anything small will do. Use buttons, erasers, markers from other board games, or simply fold up small pieces of colored paper.

2. Get a penny and a paper cup. The side of the penny with a person on it is called *heads;* the side with a building on it is called *tails.*

3. Decide which person will go first, which second, etc. One way is to flip the penny and ask everyone to call *heads* or *tails.* Those who guess incorrectly are eliminated until only one person is left. That person goes first. The person to his/her left goes second, and so on clockwise around the group.

4. To make a move, put a penny in the cup and shake it gently a few times. Then turn the cup upside down. If *heads* shows, move your marker 2 spaces. If *tails* shows, move only one space. Start at the hen house and

(moving clockwise around the board) follow the instructions on the path home.

5. The first person to get all the way round and back to the hen house is the winner. The game continues until everyone is safely home."

## Evaluation of the Program

We recorded the responses of 24 children at 4 sites. Their overall age range was 3–14, but most were 3–8. The program as a whole worked best with children 6–8.

ROSIE'S WALK is always a joy, especially with children 3–6 who understand and enjoy its humor, and respond physically to its up-beat music by tapping fingers or toes. But while ROSIE'S WALK worked with children as old as 8, those 9 or older found it babyish.

CHICK CHICK CHICK worked best with children 6 and older who liked seeing all the farm animals and particularly enjoyed it when "the egg hatched." Many appreciated the tape's humor, such as "when the cat scared the cow." A 10-year-old liked the way it was edited; he said "it was spread out and made you anticipate." However, children under 6 had trouble with CHICK CHICK CHICK. They were remarkably concerned about whether or not the new chick got together with its mother at the end (which is not shown). Typical preschoolers' questions were: "Do you think he knows he has a family?" and "Is the mommy going to get him?" Although it is possible to have children make up their own endings, this will not necessarily relieve their worries about the baby chick. For this reason, we do not recommend CHICK

CHICK CHICK for hospitalized children under 6. (Since it has great appeal for under-sixes, ROSIE'S WALK could be paired with another young children's tape, such as ONE LITTLE KITTEN, for a preschool program.)

## Comments about the Introductions

Before showing ROSIE'S WALK, it is important not only to let children know that foxes like to chase hens, but also that the fox in the videotape is pretty dumb and does not cause too much trouble. In addition to a verbal introduction, CHICK CHICK CHICK might work better with under-sevens and under-nines in poor condition if it were introduced with a series of photos of a baby chick hatching. (For a listing of suggested sources, see the long annotation of CHICK CHICK CHICK.)

## Evaluation of the Activity

This is a revision of Playroom Film Program #1 and CCTV Program #2. Through its title, its circular image, and its events, the board game was designed to reinforce the concept of going safely home. Although it had no bearing on CHICK CHICK CHICK (which was included in the program largely as a "support" for ROSIE'S WALK), the game worked unusually well. Half the test population was motivated to play it, but young children needed a fair amount of encouragement and a lot of time. Four out of 5 preschoolers simply colored the activity sheet, which they enjoyed immensely. This would be a suitable CCTV activity because it is simple, satisfying, and something a school age child can do in bed. A *four-star* program/activity!

# RULES OF THE GOING SAFELY HOME GAME

(Copyright 1985, Media Center for Children)

You may color in the board before beginning the game.

1. This is a game for two, three or four players. Each player should pick out a marker — each marker should be different. Anything small will do — use buttons, erasers, markers from other board games, or you can fold up small pieces of different colored papers.

2. You need a penny and a paper cup. The side of the penny with a person on it is called "heads"; the side with a building on it is called "tails".

3. Decide who will go first, who second, who third and fourth. One way to decide is to flip the penny and ask everyone to call heads or tails. Those who guess incorrectly are eliminated until only one person is left. That person goes first. The person on his/her left goes second and so on clockwise around the board.

3. To play the game, put the penny in the cup and shake it gently a few times. Then turn the cup upside down. If heads is showing, move your marker two spaces.
If tails is showing, only move one space. Then it is the next person's turn.
Start at the hen house and (going clockwise around the board) follow the instructions on the path.

4. The first person to get all the way round and back to the hen house is the winner. The game continues until everyone is safely home.

*Using Media to Make Kids Feel Good,* by Maureen Gaffney. Published by Oryx Press, 2214 N. Central, Phoenix, AZ 85004, 1988.

## Be the first chicken to get safely home

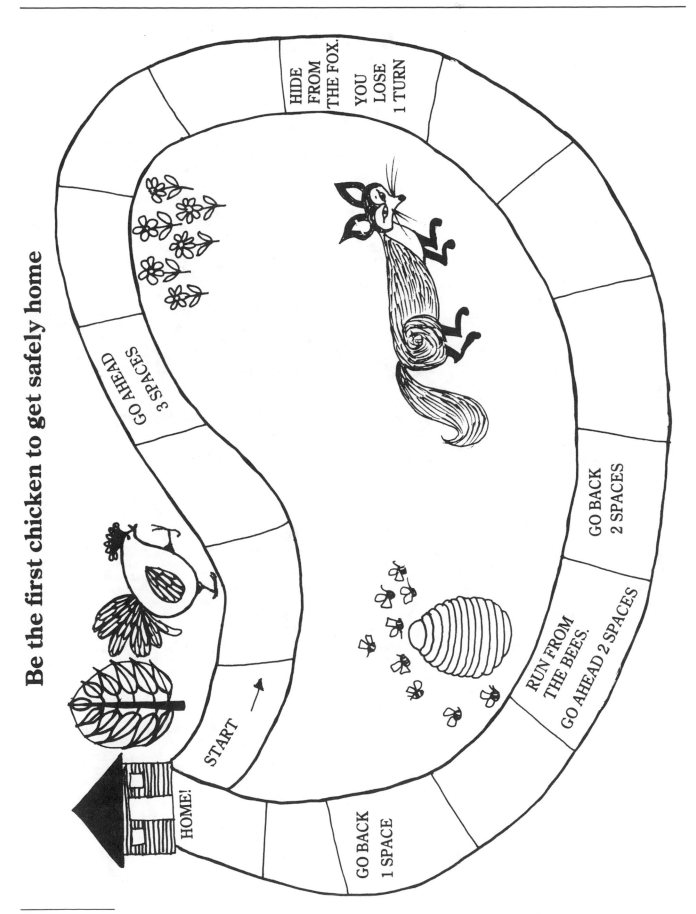

HIDE FROM THE FOX. YOU LOSE 1 TURN

GO AHEAD 3 SPACES

GO BACK 2 SPACES

RUN FROM THE BEES. GO AHEAD 2 SPACES

START

GO BACK 1 SPACE

HOME!

*Using Media to Make Kids Feel Good,* by Maureen Gaffney. Published by Oryx Press, 2214 N. Central, Phoenix, AZ 85004, 1988.

# Playroom Video Program #2

| | |
|---|---|
| **Activity:** | Drawing with a magic crayon. |
| **Materials:** | Construction paper or newsprint and crayons. |
| **Dexterity:** | Minimal. |
| **Age Level:** | 3–9. |

## HAROLD AND THE PURPLE CRAYON
(8 minutes/cel animation/narration)

Based on Crockett Johnson's picturebook, this is the droll story of an independent-minded toddler who draws himself in and out of adventures by means of his purple crayon. Very slow and low-key, the spare and monochromatic line drawings are a cross between children's artwork and coloring book illustrations.

## A VISIT FROM SPACE
(11 minutes/animation/minimal narration)

In this amusing and pleasant fantasy, a young girl uses the technique she devised to get apples from a tree to help a homesick young extraterrestrial return to outer space. Between brief introductory and closing comments by a narrator, the simple and well-structured story is communicated nonverbally through gesture and pseudo-vocalizations.

## Introduction to the First Tape

"Both videotapes are about kids who use their imaginations to solve their problems. The first one is called HAROLD AND THE PURPLE CRAYON. Does anyone know the Harold books?" (If so, ask children how he solves his problems. If not, go on.) "Harold is a very clever boy and he uses a purple crayon whenever he gets into trouble. As we watch the tape, each of us is going to hold a magic purple crayon—unless you prefer another color. Then, whenever Harold gets into trouble, we will draw something in the air to help him get out of trouble. Later we will draw on paper. For now, let's watch the story of HAROLD AND THE PURPLE CRAYON. Keep your magic crayons ready to help if he gets into trouble."

Play the tape and do an image/sound skim: "What do you remember best from that video? Does anything you saw or heard stick out in your mind?" If you can, ask how the tape made children feel. "Was there anything you didn't understand? Do you have any questions or comments about the tape?"

## Introduction to the Second Tape

"The next videotape is called A VISIT FROM SPACE. It's about a young girl who also uses her imagination. She does not have a magic crayon like Harold does, but she finds other ways to solve her problems, such as how to get apples from a very tall tree and how to help a new friend."

"Although it has a few words at the beginning and the end, mostly it has no words so you can talk out loud as you watch A VISIT FROM SPACE."

Play the tape and do an image/sound skim: "What do you remember best from that video? Does anything you saw or heard stick out in your mind?" If you can, ask how the tape made children feel. "Was there anything you didn't understand? Do you have any questions or comments about the tape?"

## Introduction to the Activity

"Now *you* can take your magic crayon and draw your own adventure, just like Harold did. Or you can draw an adventure like the one in A VISIT FROM SPACE. If you want, you can draw your favorite images or scenes from both tapes."

## Evaluation of the Program

We recorded the responses of 17 children at 4 sites. Their overall age range was 2–14, but most were 5–9. Initially we showed A VISIT FROM SPACE first. However, because it was the clear preference of the pair, showing it first dissipated children's interest in the slower and less active HAROLD AND THE PURPLE CRAYON. Consequently, we changed the screening order.

When we showed HAROLD AND THE PURPLE CRAYON first, children enjoyed labeling what Harold was drawing, anticipated what was going to happen, and were pleased that Harold got home safe and sound. For most children, the highlight of the tape was the dragon. HAROLD AND THE PURPLE CRAYON works best with viewers 3–7.

A VISIT FROM SPACE was a genuine delight and worked with the entire age range (3–14) despite the fact that over-tens found it babyish. Children were amused by the little space creatures and enjoyed the relationship between the girl and the extraterrestrial. Most children mentioned that they liked best "when he went up and got home."

Child Life staff praised this program in particular because the videotapes worked well together and effectively emphasized the going home theme. They commented on how expressive children were in their artwork—a clear indication of *four-star* status.

## Comments about the Introductions

Although the mere mention of a dragon can get children excited and involved, we do not recommend saying anything about it in introducing HAROLD AND THE PURPLE CRAYON. Such an introduction might stimulate children's imaginations so that the tape could not live up to their expectations. It is better to let children discover the dragon (who only plays a minor part) for themselves. Obviously, it could be used afterwards in children's follow-ups.

## Evaluation of the Activity

We hoped children would get metaphoric support from the tapes' young protagonists. Using a "magic crayon" was simply a device to motivate children to express themselves by drawing. (This is a variation on Playroom Film Program #8.) Over 70% of the test population did a drawing, but the videotape/activity combination worked best for children 3–9. While they enjoyed the program, older children (particularly boys) were not interested in drawing. Those who did so drew mostly from A VISIT FROM SPACE. There were many images of houses, trees, plants, flying saucers, kites, and apple cores—although dragons were also present in many children's pictures.

# Playroom Video Program #3

| | |
|---|---|
| **Activity:** | Drawing a mystery story. |
| **Materials:** | Photocopied sheets (described below), pencils, felt-tip markers. |
| **Dexterity:** | Minimal to average. |
| **Age Level:** | 10–14. |

## L'AGE DOOR
(2 minutes/line animation/nonverbal)

An unusual and somewhat existential mystery. A man goes through dozens of doors in search of something. His quest is enacted in silence until the very end when, picking up a large lid or door, the man shuts the viewer out and the sound of a slamming door is heard.

## THE CASE OF THE ELEVATOR DUCK
(17 minutes/liveaction/dialog & narration)

Based on the book by Polly Berrien Berends, this is a delightful detective story about Gilbert, a black urban preadolescent, who solves the case of what to do with a duck he finds in the elevator of his "no pets" housing project.

## Introduction to the First Tape

"Both videotapes are mysteries. Do you like mystery stories?" (Children might talk about books they have read or movies, etc.)

"The first mystery is very very short and is called L'AGE DOOR. It doesn't really have a story, but the tape itself is something of a mystery. The title gives a clue to what it's about; it names something you'll see a lot of in the tape."

"As you watch it, see if you can guess what the man in L'AGE DOOR is looking for. If you have any ideas, say them out loud because this videotape has no sound at all until the very end. In fact you can supply the dialog and sound effects yourselves if you wish."

Play the tape and do an image/sound skim: "What do you remember best from that video? Does anything you saw or heard stick out in your mind?" If you can, ask how the tape made children feel. "Was there anything you didn't understand? Do you have any questions or comments about the tape?" Then ask children what the man was looking for.

## Introduction to the Second Tape

"The next videotape is also a mystery. It is longer and tells a story about a boy named Gilbert. Gilbert lives in a city housing project with his mom and enjoys playing detective and solving mysteries. (If your group is unfamiliar with them, define a housing project as a building that is owned by the city and has strict rules about what people can or cannot do if they rent an apartment there.)

"Like the first tape, the title of the second one will give you some clues. It's called THE CASE OF THE ELEVATOR DUCK. Before we watch it, there is one thing you should know; no pets are allowed to live in Gilbert's building. His housing project even has guards to make sure that everybody obeys the rules. If anyone broke a rule, they would have to move out of the building."

"Let's watch Gilbert solve THE CASE OF THE ELEVATOR DUCK. Remember, it's okay to talk out loud during the tape."

Play the tape and do an image/sound skim: "What do you remember best from that video? Does anything you saw or heard stick out in your mind?" If you can, ask how the tape made children feel. "Was there anything you didn't understand? Do you have any questions or comments about the tape?"

## Introduction to the Activity

"How would you like to make up your own mystery story? One way to do it is to tell the story in a few steps. Let me show you a mystery story I made in pictures—one in which I am a detective." (Demonstrate as you explain the steps.)

"First, I discover there is a mystery to be solved and I decide to take the case. Second, I think of something that might solve the mystery, only it doesn't work. Third, I try something even better to solve the mystery. Fourth, I solve the mystery and my case is closed."

Present children with 4 sheets of paper (mimeographed or photocopied from your originals). On the first sheet, print the following headline: "#1. I discover the mystery and take the case." On the second, print: "#2. I think of a solution." On the third: "#3. My first guess didn't work, so I think of another." On the fourth: "#4. I solve the mystery and the case is closed."

On the sheets you provide, ask children to draw or cut out captions and make collages using magazine images. They can also write their own dialog (or the entire story) if they prefer to do that. Offer suggestions if they get stuck.

## Evaluation of the Program

We recorded the responses of 16 children at 3 sites. Their overall age range was 5–15, but most were 5–11. Although the videotapes were poorly matched, the program was carried by THE CASE OF THE ELEVATOR DUCK, which worked with children of all ages, particularly because of its captivating protagonist and amusing duck. The only problem we encountered was when we showed it on poor equipment; bad audio made the dialog almost impossible to understand. Also, when screening groups were large and boisterous they had trouble following the story because they could not hear what Gilbert was saying.

L'AGE DOOR, on the other hand, was not anywhere near as appealing as its partner and contributed nothing to the activity. Children reacted to it in a decidedly negative way. Its brevity and abstract images, coupled with a lack of sound, story, and color made it quite difficult. While the least negative response was from viewers 7–9, those under 7 neither liked nor understood L'AGE DOOR. Child Life staff at one site considered the tape to be "ominous," observing that the in-out motion of the man through the doors was too much like the chronically ill child's experience of going in and out of the hospital. They found it rather depressing, particularly because it had no clear resolution. In evaluating children's responses, we could not detect any feelings of depression; however, the tape failed to engage them in any meaningful way and many disliked it.

## Evaluation of the Activity

L'AGE DOOR was brief enough to be combined with THE CASE OF THE ELEVATOR DUCK without making the screening overlong, and it used pencil-like line animation which we hoped would motivate drawing. Making a mystery story was a "normal" children's activity with no specifically therapeutic intent. At some sites we gave children the option of telling their story in collage, but no one tried that so we dropped it.)

Despite its structure, the drawing/storytelling activity proved rather difficult—perhaps it was too conceptual. It was more than children under 9 could do by themselves. But another problem may have been that, without the stimulation of an appealing animated tape, the materials themselves (plain paper and pencils or markers) were not sufficient to motivate drawing.

While close to half the test population did some kind of drawing follow-up, only 3 (ages 11, 12, and 14) actually completed an entire mystery story—and then only with one-on-one help from adults. An optional activity for under-tens would be to give them an activity sheet with the outline of an empty elevator on it. They could color it and draw (or glue a picture of) something that one day, quite mysteriously, they might find in the elevator.

# Playroom Video Program #4

| | |
|---|---|
| **Activity:** | Drawing a mystery story. |
| **Materials:** | Photocopied sheets (described below), pencils, felt-tip markers. |
| **Dexterity:** | Minimal to average. |
| **Age Level:** | 6–12. |

## RUSSIAN ROOSTER
(3 minutes/cameraless animation/nonverbal)

This comic music video is set to an energized orchestral version of Rimsky-Korsakov's overture to "Le Coq d'Or." It tells the story of a somewhat *nebbish* rooster that looks like a chicken and manages to outwit 3 hunters. With an amusing mix of airplane and swimming metaphors, the videotape demonstrates that not only does practice make perfect—well, almost perfect—but also that the underdog sometimes comes out on top.

## THE CASE OF THE ELEVATOR DUCK
(17 minutes/liveaction/dialog & narration)

Based on the book by Polly Berrien Berends, this is a delightful detective story about Gilbert, a black urban preadolescent, who solves the case of what to do with a duck he finds in the elevator of his "no pets" housing project.

## Introduction to the First Tape

"Both videotapes have characters who solve tough problems. The first is RUSSIAN ROOSTER, a very short cartoon. It tells an unusual story about a happy-go-lucky rooster who learns to fly and sets off on a long trip. Things go pretty well until hunters try to capture him. But don't worry because the rooster outsmarts the hunters, who aren't too intelligent, and everything turns out fine. The tape has no words so you can talk out loud as you watch RUSSIAN ROOSTER."

Play the tape and do an image/sound skim: "What do you remember best from that video? Does anything you saw or heard stick out in your mind?" If you can, ask how the tape made children feel. "Was there anything you didn't understand? Do you have any questions or comments about the tape?"

## Introduction to the Second Tape

"In the next videotape, you will meet a boy named Gilbert, who lives in a New York City housing project with his mom and enjoys playing detective. Like the rooster, he has a problem to solve. His problem is solving a mystery. The title of the tape will give you an idea of what the mystery is about. The story is called THE CASE OF THE ELEVATOR DUCK."

(If your group is unfamiliar with them, define a housing project as a building that is owned by the city and has strict rules about what people can or cannot do if they rent an apartment there.)

"Before we watch the tape, there is one thing you should know; no pets are allowed to live in Gilbert's building. His housing project even has guards to make sure that everybody obeys the rules. If anyone broke a rule, they would have to move out of the building."

"Let's watch Gilbert solve his problem in THE CASE OF THE ELEVATOR DUCK. Remember, it's okay to talk out loud as you watch."

Play the tape and do an image/sound skim: "What do you remember best from that video? Does anything you saw or heard stick out in your mind?" If you can, ask how the tape made children feel. "Was there anything you didn't understand? Do you have any questions or comments about the tape?"

## Introduction to the Activity

"Would you like to make up your own mystery story, a mystery story in which you are the detective? One way to do so is to tell the story in 4 steps. Let me show you a mystery story I drew." (Demonstrate as you explain the steps.)

"First, I discover that there is a mystery to be solved and decide to take the case. Second, I find a clue. Third, I try to solve the mystery. Fourth, my case is closed."

Present children with 4 sheets of paper (mimeographed or photocopied from your originals). On the first sheet, neatly print the following head-line: "#1. I discover the mystery and take the case." On the second, print: "#2. I find a clue." On the third, print: "#3. I think of how to solve the case." On the last: "#4. My case is closed."

Ask children to draw on the sheets or cut out captions and make collages using magazine images. They can also write their own dialog or the entire story if they prefer this to drawing or collage. Offer suggestions if they get stuck; monsters or aliens and things that disappear or suddenly appear are fitting subjects for mysteries.

## Evaluation of the Program

We recorded the responses of 8 children at 2 sites. Their overall age range was 4–12, but most were 8–10. After the poor reception of L'AGE DOOR, we sought a replacement that had the same properties, particularly brevity and animation. Since we could not find another mystery, we chose a tape that had a problem-solving theme.

This genuinely agreeable pairing resulted in a highly successful program. Although we only screened the program twice, at both screenings children laughed throughout RUSSIAN ROOSTER and said they liked best "when the bird caught the hunters" and "when he was flying through the colors." Everyone responded well to Gilbert, the other characters, and the urban setting. Not surprisingly THE CASE OF THE ELEVATOR DUCK held special appeal for boys—particularly for black boys.

## Comments about the Introductions

Children need a focus and a point of view from which to experience RUSSIAN ROOSTER or it may seem too abstract. The introduction was effective in establishing an appropriate framework for the tape.

## Evaluation of the Activity

This proved to be a *four-star* program/activity. Unlike the response to Playroom Video Program #3, children were highly motivated and over half the test population did the follow-up (a simplification of the previous one). Children's stories were fascinating. Some were about pets at home. One was about a mysterious ghost who wanted food. Another (by an extremely shy 12-year-old boy) was about a mysterious shadow.

Drawing a mystery worked best with children 6–12, although the lower end of that age range needed adult assistance. The activity presented no problems for patients with IVs or in traction (who had special boards to lean on).

# Playroom Video Program #5

| | |
|---|---|
| **Activity:** | Drawing. |
| **Materials:** | White and colored paper, pencils, and markers. |
| **Dexterity:** | Minimal. |
| **Age Level:** | 9–10. |

## RUSSIAN ROOSTER
(3 minutes/cameraless animation/nonverbal)

This comic music video is set to an energized orchestral version of Rimsky-Korsakov's overture to "Le Coq d'Or." It tells the story of a somewhat *nebbish* rooster that looks like a chicken and manages to outwit 3 hunters. With an amusing mix of airplane and swimming metaphors, the videotape demonstrates that not only does practice make perfect—well, almost perfect—but also that the underdog sometimes comes out on top.

## SOLO
(15 minutes/liveaction/nonverbal)

A genuine cliff-hanger, as well as something of a metaphor for solving insurmountable problems, this well-shot dramatic story (with the look of a documentary) shows how one man makes a successful solo ascent of a rugged mountain. In a rocky crevice along the way, he finds a small tree frog. The climber carries the amphibian with him as he goes up, and releases it in a stream on the way down.

## Introduction to the First Tape

"Both videotapes are about characters who face danger. Fortunately, both characters find ways to overcome the danger and both tapes have happy endings."

"The first tape is a cartoon called RUSSIAN ROOSTER. It tells an unusual story about a happy-go-lucky rooster who learns to fly and goes on a trip. One day, however, some hunters try to capture the rooster. Things get pretty exciting, especially near the end. But don't worry, the rooster outsmarts the hunters, who aren't too intelligent, and everything turns out okay. The tape is very short and has no words so you can talk out loud as you watch RUSSIAN ROOSTER."

Play the tape and do an image/sound skim: "What do you remember best from that video? Does anything you saw or heard stick out in your mind?" If you can, ask how the tape made children feel.

"Was there anything you didn't understand? Do you have any questions or comments about the tape?"

## Introduction to the Second Tape

"The next videotape is about a mountain climber who wants to get to the top of a mountain. The tape is quite dramatic and there may be times when you think he just won't make it. It might even be a little scary, but don't worry because he does make it and the ending is happy."

"Although it looks real, like a documentary, the tape is actually a made-up story—with an actor—about how one man responds to a tough challenge. It is called SOLO, which means to do something alone. The tape does not have any words, so feel free to talk out loud. Let's watch SOLO."

Play the tape and do an image/sound skim: "What do you remember best from that video? Does anything you saw or heard stick out in your mind?" If you can, ask how the tape made children feel. "Was there anything you didn't understand? Do you have any questions or comments about the tape?"

## Introduction to the Activity

"Now you can create your favorite scene from either story. You can do it as a collage, a drawing, or a combination of both. Here are some materials to use."

Show children the materials available. Be sure they are easy to see and easy to reach. If anyone gets stuck for ideas, suggest that they depict or describe the mountain climber dangling from the cliff and almost losing his grip; the mountain climber's scene with the frog; the rooster flying away from hunters; the hunters being tricked by the rooster; or any challenge your children have had to deal with in their own lives. Children might prefer to make up a story about overcoming obstacles and illustrate it with a collage or drawing.

## Evaluation of the Program

We recorded the responses of 15 children at 4 sites. Their overall age range was 4–14, but most were 6–9. The program worked best for children 8–14 in good condition and in groups of at least 4 since the group provides emotional support that helps children enjoy its dramatic tension.

In RUSSIAN ROOSTER children related to the bird's cleverness in tricking the hunters and over-eights commented on the justice of the ending. Children especially liked "when the rooster flew away from the hunter" and "when the rooster caught the big guys."

One 9-year-old pretended the tape was a video game he was playing, which was perfect for this fast-paced work and gave the child a sense of control. An 8-year-old said the music was "scary" but all in all seemed to enjoy it.

SOLO was too sophisticated for and sometimes frightening to under-eights, but children 8–14 in good condition really enjoyed it in the context of a group.

## Comments about the Introductions

Make sure that children understand what the term solo means.

## Evaluation of the Activity

Although SOLO and THE FABLE OF HE AND SHE worked quite well together in Playroom Film Program #15, we wanted to try another partner with SOLO that would reinforce the theme of overcoming obstacles as well as motivate drawing. Unfortunately, the activity lacked both novelty and structure. Neither drawing nor storytelling appeal to older children unless they are structured in unusual ways. Only 2, both 9-year-olds, completed the activity. One drew a woman mountain climber and the other worked one-on-one with a Child Life specialist on a story about his imaginary adventures on a mountain. Discussion might be the best follow-up with preadolescents and young adolescents.

# Playroom Video Program #6

| | |
|---|---|
| **Activity:** | Collage. |
| **Materials:** | Construction paper, pencils, markers, scissors, glue-sticks. |
| **Dexterity:** | Average, except for those with IVs. |
| **Age Level:** | 7–9. |

## THE CREATION OF BIRDS

(10 minutes/cutout animation/nonverbal)

A wordless MicMac legend about the origin of birds, this tender, slow-moving videotape about the seasons makes effective use of animal symbolism, respectively the Howling Autumn Wolf and the Winter Snow Bear, and features a female protagonist.

## A STORY, A STORY

(10 minutes/cel animation/narration)

An African folktale about the origin of stories in which Ananse the Spiderman (in human form) accomplishes 3 tasks: capturing Osebo, the leopard of the terrible teeth; trapping Mmboro, the hornet who stings like fire; and catching Mmoatia, the fairy whom men never see. He does this, bringing the creatures to the sky god Nyame, in order to buy his box of stories.

## Introduction to the First Tape

"Both videotapes have to do with how things began. The first is called THE CREATION OF BIRDS. It's a MicMac legend from Canada that takes place before there were any birds on earth. The story begins in the summer when it's warm and there are lots of animals wandering around. You'll see some Native children playing with their grandfather while their parents are busy working."

"After a while, when you see a giant monster called Wind Wolf blowing all the leaves from the trees, that means autumn is coming. The wolf is a symbol for autumn. When a big white polar bear comes, what season do you think the bear stands for?" (Hopefully, children will say winter.)

"THE CREATION OF BIRDS is made from animated cutouts. We'll do an activity with cutouts later. For now, let's watch the tape. Although the writing is in French, the English translation for the title is THE CREATION OF BIRDS. It has no words, so you can talk out loud as you watch."

Play the tape and do an image/sound skim: "What do you remember best from that video? Does anything you saw or heard stick out in your mind?" If you can, ask how the tape made children feel. "Was there anything you didn't understand? Do you have any questions or comments about the tape?"

## Introduction to the Second Tape

"What would it be like if there were no stories? No one would have made the videotape we just saw if there were no stories in the world. The second videotape is an African folktale about where stories came from. It's called A STORY, A STORY and it stars Ananse the spiderman. This spiderman is not the same one you know from TV or the comics. He is a little old African—half-man, half-spider—and, although he is small, he is exceptionally smart."

"Ananse, the African spiderman, lived at a time when there were no stories on earth. So he spun a web to the sky kingdom and asked the sky god Nyame (rhymes with *Miami*) for his box of stories. Nyame said he would trade the stories for 3 things: Osebo (*o-SAY-bo*) the leopard of the terrible teeth; Mmboro (*mum-BURRO*), the hornets who sting like fire; and Mmoatia (*mwa-TEE-ah*), the fairy that people seldom see."

"Let's watch A STORY, A STORY and see if Ananse can get those 3 things for Nyame, in return for which Nyame has promised to trade the spiderman his box of stories."

Play the tape and do an image/sound skim: "What do you remember best from that video? Does anything you saw or heard stick out in your mind?" If you can, ask how the tape made children feel. "Was there anything you didn't understand? Do you have any questions or comments about the tape?"

## Introduction to the Activity

"Can you remember your favorite image or picture from either of the videotapes? Think of that image and see if you can make it into a collage by cutting out shapes and gluing them onto paper." Show children a piece of construction paper cut into a bird-like image—or whatever you like from either film—as a model.

## Evaluation of the Program

We recorded the responses of 15 children at 3 sites. Their overall age range was 3–9; most were between 6–9. This combination worked for the entire age range, but it was best with over-sixes. Because there were none available on the days we tried this program, we did not test it with over-nines, but the program would probably succeed with older children up to the age of 12.

THE CREATION OF BIRDS was the stronger of the pair and worked for the entire age range. Many children said the part they liked best was when "the girl went from sad to happy." Most children used its imagery in their collages.

A STORY, A STORY has effective repetition and wonderful music, but its images are fairly static so it is only moderately energizing. The tape is also very dialog-dependent which makes it hard for non-English speaking children and those in poor condition to follow.

## Comments about the Introductions

The discussion and questions about the wolf and the polar bear set children up for the change of seasons in the videotape. And since children seem to ignore the fact that the adults' canoes are sunk by the Wind Wolf, we do not mention it in the introduction to THE CREATION OF BIRDS. However, it is important to mention that the wolf looks like a monster, and that the title appears in French. In preparing children for A STORY, A STORY, explain that Ananse the spiderman is not the super-hero Spiderman they see on TV cartoons or in comics.

## Evaluation of the Activity

Although THE CREATION OF BIRDS had been quite effective when paired with ANANSI THE SPIDER in CCTV Program #1, we wanted to try a variation that might appeal to slightly older children. Unfortunately, no children over 9 were available on the days we tried this program.

As in the past, THE CREATION OF BIRDS proved to be the stronger tape and had a greater impact on children's collages than did A STORY, A STORY. Nonetheless, this was a *four-star* program/activity. Children were highly motivated and close to 90% of the test population made collages. Interestingly, several contained images of houses (possibly inspired by the seeking shelter theme in THE CREATION OF BIRDS).

The activity seemed most successful with children 7–9 in good condition. Children 7-9 in poor condition lacked the energy to do creative work in this mode. Preschoolers enjoyed simply experimenting with glue.

# Playroom Video Program #7

| | |
|---|---|
| **Activity:** | Collage. |
| **Materials:** | Construction paper, pre-cut trees without leaves, pencils, markers, crayons, scissors, and glue-sticks. |
| **Dexterity:** | Average, except for those with IVs. |
| **Age Level:** | 8–12. |

## THE CREATION OF BIRDS
(10 minutes/cutout animation/nonverbal)

A wordless MicMac legend about the origin of birds, this tender, slow-moving videotape about the seasons makes effective use of animal symbolism, respectively the Howling Autumn Wolf and the Winter Snow Bear, and features a female protagonist.

## THE MAGIC PEAR TREE
(5 minutes/shadow puppet animation/narration)

A slow and rather wordy Chinese folktale about selfishness which uses traditional Asian shadow-puppets. When a hungry old man asks a fruit peddler for a pear, he is coldly rebuffed. But the peddler is taught a lesson by the old man's generosity, and his magical justice.

## Introduction to the First Tape

"Both videotapes have something to do with magic and something to do with trees. The first story is called THE CREATION OF BIRDS. It's a MicMac legend from Canada and in it you will see some Native children playing with their grandfather while their parents are busy working. After a while, a giant monster Wind Wolf comes out of the water and blows all the leaves from the trees. The Wind Wolf brings autumn. Later, a giant polar bear brings winter."

"The story takes place a long time ago, before there were any birds. Watch to see what happens that is like magic. The tape has no words, so it's okay to talk out loud as you watch THE CREATION OF BIRDS."

Play the tape and do an image/sound skim: "What do you remember best from that video? Does anything you saw or heard stick out in your mind?" If you can, ask how the tape made children feel. "Was there anything you didn't understand? Do you have any questions or comments about the tape?"

Then ask, "What was the magic in the story? Who made the birds and how did he do it?" Children might say god or the Indian chief. Identify him

as Glooscap, a mythical, god-like helper to the MicMac people.

## Introduction to the Second Tape

"In the first story the magic happened when Glooscap turned tree leaves into birds. The next story also has something to do with a tree. Called the THE MAGIC PEAR TREE, it takes place in China a long time ago and uses shadow puppets dressed in traditional Chinese costumes. As the story begins, a greedy peddler is selling his fruits on a really hot day. Let's see what happens when a poor old farmer comes along. Watch for the magic in THE MAGIC PEAR TREE."

Play the tape and do an image/sound skim: "What do you remember best from that video? Does anything you saw or heard stick out in your mind?" If you can, ask how the tape made children feel. "Was there anything you didn't understand? Do you have any questions or comments about the tape?" Then ask, "What magic things do you remember from that story?"

## Introduction to the Activity

"Both tapes had magic trees in them. If you like, you can make your own magic tree collage. I cut this tree out of construction paper and glued it onto another piece of construction paper." (Demonstrate.) "What could I add to this tree that would make it look magical? What would you add?"

Encourage children to think up their own magic details or copy what they liked from the videotapes. Providing pre-cut tree shapes is helpful and sometimes essential for younger children.

## Evaluation of the Program

We recorded the responses of 10 children at 2 sites. Their overall age range was 8–15, but most were 8–12. In part because these tapes balanced each other well and in part because magic is an appealing subject, the program was an unusual success, especially with children 8–12. And although we did not test this program with anyone below 8 (none were available on the days we tried it), children 6-7 in good condition might also enjoy it.

Focusing on magic in THE CREATION OF BIRDS is a slight stretch and ignores its seasonal theme, but the tape worked wonderfully in combination with THE MAGIC PEAR TREE and, because of its lack of words, it got children talking and actively participating from the very start. THE MAGIC PEAR TREE also worked extremely well. Child Life staff at one site commented that its theme of justice was quite important to children.

## Comments about the Introductions

Because children described the Wind Wolf in THE CREATION OF BIRDS as a monster who comes out of the water, it is essential to refer to it as such in your introduction. If it is so, be sure to warn viewers that the title of the videotape is in French.

## Evaluation of the Activity

We knew that THE CREATION OF BIRDS was a fantastic motivator for collage. In this program we wanted to focus on a tree theme and encourage children to use it as a symbol in their artwork. Although pre-cut shapes did not foster great originality, participants enjoyed and benefited from the low-key atmosphere. All but one child made magic trees; the hold-out was a teenage boy. Children with IVs required assistance, but even they made collages. One child completed a tree with his left hand while his right arm was in a cast. A *four-star* program/activity!

# Playroom Video Program #8

| | |
|---|---|
| **Activity:** | Collage. |
| **Materials:** | Construction paper, pencils, markers, crayons, scissors, and glue-sticks. |
| **Dexterity:** | Average, except for those with IVs. |
| **Age Level:** | 6–14. |

## HOMMAGE A FRANCOIS COUPERIN
(2 minutes/animation/nonverbal)

Something of a classical music video, this delicate, impressionist-baroque mood piece is suggestive of spring/summer. Its subtle and exquisite ballet of butterflies and blades of grass is choreographed to a harpsichord study by French composer Couperin. There are 2 musical variations (the second more complex than the first) which are echoed visually by single and multiple images. Titles (in script) introduce "Variation 1" and "Variation 2."

## THE CREATION OF BIRDS
(10 minutes/cutout animation/nonverbal)

A wordless MicMac legend about the origin of birds, this tender, slow-moving videotape about the seasons makes effective use of animal symbolism, respectively the Howling Autumn Wolf and the Winter Snow Bear, and features a female protagonist.

## Introduction to the First Tape

"Both videotapes have something to do with the seasons. Do you have a favorite season? What pictures or images come into your mind when you

think of your favorite season?" (If no one responds, mention your favorite season/image, for example, autumn and bright orange pumpkins.)

"What do you like to do in your favorite season?" (If no one responds, you could say that in the autumn you like to go walking in the country.)

"The first tape we will see is called HOMMAGE A FRANCOIS COUPERIN. That's French. *Hommage* means that the tape is celebrating Francois Couperin, a composer of old-fashioned music. When the man who made the videotape hears Couperin's music he thinks of a season and something special that happens during that time of year. Let's watch and see what it is."

"The tape has 2 parts: "Variation 1" and "Variation 2." It has no story and no words so you may talk out loud as you watch. HOMMAGE A FRANCOIS COUPERIN is also very short."

Play the tape and do an image/sound skim: "What do you remember best from that video? Does anything you saw or heard stick out in your mind?" If you can, ask how the tape made children feel. "Was there anything you didn't understand? Do you have any questions or comments about the tape?" Then ask if children would like to see the tape again. If so, screen it. If not, go on.

## Introduction to the Second Tape

"The next videotape is called THE CREATION OF BIRDS. It's a MicMac legend from Canada that takes place before there were any birds on earth. The story begins in the summer when it's warm and there are lots of animals wandering around. You will see some

Native children playing with their grandfather while their parents are busy working."

"After a while, a giant monster called Wind Wolf comes out of the water. Wind Wolf blows all the leaves from the trees. The monster-wolf is a symbol for autumn. When a big white polar bear comes, what season do you think the bear stands for?" (Hopefully, children will say winter.)

"THE CREATION OF BIRDS is made from animated cutouts. We'll do an activity with cutouts later. For now, let's watch the videotape. Although written in French, the English translation for the title is THE CREATION OF BIRDS. The tape has no words, so you can talk out loud as you watch."

Play the tape and do an image/sound skim: "What do you remember best from that video? Does anything you saw or heard stick out in your mind?" If you can, ask how the tape made children feel. "Was there anything you didn't understand? Do you have any questions or comments about the tape?"

## Introduction to the Activity

"Now you can do a collage about your favorite season. The collage can be either a picture or a design. This is one I did." (Demonstrate.)

"Before gluing down your cutout shapes, experiment with your arrangement by putting the cutouts in different places on the background paper." (Hold up a torn or cut paper shape.) "For instance, if my shape is held like this, what does it look like? Now if it's held this way, what could it be?"

When children are ready to choose construction paper for their collages, ask them to think again about their favorite season. Tell them to concentrate on the colors they see in their minds and start their collages with those colors.

## Evaluation of the Program

We recorded the responses of 17 children at 4 sites. Their overall age range was 6–14, but most were 8–12. This program was extraordinary and overall response was exceptionally positive. Much like ISLE OF JOY (with which we would not pair it because they are too similar), HOMMAGE A FRANCOIS COUPERIN is a lovely mood piece and evoked in viewers a peaceful and relaxed frame of mind. It literally transported children, many of whom reacted in a visibly affective manner. Two very tough girls (child abuse victims) both said the music made them sad but, since they responded very well to the whole program, that may have been their interpretation of a calm-down feeling. Child Life staff were amazed, in fact, at how the girls reacted; they became very responsive and loving.

As with some of the other lyrical shorts we have shown, children thoroughly enjoyed seeing HOMMAGE A FRANCOIS COUPERIN more than once and got a great deal more from the second screening than

they did from the first. Children's own comments say it all: "The music was extraordinary!" "I liked when it came in 3-D." "When the butterflies moved, I wanted to float." "It was three-dimensional, like real." "It made me feel relaxed."

Viewers were both satisfied and challenged by THE CREATION OF BIRDS. A few did not fully understand the tape's animal symbolism, but that did not diminish their enjoyment. In most screenings children said they liked "when the girl went from sad to happy." They also liked the "monster" and enjoyed the dramatic tension it provided. Many commented favorably on both its music and its happy ending.

## Comments about the Introductions

Before we screened the tapes, children had involved discussions about their favorite seasons, their favorite seasonal images, and the things they like to do at that time of year. This provided a link between the videotapes and the activity.

Make sure to warn viewers that both titles are in French. For THE CREATION OF BIRDS it is important to discuss the symbolic animals, and to describe the Wind Wolf as a monster.

## Evaluation of the Activity

Once again we tried to tap THE CREATION OF BIRDS' power to inspire collages, only this time we focused on its seasonal theme and paired it with the delightful HOMMAGE A FRANCOIS COUPERIN.

When we asked children to do a collage of their favorite season, some used images from the pre-screening discussion. Others needed more focus or reinforcement, so we followed a line of inquiry similar to the one we used before the screening: "What's your favorite season? What do you think about when that season is here? What's your favorite thing to do then? What colors does the season make you think of?"

If children got individual help from an adult, the activity was tremendously satisfying—even uplifting. Some recalled vacations and happy times with friends and family; some did lovely abstract designs with seasonal colors.

All the test population completed this activity. Its success may have been due, in part, to the fact that seasons have universal appeal and everyone could relate to them on their own level. But part of its success was no doubt due to the lovely mood created by this combination of videotapes (which would also be quite effective as films, but we're not sure how they would do on TV). Child Life staff at all sites appreciated the peaceful, calming quality of the program, because of which they regarded it as extraordinarily valuable. A *four-star* program/activity—and then some!

# Playroom Video Program #9

| | |
|---|---|
| **Activity:** | Collage. |
| **Materials:** | Construction paper, pre-cut shapes, markers, crayons, scissors, and glue-sticks. |
| **Dexterity:** | Average, except for those with IVs. |
| **Age Level:** | 7–10. |

## MADELINE AND THE GYPSIES
(7 minutes/animation/narration)

A colorful and very verbal adaptation of Ludwig Bemelman's picturebook. In this installment of the adventures of Madeline, she gets caught on a ferris wheel with Pepito, the son of the Spanish ambassador, and spends some time with the gypsies who run the small carnival and circus. Eventually, Miss Clavel brings Madeline home.

## ANANSI THE SPIDER
(7 minutes/cel animation/narration)

A lively and colorful Ashanti folktale. In the first section, Anansi (in spider form) is rescued from trouble by his 6 resourceful sons: See-Trouble, Road-Builder, River-Drinker, Game-Skinner, Stone-Thrower, and Cushion. The second half of the tale explains how the moon came to be in the sky when Anansi could not decide which of his sons was most deserving of the bright globe he found en route home. (The running time listed above does not include the prologue. Just run past it before screening the tape.)

### Introduction to the First Tape

"The theme of this program is getting in and out of trouble. The first videotape is MADELINE AND THE GYPSIES. Does anyone know the Madeline books?" (If children do, let them share it with the group; if not, continue.)

"Madeline is a French girl who lives at a boarding school with 11 other girls. Miss Clavel is her teacher. Pepito, the Spanish ambassador's son, lives next door to the school. One day Pepito invites all the girls and Miss Clavel to the circus and carnival. That's where the trouble begins. Let's see how Madeline and Pepito get in and out of trouble. Remember, it's okay to talk out loud as you watch MADELINE AND THE GYPSIES."

Play the tape and do an image/sound skim: "What do you remember best from that video? Does anything you saw or heard stick out in your mind?" If you can, ask how the tape made children feel.

"Was there anything you didn't understand? Do you have any questions or comments about the tape?"

### Introduction to the Second Tape

"The next videotape is an African folktale called ANANSI THE SPIDER. Anansi is very clever but, like Madeline and Pepito, he gets into trouble. In this story you'll see how Anansi gets into and then gets out of trouble with the help of his six spider sons."

"I'll tell you their names and you tell me what they do best. The first is See-Trouble; what do you think he does? Next is Road-Builder; what does he do? River-Drinker? Game-Skinner? Stone-Thrower? And finally a tough one, Cushion; what does he do?"

"In the second part of the story, you'll find out how the moon got up in the sky when Anansi discovers a bright globe, which is another word for ball. He tries to decide which son to give it to. Let's watch the tape. Remember, it's okay to talk out loud as you watch ANANSI THE SPIDER."

Play the tape and do an image/sound skim: "What do you remember best from that video? Does anything you saw or heard stick out in your mind?" If you can, ask how the tape made children feel. "Was there anything you didn't understand? Do you have any questions or comments about the tape?"

### Introduction to the Activity

"Think for a minute about both tapes. Think of your favorite scene. Now let's see if you can make that scene into a collage by cutting out shapes and gluing them onto a sheet of paper."

Model the activity for children by showing them a partly finished collage of a scene from ANANSI THE SPIDER. If children are under 8 years old, supply them with pre-cut shapes.

### Evaluation of the Program

We recorded the responses of 24 children at 4 sites. Their overall age range was 3–13, but most were 3–9. Unfortunately, the tapes do not balance each other to create a cohesive program; MADELINE AND THE GYPSIES was overwhelmed by ANANSI THE SPIDER.

While MADELINE AND THE GYPSIES has some memorable images (horse, lion, and ferris wheel), children did not relate to its main characters, and none mentioned Pepito except for a girl of 4 who called him a *her*. Part of the problem may be that in video the characters are minuscule and hard to see.

On top of this, the story as a whole does not cohere. Few children understood the storyline and none discussed the plot. The program's theme of getting in and out of trouble thus lost its impact.

Children in the test sites were unfamiliar with the Madeline books, so they were not predisposed to like the tape. Those 4–7 in fair to good condition had the best response to it, but we do not recommend MADELINE AND THE GYPSIES for a video program; it works better as a film.

ANANSI THE SPIDER, on the other hand, was quite effective; the program theme was amplified by its characters' behavior and repetition. Visually strong with compelling music, it generated a happy, highly energized mood in children. Those 3–13 enjoyed it and moved to its rhythmic music. Some said they wanted to be spiders, and a few called Anansi "the mother spider." Although there was some confusion about the ending and the moon was often mislabeled, sometimes as "the sun" and sometimes vaguely as "the ball," this did not significantly diminish children's enjoyment. In all, ANANSI THE SPIDER elicited a high level of involvement and attention when it was screened, and produced a high level of motivation for the activity.

## Comments about the Introductions

As a lead-in to MADELINE AND THE GYPSIES it may be important to stress that the house where she and the other girls live is a boarding school, and that they go home when school is out.

After some experimentation, the introduction to ANANSI THE SPIDER. was best when we introduced the 6 sons by name and asked children to guess what each did. We introduced River-Drinker, for instance, and children said he drank a lot. The sons were easy except for Cushion (which children will be able to figure out when they see the videotape), but this guessing game aspect increased children's participation and improved their ability to anticipate events. Because so many children were confused, it is important to explain that the ball children see in the second part of the story is the moon and Anansi has to decide which son to give it to.

## Evaluation of the Activity

We knew ANANSI THE SPIDER worked to inspire collage (because of what its images look like—not because it uses cutout animation) so we paired it with a colorful tape about human children. Over 75% of our sample completed collages which were excellent, some quite sophisticated. Children took time doing them and most of their imagery involved horses (from MADELINE AND THE GYPSIES) and/or spiders (from ANANSI THE SPIDER).

An optional activity for very young children is to let them make spider hand movements while watching ANANSI THE SPIDER for the second time. At one site, preschoolers and young school age children whose IVs had just been removed were quite eager to do such a movement exercise.

# Playroom Video Program #10

| | |
|---|---|
| **Activity:** | Collage. |
| **Materials:** | Construction paper, pre-cut organic and geometric shapes, pencils, markers, crayons, scissors, and glue-sticks. |
| **Dexterity:** | Average, except for those with IVs. |
| **Age Level:** | 6–11. |

## ISLE OF JOY
(7 minutes/cutout animation/nonverbal)

An enchanting music video! Beginning with the image of a man in a wheelchair, this lyrical celebration of beauty moves through a series of lithographic images to vividly colored cutouts derived from the work of Matisse. Flowers and gardens, sailboats and sunbathers, swimmers and fish, lovers and birds dance across the screen to the gentle piano strains of Debussy's "L'Isle Joyeuse."

## ANANSI THE SPIDER
(7 minutes/cel animation/narration)

A lively and colorful Ashanti folktale. In the first section, Anansi (in spider form) is rescued from trouble by his 6 resourceful sons: See-Trouble, Road-Builder, River-Drinker, Game-Skinner, Stone-Thrower, and Cushion. The second half of the tale explains how the moon came to be in the sky when Anansi could not decide which of his sons was most deserving of the bright globe he found en route home. (The running time listed above does not include the prologue. Go past it before screening.)

## Introduction to the First Tape

"The first videotape, called ISLE OF JOY, is based on the cutout art of Henri Matisse. The story of how he came to make his cutouts is interesting."

"Matisse was a painter most of his life, but when he grew old he became quite ill." (Show children a photo of Matisse in a wheelchair. Several books about him have such a picture.) "While recovering, he decided to make art that would heal or help him get better. He decided to decorate the walls of his room, but he was confined to a wheelchair and painting the wall was difficult. He solved the problem by cutting shapes out of colored paper and gluing them on the walls." (Pass around some museum postcards of his cutouts.)

"The tape you are about to see has neither words nor a story. It is like a dance, maybe more like a dream of joy and beauty. As the tape proceeds, why not call out what you see. Let's watch ISLE OF JOY."

Play the tape and do an image/sound skim: "What do you remember best from that video? Does anything you saw or heard stick out in your mind?" If you can, ask how the tape made children feel. "Was there anything you didn't understand? Do you have any questions or comments about the tape?"

## Introduction to the Second Tape

"The next videotape is an African folktale called ANANSI THE SPIDER. In the first part of the story you'll meet the African folk-hero Anansi and see how he gets in and out of trouble with the help of his 6 sons."

"I'll tell you their names and you tell me what they do best. The first is See-Trouble; what do you think he does? Next is Road-Builder; what does he do? River-Drinker? Game-Skinner? Stone-Thrower? And finally a tough one, Cushion; what does he do?"

"In the second part of the story, you'll find out how the moon got up in the sky when Anansi discovers a bright globe, which is another word for ball. He tries to decide which son to give it to. Let's watch the tape. It has some words but it's okay to talk out loud as you watch ANANSI THE SPIDER."

Play the tape and do an image/sound skim: "What do you remember best from that video? Does anything you saw or heard stick out in your mind?" If you can, ask how the tape made children feel. "Was there anything you didn't understand? Do you have any questions or comments about the tape?"

## Introduction to the Activity

"Would you like to cut out some different colored designs and shapes and make a mural for the wall of your room? I started this one (demonstrate) using some shapes that look like those in the ISLE OF JOY (organic-looking shapes) and some from ANANSI THE SPIDER (geometric). You can make shapes like these or you can create your own."

## Evaluation of the Program

We recorded the responses of 10 children at 3 sites. Their overall age range was 3–13, but most were 8–13. Although preschoolers were not the program's intended audience, it even worked with them.

ISLE OF JOY is wonderfully energizing, partly because its music works so well with its colorful images. One 3-year-old with a broken leg in traction liked "the little man, his legs were cut off." Children mentioned that they liked its music and colors, and in doing their collages many preferred organic shapes (from ISLE OF JOY) to geometric ones (from ANANSI THE SPIDER) Although boys over 10 had trouble admitting it, even they liked ISLE OF JOY. However, because ISLE OF JOY is a visually demanding tape, children in poor condition—particularly those confined to bed—had an easier time with ANANSI THE SPIDER.

ANANSI THE SPIDER was a hands-down success and numerous children mentioned that they liked its music. Children, usually preschoolers and young school age children, often made spontaneous spider gestures with their hands as they watched, which would be a suitable activity for this videotape. The one difficulty was the usual confusion about the moon in the second part of the video.

## Comments about the Introductions

Telling children the names of Anansi's sons and asking them to guess what each does best makes a significant impact on children's enjoyment of the videotape. It is also important to identify the globe or ball in the second part of the story as the moon.

## Evaluation of the Activity

This was a variation on the highly successful Playroom Film Program #4. We were hoping to emphasize the musical aspects of two known collage motivators, although we did not intend to use music as the follow-up. We wanted to try this highly musical pair because pediatric patients like "musical" films—especially what we called music videos.

The activity worked very well; however, because of the wide age span, only 40% of our sample did collages. Although they enjoyed the program, older boys were not interested in the follow-up. Others were simply too young. The best age range for this *four-star* program/activity would be 6–11.

# Playroom Video Program #11

| | |
|---|---|
| **Activity:** | Collage. |
| **Materials:** | Construction and origami paper, newsprint, old wrapping paper (particularly gilt Christmas paper), crayons, markers, pencils, scissors, and glue-sticks. |
| **Dexterity:** | Average, except for those with IVs. |
| **Age Level:** | None. |

## THE STORY OF CHRISTMAS
(8 minutes/cutout animation/nonverbal)

A wordless and slow-moving nativity pageant based on the traditional story of the birth of Jesus. Jointed cutout characters, with a medieval-miniature look, move in a stately dance to medieval music. Their bright colors stand out sharply against the black background.

## THE SNOWY DAY
(6 minutes/iconographic animation/narration)

A lyrical, slow-moving sketch of a black preschooler's day of fun and exploration in the city snow. Peter spends the first day alone but the next day, when he wakes to discover that the snow is still there, he sets out with a friend with whom he can share his experiences.

### Introduction to the First Tape

"What season are we in right now?" (Hopefully children will say winter.) "What pops into your mind when you think about winter? What holidays come in the late fall or early winter?" (If they do not answer, say Hanukkah and Christmas.)

"The videotapes we're going to see take place in the winter. The first one has something to do with Christmas. It's about the very first Christmas. Let me tell you the story, because the tape has no words."

"Once upon a time, long ago, an angel told a woman named Mary that she was going to have a special baby. After a while, her husband Joseph took her on a long trip. They were very tired and needed a place to sleep, but all the hotels and motels were full. Luckily, a kind man said they could stay in his barn."

"While Mary and Joseph were settling down in the barn, an angel told shepherds that the special baby was about to be born. And three kings from distant countries saw a star so bright that they followed it and it led them to the special baby. Shep-

herds and kings all came together in the little barn where the baby was born. His mother named him Jesus."

"The tape you're about to see is rather unusual looking. It resembles old-fashioned stained-glass windows. The characters move in a slow dance. THE STORY OF CHRISTMAS has no words, so you can talk out loud as you watch."

Play the tape. During it, label the characters and explain what is happening if children are unfamiliar with the story. Point out the angel, Mary, Joseph, the shepherds, and the three kings. Also note the moment in the videotape when a flower changes color; it represents a significant passage of time.

Afterwards, do an image/sound skim: "What do you remember best from that video? Does anything you saw or heard stick out in your mind?" If you can, ask how the tape made children feel. "Was there anything you didn't understand? Do you have any questions or comments about the tape?"

### Introduction to the Second Tape

"The second videotape is called THE SNOWY DAY. Does anybody know the book? It tells a story that also takes place in the winter, but not a long time ago. This story could take place today, because it's about a boy named Peter who lives in a modern city. Peter goes out and has fun in the snow. Since the videotape has very few words, why not say out loud what Peter is doing as we watch THE SNOWY DAY."

Play the tape and do an image/sound skim: "What do you remember best from that video? Does anything you saw or heard stick out in your mind?" If you can, ask how the tape made children feel. "Was there anything you didn't understand? Do you have any questions or comments about the tape?"

### Introduction to the Activity

"Now you can draw your favorite winter activity. If you prefer, you can do a collage. Cut and paste the scene you liked or remember best from the stories you just saw."

Demonstrate how to make a collage with a partially completed scene from either tape. If children select A CHRISTMAS STORY give them dark paper for the background and make sure they have lots of bright colors for their images. Some may want to paste in shapes as well as draw or color.

## Evaluation of the Program

We recorded the responses of 13 children at 2 sites. Their overall age range was 4–10, but most were 4–8. This pairing did not work at all well and violated some of our own rules for programming in the hospital.

Not only were both tapes really slow and meditative, but they appealed to different ages. On top of this, the religious aspects of THE STORY OF CHRISTMAS were problematic for public hospitals. Our reason for trying it was to offer a Christmas program that went beyond the materialistic and sentimental hype of most commercial programs. Also, perhaps incorrectly, we regarded THE CHRISTMAS STORY as a folk-pageant told in dance, not a religious myth. (We could not find a suitable Hanukkah story or we would have tried that too.)

To a degree, older children liked THE STORY OF CHRISTMAS, but it generated no real energy for the activity. Since it seems to work better as a film, we do not recommend THE STORY OF CHRISTMAS for either TV or video programs. For younger children, it was like MADELINE AND THE GYPSIES in that they responded to separate images rather than to the story as a whole.

Preschoolers thoroughly enjoyed THE SNOWY DAY, but it was too babyish for older children. It should be paired with a tape for young children and shown exclusively in preschool programs.

## Comments about the Introductions

The lead-in to THE STORY OF CHRISTMAS was one of our longest introductions ever—we should have known better! Worse yet, it was information-giving rather than involving. Those who spoke little or no English got completely lost.

## Evaluation of the Activity

This never really got off the ground. THE STORY OF CHRISTMAS is quite beautiful—more so as a film than a video—but it did not work with pediatric patients and had no real impact on children's artwork. Two youngsters did collages based on THE SNOWY DAY. Four (ages 4, 5, and 10) used the blank-with-a-border activity sheets we developed for the program (but did not reproduce herein). And a 5-year-old made a mountain of snowballs.

# Playroom Video Program #12

| | |
|---|---|
| **Activity:** | Collage. |
| **Materials:** | Construction paper, tissue paper, pre-cut shapes (geometric and organic shapes such as clouds), stick-on stars, crayons, markers, scissors, glue-sticks. |
| **Dexterity:** | Average, except for those with IVs. |
| **Age Level:** | 3–8. |

## THE SNOWY DAY
(6 minutes/iconographic animation/narration)

A lyrical, slow-moving sketch of a black preschooler's day of fun and exploration in the city snow. Peter spends the first day alone but the next day, when he wakes to discover that the snow is still there, he sets out with a friend with whom he can share his experiences.

## THE SKY IS BLUE
(5 minutes/cutout animation/nonverbal)

Using naive and child-like cutout images, this is the saga of a young man whose kite takes him up, up, up into the starry heavens and then down, down, down to earth and home. Although he has several close calls on his journey, everything works out fine in the end.

## Introduction to the First Tape

"We are going to see stories about children who love to go outside and play. What do you like to do when you play out-of-doors?"

"The first videotape is called THE SNOWY DAY. Does anybody know the book? It is all about a boy named Peter who goes out to play after a big snowfall. What do you like to do in the snow?"

"Let's see what happens to Peter. The tape has few words, so you can talk out loud while you watch THE SNOWY DAY."

Play the tape and do an image/sound skim: "What do you remember best from that video? Does anything you saw or heard stick out in your mind?" If you can, ask how the tape made children feel. "Was there anything you didn't understand? Do you have any questions or comments about the tape?"

## Introduction to the Second Tape

"The next story happens in the spring—not in the winter. It is called THE SKY IS BLUE. It's a story about a young man who loves to play with his kite. Do you know what a kite is?" (Show a picture of or get a real kite.)

"As you will see, the kite takes the young man up, up, up to the stars—even to another planet. But don't worry, later he comes down, down, down all the way home. The tape has no words, so you can talk out loud as you watch THE SKY IS BLUE."

Play the tape and do an image/sound skim: "What do you remember best from that video? Does anything you saw or heard stick out in your mind?" If you can, ask how the tape made children feel. "Was there anything you didn't understand? Do you have any questions or comments about the tape?"

Children may want to see THE SKY IS BLUE again, so ask if they do. Be prepared to show it again immediately or after the activity.

## Introduction to the Activity

"What do you like to do when you play? Let's see if you can make a picture of yourself playing? You can either draw it or make it with cutout paper and glue. Here's my collage." (Show a collage of you playing as a child.)

## Evaluation of the Program

We recorded the responses of 15 children at 3 sites. Their age range was 2–12, but most were 2–6. This program did extremely well and worked best with those 3–8. Only very young children (2–3) in poor condition had problems staying involved.

While THE SNOWY DAY generally appeals most to under-eights, the entire sample enjoyed it. Similarly, THE SKY IS BLUE generally appeals to the same age range and yet 12-year-olds enjoyed it. Many children said that what they liked best was "the house and the dog" (a reference to going home—the happy reunion with family at the end of a journey/adventure).

## Comments about the Introductions

Asking children to talk about what they like to do in the snow significantly helped their involvement in and enjoyment of THE SNOWY DAY. It got them comfortable and ready to label. They also enjoyed talking about the things they did with their friends and families.

The introduction to THE SKY IS BLUE works as is, but you could also ask children—either before or after they see the tape—what they like to do outside in the spring. This might help create seasonal alternatives for their artwork.

## Evaluation of the Activity

This was a *four-star* variation on two successful preschool film programs (#3 and #4). In contrast to the preceding combination, THE SKY IS BLUE was an appropriate partner for THE SNOWY DAY. And although THE SNOWY DAY had a minimal impact on children's art, it effectively balanced THE SKY IS BLUE. It featured a black child while the other featured a white one, and it was realistic while the other was fantastic.

Surprisingly, considering their range, over 80% of the children in our sample completed a collage. Those with IVs and casts needed help cutting and gluing, but they did fine with some assistance. Most children used images from THE SKY IS BLUE in their artwork—lots of houses, kites, stars, and dogs—which looked fairly abstract because of the pre-cut geometric shapes.

It would be advisable to offer pre-cut representational shapes from THE SKY IS BLUE since this was the tape children preferred. As it was, we spent lots of time cutting out clouds, stars, spaceships, and people for children, who might have been more creative if those shapes had been readily available.

# Playroom Video Program #13

| | |
|---|---|
| **Activity:** | Collage. |
| **Materials:** | Activity sheets, 12″- or 18″-square felt-covered board, cardboard or store-bought tangrams, geometric and organic pre-cut paper shapes, construction paper, crayons, scissors, and glue. |
| **Dexterity:** | Average, except for those with IVs. |
| **Age Level:** | 3–8. |

## TANGRAM
(3 minutes/cutout animation/nonverbal)

A delightful music video puzzle. Using 7 angular pieces from the Chinese puzzle called a tangram (which includes a square, a rhomboid, and 5 triangles) this lyrical videotape illustrates various silhouette shapes, from fish and snail to cat and horse. Each appears briefly on-screen, moves in a characteristic way, then transforms into another shape.

## THE SKY IS BLUE
(5 minutes/cutout animation/nonverbal)

Using naive and child-like cutout images, this is the saga of a young man whose kite takes him up, up, up into the starry heavens and then down, down, down to earth and home. Although he has several close calls on his journey, everything works out fine in the end.

## Introduction to the First Tape

For demonstration, you will need poster-board or cardboard cut first into 5″ squares and then into tangram shapes. You will also need a felt- or velvet-covered board of about a foot or a foot and a half square on which to display the tangrams.

"This special puzzle with 7 pieces is called a tangram." (Place the tangram pieces randomly on the board so children can see there are several parts.)

"If I move the pieces together, I can make a shape. What shape is this?" (Demonstrate a triangle.)

"I can also make other shapes—shapes of different animals. What does this look like?" (Demonstrate a fish.)

"What's this?" (A bird.)

"This?" (A square.)

"The first videotape is a sort of video puzzle about shapes. It is called TANGRAM. Although it's very short and has no story, it shows many different shapes you can make with the pieces of a tangram. It looks like a dance of shapes."

"As you watch, why not play a game. Call out the names of the shapes as they appear on the screen. Just say what the different shapes look like, or what they remind you of. The tape has no words, so you can talk out loud as you watch TANGRAM."

Play the tape and do an image/sound skim: "What do you remember best from that video? Does anything you saw or heard stick out in your mind?"

If you can, ask how the tape made children feel. "Was there anything you didn't understand? Do you have any questions or comments about the tape?"

Then say, "What does this look like?" (Show either the bird or the rabbit from the tape.) "I'd like to see TANGRAM again, would you?" (If so, watch it again; otherwise go on.)

## Introduction to the Second Tape

"The next videotape is called THE SKY IS BLUE. Like TANGRAM it is made with different colored shapes. But it's a story about a young man who is flying his kite on a windy day. Do you know what a kite is?" (Show a picture of or get a real kite.)

"As you will see, his kite takes the young man up, up, up to the stars—even to another planet. But don't worry. Later he comes down, down, down and gets home safe and sound. The tape has no words, so you can talk out loud as you watch THE SKY IS BLUE."

Play the tape and do an image/sound skim: "What do you remember best from that video? Does anything you saw or heard stick out in your mind?"

If you can, ask how the tape made children feel. "Was there anything you didn't understand? Do you have any questions or comments about the tape?"

## Introduction to the Activity

"We have different colored construction paper in lots of pre-cut shapes and sizes. Let's make some pictures by gluing them onto bigger sheets of paper. Here is a collage I made. This is how I did it."

Demonstrate by picking a few shapes and pasting them on your already-begun collage. Ask children what else you should add. Encourage participants to copy something they liked from either tape or make up their own picture or design. Offer crayons if they want to add details.

## Evaluation of the Program

We recorded the responses of 17 children at 3 sites. Their overall age range was 2–14, but most were 4–8. This program worked exceptionally well. TANGRAM is a great opener and always gets children involved, focused, and excited.

Interestingly, all ages—even teenagers—enjoyed it and every group asked to watch it more than once. the only problem was with very young children (2–5) in poor condition who did not speak English. Without benefit of the introduction, they did not get much out of the tape.

THE SKY IS BLUE was wonderful. It's predictability encouraged children to label and anticipate the course of events. During the screening many young children spontaneously said, "He's going home." The part they liked best was "when he went home and the doggie was waiting and happy." For a babyish tape, it appealed to the entire test population (which doubtless had something to do with group dynamics).

Child Life staff treasured this program, which they said "wonderfully reinforced the going home theme" and evoked unmistakably positive responses from children.

## Comments about the Introductions

The most effective preparation for TANGRAM involved letting children identify the shapes as the facilitator actively manipulated a tangram—ending with a square, the shape that begins the videotape. Learning how to manipulate the tangram effectively requires a fair amount of rehearsal. It is, however, well worth the effort since the demonstration contributes significantly to the impact of both TANGRAM and the follow-up activity.

At some screenings we let children manipulate their own tangrams before and during a second screening. We also found that showing TANGRAM twice in a row was remarkably effective. Children were eager to identify both what they saw and what they might have missed the first time. Watching it the second time created both a better focus and more excitement.

Interestingly, when we introduced him as a young man, preschoolers thought the person in THE SKY IS BLUE was a boy; however, when we introduced him as a boy, older children said he looked more like a man. Obviously, the introduction should be modified according to the age of the audience.

## Evaluation of the Activity

This was a *four-star* variation of two successful preschool film programs (#3 and #4). To demonstrate the collage for children, we made a tangram animal and a spaceship from the THE SKY IS BLUE. We then asked children to make their own pictures using pre-cut shapes or cutting out their own.

All who saw the program did the activity, which was a true success. Younger children (2–4) were more comfortable drawing with crayons than doing collage. Six-year-olds and up made people, houses, kites, flowers, and spaceships out of geometric shapes. Since children wanted to use so many images from THE SKY IS BLUE, we decided (after the program's first try-out) to include organic-looking shapes, such as kites, clouds, people, dogs, boats, and spaceships.

As an option, older children (10–16) might enjoy making the tangram shapes on the tangram puzzle activity sheet which follows.

## TANGRAM PUZZLE

A tangram is a puzzle. To play, you could cut the square in center of this page along the dotted lines into 7 pieces, or you could make a tangram puzzle of your own out of colored paper, using this one as a guide.

Using the tangram shapes, copy the black figures on this page. The line drawings show you how the tangram pieces were arranged. **Remember, each figure must include all seven tangram pieces.** Or, you can make up your own shapes and make silhouettes, using as many pieces as you like.

*Using Media to Make Kids Feel Good,* by Maureen Gaffney. Published by Oryx Press, 2214 N. Central, Phoenix, AZ 85004, 1988.

# Playroom Video Program #14

| | |
|---|---|
| **Activity:** | Making shadow puppets. |
| **Materials:** | Activity sheets, 12"- or 18"-square felt-covered board, cardboard or store-bought tangrams, 18"-square sheet of ¼" thick translucent lucite, strong flashlight, masking tape, geometric and organic pre-cut paper shapes, construction paper, crayons, scissors, glue, brads, a hole puncher. |
| **Dexterity:** | Considerable, may be difficult for those with IVs. |
| **Age Level:** | 5–11. |

## TANGRAM
(3 minutes/cutout animation/nonverbal)

A delightful music video puzzle. Using 7 angular pieces from the Chinese puzzle called a tangram (which includes a square, a rhomboid, and 5 triangles) this lyrical tape illustrates various silhouette shapes, from fish and snail to cat and horse. Each appears briefly on-screen, moves in a characteristic way, then transforms into another shape.

## JACK AND THE BEANSTALK
(12 minutes/silhouette animation/narration)

Based on the traditional folktale about a naive young man who trades his poor mother's only pig for a sack of beans, this charming tape uses an unusual type of shadow puppet animation. Although he has only one encounter with the cruel giant, things work out quite well in the end for the irrepressible Jack and his mother.

## Introduction to the First Tape

For demonstration, you will need poster-board or cardboard cut first into 5" squares and then into tangram shapes. You will also need a felt- or velvet-covered board of about a foot or a foot and a half square on which to display the tangrams.

"The first videotape is sort of a puzzle about shapes. Do you like puzzles?" (Pause for their response.)

"I like puzzles—especially the tangram. Here are the 7 pieces of the tangram." (Place the pieces randomly on the board so children can see there are several parts.)

"If I move the pieces together, I can make a shape. What is this?" (Demonstrate a triangle.)

"I can also make other shapes—shapes of different animals. What does this look like?" (Demonstrate a fish.)

"What's this?" (A bird.) "This?" (A square.)

"The first tape is called TANGRAM. Although it's very short and has no story, it shows many different shapes you can make with the pieces of a tangram. It looks like a dance of shapes."

"As you watch, why not play a game. Call out the names of the shapes as they appear on the screen. Just say what the different shapes look like, or what they remind you of. The tape has no words, so you can talk out loud as you watch TANGRAM."

Play the tape and do an image/sound skim: "What do you remember best from that video? Does anything you saw or heard stick out in your mind?" If you can, ask how the tape made children feel. "Was there anything you didn't understand? Do you have any questions or comments about the tape?"

"Would you like to see TANGRAM again?" (If children say yes, screen it again and encourage them to label the images; otherwise, go on.)

## Introduction to the Second Tape

"The second videotape looks unusual because it's made with shadow puppets. Do you know what a shadow puppet or silhouette puppet is?" (Demonstrate with cutouts and a sheet of lucite.) "Although you can tell which character is which, shadow puppets are strange looking because you never really get to see their faces or their eyes."

"The tape we are about to see tells the story of JACK AND THE BEANSTALK. Does anyone know that story?" (If they do, let different children tell parts of it. After each segment ask the next child: "And then what happened?" If they don't, continue.)

"In this story a young man trades his poor mother's only pig—and in this version it is a pig, not a cow—for a sack of beans which grow into a gigantic beanstalk. Jack climbs the beanstalk and finds himself at the house of a monstrous giant who likes to eat young men. But Jack is clever and everything turns out fine in the end."

"Although the tape has words, it's okay to talk out loud as you watch, and be sure to ask if you don't understand something. Remember, because this story uses shadow puppets you won't see any of the characters faces or eyes—just the outline of their bodies. Let's watch JACK AND THE BEANSTALK."

Play the tape and do an image/sound skim: "What do you remember best from that video? Does anything you saw or heard stick out in your mind?" If you can, ask how the tape made children feel.

"Was there anything you didn't understand? Do you have any questions or comments about the tape?"

## Introduction to the Activity

"Here is a shadow puppet activity sheet and some tangram shapes (see Tangram Puzzle activity sheet following Video Program #13) for you to make puppets with. You can attach the shapes with brads, like I've done here." (Demonstrate.)

"Make any kind of character you like."

## Evaluation of the Program

We recorded the responses of 25 children at 4 sites. Their overall age range was 3–12, but most were 5–9. This program worked exceedingly well for the entire population, despite the fact that TANGRAM appealed more to the lower and JACK AND THE BEANSTALK appealed more to the upper end of that age range. The only ones who had trouble with TANGRAM were boys, 11 and up, who thought it babyish.

Showing TANGRAM first was really effective in terms of this pairing. Children thoroughly enjoyed labeling things they recognized—even throughout a second viewing (during which they saw things they had missed the first time). It was highly involving and rescreening it enhanced group rapport.

JACK AND THE BEANSTALK was phenomenally well-received. Most children knew the story and enjoyed anticipating the course of events, particularly the appearance of the "giant monster." The narrator has a British accent and often talks over the music, so some words got lost; however, children were familiar enough with the storyline and could figure out what was happening from the visuals. Children relished its dramatic tension and commented favorably on the tale's "justice." Generally, it produced great feelings of satisfaction.

## Comments about the Introductions

TANGRAM worked best when, prior to the screening, the facilitator arranged a tangram into different shapes (ending with the square which begins the tape) and asked children to identify them. This was the best way to get children verbalizing and involved.

Learning how to manipulate the tangram effectively requires a fair amount of rehearsal. It is, however, well worth the effort since using it contributes significantly to the impact of both TANGRAM and the follow-up.

For JACK AND THE BEANSTALK, letting those who knew it tell the story was effective. But children must be warned that they will not see any of the characters' eyes; without such a warning (the first time we tried this) we got many complaints about that. Their complaints notwithstanding, viewers were intrigued by the shadow puppets.

## Evaluation of the Activity

We asked children to make shadow puppets using tangram or human shapes (from the preceding activity sheets), hole punchers, and brads. We showed them a person but told them they could do anything they had seen in the tapes or invent their own special puppet. We helped those who wanted to use the activity sheets.

Puppet-making turned out extremely well. Some children made monsters. Two made people and added the eyes that were missing in the tape. Others did animals. A 12-year-old did a mother with a carriage. Because they were beyond their abilities, preschoolers did not attempt the puppets, but they had fun gluing different shapes on paper.

Young children needed assistance with the hole punchers, as did those with IVs, but they completed the activity successfully. This *four-star* program/activity seemed highly satisfying for everyone.

# SHADOW PUPPET

To make puppet screen:

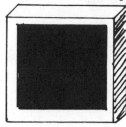

You will need lightweight cardboard or dark colored construction paper, scissors, a hole punch, paper fasteners, waxed paper, glue or tape, the lid of a box and a flashlight

1. Cut out the center of a box lid to make a frame.

2. Tape or glue waxed paper to the frame.

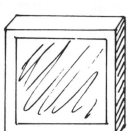

To make a shadow puppet :

1. Trace the outlines of the template (on next page) on cardboard or paper. Cut out the pieces.

2. With the hole punch, make a hole at the top of each arm and leg and a hole at each shoulder and hip on the body.

3. Fasten the arms and legs to the body with the paper fasteners.

3.

4. Arch the puppet so it looks like the letter C from the side and  paste the top of the head and the tip of the toes to the back of the of the waxed paper screen.

5. Now hold the flashlight behind the puppet and move the light up and down, or from side to side and watch how the puppet seems to leap and jump about.

4.

If you want, you can make more than one puppet.

5.

*Using Media to Make Kids Feel Good,* by Maureen Gaffney. Published by Oryx Press, 2214 N. Central, Phoenix, AZ 85004, 1988.

# SHADOW PUPPET

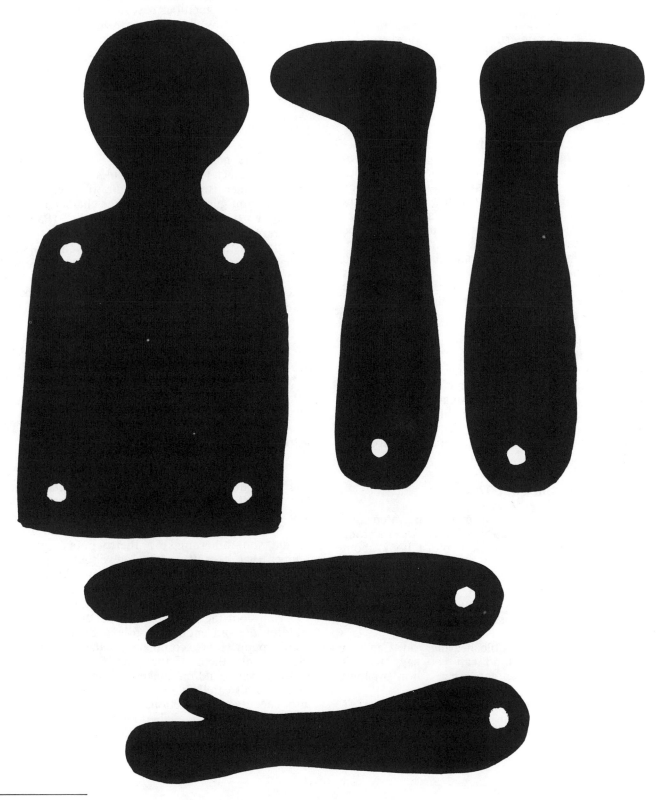

*Using Media to Make Kids Feel Good,* by Maureen Gaffney. Published by Oryx Press, 2214 N. Central, Phoenix, AZ 85004, 1988.

# Playroom Video Program #15

| | |
|---|---|
| **Activity:** | Making paper bag puppets. |
| **Materials:** | Activity sheets, paper sandwich bags, construction paper, markers, scissors, and glue-sticks. |
| **Dexterity:** | Average, except for those with IVs. |
| **Age Level:** | 3–12. |

## PIERRE
(6 minutes/line animation/song)

In this delightful music video send-up of cautionary tales (based on the picturebook by Maurice Sendak), Carole King sings about a preschool boy who says "I don't care!" to everything. Pierre refuses to cooperate or to be neat. He is so laissez-faire that he doesn't care to go out with his parents, and he doesn't even care when he gets swallowed by a lion. His parents, however, do care and they rush him to the doctor who shakes the boy out from the lion's mouth, alive and better than ever. After that, of course, Pierre learns to care, and the lion becomes his friend.

## A CHAIRY TALE
(10 minutes/liveaction/nonverbal)

This humorous and sometimes slapstick, black-and-white mime-drama about reciprocation is enacted by a man and an animated chair. Ravi Shankar did the compelling raga-like score for this classic videotape in which, after learning that not all chairs can be taken for granted, a man practices the golden rule.

### Introduction to the First Tape

"In this program you will meet some interesting characters. First is a boy named Pierre. Does anyone know Pierre? Maurice Sendak wrote a book about Pierre, who doesn't care."

(Hold up a paper bag puppet colored to resemble Pierre. Have him say, in a special character voice that gets progressively louder: "I don't care!" Say it a few times and ask children to say it along with the puppet.)

"Pierre is having trouble hearing you. Can you talk any louder? How loud can you say, 'I don't care!'? Pierre doesn't even care when a lion swallows him." (Have puppet say, "I don't care!")

"My, my! But don't worry, because Pierre's mom and dad rush him to a doctor and Pierre comes out safe and sound at the end. Let's watch PIERRE."

Play the tape and do an image/sound skim: "What do you remember best from that video? Does anything you saw or heard stick out in your mind?" If you can, ask how the tape made children feel. "Was there anything you didn't understand? Do you have any questions or comments about the tape?"

Ask children if they want to see PIERRE again. If they do, rescreen it; if not, go on.

### Introduction to the Second Tape

"In the next videotape you'll meet a pair of unusual characters. One is a man who likes to read and the other isn't even human. If I tell you the title, can you guess what the other character is? The title is A CHAIRY TALE. A chair-y tale." (Pause for their responses, if any.)

"It tells the story of a man who wants to sit on a chair and read a book but the chair has ideas of its own and tries to let the man know. The tape is black and white and has no words so you can talk out loud. Let's watch A CHAIRY TALE and discover what the chair wants."

Play the tape and do an image/sound skim: "What do you remember best from that video? Does anything you saw or heard stick out in your mind?" If you can, ask how the tape made children feel. "Was there anything you didn't understand? Do you have any questions or comments about the tape?"

### Introduction to the Activity

"Here are some paper bags and other materials you can make puppets with. You can make puppets like these if you want to." (Hold up Pierre puppet and a girl puppet made from paper sandwich bags.)

"Think a bit about what you'd like to do. Would you rather make a Pierre puppet or a girl puppet that doesn't care? How about a lion who doesn't care? Perhaps you'd rather make a puppet who cares. Or a puppet who thinks things are unfair—like the chair did in A CHAIRY TALE."

Hand out the paper bag puppet activity sheets if children are old enough to follow them. After children's puppets are completed, encourage them to interact with them. If they chose a character from PIERRE, help children make up dialog so they can say, "I don't care!" If they focus on A CHAIRY TALE, also encourage interaction. For instance, when toy cars or trucks are available, let the car tell the puppet something like, "I'm tired of doing all the driving, will you give me a ride?"

## Evaluation of the Program

We recorded the responses of 27 children at 4 sites. Their overall age range was 2–12, but most were 4–8. Both tapes were manifestly therapeutic and the program was a success despite the fact that older children were put off by PIERRE—and showing it twice turned some off completely. (Because of this, it might work better to use A CHAIRY TALE in school age programs and keep PIERRE strictly for preschoolers.)

Children who knew the book responded most enthusiastically to PIERRE, and, with the exception discussed below, its effect was quite positive. The tape was great for children in isolation or in traction. (One 3-year-old in traction wiggled her legs and pointed to them when Pierre was upside down in the chair.) Afterwards, most children said it was a pretend story and they knew that Pierre really did care. However, the ending where Pierre finally cares is such a short moment that it was missed by some (notably, those discussed below). It helps if an adult can point it out after the screening.

PIERRE elicited negative responses from 3 boys (4–6) in poor condition. One of them, a 4-year-old, was shy and withdrawn and expressed initial anxiety about the lion's "chewing Pierre," although he was relieved at the end. The 6-year-old (who was considered to be suicidal) responded by acting out and saying over and over again, "I don't care! I don't care!" The other 4-year-old said the tape made him feel sad because Pierre didn't care; then he talked about his grandmother and asked, "How come Mommy didn't come yesterday?" These boys were trying to cope with many things and PIERRE touched on their fears or negative feelings. Because of this, and because of the need to reinforce the ending, PIERRE should only be used in adult-supervised situations where its therapeutic potential can be maximized. We do not recommend it for TV.

Younger children delighted in the chair's magical and inexplicable movements, but A CHAIRY TALE also worked very well with older children (for whom there are few appealing titles). Viewers exhibited a high level of energy and excitement and had great fun trying to figure out what the chair wanted.

## Comments about the Introductions

So that very young children will enjoy PIERRE, it might help to read them the book just prior to or the day before screening the videotape. Another option would be to play the part of Carole King's "Really Rosie" record which includes "Pierre." The introduction for A CHAIRY TALE was effective in motivating children to guess what the chair wanted, something they really enjoyed.

## Evaluation of the Activity

This was a *four-star* revision of Playroom Film Program #6. We gave children paper bags to make puppets, either by drawing or gluing on cutout paper. This worked for children 3–12 and, despite the activity sheet model, children made a wide range of puppets—from Santa Claus and Michael Jackson to a deceased but fondly remembered family pet. A 12-year-old who was fantasizing pleasant events, including her wedding, said hers was "a funny man in a tuxedo." Older boys did not want to do the activity at all, but they played with the sample puppets we brought.

# PAPER BAG PUPPET

To make a paper bag puppet you need: a small paper bag, glue, scissors, and colored construction paper.

1. Cut out of paper 2 eyes, a nose, 2 lips and hair.
2. Glue the hair, eyes, nose, and the upper lip onto the flap at the bottom of the paper bag.
3. Glue the bottom lip to the side of the bag just under the flap.
4. Put your hand inside the bag and move the flap up and down to make the puppet talk.

If you want, you can make a crown so the puppet can be a king or queen or princess or prince.

Instead of cutting and gluing the eyes, nose and mouth, you can draw them with crayons.

 2 lips  2 ears   2 eyes

 2 arms

To make Curious George:

1. Cut 2 ears, a tail, 2 lips and 2 arms from construction paper.
2. Glue the eyes, nose, ears and one lip to the flap on the bottom of the bag, and the other lip just under the flap. Now glue the arms and the tail to the bag.

To make the puppets talk put your hand inside the bag and move the flap up and down.

*Using Media to Make Kids Feel Good,* by Maureen Gaffney. Published by Oryx Press, 2214 N. Central, Phoenix, AZ 85004, 1988.

# Playroom Video Program #16

| | |
|---|---|
| **Activity:** | Making finger puppets. |
| **Materials:** | Activity sheets, construction paper, tissue paper, small scraps of light-weight material, yarn, pipe cleaners, aluminum foil, markers, crayons, pencils, scissors, and glue. |
| **Dexterity:** | Considerable; difficult with IVs. |
| **Age Level:** | 6–12. |

## HANDS
(3 minutes/animated photographs/nonverbal)

Black-and-white photographs were tinted blue in this zany celebration of those great performers— human hands. First the thumb, then the index finger, then one, then a pair of hands perform their tricks from clapping and waving to finger plays. Cue-cards introduce each section, following which there is a quick, then an even quicker, reprise to the accompaniment of an odd mix of found sounds. (Before screening this, check with hospital staff and make sure no children in the scheduled group have epileptic tendencies, since the tape's stroboscopic images might trigger a seizure.)

## THE PRINCESS AND THE PEA
(10 minutes/puppet animation/dialog & narration)

In this droll romance, a young man finds the woman of his dreams despite a preposterous test engineered by his mother. Although the basic plot was adapted from an enigmatic Hans Christian Andersen tale, the filmmaker has fleshed out the characters with subtle wit, telling parent-child interactions, and non-stereotypical details such as Princess Jana's knowledge of astronomy. Imaginative attention to detail has been lavished on the handmade props and styrofoam puppets. And its quaint appearance contrasts with the videotape's sweet tone, resulting in a low-key and pleasantly burlesque fairytale.

## Introduction to the First Tape

"Both videotapes are made with puppets. The first one uses an unusual puppet—the hand. Do you think a hand all by itself can be a puppet? How?" (Model a rabbit-head shadow puppet.)

"What else can hands be? What types of things can hands do besides be puppets?" (If children with IVs seem debilitated by them you might point that out and talk about the kinds of things you cannot do when your hand is in an IV.)

"The first tape is called HANDS and it stars a pair of hands. The director wanted to show us a close-up of hands and what they can do. But I should warn you that not only is this tape short and sometimes very fast, the sounds do not always match what you see. It is rather odd indeed. On top of all this, the videotape has no story and no words, so you can talk out loud as you watch HANDS."

Play the tape and do an image/sound skim: "What do you remember best from that video? Does anything you saw or heard stick out in your mind?" If you can, ask how the tape made children feel. "Was there anything you didn't understand? Do you have any questions or comments about the tape?"

## Introduction to the Second Tape

"The next videotape is called THE PRINCESS AND THE PEA. Does anyone know that story?" (Most children won't, so review the storyline.)

"It's all about a prince who meets a princess and wants to marry her. Now I have to ask you a question: If I said I was a princess, how would you know if I was a *real* princess?" (Children might say something like a real princess would be wearing a crown, or who knows what else. It's an effective question for opening the discussion.)

"Does saying I'm a princess, *mean* I'm a real princess? In the next tape, which is based on a story by Hans Christian Andersen, there is a test to make sure that a princess who says she is, actually is a princess. The prince's mother wants to make sure that her son marries a real princess, so she sets up a most unusual test."

"Styrofoam puppets are used in the tape. You won't be able to see the puppeteers' hands, but you will see the strings and some rods which hold the puppets up. Remember, it's okay to talk out loud as you watch THE PRINCESS AND THE PEA."

Play the tape and do an image/sound skim: "What do you remember best from that video? Does anything you saw or heard stick out in your mind?" Ask how the tape made children feel. Ask if there was anything they didn't understand. Ask if they have any questions or comments.

Find out if children know what the test was, and if they mention the pea, as they probably will, ask if they think it was a fitting test, and why.

## Introduction to the Activity

"Here is an activity sheet so you can make a special type of puppet—not a hand puppet, not a styrofoam marionette, but a finger puppet."

Make a few model puppets to demonstrate. Help children figure out the activity sheets. Be sure that their add-on materials are attractively displayed and limit the number of items (to 5 or so) children can take at one time, but tell them they can always go back for more later.

## Evaluation of the Program

We recorded the responses of 31 children at 4 sites. Their overall age range was 4–14, but most were 6–10. This program was a genuine success with the entire test population. HANDS is demanding yet children were fascinated by and became visibly involved in it. Many moved their hands as they watched it. Despite this, the tape did not exactly focus children's energies and they were confused by the strange sound effects, which did not match the images shown. Almost everyone complained that it was too short, and in this case it meant they wanted more. Older boys enjoyed the sounds, like the burps and pigs, etc. One 11-year-old with a tumor in his hand, gave the videotape a super rating; he was very positive and uplifted by it. Other comments were that is was "weird" and "good but gross." Two boys said it was like a music video.

Although it came as no surprise, THE PRINCESS AND THE PEA was the clear preference of the pair. Everyone was delighted by the tape and older children became as involved in its technical aspects as in its story. Many mimicked the characters, particularly the queen with her "purple hair and long nails" and "the way she talked." Child Life staff at one site were pleasantly surprised at children's positive response to the queen; they thought she might represent a negative mother-figure but children found her truly amusing and liked her a great deal.

THE PRINCESS AND THE PEA was quite effective in getting children to anticipate and to verbalize; many expressed their opinions about the test: "It was crazy, no one would feel a pea." "Anyway, it wasn't a pea, it was a pearl because a pea would have broken."

## Comments about the Introductions

The preparations for both tapes got children effectively involved. The one for HANDS encouraged children's active participation in discussing what hands can do, principally out of the ordinary things. Just be careful not to go too far or the videotape will seem like a letdown, as it was in one screening where a group spent 15 minutes making shadow puppets and discussing what hands could do prior to seeing the tape. Since it did not follow through on that theme, children were disappointed.

## Evaluation of the Activity

Although THE PRINCESS AND THE PEA had nothing to do with finger puppets, its droll and handmade look helped motivate the activity, as did HANDS to a lesser extent. Making finger puppets was a thoroughly effective follow-up.

We demonstrated how to make a queen and a prince and helped children with the activity sheets. Energized largely by THE PRINCESS AND THE PEA, over 90% of the test population made puppets. It was a phenomenal group activity—most appealing to children 6–12, but even 14-year-old boys got involved.

A *four-star* program/activity and then some!

# FINGER PUPPET

You will need lightweight cardboard, scissors, crayons, colored paper and glue or tape.

1. Draw outline of the body on stiff paper or lightweight cardboard.
Cut it out and then cut out 2 holes at the bottom, just big enough to put your fingers through.

2. Draw and color a face, hair and clothes. Or you can cut hair and clothes from colored paper and glue them on.

3. Put your fingers through the holes from the back to make the puppet walk and dance.

*Using Media to Make Kids Feel Good,* by Maureen Gaffney. Published by Oryx Press, 2214 N. Central, Phoenix, AZ 85004, 1988.

# Playroom Video Program #17

| | |
|---|---|
| **Activity:** | Making an egg-carton dragon. |
| **Materials:** | Papier-mache egg cartons, construction paper, crayons, markers, scissors, and fast-drying glue. Paint is optional; so are children's blocks. |
| **Dexterity:** | Average, except for those with IVs. |
| **Age Level:** | 3–8. |

## THE MOLE AND THE TELEPHONE
(7 minutes/cel animation/nonverbal)

In the further adventures of this animal *every-child*, Mole uncovers an old-fashioned telephone while burrowing in a garden. When the receiver starts making sounds, Mole tries to figure out what the strange creature wants. Mole feeds it, scolds it, wraps it to keep it warm, and finally cradles it. When it snores, Mole manages to quiet it and, snuggling beside it, goes to sleep also.

## TCHOU TCHOU
(15 minutes/object animation/nonverbal)

A slow-moving but dramatic fantasy made entirely from children's colored wooden blocks. A boy and a girl (either playmates or siblings) amuse themselves in a playground until a block-dragon threatens their security. The child characters build a fort in self-defense, but the dragon knocks down the walls. In the end, however, the children outwit the dragon and tame it, even making it part of their play by turning it into a choo-choo train.

### Introduction to the First Tape

"The first videotape is all about a little animal called a mole. Does anyone know what a mole is? It's like a mouse with no ears and almost no tail. Moles have blackish backs and white bellies. They love to dig tunnels and holes in gardens or lawns."

"Do you think a mole would know what a TV is? What would a mole do with a TV set? What about a telephone? We're going to see a videotape called THE MOLE AND THE TELEPHONE. Let's see what a mole does the first time it discovers an old-fashioned telephone. The tape has no words so you can talk out loud as you watch THE MOLE AND THE TELEPHONE."

Play the tape and do an image/sound skim: "What do you remember best from that video? Does anything you saw or heard stick out in your mind?" If you can, ask how the tape made children feel.

"Was there anything you didn't understand? Do you have any questions or comments about the tape?"

### Introduction to the Second Tape

"The second videotape, TCHOU TCHOU, is a make-believe story that uses blocks. It's about a boy, a girl, and a dragon. What is a dragon? What do dragons do?"

"The dragon in TCHOU TCHOU is a little scary, but mostly it makes a big mess. At first the boy and girl are not sure what to do about the dragon, but in the end they figure out a way to make everything okay."

"During this tape, whenever we see the dragon coming we're going to yell *boo*." (Practice with children.) "And whenever the dragon leaves, we're going to shout *hooray*." (Practice this.)

"Now that we're ready for the dragon, let's watch the tape. It has no words, so you can talk out loud as you watch TCHOU TCHOU."

Play the tape and do an image/sound skim: "What do you remember best from that video? Does anything you saw or heard stick out in your mind?" If you can, ask how the tape made children feel. "Was there anything you didn't understand? Do you have any questions or comments about the tape?"

### Introduction to the Activity

"If you want to, you can make your own dragon out of an egg carton. Here is one I made." (Demonstrate.) "As you can see, I painted the outside of the carton with bright colors and then glued on a long red tongue and some teeth. I've brought some construction paper you can cut out to decorate your dragon."

Before the program, split the egg-cartons lengthwise so that the part that holds the eggs can become a 6-scaled dragon. Unless you have a poultry farm nearby, it may take a while to save the empty egg-cartons, so ask your friends and colleagues to help. Restaurants (perhaps even the hospital cafeteria) may have wide papier-mache egg-cartons which you can split into several dragons.

Children will need a fair amount of help to do this, and the process must be modeled before they begin. When their dragons are dry, encourage children to play with them, and to incorporate blocks into their dramatic play with the dragons. An alternative would be for children to simply go to the block corner and play dragon with the blocks.

## Evaluation of the Program

We recorded the responses of 15 children at 3 sites. Their overall age range was 3–13, but most were 3–8. This program was marvelous. Although TCHOU TCHOU was the clear favorite, THE MOLE AND THE TELEPHONE was perfect for children 3–8 (including those who did not speak or understand English).

Under-nines found the mole character extremely appealing and enjoyed labeling and guessing what it was doing with the phone. They seemed highly satisfied when mole put the telephone to sleep like a baby. A girl of 5 captured the overall response when she said, "If I had a mole at home, I'd love it and squeeze it and take care of it."

TCHOU TCHOU's age range was a little older, from 5–13. The test groups were engrossed by the block characters, the story, and the highly dramatic music. Children also understood how the block boy and girl solved their problem with the dragon. As an 8-year-old boy said, "They switched him around, that's why they call him Tchou Tchou."

At one screening, older children were too self-conscious to boo and cheer as we suggested, so they asked us to do it. At other sites everyone participated in the booing and cheering.

Sevens and older noticed many details (such as the boy's sneakers and the basketball). They verbalized a great deal, freely expressed their feelings (of loss, when the girl appears to be missing), and enthusiastically anticipated the dragon's return.

## Comments about the Introductions

Getting children to participate with *boos* and *hoorays* during the screening of TCHOU TCHOU was a highly effective device, both to offset any fears they might have had and to foster group rapport. We strongly suggest that it be done with all children under 8.

## Evaluation of the Activity

This is a variation on Playroom Film Program #5 in which we replaced the earlier mole film with one that we hoped would be less confusing. Because it was the stronger tape and featured a scary dragon, we based the activity on TCHOU TCHOU. Making an egg-carton dragon was remarkably appealing and over 70% of the test population undertook it. Children could not wait to make their dragons or "monsters," which in some way may have fed into their need for control.

We modeled a simply painted, green egg-carton dragon. After they had made their own, we encouraged children to engage in dramatic play. Where blocks were available, we also encouraged play with them. At one site, a few preschoolers (3–5) became successfully engaged in block play, but most children were disinterested in dramatic play and focused on creating their own dragons. Over-nines found neither activity appealing, although they did enjoy the screening—particularly TCHOU TCHOU.

There were no problems in terms of children's physical conditions as long as adult help and encouragement were readily available. For children up to 8/9, this was a *four-star* program and then some!

# Playroom Video Program #18

| | |
|---|---|
| **Activity:** | Making musical instruments. |
| **Materials:** | Paper cups, dried rice or macaroni, waxed paper, rubber bands, construction paper, markers, crayons, and scissors. |
| **Dexterity:** | Average, except for those with IVs. |
| **Age Level:** | 5–10. |

## KUUMBA
(8 minutes/cutout animation/dialog & narration)

A contemporary origins tale from Trinidad which explains how an ingenious boy invented the steel drum the night before the parade and carnival celebrations held in conjunction with Mardi Gras. The videotape makes excellent use of sound and Caribbean music and gives a positive image of the black family. Although somewhat primitive-looking, the child-made artwork is appealing.

## GERALD McBOING BOING
(7 minutes/cel animation/narration)

A classic cartoon, narrated in verse (written by Dr. Seuss), this is the sometimes poignant tale of a handicapped boy who eventually finds a place for himself in the world. From the day he uttered his first sound, Gerald McCloy was unable to talk; he could only go "beep-beep" or "boing-boing." Because of this, he is rejected by his neighbors, his peers, and his local school. Gerald's handicap becomes an asset, however, when he is hired by a radio station to make sound effects.

## Introduction to the First Tape

"This program is all about special sounds. Do any of you know a special sound? Can you make that sound?" (If they seem stuck, name and imitate a musical sound you like.)

"The first videotape is called KUUMBA. It's about a boy named Simon. He lives on a Caribbean island where everyone is preparing for the Mardi Gras carnival. There will be parades and dancing and beautiful costumes, and Simon wants to find a special sound to make music during the carnival parade. Let's see what he finds. Remember, it's okay to talk out loud as you watch KUUMBA."

Play the tape and do an image/sound skim: "What do you remember best from that video? Does anything you saw or heard stick out in your mind?" If you can, ask how the tape made children feel. "Was there anything you didn't understand? Do you have any questions or comments about the tape?"

## Introduction to the Second Tape

"The next videotape is called GERALD McBOING BOING. Unlike Simon, Gerald doesn't go looking for them because he makes special sounds naturally. In fact, Gerald cannot talk, he just makes special sounds; and at first this causes him some problems. Let's discover what happens as we watch—and listen to—GERALD McBOING BOING."

Play the tape and do an image/sound skim: "What do you remember best from that video? Does anything you saw or heard stick out in your mind?" If you can, ask how the tape made children feel. "Was there anything you didn't understand? Do you have any questions or comments about the tape?"

Ask children to think of their favorite sound in GERALD McBOING BOING. "Can you imitate it?"

## Introduction to the Activity

"Now you can make special sounds by making an instrument like Simon did. Here are some materials you can use. If you prefer, you can simply draw an imaginary instrument and the group will guess what sound it would make."

Demonstrate both activities. For one, use a paper cup and rice or macaroni to make a maraca; for the other, draw an imaginary instrument and make up a sound for it.

## Evaluation of the Program

We recorded the responses of 15 children at 4 sites. Their overall age range was 3–12, but most were 6–9. The tapes worked remarkably well together, with neither the clear preference. Both were enjoyed by all (except for under-fours who could not follow the stories) and both were screened several times at children's request. Everyone related to the boys' problems and was pleased by their resolution.

KUUMBA was a true success and this seemed to be the best pairing for it of all the combinations we tried. Children moved to its music and got very involved in the story. West Indian children (we had 3) especially appreciated it and identified with the character of Simon.

Children eagerly anticipated the sounds in GERALD McBOING BOING and joined Gerald in making them, particularly during a second or third screening (at children's request). A boy of 9 said he liked Gerald's ability to "overcome his difference." Hospital staff all commented on this aspect of the tape and were pleased that children related to it. GERALD

McBOING BOING would work both in film and on TV—as would the entire program.

## Comments about the Introductions

We did not say anything about Gerald's leaving home or going through a sad period. Nonetheless, those events did not seem to upset children who enjoyed and understood the story without being warned about them.

## Evaluation of the Activity

This is a revision of Playroom Film Programs #9 and #16 as well as CCTV Program #13. We wanted to find a better partner for KUUMBA and develop an activity that drew on what it had to offer. Previous experience indicated that although it used cutout animation, its theme and its music were the tape's strong points—not its imagery.

We provided paper cups and fillings for them so children could make maracas. Close to 70% of our sample did the activity which worked best with those 5–12. The over-tens were largely girls; although they enjoyed the videotapes, boys over 9 shied away from creating an instrument and seemed embarrassed by the idea.

A number of children drew their instruments, but actually making one seemed to generate more excitement and satisfaction. The best variation involved paper cups. After they had decorated the outside of their cup, children filled them with rice or macaroni and made a "skin" by stretching waxed paper, secured by a rubber band, over the top. (Making a comb and waxed paper kazoo, which we tried initially, was too difficult and became a frustration rather than an enjoyment.) We also took advantage of anything remotely musical that we found in the playroom.

In one remarkably constructive session, children found a few instruments in the room, made others, and then everyone sat around and sang. They sang "Old MacDonald" then traded instruments and sang some more; some even made up their own songs.

Children in poor condition were not up to this activity. They enjoyed the tapes but could not get sufficiently energized to attempt the instruments. Although older girls would probably enjoy it, the best age for this *four-star* program/activity is 5–9.

# Playroom Video Program #19

| | |
|---|---|
| **Activity:** | Mask-making. |
| **Materials:** | Uncoated white paper plates, tongue depressors (to hold masks from the bottom), construction paper, tissue paper, yarn, crayons, markers, masking tape, glue-sticks, and a stapler. |
| **Dexterity:** | Average, except for those with IVs. |
| **Age Level:** | 6–13. |

## THE MASKMAKER
(7 minutes/liveaction/nonverbal)

As Bip, Marcel Marceau acts out the tale of a maskmaker who enjoys the disguise wearing a mask allows, until a jovial mask sticks and he cannot remove it. (The running time listed above does not include the tedious spoken introduction Marceau gives preceding his performance. As we do in nonhospital situations, just run past the introduction before screening the tape.)

## WHERE THE WILD THINGS ARE
(8 minutes/animation/narration)

An unusual and slightly overdone production based on the picturebook by Maurice Sendak. This is the story of what happened the night Max wore his wolf suit. When his mischief gets out of hand, Max's mother (who is not seen) sends him to bed without dinner. The boy's imagination turns his room into a jungle where the wild things live. The beasts recognize Max's wildness and make him their king, but after a wild rumpus he gets bored. So Max returns to his real room where his supper is waiting.

## Introduction to the First Tape

"The program we are going to see is about feelings and imagination. Feelings are like the weather because sometimes they change from day to day. Do you feel the same way all the time?"

"The first videotape is called THE MASKMAKER. It is about a man who makes masks. What is a mask? Why do people use them?"

"In the story, the man makes many masks—all expressing different feelings. He likes to wear different masks so no one will know how he really feels. One time he puts a mask on but cannot get it off. He tries and tries but it won't budge. Finally he has to destroy the mask to get it off and realizes that it is best to be himself."

"In the tape the actor who plays the maskmaker is a mime. A mime doesn't talk or use anything but movement and facial expression to let you know what is happening, so you have to watch very carefully."

"The tape doesn't have a real ending, so let's make up our own. Since it has no words, you can talk out loud as you watch THE MASKMAKER."

Play the tape and do an image/sound skim: "What do you remember best from that video? Does anything you saw or heard stick out in your mind?"

If you can, ask how the tape made children feel. "Was there anything you didn't understand? Do you have any questions or comments about the tape?"

Ask children how they would feel if they had to wear one mask, expressing the same feeling, all the time. "How do you think the story ends?"

### Introduction to the Second Tape

"The next videotape is called WHERE THE WILD THINGS ARE. Does anyone know the book?"

"It's a story about a young boy who has many different moods or feelings. Sometimes Max is happy and loving; at other times he's unhappy and angry and thinks about monsters."

"This story tells what happens to Max—in his imagination—one night when he's in a bad mood. Remember, it's okay to talk out loud as you watch WHERE THE WILD THINGS ARE."

Play the tape and do an image/sound skim: "What do you remember best from that video? Does anything you saw or heard stick out in your mind?" If you can, ask how the tape made children feel. "Was there anything you didn't understand? Do you have any questions or comments about the tape?"

Discuss how Max's mood changed and how he decided he did not want to be king of the wild things. Ask children what they thought about the monsters.

### Introduction to the Activity

"Masks can be made from different things and they can express different feelings. Here are some paper plates you can use to make your own paper plate mask, if you like. Before you begin, why not think about what feeling you want your mask to have. Will it be happy? Angry? Sad? If you wish,

you may make one of the characters from the tapes we just saw."

Show children a pair of simple, contrasting paper plate masks that you have already made.

### Evaluation of the Program

We recorded the responses of 22 children at 4 sites. Their overall age range was 5–17, but most were 5–12. This program was highly provocative and very effective for a supervised playroom situation. Children said that THE MASKMAKER was funny, sad when "he couldn't get the mask off," and both "because he had to destroy his happy face; but he can make another." The tape needs adult staff input, however, partly because its ending is not clearly resolved.

Our test population said "it was scary because of the monsters" but they thoroughly enjoyed WHERE THE WILD THINGS ARE. It is also best shown in a supervised situation where an adult can provide the reassurance that will let children enjoy the monsters as well as help children discuss their fantasies/fears.

No one had difficulty with the program and the more children there were in a screening, the better it was. Child Life staff at one site liked the program specifically for the playroom because it was so evocative, although staff at another site had reservations about WHERE THE WILD THINGS ARE—both book and tape—because of its monsters and scary qualities.

### Comments about the Introductions

It is essential to warn viewers about THE MASKMAKER's ambiguous ending, and since so many children mentioned monsters and scary feelings in their responses to WHERE THE WILD THINGS ARE, it may be advisable to talk about them after that.

### Evaluation of the Activity

Having determined by trial and error that paper plates worked better than anything else for mask-making, we tried another mask activity. This time children 6–13 enjoyed it and the process was quite therapeutic in some instances, such as when a 6-year-old abuse victim created a crying mask because, she said, the program made her sad. A girl with a cleft palate made a funny clown mask. A boy of 6 who was very controlled copied our model masks exactly. Another boy of 5 did a scary mask.

Adolescents did not want to make masks despite the fact that THE MASKMAKER appealed to them. It would be an appropriate tape for that age group if followed by discussion rather than artwork.

# Playroom Video Program #20

| | |
|---|---|
| **Activity:** | Drawing a place to be alone. |
| **Materials:** | Paper, pencils, and markers. |
| **Dexterity:** | Minimal. |
| **Age Level:** | 7–13. |

## BEING BY MYSELF
(6 minutes/liveaction/dialog & narration)

In this slice-of-life documentary portrait, preadolescent Lori Morris talks about her life in Maine and what it's like to be part of a large family. Sometimes, Lori feels a need to take time off from her job as a waitress in the family's seafood restaurant in order to get away by herself. Although she enjoys her family and respects her hard-working parents, Lori dreams of living alone someday—perhaps in response to the pressures in such a large, close-knit family.

## OH BROTHER, MY BROTHER
(14 minutes/liveaction/dialog & narration)

Made by the subjects' parents, this heart-warming portrait of brotherly love and ambivalence combines the best aspects of a poignant drama and a funny home movie. The story revolves around an older brother's attempts to convince his newly independent younger brother to kiss him and say "I love you." Six-year-old Josh earnestly pursues his goal while engaged in everyday activities, ranging from jumping in leaves to building a tower with blocks, but it is 2-year-old Evan who gets the last word.

## Introduction to the First Tape

"Both videotapes are about families and about how sometimes you want to be with them, while sometimes you want to be by yourself. Do you have a special place you like to go when you need to be alone?"

"The first tape is called BEING BY MYSELF. It's a real-life documentary about a girl named Lori who lives in Maine and is part of a very large family. Let's watch BEING BY MYSELF."

Play the tape and do an image/sound skim: "What do you remember best from that video? Does anything you saw or heard stick out in your mind?"

If you can, ask how the videotape made children feel. "Was there anything you didn't understand? Do you have any questions or comments about the tape?"

## Introduction to the Second Tape

"The second videotape is about real brothers. Evan is 2 and Josh is 6. In the first tape, Lori sometimes wanted to get away from her family and be by herself. In this one, Josh likes to do some things with his younger brother and tries to convince him that people can love more than one person at a time. But Evan has just turned 2 and children that age are sometimes fiercely independent, so Evan says *no* to just about everything Josh suggests."

"You were once 2. How do you think you said *no* when you were that age." (Let children say no a few times. Ask them to say it louder each time.) "Okay, let's watch OH BROTHER, MY BROTHER."

Play the tape and do an image/sound skim: "What do you remember best from that video? Does anything you saw or heard stick out in your mind?" If you can, ask how the tape made children feel. "Was there anything you didn't understand? Do you have any questions or comments about the tape?"

Ask if saying *no* and getting away by yourself are related in any way. Discuss being 2 years old and how for a child of that age saying *no* may be his/her only power.

## Introduction to the Activity

"Have you ever done something really special with a sister or brother or a best friend? Are there special places you like to go with them? See if you can think of a such a place in your mind, then draw a picture of it or describe—either in writing or just by talking—a special place you go with someone special."

If children want to talk about their thoughts or memories, encourage them to do so. If they are hesitant to draw or write about their own experiences, suggest they talk about their favorite scene from either tape.

## Evaluation of the Program

We recorded the responses of 18 children at 3 sites. Their overall age range was 5–13, but most were 7–11. Thematically, these tapes balance each other well but the first one had a few drawbacks. BEING BY MYSELF appealed quite a bit to girls 7–12, but younger children did not understand it and older boys had a fairly predictable resistance to a videotape about a girl. While children related well to the theme of needing a place to be alone (to think, play, plan, or daydream) and generally liked Lori, the tape's structure—it seemed to have no beginning and no resolution—made it hard to grasp.

Many children also had trouble understanding Lori's New England accent, and her soft voice was difficult to hear. Most children's comments had to do with either liking the lobsters or the birthday party. Preadolescent boys were a tough audience for this tape, but even they responded well to Lori. When asked how the tape made him feel, a 9-year-old boy captured the overall feeling by saying, "Outside boring, inside happy."

OH BROTHER, MY BROTHER was a phenomenal success for all ages (5–13) as well as several younger children who were not counted in our statistics. Focusing the introduction on saying *no* and how 2-year-olds behave somehow overcame older children's bias against a tape about "babies." Child Life staff at one site were astonished at older boys' positive response. They added that while BEING BY MYSELF had some structural flaws its theme was terrific.

## Comments about the Introductions

The prelude to BEING BY MYSELF worked very well. It elicited involved discussions about favorite places to be alone, which really helped this low-key tape. Emphasizing Evan's saying *no* in presenting OH BROTHER, MY BROTHER provided children with a focus and facilitated their anticipation of events. At every screening they roared with laughter whenever Evan said *no*.

## Evaluation of the Activity

We wanted to encourage children to visualize a special place where they could be alone—and draw or write about it. But the activity was hard to evaluate. It succeeded at only one screening with boys 7–13. At that session, a boy wrote a sweet paragraph about his room and being able to think about things there. Although the others would neither draw nor write, many told us about their favorite places to be alone. Obviously, a good alternative—and perhaps the better plan—would be to ask children to talk about their special hideaways.

Because of a scheduling conflict, we could not attempt the activity with one group. And at one particularly large screening with 9 children, the group got interested in playdough. We suggested making a scene from the videotapes and they all worked on making a restaurant, including tables, chairs, menus, and food. This was instrumental in bringing the group together and was enjoyed by everyone from preschoolers to teenagers.

If we had more data on this activity, we might be able to recommend it. As it is, we can only say that it—or some variation on it—is worth trying.

# Playroom Video Program #21

| | |
|---|---|
| **Activity:** | Drawing a family portrait. |
| **Materials:** | White paper, pre-cut construction paper frames, pencils, markers, crayons, and glue-sticks. |
| **Dexterity:** | Minimal. |
| **Age Level:** | 5–9. |

## MY BIG BROTHER
(6 minutes/liveaction/dialogue & narration)

In this slice-of-life documentary, Dexter Maxwell, a black preadolescent from New York City, talks about his life. Among the things he shares are playing stoop ball on the streets, traveling by subway to where his mother works, and taking dance class. An only child with a single parent, Dexter wanted male companionship, so he applied for a Big Brother through the national program of that name.

## OH BROTHER, MY BROTHER
(14 minutes/liveaction/dialog & narration)

Made by the subjects' parents, this heart-warming portrait of brotherly love and ambivalence combines the best aspects of a poignant drama and a funny home movie. The story revolves around an older brother's attempts to convince his newly independent younger brother to kiss him and say "I love you." Six-year-old Josh earnestly pursues his goal while engaged in everyday activities, ranging from jumping in leaves to building a tower with blocks, but it is 2-year-old Evan who gets the last word.

## Introduction to the First Tape

"Both videotapes are about families. The first one, called MY BIG BROTHER, is about Dexter Maxwell. He is 12 years old and lives with his mom in New York City. Let's watch MY BIG BROTHER."

Play the tape and do an image/sound skim: "What do you remember best from that video? Does anything you saw or heard stick out in your mind?" If you can, ask how the tape made children feel. "Was there anything you didn't understand? Do you have any questions or comments about the tape?"

Discuss Dexter's desire for a brother and how brothers and sisters can be both fun and annoying.

## Introduction to the Second Tape

"The next videotape is about real brothers who are much younger than Dexter. Evan is 2 and Josh is 6. In the first tape Dexter had a problem because he didn't have a brother. In this tape, a boy has the opposite problem. Sometimes it's a problem to have a brother."

"Evan has just turned 2 and children that age are sometimes fiercely independent, so Evan says *no* to just about everything Josh suggests."

"You were once 2. How do you think you said *no* when you were that age." (Let children say *no* a few times. Ask them to say it louder each time.) "Okay, let's watch OH BROTHER, MY BROTHER."

Play the tape and do an image/sound skim: "What do you remember best from that video? Does anything you saw or heard stick out in your mind?" If you can, ask how the tape made children feel. "Was there anything you didn't understand? Do you have any questions or comments about the tape?"

"Do you think those brothers love each other—even though they had some fights? Why wouldn't Evan say he loved Josh?" Discuss how for a child of 2 saying *no* may be his/her only power.

## Introduction to the Activity

"Both tapes were family portraits. A portrait is a picture of one or more special people. Now it's your turn to make a portrait. You can draw a picture of someone in your family, or your whole family, or your best friend."

Before children begin, show them a portrait you drew. Be honest about who it is and how you feel about them. However, be careful not to draw it too well or you will intimidate children.

## Evaluation of the Program

We recorded the responses of 11 children at 3 sites. Their overall age range was 3–11, but most were 6–8. This combination worked quite well and the impact of the program was noteworthy. It raised many issues, including ambivalent feelings about home and about being hospitalized for a long time, which were important to address. Child Life staff regarded the program as effectively therapeutic.

MY BIG BROTHER had the same structural flaws as BEING BY MYSELF (too short, too unstructured), but when children saw it for the second time (we rescreened the entire program), they enjoyed it better. While none seemed to respond to the big brother character, they did respond to Dexter's wanting a big brother, and to Dexter himself. He was generally engaging—especially so with urban and black children. Ratings were all good, super, and super good.

OH BROTHER, MY BROTHER appealed to all viewers—older children as well as preschoolers.

## Comments about the Introductions

After some experimentation, we learned that the most effective preparation for MY BIG BROTHER was the one that focused simply on Dexter and his life. The introduction for OH BROTHER, MY BROTHER was quite effective in involving children. It focused them on Evan, and how 2-year-olds exercise control. It also gave older children an anticipatory focus; they broke into gales of laughter every time Evan said *no*.

## Evaluation of the Activity

This is a *four-star* variation on the previous program. Where that was all white and part female, this was part black and all male. Where that was about getting away by oneself, this was about belonging. Over 70% of our sample did the activity and all drew pictures of their families or close friends, but older youngsters were reluctant to talk about their families. One boy who was initially resistant finally decided to share his family with us. He carefully studied a picture of himself and his sister at summer camp and drew a portrait.

# Playroom Video Program #22

**Activity:**  Modeling playdough.
**Materials:**  Playdough. Activity sheet optional.
**Dexterity:**  Minimal-average, except with IVs.
**Age Level:**  3–13.

## WORM DANCES
(3 minutes/clay animation/nonverbal)

An upbeat scat and percussion music video in which one primal playdough shape turns into another. The colorful, eye-pleasing transformations and delightful wiggling to a carefree soundtrack make this videotape a perfect lead-in to clay or playdough activities.

## WHAZZAT?
(10 minutes/clay animation/nonverbal)

Six lively clay creatures change shape and move about, helping each other explore their environment. When the friends discover an unknown creature (in the section based on the Arab/Indian tale about the blind men and the elephant), they each describe it nonverbally from a different point of view. After 5 of them have depicted what they know about it, the group pools its resources and figures out what the creature is. In unison, all shout "ELEPHANT," the only word in this joyful classic.

## Introduction to the First Tape

"Both videotapes in this program were made with playdough. The first is very short. It's called WORM DANCES. It has no words and no story, just little pieces of clay that move and wiggle in all sorts of ways. You can talk as you watch WORM DANCES."

Play the tape and do an image/sound skim: "What do you remember best from that video? Does anything you saw or heard stick out in your mind?" If you can, ask how the tape made children feel. "Was there anything you didn't understand? Do you have any questions or comments about the tape?"

Then say, "You know I'd love to see WORM DANCES again. Would you?" If they say yes, remind them they can talk during the tape.

After the second screening, say: "What do you remember after watching twice? Did anything seem different to you? Did you see anything this time you did not see before?"

## Introduction to the Second Tape

"The next videotape is called WHAZZAT? Like WORM DANCES it is made out of playdough, but it has a story about some funny little creatures who go on a trip. What is interesting about them is that they cannot see. All of them are blind."

"In the first part of the story the little creatures run into a few problems and in the second part of the story they come across a big, unfamiliar animal. By working together and helping each other, they solve all their problems and identify the animal."

"Just remember that things may look a bit scary at times but everything works out fine in the end. Since the tape has no words, it's okay to talk out loud as you watch WHAZZAT?"

Play the tape and do an image/sound skim: "What do you remember best from that video? Does anything you saw or heard stick out in your mind?" If you can, ask how the tape made children feel. "Was there anything you didn't understand? Do you have any questions or comments about the tape?"

## Introduction to the Activity

"Here is some playdough you can use to make your own creatures. I'll start by making the little bear on the activity sheet. Later I might get some other ideas of things to make."

Demonstrate a primitive looking animal. Suggest that children make a creature from their own imaginations, from the tapes, or from the activity sheet.

## Evaluation of the Program

We recorded the responses of 29 children at 4 sites. Their overall age range was 2–13, but most were 5–8. This was an absolute success. The program engaged, relaxed, and entertained children and motivated a follow-up that allowed many outlets for self-expression. All Child Life specialists from all hospitals thought it was great!

Younger children (2–6) especially enjoyed WORM DANCES, but older ones did too. Preschoolers delighted in the worms and "wiggling things." WHAZZAT? was more appealing to children 5 and older who could better understand the story. Those 2–4 had some trouble following the storyline, but they related to it on a visceral level; just watching the clay move and change was satisfying. In addition, everyone personalized the clay characters. Many children referred to the purple slowpoke in their comments: "They forgot him!" came up spontaneously in every screening.

## Comments about the Introductions

When preparing very young children for WHAZZAT?, it is important to warn them that the characters get into trouble that might be a little scary. Tell children not to worry because everything works out fine in the end.

## Evaluation of the Activity

This is the same winning, sculpture-inspiring pair we had used in Playroom Film Program #7 and CCTV Program #12. We gave children 4 different colors of playdough and activity sheets, showing steps to make a horse and a bear. We usually modeled one animal for them and then encouraged them to make their own figures either from the tape or their imaginations.

Demonstrating helped children get started and built up their confidence in their own abilities. Interestingly, they seemed encouraged by the fact that we were not accomplished artists. To a marked degree they enjoyed being able to tell us that the bears we made "didn't really look like bears."

Close to 95% of our sample participated and the activity was especially conducive to positive group dynamics. At the end of one session, children made a wonderful display by spontaneously putting all their creations together in the middle of the table.

Food was the focus in every group. We got lots of burgers, hot dogs, pizza, spaghetti and meatballs, and milk shakes. (Since food or the lack of it is a major issue for hospitalized children, this activity gives them a chance to deal with it.) But, their work also reflected other needs, including family pets. An angry 5-year-old wanted to "karate chop" his playdough horse and asked for a plastic hammer. He had a great time banging and squashing the clay.

This was a *four-star* program/activity and then some!

# CLAY CREATURES

To make a horse or dog:

1. Take a small fistful of clay and roll it between your hands into the shape of a pencil. Carefully bend it into the shape of a rainbow to make the body.

2. Make a head by rolling another smaller piece of clay into the shape of a short fat crayon. Stick it onto one end of the body.

3. Roll an even smaller piece of clay into a tail and stick it onto the other end of the body.

4. Pinch two little pieces of clay and stick them on top of the head for ears. Roll two small beads of clay for eyes.

To make a bear:

1. Take a small fistful of clay and roll it between your hands into the shape of a crayon. Carefully bend it to an upside down V to make the bear's legs.

2. Roll another handful of clay into a nice round ball and stick it on top of the legs to make the body.

3. Make a smaller ball for a head and two small crayon shapes for the arms.

4. Pinch two little pieces of clay for ears and make three small beads for the bear's eyes and nose.

*Using Media to Make Kids Feel Good,* by Maureen Gaffney. Published by Oryx Press, 2214 N. Central, Phoenix, AZ 85004, 1988.

# Playroom Video Program #23

| | |
|---|---|
| **Activity:** | Sculpting with playdough. |
| **Materials:** | Shoe box tops, tongue depressors, coffee stirrers, plastic knives (for sculpting), and playdough. |
| **Dexterity:** | Average to considerable; difficult with an IV. |
| **Age Level:** | 6–12. |

**SOPHIE AND THE SCALES**
(10 minutes/pixillated liveaction/nonverbal)

A stylized slapstick comedy in which a young girl fights back when an ill-natured piano teacher goes too far. Initially, Sophie, who looks like a little doll, appears docile and timid, but a mischievous side of her personality emerges when she is alone with her bizarre piano teacher. Later, after the humorless tutor has literally thrown her out the door, Sophie returns and, in a wish-fulfilling scene, turns the tables and throws the teacher around the room. This done, Sophie picks up her things and returns home, once again behaving like a perfect little doll.

**THE FABLE OF HE AND SHE**
(11 minutes/clay animation/dialog & narration)

A delightful tale in which the inhabitants (Hardibars and Mushamels) of the imaginary island of Baramel change their attitudes about sex-defined job roles as a result of a natural disaster. The unusual names (chopachucks, mushmoos, pompomberries, reverse-a-quake), the imaginative bas-relief playdough animation, and the amusing storyline give this tape universal appeal.

## Introduction to the First Tape

"Has someone ever done something that bugged you so much or made you so mad you wanted to make them stop or go away?" (Hopefully children will respond, if not, relate a time when such a thing happened to you. If they do respond, ask them what they did about it. Did they ever wish they could be like the Incredible Hulk and change physically?)

"In the videotape we are about to see you will meet an old-fashioned girl named Sophie. She is very good and somewhat timid. Every day she takes piano lessons from a weird piano teacher who is extremely strict and something of a bully."

"Let's see what happens to Sophie when she reaches her limit. You should know that the tape looks unusual because real people act out the characters' parts but they move like puppets. It's sort of

weird! You'll see heavy make-up, funny wigs, and jerky movements all designed to make you think of puppets or dolls. Since it has no words, it's okay to talk out loud as you watch SOPHIE AND THE SCALES."

Play the tape and do an image/sound skim: "What do you remember best from that video? Does anything you saw or heard stick out in your mind?" If you can, ask how the tape made children feel. "Was there anything you didn't understand? Do you have any questions or comments about the tape?"

## Introduction to the Second Tape

"The next videotape shows another way of solving problems: cooperating and working things out together. It is called THE FABLE OF HE AND SHE. The story takes place on an island called Baramel. Like those in the earlier tape, the creatures in this are unusual. They are little clay creatures. The blue hardibars are men, and red/pink mushamels are women in THE FABLE OF HE AND SHE."

Play the tape and do an image/sound skim: "What do you remember best from that video? Does anything you saw or heard stick out in your mind?" If you can, ask how the tape made children feel. "Was there anything you didn't understand? Do you have any questions or comments about the tape?"

## Introduction to the Activity

"Here is some playdough and box tops so you can create your favorite scene or image from the tapes we just saw. If you prefer, you can make something from real life or a dream."

To help children get started, show them a scene you have already begun. If children get stuck, ask them to name their favorite scene from the tape and describe everything they can remember about it. Then let them start with the easiest thing to make from that scene.

## Evaluation of the Program

We recorded the responses of 22 children at 4 sites. Their overall age range was 4–16, but most were 6–10. Interestingly, this produced the most obviously therapeutic results of any program, a consequence attributable largely to SOPHIE AND THE SCALES. However, SOPHIE AND THE SCALES needs careful handling. The introduction must focus children on the humor of the piece and help them understand the theme because, stylistically, the tape is quite unusual. Most children responded to its story by saying that the teacher "deserved it" when Sophie beat her up. Child Life staff at one site thought it was wonderful—particularly for abused children.

A 6-year-old abuse victim remembered "the teacher because she was so mean" and said she was ugly, then she made a playdough portrait of the teacher's face in a very careful and detailed manner. And a 10-year-old who just had an appendectomy observed, "In real life, children can't hit their teachers because they will get in trouble." He then sculpted a giant playdough needle with blood coming out of it and said, "I'm gonna give this shot to the doctor."

A girl of 10 with a severe blood disorder had been through a great deal of surgery. Generally she was quiet and passive, but after seeing SOPHIE AND THE SCALES she became quite animated and mentioned 3 times that the teacher was mean; she personalized the experience by saying over and over, "I'd give her a piece of my mind." Child Life staff were delighted at her response.

None of the children who saw SOPHIE AND THE SCALES had a bad reaction; all laughed, enjoyed the slapstick, and liked the theme of revenge. Girls generally related better to the tape than boys (because of the character, Sophie) but it was fine for all ages, 7 and over. However, we do not recommend SOPHIE AND THE SCALES or the program for TV or anything but an adult supervised screening.

THE FABLE OF HE AND SHE was a fitting antidote to the first tape and was also extraordinarily well-received. Children in general do not respond to the message about sex-role reversal, but they seem to love the characters, how the clay moves, the drama of the storms, and the fun of the contest. It was great for all ages, and older children often expressed interest in its animation technique.

## Evaluation of the Activity

Because working with playdough is so physical, we thought it would be a good follow-up to SOPHIE AND THE SCALES. By itself, however, it is doubtful it could motivate a clay activity (puppetry might be easier). For this reason, we paired SOPHIE AND THE SCALES with THE FABLE OF HE AND SHE—a pairing that also made sense in terms of program balance.

We supplied children with playdough (white, red, blue, and yellow) and shoe box tops and asked them to create their favorite scene or image from either tape using a bas-relief modeling technique (similar to that used in THE FABLE OF HE AND SHE). We demonstrated with our own simple, unfinished scenes.

Over 70% of our sample completed a sculpture and, partly because working with clay is minimally frustrating, the activity allowed participants a significant emotional release. Children who were most excited about the revenge theme did pictures of Sophie, the teacher, or things like the giant needle. Five did artwork relating specifically to the piano teacher.

The others drew on THE FABLE OF HE AND SHE and had considerable fun creating islands with worms on them and assorted images they had seen in the tape. In some of our screenings, a number of children worked together, something which fostered a positive group spirit.

Over-twelves, particularly boys, did not want to work with playdough and children under 5 did not create pictures, although they were quite interested in manipulating the playdough and watching it make different colors when combined.

This was a *four-star* program/activity for children 6–12.

# Playroom Video Program #24

<table>
<tr><td>Activity:</td><td>Box art.</td></tr>
<tr><td>Materials:</td><td>Shoe boxes and tops, styrofoam packing peanuts, pipe cleaners, wooden thread spools, wooden clothes pins, felt scraps, patterned paper, cardboard, construction paper, markers, scissors, and glue (preferably fast-drying).</td></tr>
<tr><td>Dexterity:</td><td>Considerable; difficult with IVs.</td></tr>
<tr><td>Age Level:</td><td>6–12.</td></tr>
</table>

### CAPTAIN SILAS (Short Version)
(7 minutes/object animation/narration)

Making imaginative use of a large cast of peanuts and household objects such as blue-tinted popcorn (the sea), a shaving brush (dolphin), and a wing tip shoe (boat), this droll videotape presents a delightful miniature world in which merchant-sailor Silas makes his living by trading trucks (made from thread spools) for sugar cubes (the principal building material used on Truck Island).

### CURIOUS GEORGE GOES TO THE HOSPITAL
(15 minutes/puppet animation/dialog & narration)

Based on the picturebook by Margret and H. A. Rey, this chapter of the adventures of the child-monkey and his surrogate parent (the man with the yellow hat) tells about when George swallows a jig-saw puzzle piece and goes to the hospital, where he stays 2 nights, to have it removed. Hospital procedures are described quite accurately, and the irrepressibly curious monkey manages to make amusing mischief.

### Introduction to the First Tape

"Both of the stories are about characters much smaller than you. In fact all the characters from the first videotape, called CAPTAIN SILAS, could fit in this shoe box (show shoe box), and they are about the size of peanuts." (Show styrofoam peanuts.)

"Captain Silas is the captain of a boat. Let's take a look at how he lives. It's okay to talk out loud as you watch CAPTAIN SILAS."

Play the tape and do an image/sound skim: "What do you remember best from that video? Does anything you saw or heard stick out in your mind?"

If you can, ask how the tape made the children feel. "Was there anything you didn't understand? Do you have any questions or comments about the tape?"

### Introduction to the Second Tape

"The next videotape is called CURIOUS GEORGE GOES TO THE HOSPITAL. Does anyone know who Curious George is?" (They may, but if not, say he is a little monkey who has many adventures).

"In the tape we are about to see, George gets sick and has to go to the hospital. But don't worry, he gets better and goes home in the end. Let's watch CURIOUS GEORGE GOES TO THE HOSPITAL."

Play the tape and do an image/sound skim: "What do you remember best from that video? Does anything you saw or heard stick out in your mind?" If you can, ask how the tape made children feel. "Was there anything you didn't understand? Do you have any questions or comments about the tape?"

### Introduction to the Activity

"Both videotapes were about tiny characters and their worlds. Now it's your turn to make a small or miniature world, if you want to. Here are some shoe boxes that you can paste things into like a diorama or a model house. (Demonstrate.) You can make your favorite scene from either of the tapes or make up your own little world."

Because the materials themselves often serve as direct inspirations to the children, make sure each type of material is easy to see and in its own container (such as a shoe box top). Show them a nearly finished shoe box world. Add a styrofoam peanut and/or a pipe-cleaner monkey. Children will need a fair amount of help with this, so recruit some extra adults. Boxes can be covered on the outside with different colored paper.

### Evaluation of the Program

We recorded the responses of 17 children at 3 sites. Their overall age range was 4–10, but most were 8. Both videotapes involve stories that start at home and end at home, and the program was truly successful with the entire test population.

CAPTAIN SILAS invited children to discover the numerous small objects used so imaginatively in this clever animation. However, because we were worried about the length of the program, we stopped CAPTAIN SILAS just after he takes his groceries home following the successful first voyage. (This is what is meant by "short version" above.) Although the short version has a visual conclusion without a corresponding narrative closure (which is not altogether satisfying), it was better for this program than showing the entire tape. We recommend showing only half of CAPTAIN SILAS if you intend to pair it with another long tape.

CURIOUS GEORGE GOES TO THE HOSPITAL was the best received videotape of all the titles we showed. Everybody wanted to see it again and again. At children's insistence, we screened it 5 and 6 times in a day. It depicts a delightful, nonthreatening hospital situation.

## Evaluation of the Activity

This is a *four-star* revision of Playroom Film Program #10 and CCTV Program #8. Although children were quite enthusiastic about the box art, they had to be in good to excellent condition to complete their boxes and they needed substantial assistance. Of the school age children who saw the program, 80% completed a box. The activity worked best for ages 6–10 in good (or better) condition and without IVs. Although we did not have any in this test population, it would also probably work with those 10–12.

Only 2 children did scenes from the movies; one did a scene about George and one created a scene with the red sea monster from CAPTAIN SILAS. Three did a scene of their home or a room in their house or apartment (which the boxes themselves may suggest).

Because box art requires so much dexterity, children with IVs may get discouraged, but they can do it if they have sufficient energy and if they get one-to-one help from an adult (including parents). Also, make sure to use adult shoe boxes; anything smaller will be too narrow for children to get their hands into.

It is essential to show children a model before they begin. The idea that the box is to be used as a stage viewed from the side needs to be reinforced with a visual aid. And if the activity is to run smoothly, it is important to have the objects well organized visually before children come to select them and to limit the number of objects they can take initially. To forestall hoarding and to prevent children from being overwhelmed, we allowed them to take only 10 objects at first; when they had used that batch, they could take 5 more each time they needed new supplies. To help children focus, we put the materials on a table that was separate from the area they were working in. We also used the shoe box tops as trays—both to hold children's own supplies and to separate small objects on the materials table.

If you have enough time before starting the activity, it would be desirable to play a game with children to inspire them to use objects imaginatively in their artwork. Give everyone an object and ask them to imagine what, besides its intended function, it could be used for or what, besides what it is, it looks like.

At one session we gave children styrofoam peanuts (although almost anything in the playroom could be used). They had a wonderful time turning the peanuts in different ways and looking at them from different angles. They said the styrofoam forms could be snakes, skates, peanuts, and shoes. Then they started making various letters of the alphabet with them.

*The Fable of He and She.* Courtesy: Learning Corporation of America.

*Whazzat?* Courtesy: Encyclopedia Brittanica Educational Corporation.

*Tchou Tchou.* Courtesy: Encyclopedia Brittanica Educational Corporation.

# Appendices

# APPENDIX A:

# Survey of Media Use in Children's Hospitals and Pediatric Wards in the USA and Canada

## by the Staff of the Media Center for Children

As part of the Hospitalized Children's Media Project, the Media Center for Children (MCC) surveyed children's hospitals and pediatric wards in the US and Canada to learn how media is used with nonpsychiatric child in-patients. In late 1983 MCC mailed a 3-page questionnaire to an in-house hospital list as well as to selected members of the Association for the Care of Children's Health. In the spring of 1985, MCC sent a modified 2-page survey, more focused on closed-circuit television, to an additional 15 hospitals.

Since it was impractical to determine beforehand which staff person within an institution was responsible for media, the questionnaires were sent to several people at each hospital: the Director of Child Life (if that position existed), the Chief of Pediatric Nursing, and/or the Head Nurse. Usually, only one person from each hospital returned the questionnaire, but when two were returned by the same institution, we collated the information and treated it as a single response.

Forty-four hospitals responded to the first questionnaire and 8 responded to the second (both are included in appendix). There were a total of 52 responses from hospitals in 22 states, 5 Canadian provinces, and the District of Columbia.

The questionnaires were intended to amplify a series of telephone interviews Deirdre Boyle conducted with the staff of 21 children's hospitals and/or pediatric wards in 1982. Boyle's data were documented in her article, "Hospitalized Children and Media: A Survey" (*Young Viewers* 6:4). We were

hoping to get a broader picture of the issues and problems Boyle had identified. As it turns out, however, our statistics are no more revealing than Boyle's narrative, but they do provide a general overview of how and what sort of media is used for the education, orientation, and enrichment of hospitalized children.

### Television Use

Television and video monitors are ubiquitous in the children's rooms and wards of hospitals. While the second survey did not ask about the distribution of television sets, all but 5 hospitals responding to the first survey indicated that they had at least one TV set per patient room and usually at least one in a playroom or lounge area as well. The first survey also indicated that television sets were provided free in 64% of the hospitals which responded; the rest had a nominal fee that could be waived for needy children.

Beyond the number of sets in hospitals, their size makes them a presence to be reckoned with. The majority of hospitals (60.4%) have television sets with screens 19″ or larger. However, while sets are plentiful and physically impressive, good commercially broadcast programs for hospitalized children are not.

The paucity both day and night of child-appropriate broadcast programming was frequently mentioned by those surveyed. And while roughly

45% of the surveyed hospitals have cable hook-ups, cable viewing is generally limited to adults. In addition, available programs either pose considerable problems for hospitalized children, because of their content or emotional tone, or do nothing to alleviate or clarify the usually painful and confusing experience of hospitalization. Because of this, many hospitals try to avoid commercial broadcasting by offering pediatric patients nontheatrical or educational media as an alternative. Using educational media on a hospital's closed-circuit TV (CCTV) system becomes a problem, however, if hospitals charge a rental fee for television sets. Educational rights and rates are only applicable when no fee is charged for viewing such programs.

## Alternative Media

Virtually all hospitals responding to our questionnaires indicated they use some form of alternative media with children. The most widely used format is 16mm film (67%), followed by radio and TV video games (both 55.8%), ¾-inch video (51.9%), and ½-inch VHS videocassettes (44.2%). Other media, such as records/tapes, 8mm film, slide shows, arcade videogames, videodisc, and ½-inch Beta videocassettes were also used, but to a lesser extent.

Thirty-nine hospitals, 75% of those responding, use 16mm film or videocassettes with children on a regular basis (daily or weekly) in the playroom and/or over CCTV. An additional 7 use film and videotapes with children but did not indicate if they do so on a regular basis. And 6 use only radio or video games with children in the playroom.

Fifty-eight percent of the hospitals screen one to 10 films or tapes per week. These are usually educational and entertainment shorts as well as features, and they are often repeated more than once. Twenty-one percent of those surveyed (almost exclusively those with CCTV programming for children) program 30 or more titles a week.

Alternative media is usually used for a number of reasons, including enrichment/entertainment, education, therapeutic benefits, public relations, and to record children's activities. However, the majority of hospitals (55.9%) said they use alternative media for a combination of entertainment and education.

## Programming Sources

Sources for children's media are varied, but most hospitals use what they call donated films and tapes (69%) and/or borrow works from their public library (63.5%). Fifty-nine percent of those surveyed also rent or buy from educational/nontheatrical distributors; however, since film/videotape budgets are generally small, the overall number of works obtained from the latter source is also small.

Rental budgets range from $50 a year at St. Joseph's in Hamilton to $2,800 annually at the St. Paul Children's Hospital in Minnesota. Only 28% have a budget to purchase media. The 2 largest purchasing budgets were reported by Tod Babies' Hospital in Youngstown which allocates approximately $1,500 annually to buy films and videotapes, and Grady Memorial in Atlanta, which has an annual budget of $5,000.

Thirty-four hospitals (65%) actually own films or videotapes, although such collections often include more than children's media. Of these, the majority own between one and 30 films/tapes. Eight of those with CCTV programming for children own 75 or more films/tapes.

## Evaluation and Selection

Eighty-five percent of the institutions surveyed have a structured selection and evaluation process for any media (except television) that is programmed or shown to children in the hospital. This responsibility is assumed by different hospital staff members—often a committee—from the director of nursing education, director of pediatric nursing, and head nurse, to education consultants, health care experts, pediatricians, media coordinators, and Child Life staff. However, in 35% of those surveyed, Child Life directors or therapists were solely responsible for media selection. In another 12%, it was the sole responsibility of recreation/play therapists/supervisors.

A majority (73%) of respondents have some sort of criteria for selecting the films and tapes they show to pediatric patients. The 5 most frequently cited had to do with the work's appropriateness to the age and developmental level of children, educational value, entertainment value, popularity and appeal, and hospital-appropriateness. Other considerations were subject matter, applicability to the needs of the patients, lack of violence and negative stereotypes, technical quality, price, running time, accuracy, and emotional tone.

A disappointingly small percentage (38.5%) said they conduct follow-up evaluations of their media programs. We assume from the few hospitals that elaborated about why they do not conduct follow-ups that lack of staff and a shortage of time makes formal evaluation difficult. What follow-ups exist vary from informal comment sheets to discussions with staff, patients, and/or parents.

## Programming Problems

Approximately 42% experienced problems with their children's media programs. The most frequently cited ones were lack of funding, overworked staff with limited time to screen and preview, lack of age- and institution-appropriate materials, and the tendency among some staff to use television as a background in the room when children really need other stimulation.

Difficulties with hardware, software, and suppliers were not uncommon. A number of hospitals mentioned that libraries and even distributors may make substitutions when selected titles are unavailable. Sometimes works arrive in poor or unusuable condition, and projectors/monitors break down, especially those which receive heavy use.

## CCTV Systems

Twenty-six (half the hospitals) had or were about to install CCTV systems for transmitting programs to pediatric patients at the time of our surveys. Another 16% had CCTV but either did not use it for children or did not indicate that they did so.

Hospitals use CCTV with children for one or more of 3 ends: health education, recreation, and hospital/surgical orientation. CCTV programming for children is usually available on only one channel, but Children's Hospital/National Medical Center in Washington has 2 channels for children, and Children's Orthopedic Hospital in Seattle has one in-house channel for young children and another for adolescents/adults.

Roughly half the hospitals with CCTV for children program 7 to 16 hours a day, beginning between 6:00 and 9:00am, and ending between 5:00 and 8:00pm. The other half program one to 6 hours a day, usually in the afternoon, beginning at noon or 12:30pm.

While program times vary, scheduling considerations seem rather consistent. Among the factors CCTV programmers work around are staff availability; the hours children are awake; avoiding conflict with Child Life and other programs; scheduling something at lunchtime, rest periods, or other times when children are supposed to be in their rooms; and times of the day when good or acceptable commercial programming is lacking.

Most hospitals said they repeat their programming every week or 2 weeks, which generally corresponds to the average stay of pediatric patients in the hospitals we surveyed. Some, however, repeat programs daily.

## CCTV Transmission

The actual transmission of closed-circuit programming is handled by different departments and/or individuals in different hospitals. Audiovisual/media departments transmit children's CCTV in about 42% of those surveyed. Other hospitals delegate this responsibility to Child Life staff, Recreation/Therapy, Training, Education and Communications, or an outside TV/video service. But regardless of who or what department is responsible, they usually do more than transmit. In addition to activating the system, changing tapes, and transmit-

ting the programs, some of these departments and/or individuals also plan, schedule, purchase, and produce children's programming.

## Self-Generated Programming

While self-generated CCTV programming is becoming more widespread, only 16 (or 65%) of the 26 hospitals with CCTV programming for children develop their own in-house programming and have a staff position for this purpose. One uses an outside consultant. Cardinal Glennon Memorial in St. Louis and Miller Children's Hospital in Long Beach have both a full-time and a part-time staff person working on the development of programming for children. All Children's in St. Petersburg, Grady Memorial in Atlanta, Le Bonheur in Memphis, Kapiolani/Children's Medical Center in Honolulu, Minneapolis Children's, and Sacred Heart in Spokane all have a full-time staff person working on in-house program development. The remaining hospitals with programming positions use either one or 2 part-time staff or various staff people who work for varying amounts of time each week.

Typically, production facilities and equipment are not extensive; they often consist of a portable ½-inch video unit or a simple ¾-inch system. However, a number of hospitals actually have studios, some of which are upgraded closets and some of which are first-rate professional facilities. Among those with large studios and full production facilities are Grady Memorial, Le Bonheur, Lutheran General in Park Ridge, IL and Minneapolis Children's.

Salaries of the staff people responsible for program development are usually paid out of a department budget such as biomedical communications, nursing or nursing education, AV/media services, training and education, Child Life or pediatrics, while in-house generated programming itself is usually funded either from the general hospital budget, from grants and donations, or from a combination of both.

## Interactive Programming

Seven hospitals have interactive components in their self-generated programming:

- At Cardinal Glennon Memorial Hospital for Children a puppet host addresses children individually and children both appear in the program and assist with production.
- Children's Hospital/National Medical Center has been experimenting with having children tape each other and with playing games between patient rooms via CCTV monitors.
- Children's Hospital/Health Sciences Center in Winnipeg has daily live broadcasts with a puppet host called No-name from Monday through Friday. Child patients are visited before the show and many are greeted on-air during the show.

Children may both appear on the show and participate in games, crafts, jokes, and songs, etc.

- Johns Hopkins Hospital in Baltimore was planning to involve children in the shooting of CCTV programs. At the time of the survey, they were also planning a live Bingo show with a call-in winner.
- At Lutheran General Hospital in Park Ridge questions are posed on-air for audience reflection, and hospital-generated print materials are used for follow-up.
- At Minneapolis Children's Medical Center viewers interact with on-air talent via telephone to play educational games.
- The puppet, Freckle Face, is the hospital heroine at Sacred Heart Medical Center in Spokane. The hospital uses Freckle Face and a detective friend to tell stories about the fears children experience with hospitalization. Children see the story on closed-circuit television and then use puppets for play therapy afterwards.

Although Swedish American Hospital in Rockford said its CCTV programming was not specifically geared to children, it does broadcast a bingo program for children once a week via CCTV. The Children's Hospital in San Diego had a very successful interactive puppet program called the "Socky Show" that was produced in-house and shown daily. Unfortunately, production was curtailed when its budget was cut. At the time of the survey, however, the hospital was still airing tapes of the original series.

## Making Programs Available to Other Institutions

In our second survey, we asked if hospitals' CCTV programming was available to other institutions. The following institutions said yes (although the list is by no means complete since this question was not included in the first survey):

- Children's Hospital and Health Center in San Diego makes programming available on an individually determined basis. Contact: Tom Zamerick, Coordinator of Medical Television (619) 576-5815.
- Children's Hospital/Health Sciences Center in Winnipeg will copy samples of its programs for institutions that send a blank tape. It also has printed information on how to set up a CCTV station and use CCTV in the hospital. Contact: Donna Lozan, CCTV/Child Life Department (204) 787-2728.
- Miller Children's Hospital/Memorial Medical Center in Long Beach makes some of its programs available for purchase. Contact: Dorothea Passios, Child Life Department (213) 595-3234.
- University Medical Center in Tucson offers some of its programming for purchase. Contact: Mary

Gibson, Biomedical Communications Marketing Department (602) 626-7343.

- Warren General Hospital in Warren, OH makes some of its programming available to local hospitals on request. Contact: Renee Bokis, Head Nurse (216) 373-9000.

Both Children's Hospital/National Medical Center and Grady Memorial are planning to make their programming available to other institutions in the near future.

## Priorities

We asked hospitals what their greatest needs were in terms of CCTV programming, and roughly 70% responded. In addition to funding support, which was mentioned throughout the survey and not just in response to this question, 5 other areas were consistently ranked as priorities. They include information on using media creatively with hospitalized children; information on what media materials are available for children; better commercially produced media for entertainment and recreation; participatory programs with activity suggestions for children; and information about what other hospitals are doing in this area.

Access to hospital-appropriate materials, and information on programming materials for hospitalized children were also frequently mentioned. Interestingly, equipment to create self-generated programming and information on how to make TV participatory were not high priorities for most hospitals at the time of our survey, perhaps because those for whom it was a priority had already obtained their equipment or developed their programs.

## A Special Problem

One of the most persistent problems cited was the tendency of parents and floor staff to turn from child-appropriate television programs to others, particularly soap operas, that appealed to their own adult tastes. This corroborates Boyle's findings. Anne Williamson of the Seattle Children's Orthopedic Hospital suggested to Boyle that parents' lack of cooperation in keeping child-appropriate media on television was due to the fact that hospitalization is a stressful situation for parents as well and perhaps causes them to be less sensitive to what is and is not appropriate programming for hospitalized children. In contrast to other types of programming, however, Boyle found that live, in-house productions often generate enough enthusiasm and recognition on the part of both children and parents to keep the dial tuned to them.

Although our survey did not ask about parents' cooperation in keeping child-appropriate programs on television when available, we did ask about staff. Interestingly, the 9 hospitals which generate their own CCTV programs for children—often interactive, live programs—reported the highest level of staff cooperation in keeping such programs on. Seven of these said staff were extremely cooperative; one said staff were moderately cooperative; and one did not respond. Half of those with CCTV programming specifically for children, though not necessarily live or interactive, indicated that staff were extremely to moderately cooperative. The rest either did not respond or reported that staff were minimally cooperative.

## Conclusion

Despite the problems and obstacles associated with effective use of media in hospitals, there is agreement among pediatric professionals about the need for an alternative to broadcast television programming for hospitalized children. Most hospitals with alternatives to commercial television (whether in the playroom or on CCTV) seem to agree with Kathleen Vrabel, Director of the Child Life and Education Department at Tod Babies' and Children's Hospital that media can have "fantastic benefits if monitored properly." While several hospitals qualified their positive comments on media with reminders that it should not be overused or used as a substitute for contact with people, a majority of alternative media users commented on its therapeutic value; its potential as a tool for communicating with children; its ability to educate,

entertain, and relax children and their families; and its role in alleviating some of the pain and anxiety of hospitalization.

But there is also agreement that more work must be done to support the effective use of media in hospitals. The need to educate parents and staff about the impact of both appropriate and inappropriate media surfaced as an important issue in our survey. Also, among the hospital staff we surveyed, there was unanimous agreement that a media clearinghouse would be helpful. Such a clearinghouse could make a significant contribution towards removing the biggest obstacles to effective and appropriate media use in hospitals—lack of staff and staff time, lack of funding, and lack of information about available and hospital-appropriate media—if the clearinghouse provided reviews and bibliographies, acted as a search service, and provided information on available materials as well as on the creative and positive uses of media. Recommended programs that had been previewed and evaluated by the clearinghouse could be helpful in preventing individual hospitals from reinventing the wheel.

Some respondents also suggested that it would be helpful if the clearinghouse could act as a distribution resource and make appropriate media available at reasonable prices. Such a clearinghouse could, in fact, facilitate a process that is often too costly and too time-consuming for pediatrics staff to assume without outside help and without the benefits of shared information.

# HOSPITALS THAT RESPONDED TO THE MCC SURVEY

Institutions with one asterisk have CCTV programming geared specifically for children. Those with 2 asterisks program self-generated materials for children.

**A.I. du Pont Institute**
PO Box 269, Wilmington, DE 19899
*Contact:* Terry Lastowka,
Child Life Department, (302) 651-4848

**Alberta Children's Hospital**
1820 Richmond Road SW, Calgary, Alberta T2T 5C7
*Contact:* Janice Robertson,
Recreation/Child Life, (403) 229-7000

**All Children's Hospital\***
801 Sixth Street South, St. Petersburg, FL 33701
*Contact:* Judi Victucci, Pediatric Clinical Specialist,
Nursing Education (813) 899-7451

**Cardinal Glennon Memorial Hospital for Children\*\***
1465 South Grand Boulevard, St. Louis, MO 63104
*Contact:* Mary Klausen,
Child Life Department, (314) 577-5600

**Cedars-Sinai Medical Center**
8700 North Beverly Boulevard, Los Angeles, CA 90048
*Contact:* Robert Morrison,
Pediatric Play Therapy, (213) 855-4431

**Children's Hospital\***
345 North Smith Street, St. Paul, MN 55408
*Contact:* Meg Katzman,
Child Life Department, (612) 298-8666

**Children's Hospital & Health Center\***
8001 Frost Street, San Diego, CA 92123
*Contact:* Tom Zamerick,
Coordinator of Medical Television, (619) 576-5815;
Linda Lederer,
Coordinator of Child Activity Program, (619) 576-5821

**Children's Hospital/Health Sciences Center\*\***
700 William Avenue, Winnipeg, Manitoba R3E OX3
*Contact:* Donna Lozan,
Coordinator of Children's Hosptial TV,
Child Life Department (204) 787-2728

**Children's Hospital Medical Center**
300 Longwood Avenue, Boston, MA 02115
*Contact:* Myra Fox,
Director of Patient Activity, (617) 735-6551

**Children's Hospital Medical Center**
51st & Grove Streets, Oakland, CA 94609
*Contact:* Ron Anderson,
Media Specialist, (412) 428-3053

**Children's Hospital/National Medical Center\*\***
111 Michigan Avenue NW,
Washington, DC 20010
*Contact:* Tom Thompson,
Director of New Horizons, (202) 745-3225

**Children's Hospital of Eastern Ontario**
401 Smyth Road, Ottawa, Ontario K1H 8L1
*Contact:* Denise Alcock,
Director of Nursing, (613) 737-2321

**Children's Hospital of New Jersey**
15 South 9th Street, Newark, NJ 07107
*Contact:* Carol Rothman,
Child Life Department, (201) 268-8322

**Children's Hospital of Philadelphia\***
34th & Civic Center Boulevard,
Philadelphia, PA 19104
*Contact:* Frances Ritter,
Director, Child Life Department, (212) 596-9258

**Children's Hospital of Pittsburgh\***
125 DeSoto Street, Pittsburgh, PA 15213
*Contact:* Stephanie Stein,
Child Life Department, (412) 647-5022

**Children's Hospital of the King's Daughters\***
800 West Olney Road, Norfolk, VA 23507
*Contact:* Judy Andresky,
Associate Director of Nursing,
(804) 628-3870

**Children's Orthopedic Hospital & Medical Center***
PO Box C 5371, Seattle, WA 98105
*Contact:* Denise Fralick,
Volunteer Manager, (206) 526-2155;
Michael Rothenberg, M.D.,
Child Psychiatry & Behavioral Medicine, (206) 526-2164

**Clara Maass Medical Center**
1 Franklin Avenue, Belleville, NJ 07109
*Contact:* Robert Califano,
Recreation Therapy, (201) 450-2117

**Glenn R. Frye Memorial Hospital**
420 North Center Street, Hickory, NC 28601
*Contact:* Lorraine Moore,
Recreation Therapy, (704) 324-3380

**Grady Memorial Hospital***
80 Butler Street SE, Atlanta, GA 30335
*Contact:* Kathleen Doberstein, Director,
Patient Education/Media Services (404) 589-3760

**James Lawrence Kernan Hospital**
2200 North Forest Park Avenue, Baltimore, MD 21207
*Contact:* Chris Brown,
Child Life Department, (301) 448-2500

**Johns Hopkins Hospital****
600 North Wolfe Street, Baltimore, MD 21205
*Contact:* Jerriann Wilson,
Child Life Department;
Nancy Andrews,
Child Life Video Producer, (301) 955-6276

**Kapiolani/Children's Medical Center***
11319 Punahou Street, Honolulu, HI 96826
*Contact:* Lynn Okamura,
Play Therapy/Nursing, (808) 947-8511

**Kunstadter Children's Hospital***
Michael Reese Hospital, 29th & Ellis Avenue
Chicago, IL 60619
*Contact:* Claire Coen,
Director of Child Life Program, (312) 791-4270

**Le Bonheur Children's Medical Center****
One Children's Plaza, Memphis, TN 38103
*Contact:* Rita Ross,
Child Life Department, (901) 522-3306

**Lutheran General Hospital****
1775 Dempster, Park Ridge, IL 60068
*Contact:* Linda Bieschke,
Child Life Department, (312) 696-7747;
George Patay,
Media Services Department, (312) 696-5553

**Madison General Hospital**
202 South Park Street, Madison, WI 53715
*Contact:* Jill Case-Wirth,
Patient Education, (608) 267-6193

**Maine Medical Center**
22 Bramhall Street, Portland, ME 04102
*Contact:* Helen Leddy,
Pediatrics Department, (207) 871-2695

**Miller Children's Hospital***
Memorial Medical Center of Long Beach,
PO Box 11428, Long Beach, CA 90801-1428
*Contact:* Teri Garrett, Child Life Specialist;
Dorothea Passios,
Child Life Department, (213) 595-3234

**Minneapolis Children's Medical Center****
2525 Chicago Avenue, Minneapolis, MN 55404
*Contact:* Donna Johnson,
Director of Media Services, (612) 874-5932;
Sheila Palm,
Child Life Department, (612) 874-6259

**Montreal Children's Hospital***
2300 Tupper Street, Montreal, Quebec H3H 1P3
*Contact:* Michelle Viauchagnon,
Child Life & School Services, (514) 934-4400

**North Carolina Memorial Hospital***
Manning Drive, Chapel Hill, NC 27514
*Contact:* Darl Pothoven, Supervisor,
Pediatric Recreational Therapy, (919) 966-2301

**Orlando Regional Medical Center**
1414 South Kuhl Avenue, Orlando, FL 32806
*Contact:* Carla Chesser,
Child Life Program, (305) 841-5111

**Rhode Island Hospital**
593 Eddy Street, Providence, RI 02902
*Contact:* B. J. Seabury,
Child Life Department, (401) 277-8278

**Royal Alexandra Hospital's Children's Pavillion**
10240 Kingsway, Edmonton, Alberta T5H 3V9
*Contact:* Barbara Geyer,
Director of Nursing, (403) 477-4602

**Sacred Heart Medical Center****
West 101 & 8th, Spokane, WA 99220
*Contact:* Gracia Anderson,
Pediatric/Child Life, (509) 455-4648

**St. Joseph's Hospital**
50 Charlton Avenue East, Hamilton, Ontario L8N 4A6
*Contact:* Margo Winton,
Child Life Department, (416) 522-4941

**St. Joseph's Hospital & Medical Center**
PO Box 2071, Phoenix, AZ 85001
*Contact:* Martha Frisby,
Pediatrics Department, (602) 285-3221

**St. Mary's Hospital***
200 Jefferson SE, Grand Rapids, MI 49503
*Contact:* Clare Siska,
Child Life Coordinator, (616) 774-6538

**St. Peter's Medical Center**
254 Easton Avenue, New Brunswick, NJ 08903
*Contact:* Donna Dziedzic,
Pediatrics Department, Child Psychiatric Nursing,
(201) 745-8600

**Shriners Hospital for Children**
2211 North Oak Park Avenue, Chicago, IL 60635
*Contact:* Joanne Woiteschek, Acting Director,
Patient Care Services, (312) 622-5400

**Shriners Hospital for Crippled Children**
1645 West 8th, Erie, PA 16505
*Contact:* Donna Martin,
Child Life Department, (814) 452-4164

**Sinai Hospital**
Belvadere & Greenspring, Baltimore, MD 21215
*Contact:* Laura Cohen, Child Life Specialist,
Pediatrics Department, (301) 578-5800

**Swedish American Hospital**
1400 Charles Street, Rockford, IL 61101
*Contact:* Elaine Johnson,
Child Life Department, (815) 968-4400

**Tod Babies' & Children's Hospital***
500 Gypsy Lane, Youngstown, OH 44501
*Contact:* Kathleen Vrabel, Director,
Child Life & Education, (216) 747-1444

**Tuft's New England Medical Center**
Box 444, Boston, MA 02111
*Contact:* Kristine Angoff, Play Program,
Boston Floating Hospital, (617) 956-5232

**U. C. Davis Medical Center**
2315 Stockton Blvd (# 5001), Sacramento, CA 95817
*Contact:* Connie Baker, Director of Child Life Program,
Clinical Social Services, (916) 453-2173

**University Hospital**
Saskatoon, Saskatchewan S7N 0X0 Canada,
*Contact:* Shirley Patola,
Pediatric Out-Patients, (306) 966-8108

**University Hospital of Jacksonville***
655 West 8th Street, Jacksonville, FL 32216
*Contact:* Leslie Hutchins,
Child Life Department, (904) 350-6899

**University Medical Center***
1501 North Campbell Avenue, Tucson, AZ 85724
*Contact:* Gayle Sumida, Media Specialist,
Biomedical Communications, (602) 626-7343

**University of Missouri**
Columbia Hospital,
One Hospital Drive, Columbia, MO 65201
*Contact:* Ginny Morgan or Theresa Schulte,
Child Life Services, (314) 882-8172

**Warren General Hospital***
667 Eastland Avenue SE, Warren, OH 44484
*Contact:* Media Review Committee,
Department of Education, (216) 373-9000

# media center for children

July 1, 1983

Attention Child Health Care Professionals:

Are you concerned about the quality and quantity of media that children in your care are exposed to while in the hospital? If so, would you take some time to complete the enclosed questionnaire?

As part of our Hospitalized Children's Media Project, the Media Center for Children (MCC) is conducting a survey among hospitals in the US and Canada regarding their use of media with in-patients (non-psychiatric) in pediatrics wards and children's hospitals. With your input, MCC will develop a report which can serve as a first step in improving the media children see in hospitals.

Before going any further, I should explain that the Media Center for Children is a non-profit educational organization which gathers and publishes information about children's media for the general public. With funding support from the Association for the Care of Children's Health (ACCH), the National Endowment for the Arts, the New York State Council on the Arts, and several foundations, MCC is studying "the state of the art" of hospitalized children's media. Results of the survey, as well as in-hospital evaluations of MCC-developed playroom and CCTV programs, will be published in a special hospital issue of Young Viewers, MCC's magazine.

Our primary goal in undertaking the Hospitalized Children's Media Project is to give the people who work with children in hospitals, as well as the children themselves, some input into the evaluation and development of media for hospitalized children. A secondary goal is to provide health care professionals with information about model programs and different sources of hospital-appropriate children's media.

We can do none of this, however, unless we know what people in the field are doing already. That's where you come in. Whether you're using media a great deal or only a little, it is important for us to know. And, perhaps more importantly, we want to know what you would do if money were not a problem.

Please complete as many questions as you can on the attached pages, and return the form to us. If sections are unclear, or if you would like more details, call me or Jane Rayleigh at 212/679-9620 on Tuesdays or Wednesdays. We will be happy to discuss the questionnaire or the project with you.

Also enclosed, for your information, is an MCC brochure.

With sincere thanks for your cooperation,

Maureen Gaffney
Executive Director

**3 West 29th Street    New York City NY 10001    212/679-9620**

MEDIA CENTER FOR CHILDREN
SURVEY OF MEDIA FOR HOSPITALIZED CHILDREN

Name _____ Phone ( ___ ) _____ Ext: _____

Department _____

Hospital _____

Address _____

---

PEDIATRICS POPULATION

- Number of beds in pediatrics ward _____
- Average length of child's stay _____
- Ethnic breakdown:  Euroethnic _____ %   Black _____ %
  Hispanic _____ %   Asian _____ %
  Mid-Eastern _____ %   Other _____ %

---

MEDIA UTILIZATION

- What types of media do you use in the playroom?
  16mm film _____      3/4" video _____
  1/2" VHS _____      1/2" BETA _____
  videodisc _____      arcade video games _____
  TV video games _____      radio _____
  don't use media _____      other _____

- Do you use media for education/orientation ___   entertainment ___   other ___

---

MONITORS/TELEVISION SETS

- Number of sets per patient room _____
- Number of beds per room _____
- Number of sets in playrooms _____   in lounges _____   total in children's area _____

- Approximate screen size of sets in children's rooms _____
- Is the speaker on the monitor _____   in a hand-held personal unit _____

- What is cost per day for television/monitor rental? $ _____   Free _____
- Are there exceptions? (Please explain) _____

- Who maintains/repairs monitors? _____
- Describe any persistent technical problems _____

---

PROGRAMMING

- Do you have a cable hook-up?  No ___  Yes ___    With whom? _____
- What percentage of your programming is cable _____ %; local/network television _____ %

- Do you use donated films/tapes?                          No ___  Yes ___
- Do you borrow films/tapes from the public library?       No ___  Yes ___
- Do you rent films/tapes from distributors?               No ___  Yes ___
- Do you buy films/tapes from distributors?                No ___  Yes ___
- Do you rent Beta/VHS tapes from electronics/video stores? No ___  Yes ___

- What is your budget for film/tape rental? _____ for film/tape purchase? _____
- How many films/tapes do you own? _____
- How many films/tapes do you use per week? _____
- What do you use most?  feature films ___   shorts ___   educational programs ___   other ___

---

EVALUATION/SELECTION

- What is the title and professional background of person who evaluates and selects
  programming which is not created in-hospital? _____

- What is the criteria used for selecting programming? _____

- What evaluation follow-up do you use? _____

- Describe any problems _____
  _____
  _____

## CLOSED-CIRCUIT SYSTEM

- Do you have a closed-circuit system? No ____ Yes ____
- Approximate cost to set up entire system $ _____ ; to set up pediatric system $ ____
- How do you use it?   health education _____       recreation _____
                hospital/surgery orientation _____       other _____
- What hours is closed-circuit programming offered? _____
- Why those hours? _____
- How often do you repeat programming? _____
- How many channels do you use with children? _____
- What department is responsible for transmitting programming? _____
- What are their responsibilities? _____
- Who is responsible for repair/maintenance of system? _____
- What is title and professional background of person who develops self-generated programming? _____
- Is s/he staff ___ or outside consultant ___, number of work hours per week _____
- What department/division pays their salary? _____
- Do you have production capabilities? No ___ Yes ___ (Please describe) _____
- How is your program supported? _____
- What are your greatest needs in terms of closed-circuit television programming?  Please rank those that apply.

  ___ Trained staff
  ___ Funding support
  ___ Information on what media materials are available
  ___ Information on how to program materials for hospitalized children
  ___ Information on how to use media creatively with hospitalized children
  ___ Information on how to make television participatory
  ___ Information on what other hospitals are doing in the same area
  ___ Equipment to create self-generated programs
  ___ Better commercially-produced materials for entertainment/recreation/enrichment
  ___ Better access to hospital-appropriate materials
  ___ Education program for parents
  ___ Education program for staff
  ___ Participatory programs with activity suggestions for children

- Does your hospital-generated programming have an interactive component?  If so, please describe.

- How cooperative is your staff in keeping child-appropriate programming on when it is available?  extremely ___   moderately ___   minimally ___
- Please describe problem areas.

COMMENTS
- If a children's media clearinghouse were established, how best could it help you?

- What advice would you give other hospitals interested in developing a closed-circuit program for children?

- Any comments about using media, in general, with hospitalized children?

- Would you or someone from your staff be interested in attending a seminar on media for hospitalized children in 1984? No ___   Yes ___

- If so, who? _____

Thank you for taking time to participate in this survey.  Please return completed questionnaire -- by September 15, 1983 -- to:  Maureen Gaffney
       Media Center for Children
       3 West 29 Street
       New York  NY 10001
       (212) 679-9620

# media center for children

9 May 1985

Dear Child Health Care Professional:

If you are concerned about the quality and quantity of media that children in your care are exposed to while in the hospital, would you please take a few minutes to complete the enclosed questionnaire?

As part of our Hospitalized Children's Media Project, the Media Center for Children (MCC) has conducted several surveys among hospitals in the United States and Canada regarding their use of media with in-patients (non-psychiatric) in pediatrics wards and children's hospitals. The input we have received is being made part of a report which can serve as a first step in improving the media children see in hospitals.

Before going any further, we should explain that the Media Center for Children is a non-profit educational organization which gathers and publishes information about children's media for the general public. With funding support from the Association for the Care of Children's Health (ACCH), the National Endowment for the Arts, the New York State Council on the Arts, and several foundations, MCC is studying "the state of the art" of hospitalized children's media. Results of our surveys, as well as in-hospital evaluations of MCC-developed playroom and CCTV programs, will be published this summer in a special Hospital Programmers Handbook.

Our primary goal in undertaking this project is to give the people who work with children in hospitals, as well as the children themselves, some input into the evaluation and development of media for hospitalized chidlren. A secondary goal is to provide health care professionals with information about model programs and different sources of hospital-appropriate children's media.

The enclosed questionnaire explores several aspects of closed-circuit television programming for pediatric patients. We are anxious to include the results of this survey in our report, and for this reason request that you complete the questionnaire and return it to us as quickly as possible -- but by May 24th at the latest. Many of the questions require only checking an appropriate answer or a very brief bit of information. If we don't hear from you in two weeks, we'd like to phone you to collect the information -- it's that important!

We greatly appreciate your assistance with this project and would be pleased to give you more information if you want it.

With sincere thanks for your cooperation,


Maureen Gaffney                    Jane Rayleigh
Executive Director                 Research Consultant


**3 West 29th Street    New York City NY 10001    212 / 679-9620**

## MEDIA FOR HOSPITALIZED CHILDREN
## CLOSED-CIRCUIT TELEVISION (CCTV)

- Who is in charge of CCTV for pediatric patients?

    Name _____ Title _____

    Department _____ Phone (      ) _____

    Hospital _____

    Address _____


- When did hospital set up CCTV system? _____
- How was initial set-up cost funded? _____
- Approximate cost to set up entire system? $ _____ Pediatrics CCTV system? $ _____
- What size is CCTV-monitor screen?  ____under 7"  ____under 12"  ____under 19"  ____over 19"
- Who is responsible for repair/maintenance of system? _____
- Are there any persistent problems? _____
- What department is responsible for transmitting programs? _____
- What are their responsibilities? _____


- What hours are CCTV programs for children offered? _____
- Why those hours? _____
- How often do you repeat children's programming? _____
- How many channels are available for children? _____
- How do you use CCTV with children?
    _____health education                    _____recreation (with activities)
    _____hospital/surgery orientation        _____recreation (without activities)
    _____to keep children occupied           _____other
- How cooperative is staff in keeping child-appropriate programming on when it is available?
    _____extremely        _____moderately        _____minimally


- What is the name, title, and professional background of person who evaluates and selects
  programming not created in-hospital? _____
  _____

- What criteria is used for selecting programming? _____
  _____

- What evaluation follow-up do you use? _____
  _____

- Describe any problems. _____


- What format do you use?  ___VHS  ___Beta  ___3/4"  ___videodisc  ___16mm film
- What is annual budget for video/film rental? $ _____  Video/film purchase? $ _____
- How many tapes/discs/films does hospital own? _____
- How many works do you use per week? _____
- What do you use most?  ___feature films  ___shorts  ___educational programs  ___other


- Do you use donated video/film?                    ___No    ___Yes
- Do you borrow video/film from public library?     ___No    ___Yes
- Do you rent works from distributors?              ___No    ___Yes
- Do you buy works from distributors?               ___No    ___Yes
- Do you rent VHS/Beta tapes from video clubs?      ___No    ___Yes

- What is the name, title, and professional background of person who develops in-hospital programs? _____
- Is s/he ___ staff or ___ outside consultant? Number of work hours per week? _____
- What department/division pays his/her salary? _____
- Describe your production capabilities? _____
_____
- What staff or outside consultants are involved with production? _____
_____
- How is self-generated programming funded? _____
_____
- Does your hospital-generated programming have an interactive component? Please describe:

- Is programming developed in your hospital available to others? ___ No ___ Yes
- Under what terms/conditions? _____
_____
- Are print or other materials available with tapes? Please describe: _____
_____
- Who should other hospital media programmers contact for available works/materials?
Name _____ Phone ( ) _____
Department _____

- Other than funding support, what are your greatest needs in terms of CCTV programming? Please rank all that apply.

    ___ information on what materials are available
    ___ information on how to program materials for hospitalized children
    ___ information on how to use media creatively with hospitalized children
    ___ information on how to make television participatory
    ___ information on what other hospitals are doing in the same area
    ___ equipment to create self-generated programs
    ___ better commercially produced works for entertainment/recreation/enrichment
    ___ better access to hospital-appropriate materials
    ___ participatory programs with activity suggestions for children

- What advice would you give other hospitals interested in developing a CCTV program for children?

Please mail completed form by May 24 to: Jane Rayleigh, Media Center for Children, 3 West 29 Street, New York NY 10001. (212) 679-9621.

# APPENDIX B:

# TV in Pediatric Wards: Is It Worrisome or Worthwhile?*

## by Elizabeth Crocker

In September 1982, at the annual meeting of the Canadian Association of Paediatric Hospitals in Vancouver, it was agreed that a study should be carried out to determine "the state of the art" of television services and programming for patients in Canadian children's hospitals. The Canadian Institute of Child Health agreed to undertake the study, the Hospital for Sick Children Foundation agreed to fund it, and I was hired to research and document it. I was past director of Child Life at the Izaak Walton Killam Hospital for Children in Halifax and had developed an in-house television channel there. This report gives a factual account of the present situation in Canadian children's hospitals and suggests some areas of cooperation for the future.

## Overview

Television surrounds us. For more than 3 decades, North Americans have been drawn towards entertainment, news, and sports in the comfort of our own homes. Some of us may remember a time when there was no television, but our children have only known a world where television exists.

For a number of years, researchers have been trying to determine the effects of television on children and to quantify the amounts of television being watched by children of different ages. As with any field of research, studies with a range of findings have emerged. In spite of these differences, however, certain generalizations can be made:

- Excessive television viewing can displace other activities and disrupt a young child's development of verbal skills or hurt the academic achievement of school age children.
- Connections exist between violence on television and violence in society—and violence on television can stimulate children to be more aggressive and violent.
- Exposure to prosocial television leads children to be more helpful, sharing, cooperative, and empathetic; further, children who watch these programs are inclined to be more productive in their fantasy, more imaginative in their play, and more creative in general; these children are also less likely to hold ethnocentric or sex-stereotyped beliefs.
- Young children cannot always differentiate between what they see on TV and what is real.
- Children's television viewing peaks in early adolescence and then sharply declines. Actual viewing hours per week range from 20 to 50 hours depending on the study, where it was done, and the socioeconomic levels and ages of the groups sampled. It is estimated that one-quarter of

---

school-age children spend more than 25% of their normal waking hours watching television.

- The percentage of air time devoted to children's programming on most networks is extremely small. For example, PBS allots 27% while most other networks fall somewhere between 4% and 8%. Most of what is categorized as children's programming is for preschoolers; material for school-age children is almost nonexistent.
- Because of vast developmental differences between preschoolers, early school-age children, and preadolescents, there is no such thing as a mass child audience.

Research findings lead one to conclude that while television can, without doubt, offer a range of information, entertainment, and stimulation, it also offers a great deal of violence, advertising, and race/role/age stereotypes. Television does all this in program packages that, for the most part, are not designed for children.

Many groups that work with children worry about this. The American Academy of Pediatrics has gone so far as to express its concern about the effects of television on children in general, but when we look at what happens in hospitals with respect to television viewing, the problems are magnified.

It is estimated that one in 15 children is hospitalized each year, and it is fairly well accepted that hospitalization sets up stress, anxiety, and fear in both children and their families. Most hospitals, in an attempt to provide a familiar and pleasant experience for children, have made television completely accessible to pediatric patients. As a result, children in hospital watch television as only second choice to visitors or recreational activities. Often the television is on in the background while the child does something else.

Even though watching television may not be children's first choice of activity, the amount they watch is enormous. Studies that have attempted to quantify viewing patterns have found that each day children watch TV for approximately 4 hours just between 9:00am and 5:00pm, and for nearly 6 hours if in isolation. The time spent watching TV escalates on weekends due to fewer medical tests/procedures and reduced play programs. One American study calculated that children were watching television in excess of 8 hours a day!

Despite the possibility that television may be convenient and familiar (and therefore reassuring), is it safe to assume that all those hours are developmentally appropriate, worthwhile, and stress-reducing? Instead, could it be that all those hours are harmful and even detrimental to the concept of good health?

Imagine, for a moment, the hospitalized child who watches 4 or 5 hours of television in the daytime (not including what she or he watches at night). What is he or she watching? Talk shows where the guests may be clarifying the categories of assault and rape; game shows where guests squeal as they break balloons and win refrigerators; news with its often gruesome depiction of events; advertisements for anything from cleaning agents to life insurance to protect you from a range of potential disasters; and soap operas with conflict-, sex-, trauma-, and often death-dependent plots.

If people are concerned about the effects of television on children, their concern should be doubled or tripled when they examine what's happening in hospitals. The line from the Hippocratic Oath that says "First do no harm..." has relevance for the issue of television in hospitals. Does it make sense to attend to the organic concerns of a patient and not address other behaviors that may not be in the patient's best interests?

Many pediatric hospitals no longer allow smoking in their buildings and advise people that they have a "no smoking" policy because they are health institutions; many hospitals support car restraint legislation and educate patients and their parents about the value of safety seats and belts. A number of Canadian pediatric hospitals have been so concerned about the potentially worrisome effects of television, that they have developed alternatives that they feel are healthy and worthwhile.

When or if hospitals decide that they do not want to maintain the *status quo* with respect to television, there are a number of options open to them:

- Eliminate television altogether. This is not a highly desirable solution because it does not recognize that some television can be worthwhile, relaxing, informative, and therapeutic (in that it is a normal activity that the patient can associate with his or her nonhospital world).
- Provide program alternatives and black out all other, regular channels. This solution has problems because there are occasional good programs on the regular channels and having only one channel does not allow for different tastes and ages to be satisfied at the same time.
- Provide program alternatives that will complement and/or compete with regular programming.
- Offer more human alternatives such as additional recreational activities so that television is a less preferred option for pediatric patients.

## Goals of the Study

The purpose of this study was to determine which Canadian pediatric hospitals have chosen to establish a closed-circuit channel with programming geared to children; whether the new channels have been successful in meeting their objectives; whether other hospitals are contemplating establishing a channel; and whether there are ways Canadian pediatric hospitals can work together to share resources and experiences. Phrased differently, this study was to identify Canadian hospitals' concerns about television, find out what people are doing about them, and suggest possibilities for the future.

## Procedure

Letters were sent to all Canadian pediatric hospitals asking them to identify who should be called to discuss technical questions related to equipment and hardware as well as programming questions. In many cases, more than one person was identified as having relevant information.

A rough questionnaire was developed which served as a guide for telephone interviews with representatives from each hospital. In every case, respondents were very helpful and very interested in the study.

The telephone interviews provided information about who is doing what right now and what people's plans are for the future. They also raised other questions that needed to be resolved—questions such as sources for materials, and the legality of off-air taping.

## The Current Picture

Eleven Canadian hospitals were contacted. Of these, 6 have the wiring and equipment to have a closed-circuit channel for children, but 2 are not operational—in one case, the hospital is new and other issues are more pressing and, in the other, internal disagreement over the role of television has stalled activities. Of the 4 hospitals doing some programming, 2 are very active, one is becoming more active, and one is doing very little.

In hospitals with their own channels, the main motivating factors were a feeling that children were watching a great deal of television and that most of it could not be called "children's programming"; the availability of some money, usually from an external or donated source; and the existence of staff who were eager to establish a closed-circuit channel.

Great ranges were found in the amount of money spent to set up and operate a hospital "channel," in the equipment used, and in which staff members become involved in operating the channels. Only the Winnipeg hospital is currently producing a live program daily; it is called "The Good Day Show."

Actual programs being aired and sources for programs also differed between hospitals. For example, one hospital raved about how inexpensive Disney tapes are to buy while another hospital indicated they were looking for a source of Disney tapes.

## Issues, Concerns, and Questions

A variety of issues, concerns, and questions were raised during the course of this study.

*What is the playing life of a tape?*
Distributors' answers to this question ranged from 150 plays to 400 plays. One hospital makes a copy of each new tape it buys; it then uses the copy and when it begins to fade from use, another copy is made from the original.

*What is the storage life of a tape?*
If tapes are stored under good conditions, their life should be indefinite. Tapes should be kept at room temperature in a room that is neither too damp or too dry. Tapes should also be stored on nonmagnetic, nonsteel shelving such as wood or aluminum.

*How valuable is the extended-play feature on VCRs?*
Generally, people have found the image quality on extended play to be very poor. Winnipeg uses a "stacker" to set up as many as 4 tapes programmed to go on at different times; Halifax has 2 VCRs, so it can set up dual 2-hour tapes.

*Should hospitals have equipment acquisition policies?*
There are a number of good reasons why hospitals should be aware of what video equipment is being bought by different departments. If various pieces of equipment are compatible with one another, one department can sometimes use another department's equipment. If more than one department wants video equipment, it may be possible to negotiate a better price by buying everything from one source.

*What's the minimum equipment needed for a CCTV channel?*
Presuming that the hospital already has coaxial cable, one needs a VCR, a channel block, and a modulator to establish a closed-circuit channel. This equipment can be obtained and installed for under $5,000.

*What type of equipment should one buy?*
There is some debate as to the relative merits of ½-inch *versus* ¾-inch and different companies' products. After talking to a number of people, the consensus is that ½-inch equipment is more than adequate for closed-circuit channels in hospitals and that unless one were to do a great deal of production, the expense incurred by ¾-inch equipment is not worth it. Too, there is more available in ½-inch software—and for less money—than in ¾-inch.

Having said all that, however, it might be that a hospital would choose to go the ¾-inch route if all other pieces of video equipment already in the hospital as well as in the neighboring university were ¾-inch.

The 3 major companies are Sony, Panasonic, and JVC. It might be worthwhile to determine what capabilities you want your equipment to have and then bargain for the best price.

### Service contracts are expensive—are they worthwhile?

Hospitals should have regular monthly maintenance checks of their video equipment. In the long run, this is usually cheaper and more convenient than responding to crises. Bargain for a maintenance and service contract.

### What is a lease-buy plan?

In 5 provinces, it is possible to lease-buy video equipment over a 3-year period at little more than the original outright cost. This plan is handled in Ontario through TV Ontario, in the Maritime provinces through the Departments of Education, and in Newfoundland through the Department of Education. Such plans apply to video equipment, cameras, batteries, and tapes. For example, a SLO-323 Betamax Videocassette Recorder/Player in the Maritimes could be bought outright for $1,860 (in Canadian dollars), but through a lease-buy plan, paying over 3 years, it would cost $2,248.

### How can a closed-circuit TV channel be funded?

In most cases, existing hospital channels were funded through financial or equipment donations and external funding such as foundations or lotteries.

### What are the benefits of live programming?

The live programs at both the children's hospital in Winnipeg and in Minneapolis have a number of strengths. First, the host of the program visits every patient before the show to find out if the child has any messages, pictures, or toys he or she wants to show on the program. The value of this personal visit cannot be overestimated. By talking to children on the program, children see television as an interactive process; in fact, in both places, children can actually call the program or be on it in person. Most children feel the power of television and with these live programs, they can participate.

Live programs can also reach children in ways that might make a big difference in a child's compliance with treatment, or eating patterns or general morale. For example, if *No-name* (the Winnipeg puppet who adores food) told a patient who was not eating that if the child did not eat his supper he (No-name) might eat it all himself, there is a good chance the child would eat so he could proudly tell No-name the next day.

A live program also helps personalize the hospital. Doctors can be hosts for a phone-in show.

Cameras can explore various areas of the hospital. And special guests can visit everyone over the air. The potential of live programming is only limited by staff and imagination.

### Can volunteers play a role in a closed-circuit channel?

Volunteers are used in the production of the live programs in both Winnipeg and Minneapolis. They tour the wards, act as hosts, and provide special entertainment or craft-teaching skills. With a well-trained, dedicated group it would be possible to run a closed-circuit channel entirely with volunteers; however, some continuity would be desirable so that the volunteers could be alerted to patients who were experiencing some sort of difficulty.

### What are the pediatric viewing characteristics?

Hospitalized children's viewing patterns have the following characteristics: children watch more TV in hospital than at home; children regress somewhat in their taste of programs, just as they often show some regression in their preference for leisure activities (for example, children who would normally feel a certain program was too juvenile might find it comforting in the hospital); hospitalized children prefer less fast-paced programs than they normally watch at home—which is a likely result of the fact that the hospital environment is extremely (and often unpleasantly) stimulating and if television programs are too fast they can be overwhelming.

### Is a room monitor better than an individual monitor?

The disadvantage of a room monitor is that there may be several patients in the room and they may not all have the same preferences in programs. The disadvantage of the individual bedside monitors, however, is that television viewing becomes a solitary occupation, further isolating the patient from social interactions. Although individual monitors are quieter, the disadvantage of isolation outweighs the noise advantage. Hospitals that rent television sets to patients must be careful in using rented [and sometimes even purchased] videotapes since there is usually a stipulation that video materials be shown free of charge; if there is a fee for the sets, it could be argued that the hospital is charging admission for the program and the price of rental/purchase would be raised.

### Does it matter when one schedules CCTV programs?

It is wise to determine what programs are being shown on the other channels as one would not want to compete with an existing program of quality; at the most, one would only want to schedule a videotape that would appeal to a different age group. It is important to be aware of patient schedules and routines; for example, if preschoolers routinely have naps after lunch, that would not be an appropriate time to play a tape geared for them. If patient days are usually full of treatments, procedures, and a host of recreational activities, then it would be wise to schedule only short programs during the day and save feature-length movies for evenings or weekends.

### Is it legal to use TV programs taped off-air?

Technically speaking, it is not legal unless you have permission to do so. For example, hospitals in Ontario can use programs recorded off-air from TV Ontario, but hospitals in the rest of the country would be breaking copyright laws if they taped a program from "Galaxy" (a package of programs put together by TV Ontario). It has been suggested that it might be possible to make some sort of agreement with ACTRA and the American Federation of Musicians which would enable hospitals to tape Canadian programs from CBC, but unless this were negotiated, it is illegal to tape off-air even from CBC. Some have tried to argue that an off-air taping would actually be "for home use"—the hospital being children's home-away-from-home. In law, this argument holds little weight.

The question has been raised as to whether it is even legal to show rented videos on hospital closed-circuit channels. A safeguard would be to get a letter in writing from the rental company stating they are aware the hospital intends to show the tape on their closed-circuit channel and that no fee will be charged. (As indicated above, however, renting television sets might present significant problems with respect to televising rented tapes.)

### Who should decide what to show on CCTV?

If programs have not been tested with children before, it is a good idea to have some children be part of any review process. While it may be ideal for a multi-disciplinary committee to review all program content, the reality is that this is an enormously time-consuming task. Realistic alternatives would be to have one department (such as the Child Life Department), which is normally child-centered and cognizant of child development, determine what goes on TV or to have a national clearinghouse that would, using a committee structure, review software and make recommendations to hospitals. In either case, it would be helpful to establish selection guidelines.

The Committee on Children's Television in San Francisco has developed "General Guidelines for Selecting Television Programming for Children" (included at the end of this report).

### Is a CCTV channel better than mobile VCR units?

A closed-circuit channel has the advantage of being able to reach a large number of patients at one time whereas mobile units allow very specialized programs to be shown to patients, such as those having dialysis. Having mobile VCRs also enables hospital school teachers to use certain videotapes in school lessons. Thus, mobile units mean one can individualize the uses and program content. On the other hand, the reach of closed-circuit should not be underestimated. It would be virtually impossible to have enough mobile units to do what a CCTV channel can do. Too, it is very time-consuming to wheel around more than 4 or 5 mobile units. In the best of worlds, one would have a closed-circuit channel and some mobile units. However, if one has to make a choice, there is no question that it is far more powerful and efficient (and perhaps even more personal if one considers the potential of live CCTV programming) to have a closed-circuit channel.

### Do children watch CCTV programs? Do they make a difference?

After Winnipeg's CHTV channel was introduced, a research study was conducted to determine if it had had any impact. It was observed that there was an increase in total viewing hours, but almost half of those hours were spent watching CHTV. Since there had not been a decrease in other activities, it was assumed that CHTV was, to some degree, filling a void. Interestingly, the amount of time pediatric patients spent watching specifically children's programs increased from 43 to 147 minutes, and the amount of time spent watching daytime soap operas decreased from 43 to 17 minutes. In terms of audience figures, 8 out of 10 patients watched the live programming at 1:00pm—93% of whom were between the ages of 5 and 11 (the program's target audience). In addition, 45% of the patients spontaneously named CHTV as the feature of the hospital they liked best.

A 1983 study by Guttentag, Albritton, and Kettner showed that, with the introduction of a high quality closed-circuit channel that had a live program, children were more active in their selection of programs, became more discriminating viewers, and saw fewer advertisements, stereotypes, and violence because they were watching a greater number of programs geared specifically for children.

## Potential for Cooperation

Each hospital in the study was asked if any role could be seen for a clearinghouse with respect to television. The unanimous response was yes. People in the field would very much like to have the benefits of an organization (which could preview huge numbers of films and tapes, review them, and recommend ones for purchase) and a newsletter that would share information about hardware, software, and programming hints or tips. No one felt there would be any value in the clearinghouse's owning tapes since hospitals would want to have ready access to anything that was good. The advantage of having someone else preview tapes for hospital staff is that previewing is both expensive and time-consuming.

Another potential for cooperation between Canadian pediatric hospitals would be to go in a unified way to groups like ACTRA and CBC to discuss the possibility of special status with respect to taping off-air.

Canadian pediatric hospitals could further cooperate to everyone's advantage by collectively bargaining for a year's worth of equipment or blank tapes. It is likely that a better price could be obtained for such a bulk purchase.

Some group prices might also be obtained for actual programs. For example, the National Geographic has an arrangement whereby one can get a far better individual price for a program if one buys the rights to duplicate a certain number of copies. In many cases, companies that sell or rent programs indicated they would be willing to discuss the possibility of better prices for multiple orders.

## Conclusion

One is left with the original question: "Is television in pediatric hospitals worrisome or worthwhile?" The conclusion of this study is that to maintain the *status quo* with respect to hospital viewing is worrisome. Children are watching too much of what is not geared for and may be harmful to them. A closed-circuit channel is not very difficult or expensive to establish and enables hours of alternative, high quality, commercial-free, and specifically children's programming to be available to pediatric patients. The benefits of a closed-circuit channel are perhaps greatest for those children who must be in isolation and/or on bed rest, but they are also significant for all patients. Having a live program as part of one's offerings on a closed-circuit channel has proven to have significant benefits and should be a goal.

Some concern has been expressed by selected individuals that there may be a danger of having machines replace people—in hospitals' turning to television as an inexpensive way of entertaining children and therefore cutting back on Child Life programs. It should be stated, therefore, that the establishnent of a closed-circuit channel should always follow the establishment of Child Life services because human interactions are always better than media. A closed-circuit channel complements existing recreational programs and extends what personnel can do; by itself, however, television is not enough.

Related to this issue is the question "Should we expand our Child Life services or introduce a closed-circuit channel if our funds are limited?" Each hospital will have to answer this question in its own way, depending on its existing programs for children and the degree to which current television offerings and viewing patterns present a problem.

## Recommendations

It appears that if the Canadian Association of Paediatric Hospitals wants to pool some of its resources, it could do a great deal to further the cause of quality television experiences for pediatric patients.

A newsletter would do a lot to share information with people working in this field. A service which reviews video catalogs and tapes would save individuals a vast amount of time and money. Consolidated buying of hardware and/or software would yield significant savings.

People in hospitals with existing channels are looking for ways to share information, to improve their service and expand their offerings; people without existing channels are looking for guidance about what to do and how best to do it.

The Canadian Association of Paediatric Hospitals appears to be in an excellent position to help. Television is not going to go away. What is important then is to make it into something worthwhile, something that will reflect the policies and philosophies of pediatric hospitals, something that will foster rather than hinder child growth and development.

## References

Boyle. "Hospitalized Children and Media: A Survey," *Young Viewers* 6 (4): 1983.

Guttentag, Albritton, and Kettner. "Daytime Television Viewing by Hospitalized Children," *Pediatrics* 68 (5): 1981.

Guttentag, Albritton, and Kettner. "Daytime Television Viewing by Hospitalized Children: The Effect of Alternative Programming," *Pediatrics* 71 (4): 1983.

McCain and Crump. "Television Viewing and the Hospitalized Child," *Pediatric Nursing*, 1983.

Murray. *Television and Youth: Twenty-Five Years of Research and Controversy.* (Boys Town, NE: Boys Town Center for the Study of Youth Development, 1980)

Rothenberg. "Television and Children," *Pediatrics in Review* 1 (10): 1980.

# Guidelines for Selecting Television Programming for Children

**by**
**The San Francisco Committee on Children's Television**

- Does the program appeal to the audience for whom it was intended? (A program for twelve-year-olds should be different from a program for six-year-olds.)

- Does the program present racial groups positively and does it show them in situations that enhance the Third World child's self-image? (Who has a lead role? Who is the professional or leader and who is the villain?)

- Does the program present gender roles and adult roles positively? (Are the men either superheroes or incompetents? Are the women flighty and disposed to chicanery? Are teenagers portrayed with adult characteristics?)

- Does the program present social issues that are appropriate for the child viewer and perhaps are something a child can act on at a child's level? (Litter vs. atomic fallout; pet care vs. saving wolves.)

- Does the program encourage worthwhile ideals, values, and beliefs?

- Does the program present conflict that a child can understand and does it demonstrate positive techniques for resolving the conflict?

- Does the program stimulate constructive activities and does it enhance the quality of a child's play?

- Does the program separate fact from fantasy? Does it separate advertisements from program content?

- Does the program present humor at a child's level? (Or is it adult sarcasm, ridicule, or adult remembrances of what s/he thought was funny from his/her childhood?)

- Does the program have a pace that allows the child to absorb and contemplate the material presented?

- Does the program have artistic qualities?

# 1982/83 Status of Canadian Hospitals' CCTV

[This replaces a graph contained in the original report.]

**Alberta Children's Hospital** in Calgary, Alberta has no CCTV channel. Television sets are in day rooms and can be rented by children in isolation. Three TV channels are available.

**Children's Hospital** in Vancouver, British Columbia has no CCTV channel. Several mobile VCR units are used by Child Life. Television sets are in each patient room. Five TV channels are available to patients.

**Children's Hospital, Health Sciences Centre** in Winnipeg, Manitoba has a CCTV channel—Channel CHTV—which started in 1980. Two Child Life staff members are responsible for program content. Channel CHTV airs for 9 hours a day, 55 hours a week and has one hour of live programming a day. A stacker is used to program up to 4 tapes at a time. Format is ½-inch Beta. Television sets are in each patient room. Three other TV channels are available.

**Children's Hospital of Eastern Ontario** in Ottawa, Ontario has a CCTV channel, but the system is presently on hold. When in use, Child Life staff would be responsible for program content. Production capabilities exist. Currently the hospital is using ½-inch VHS and ¾-inch mobile units.

**The Hospital for Sick Children** in Toronto, Ontario has a CCTV channel—Channel HSC-TV—which began operating in 1982. The manager of internal TV and production is responsible for program content. The channel has production capabilities and is also used by nursing for pre-op teaching as well as by the chaplain on Sundays. The channel airs 6 hours a day, 30 hours a week. Format is ½-inch Beta although there are some mobile VHS units. Television sets are located in each patient room. Eleven other channels are available.

**I.W.K. Hospital for Children** in Halifax, Nova Scotia has a CCTV channel—Channel TV4U—which started in 1981. Child Life staff is responsible for program content. The channel has production capabilities but is limited by staff time. It airs 8 hours a day, 52 hours a week. Format is ½-inch VHS. TV sets are in each patient room; a mobile VCR is used in school. Two other channels are available.

**The Janeway Hospital** in St. John's, Newfoundland has no CCTV channel. It does have a ¾-inch VCR in the OPD and is waiting for cable to be laid. Television sets are in most rooms. Two channels are available to patients.

**Montreal Children's Hospital** in Montreal, Quebec has CCTV, Channel 9; it was hooked up in 1979 but only began operating in 1986. The coordinator of the AV department is responsible for program content. The channel airs 6 hours a day; production capabilities exist. Format is ½-inch VHS. Each patient bed has a TV set. Although 12 other TV channels are available, poor reception reduces the number of functional channels to 8.

**Ste. Justine Hospital** in Montreal, Quebec has no CCTV channel and currently has no plans for such a system. Television sets are provided in playrooms and in some patient rooms.

**University of Alberta Hospital** in Edmonton, Alberta has no CCTV channel but does have a video disk player with a large screen. Television sets can be rented per bed. Three TV channels are available to patients.

**War Memorial Children's Hospital** in London, Ontario has no CCTV channel but it does have a VCR on a mobile cart that utilizes ½-inch video. Television sets are available in each patient room.

# Sources for Children's Hospital Programs

**American Women in Radio & Television, Inc. (AWRT)**
c/o Amy Addison-Licameli
National Chair of Soaring Spirits
Program Director, WNYE-TV
112 Tillary Street, Brooklyn, NY 11201
(718) 596-4425

Through AWRT's Soaring Spirits Project, 85 hospitals in the US and Canada—if they are approved AWRT sites—can receive tapes of a variety of programs on loan, the only charge being the cost of the blank tape, dubbing, and shipping charges. The price is $44 (US) for each hour-long tape. Some of the programs available from AWRT include FREE TO BE... YOU AND ME as well as episodes from "The Big Blue Marble," "Lassie," "Charlie Brown," and "Wild Kingdom." Normally AWRT sites only exist where there are AWRT chapters but Ms. Addison-Licameli thought a special status could be arranged if national organizations wanted to write to her. [*Editor's Note:* Tapes must be carefully previewed, however, since not all are appropriate for hospitalized children. For example there is one segment of "Lassie" which features a burning barn that terrified burn victims. And there is a "Wild Kingdom" episode in which a woman doctor does not effectively sedate a huge cat (who was perhaps more than usually stimulated by the presence of the camera crew) and viewers watch as the cat hangs precariously from a tree while the narrator casually comments that things did not work out as expected.]

**Candle Corporation**
10880 Wilshire Boulevard (Suite 2404)
Los Angeles, CA 90024
(213) 207-1400

**Environmental Video, Inc.**
1731 North Sepulveda Boulevard
Manhattan Beach, CA 90266
(213) 546-4581

$35 (US) can get you a 30-minute cassette of "exotic tropical fish in an aquarium setting with a soothing bubble soundtrack" from Candle Corporation, although both companies distribute other plotless videos [video wallpaper] which would be ideal for babies and clinic waiting areas.

**Coronet Instructional Media**
200 Suiteelcase Road East
Markham, Ontario L3R 1G2
(416) 475-0557

The Halifax hospital purchased "Healthwise," a 13-part series of 15-minute programs. The series seemed expensive but the hospital has been extremely happy with them. Sample program titles include ALLERGY? ALLER-CHO!; CLEAN POWER; HELLO HOSPITAL; and THE STOMACH STORY.

**Family Communications**
4802 Fifth Avenue, Pittsburgh, PA 15213
(412) 687-2990

Mr. Rogers' programs have a strong prosocial impact on children. A number of video programs are available such as HAVING AN OPERATION; WEARING A CAST; A VISIT TO THE EMERGENCY DEPARTMENT; WHAT IS LOVE; DEATH OF A GOLDFISH; I AM, I CAN, I WILL; MOVING; and many more.

**Gordon Watt Films**
3241 Kennedy Road (Unit 3)
Scarborough, Ontario M1V 2J8
(416) 291-9321

This distributor represents Churchill Films as well as others in Canada. Churchill has released a 15-minute video of CURIOUS GEORGE GOES TO THE HOSPITAL ($450). They also have the 26-minute, Academy-award winning film/video GRAVITY IS MY ENEMY ($535). A separate fee schedule for duplication rights exists so it is possible that if several copies of the same title are ordered, films could be less expensive.

**Great Plains National (GPN)**
Box 80669, Lincoln, NE 68501
(800) 228-4630

Hospitals can obtain off-air taping rights of programs (such as "Reading Rainbow") for CCTV use. GPN needs to know the size of the hospital audience, since size determines the fee. The minimum fee for any program's taping rights is $35 (US). GPN has a Joint Purchase Buying Policy whereby a group may buy a master set of a particular program and is then charged a nominal fee for each dub it makes for group members.

**International Tele-Film Enterprises**
47 Densley Avenue,
Toronto, Ontario M6M 5A8
(416) 241-4483

    This distributor represents a host of producers and carries hundreds of programs, including those from the "Paddington Bear Series," "Cartoon Classics," and "Storytime Readings," as well as features like THE CHILDREN OF THEATRE STREET, and numerous programs on health, values, and development that are all geared to children. Duplication rights can be negotiated.

**Kid's Corner, Ltd.**
2027 North Tejon,
Colorado Springs, CO 80907
(303) 475-2499

    Excellent programs involving music, puppets, and occasional shots of real situations. Current titles: WELLNESS: IT'S NOT MAGIC; JASPER GOES TO THE HOSPITAL; THE DAY OF JASPER'S OPERATION; I'M A LITTLE JEALOUS OF THE BABY; and MY BROTHER IS SICK.

**Local Public Libraries**

    Libraries are building collections of videotapes that might be available for hospital use.

**Magic Lantern**
872 Winston Churchill Boulevard
Oakville, Ontario L6J 4Z2
(416) 844-7216

    Magic Lantern represents over 65 producers and carries over 3,000 titles, with 100 new children's titles added each year. License fees are based on the size of the hospital and the number of programming hours. For example, last year Magic Lantern put together a package of 17 hours of video programming for the Children's Hospital of Eastern Ontario, giving the hospital unlimited use of those programs for the year for just over $1,200. Videos are also available for purchase and consortium buying or group purchases would yield lower prices. Magic Lantern represents Walt Disney in Canada.

**National Film Board of Canada (NFBC)**
1251 Avenue of the Americas
New York, NY 10020
(212) 586-5131

    NFBC has a number of programs now on videotape. For Canadian institutions, they are also willing to have films copied onto video for the cost of the tape and dubbing fee.

**National Geographic Society**
211 Watline Avenue (Suite 210)
Mississauga, Ontario L4Z 1P3
(416) 279-9999

**National Geographic Society**
17th & M Streets, NW, Washington, DC 20036
(202) 875-7000

    National Geographic has a number of excellent, high-quality films/videos for children at all age levels. Centralized buying of a number of prints reduces the unit cost. For example, the 28-minute MAN THE INCREDIBLE MACHINE costs $525 (Canadian). Their duplication policy and fee schedule would bring the unit cost down to approximately $130 if 5 prints were ordered.

**TV Ontario Marketing**
Box 200, Station Q, Toronto, Ontario M4T 2T1
(416) 484-2600

    TV Ontario has an enormous number of programs available that it has made itself or that it represents in Canada. These programs are readily available for dubbing costs only in the province of Ontario. In the rest of Canada the price of a program is usually $240 for every 30 minutes; some programs are more expensive. However, different provincial Departments of Education may have purchased programs from TV Ontario and, if so, would have paid for the closed-circuit television rights within that province. Consequently, hospitals should always check with their own provincial Department of Education to see if a program is available. Tapes can also be rented at the rate of $55 each ($40 each for 10 or more).

## Additional Resources

**BBC Television Distributors**
55 Bloor Street West (Suite 1220)
Toronto, Ontario M4W 9Z9
(416) 585-2583

**Children's Television International**
Three Skyline Place (Suite 1100)
5201 Leesburg Pike
Falls Church, VA 22041
(703) 321-8455

**Medical Media Center**
222-A Kingston Road (Suite 203)
Scarborough, Ontario M1N 1T8
(416) 265-3334

**The Production House, Inc.**
Pond Street
Essex, MA 01929
(617) 281-3087

**Television Licensing Center (TLC)**
5547 North Ravenswood
Chicago, IL 60640
(800) 323-4222

# APPENDIX C:
# MCC Hospital Evaluation Form

FORM FOR EVALUATING MCC'S HOSPITALIZED CHILDREN'S FILM/VIDEO/CCTV PROGRAMS

Program Title _____ Running Time _____

    Titles of Films/Tapes #1 _____ _____ min    Film/Videotape

                 #2 _____ _____ min    Film/Videotape

                 #3 _____ _____ min    Film/Videotape

---

- **MEDIA FORMAT**     TV Monitor in Children's Room     Video Monitor in Playroom/Lounge/Library
  16mm Film in Playroom/Library

- **SITE**     Bellevue    Children's    Downstate    New York    St Luke's/Roosevelt

- **POPULATION**     _____ Total number of children with whom program was evaluated

  Ethnic Breakdown     _____ Asian/Arabic    _____ Black    _____ Euroethnic    _____ Hispanic    _____ Native

  Age Range     _____ to _____ years of age

  Average Age     _____

- **CONDITION**     Number of children rated   Excellent _____   Good _____   Fair _____   Poor _____

- **CONCENTRATION**     Greatest number of children were between ages _____ and _____

  Median Age     _____ (Midpoint of age-range of greatest concentration)

---

ATTRIBUTES OF FILMS OR TAPES IN THE PROGRAM BEING EVALUATED  [Circle those attributes that apply]

| | TITLE #1 | TITLE #2 |
|---|---|---|
| **SOUND** | Dialogue    Nonverbal<br>Narration    Silent | Dialogue    Nonverbal<br>Narration    Silent |
| | Effects only/Effects & Music | Effects only/Effects & Music |
| | Music     Effective/Disconcerting | Music     Effective/Disconcerting |
| Sound Density | High   Medium   Low | High   Medium   Low |
| Audibility | Good   Fair   Poor | Good   Fair   Poor |
| **IMAGES** | Liveaction<br>Animation    Representational/Abstract | Liveaction<br>Animation    Representational/Abstract |
| | Clear/Muddy Colors<br>Legible/Illegible Images | Clear/Muddy Colors<br>Legible/Illegible Images |
| Visual Density | High   Medium   Low | High   Medium   Low |
| Visual Quality | Good   Fair   Poor | Good   Fair   Poor |
| **STRUCTURE** | Narrative*   Based on a book<br>Associative   Catalog | Narrative*   Based on a book<br>Associative   Catalog |
| | Simple Format/Complex Format | Simple Format/Complex Format |
| | Too reduced to be clear<br>Amplified nicely with repitition<br>Too much going on | Too reduced to be clear<br>Amplified nicely with repitition<br>Too much going on |
| | Clear     Confusing | Clear     Confusing |
| **SUBJECT/THEME** | Appropriate/Inappropriate   Describe: | Appropriate/Inappropriate   Describe: |

*Definition:  Who and where/when is established.  A problem emerges and is clearly resolved -- the <u>what</u>.

| | TITLE #1 | TITLE #2 |
|---|---|---|
| ● TREATMENT | Story or information is conveyed via:<br>  Soundtrack  Images  Both<br>Effective/Ineffective for this audience | Story or information is conveyed via:<br>  Soundtrack  Images  Both<br>Effective/Ineffective for this audience |
| ● PACE | Slow  Moderate  Rapid<br>Effective/Ineffective | Slow  Moderate  Rapid<br>Effective/Ineffective |
| ● EDITS/CUTS | Long takes  Quick cuts<br>Effective/Confusing | Long takes  Quick cuts<br>Effective/Confusing |
| ● MOOD | What mood did children experience?<br><br>Appropriate/Inappropriate | What mood did children experience?<br><br>Appropriate/Inappropriate |
| ● LENGTH/DENSITY<br><br>Comments: | Appropriate ratio of material to length<br>Too short to cover material adequately<br>Too long for this audience | Appropriate ratio of material to length<br>Too short to cover material adequately<br>Too long for this audience |
| ● PROGRAM THEME | Did/Did not reinforce program theme | Did/Did not reinforce program theme |
| ● POSITION<br><br>Comments: | Did/Did not work well as lead-in<br>Did/Did not work well when repeated<br>Requires/Benefits from two viewings | Did/Did not work well as second film/tape<br>Did/Did not work well when repeated<br>Requires/Benefits from two viewings |
| ● STRONG POINTS | | |
| ● WEAK POINTS | | |
| ● INTRODUCTION<br><br>Comments: | Appropriate/Inappropriate<br>Sufficient/Insufficient/Overwhelming | Appropriate/Inappropriate<br>Sufficient/Insufficient/Overwhelming |
| ● ACTIVITY<br>Comments: | Did/Did not help motivate activity | Did/Did not help motivate activity |

|  | TITLE #1 | TITLE #2 |
|---|---|---|
| ● VIDEO TRANSFER<br>Describe: | Quality   Acceptable/Unacceptable | Quality   Acceptable/Unacceptable |
| ● AGE RANGE | For what ages did title work best? | For what ages did title work best? |

● PARALLELS BETWEEN EITHER TITLE AND OTHERS IN THE HOSPITAL SERIES

● APPROPRIATENESS OF CONTENT OR TREATMENT FOR HOSPITALIZED CHILDREN

● ANY COMMENTS BY HOSPITAL STAFF REGARDING EITHER TITLE

● SCREENING CONDITIONS    Good  Fair  Poor    How did such conditions affect responses?

● IMPACT OF PHYSICAL SPACE OR ENVIRONMENT ON SUCCESS OF OVERALL PROGRAM

● IMPACT OF ENVIRONMENT OR CHILDREN'S DISABILITIES ON SUCCESS OF ACTIVITY

● FOR WHICH POPULATION SEGMENTS DID THE PROGRAM AS A WHOLE WORK BEST -- AND WHY?

● DID THE TWO FILM/TAPE TITLES BALANCE EACH OTHER TO CREATE A COHESIVE PROGRAM?

- DOES THE PROGRAM AS A WHOLE, OR INDIVIDUAL TITLES IN THE PROGRAM, REQUIRE FURTHER TESTING?

- HOW SIGNIFICANT WAS THE PRESENCE OF TRAINED ADULTS

- ACTIVITY ATTRIBUTES    [Circle those which apply]

| | | |
|---|---|---|
| Type | Drawing  Coloring  Collage  Assemblage  Storytelling  Game  Puzzle  "Clay" | |
| | Other: | |
| Materials | Crayons  Pencils  Markers  Paper  Scissors  Glue  Boxes  Objects  Magazines | |
| | Other: | |
| Complexity | Simple    Moderately Complex    Difficult | |
| Age Level | Young    Middle    Mature | |
| Physical Demands | Minimal Dexterity    Average Dexterity    Considerable Dexterity | |

- APPROPRIATENESS IN TERMS OF CHILDREN'S PHYSICAL AND EMOTIONAL CONDITIONS

Activity worked for those    in wheelchairs    in traction    confined to bed    with i.v. splint _____

- AGE RANGE OR POPULATION SEGMENT FOR WHOM ACTIVITY WORKED BEST.   EXPLAIN:

If this differed from the population for whom program worked best, what changes are recommended?

- SUMMARY OF OVERALL CCTV PROGRAM RESULTS FROM EVALUATION SHEETS

| | | | | | |
|---|---|---|---|---|---|
| Interest | 0 | 1 | 2 | 3 | 4 |
| Involvement | 0 | 1 | 2 | 3 | 4 |
| Enjoyment | 0 | 1 | 2 | 3 | 4 |
| Attention Sustained for Show's Duration | 0 | 1 | 2 | 3 | 4 |
| Made Comments During Show | 0 | 1 | 2 | 3 | 4 |
| Discussed Program Afterwards | 0 | 1 | 2 | 3 | 4 |
| Motivation to do Activity | 0 | 1 | 2 | 3 | 4 |
| Completed Follow-up Activity | 0 | 1 | 2 | 3 | 4 |
| Able to Work without Adult Assistance | 0 | 1 | 2 | 3 | 4 |

PROBLEMS:

# APPENDIX D:
# Children's Illnesses
### (Total = 98.8%)

| | |
|---|---|
| 14.8% | Kidney Disease, Urinary Disorder |
| 07.7% | Sickle Cell Anemia |
| 06.8% | General Surgery |
| 06.4% | Cancer, Leukemia |
| 05.6% | Blood Disorder |
| 05.0% | Child Abuse |
| 04.6% | Infection, Abcess |
| 04.4% | Broken Bones |
| 04.2% | Heart Ailment |
| 03.7% | Appendicitis |
| 03.5% | Asthma |
| 03.3% | Bowel Disorder, Colitis |
| 03.3% | Burns |
| 02.4% | Multiple Trauma from Auto Accident |
| 01.6% | Spina Bifida |
| 01.5% | Diabetes |
| 01.5% | Failure to Thrive |
| 01.4% | Abdominal Pains |
| 01.4% | Hypertension |
| 01.0% | Reconstructive Surgery |
| 01.0% | Seizures |
| 00.9% | Attempted Suicide |
| 00.8% | Arthritis |
| 00.8% | Developmental Retardation |
| 00.8% | Ingestion of Foreign Matter |
| 00.8% | Physiological Underdevelopment |
| 00.7% | Cystic Fibrosis |
| 00.7% | Eye Injury |
| 00.7% | Muscular Disability |
| 00.7% | Shunt Placement for Hydrocephalus |
| 00.6% | Hodgkins Disease |
| 00.6% | Immunological Problems |
| 00.6% | Pneumonia |
| 00.6% | Rheumatic Fever |
| 00.5% | Memingitis, Degenerative Neuorological Problems |
| 00.5% | Tonsilectomy |
| 00.4% | Hernia |
| 00.3% | Chicken Pox Complications |
| 00.3% | Observation |
| 00.3% | Hepatitis |
| 00.3% | Hormonal Imbalance |
| 00.3% | Bone Disease |
| 00.3% | Vaginal Problems |
| 00.2% | Eczema |
| 00.2% | Emotional Disorder |
| 00.2% | Thalocemia |
| 00.1% | Cataracts |
| 00.1% | Deafness |
| 00.1% | Diema |
| 00.1% | Harrington Rod |
| 00.1% | Polycystic Ovaries |
| 00.1% | Tracheotomy |

# Selected Resources

# RECOMMENDED PRINT RESOURCES

Adams, Margaret A., M.S., "A Hospital Play Program: Helping Children with Serious Illness." *American Journal of Orthopsychiatry* 46 (3), 1976: 416–424.

Adler, Renata. "Afternoon Television: Unhappiness Enough, and Time." *Television: The Critical View*, edited by Horace Newcomb. New York: Oxford University Press, 1979: 75–86. (Originally published in *The New Yorker*, February 12, 1972.)

Altshuler, Anne, R.N. *Books That Help Children Deal with a Hospital Experience.* Washington, DC: US Department of Health, Education, and Welfare, 1978.

Anderson, Peggy. *Children's Hospital.* New York: Harper & Row, 1985.

Andrews, Nancy, editor. *Alternative Uses of Television and Videotape for Hospitalized Children and Adolescents.* Washington, DC: Association for the Care of Children's Health, 1986.

Axline, Virginia Mae. *The Principals of Non-Directive Play Therapy.* New York: Random House, 1947.

Belmont, Herman S., M.D., "Hospitalization and Its Effects upon the Total Child." *Clinical Pediatrics* 9 (8), 1970: 472–483.

Bergmann, Thesi, and Freud, Anna. *Children in the Hospital.* Madison, CT: International Universities Press, 1975.

*Child Life Activities: An Overview.* Washington, DC: Association for the Care of Children's Health, 1981.

*Closed Circuit Television and Patient Education: A Resource Manual.* Chicago, IL: American Hospital Association, 1982.

Boyle, Deirdre. "Hospitalized Children and Media: A Survey." *Young Viewers* 6 (4), 1983: 9–10. (Reprinted in *Young Viewers* 7 (4) as well.)

Brody, Jane E., "New Focus on Emotions of Child in Hospital." *The New York Times*, Tuesday, September 21, 1982: C1, C12.

Dreyer, Sharon. *The Bookfinder (Volumes 1–3): A Guide to Children's Literature about the Needs and Problems of Youth Aged Two to Fifteen.* Minneapolis, MN: American Guidance Service, 1977/81/85.

*Educational Resources for Pediatric Health Care.* Washington, DC: Association for the Care of Children's Health, 1986. (This is a free pamphlet.)

Fassler, Joan. *Helping Children Cope: Mastering Stress through Books and Stories.* New York: Free Press/Macmillan, 1978.

Gaffney, Maureen, "Finding the Proper Balance: Planning Film/Activity Programs." *Young Viewers* 5 (3), 1982: 27–28.

Gaffney, Maureen, and Laybourne, Gerry Bond. *What to Do When the Lights Go On: A Comprehensive Guide to 16mm Films and Related Activities for Children.* Phoenix, AZ: Oryx Press, 1981.*

Guttentag, Deborah N. Waldner, Ph.D.; Albritton, William L., M.D./Ph.D.; and Kettner, Ruth B., "Daytime Television Viewing by Hospitalized Children." *Pediatrics* 68 (5), 1981: 672–676.

Guttentag, Deborah N. Waldner, Ph.D.; Albritton, William L., M.D./Ph.D.; and Kettner, Ruth B., "Daytime Television Viewing by Hospitalized Children: The Effect of Alternative Programming." *Pediatrics* 71 (4), 1983: 620–625.

Guttentag, Deborah N. Waldner, Ph.D. and Kettner, Ruth B., "Closed Circuit Television: A Unique Tool." *Children's Health Care* 12 (1), 1983: 25–28.

"Half-Inch Video." *Young Viewers* 7 (1), 1984.*

"Hospital Programs." *Young Viewers* 7 (4), 1984.

*The Hospitalized Child Bibliography.* Washington, DC: Association for the Care of Children's Health, 1979.

*Ideas for Activities with Hospitalized Children.* Washington, DC: Association for the Care of Children's Health, 1982.

Johnson, Larry D., "Minneapolis Children's Hospital Channel Performs Valuable Services on Low Budget." *Community Television Review*, January 1981: 9–11.

Lima, Carolyn W. *A to Zoo: Subject Access to Children's Picture Books.* New York: Bowker, 1986.

McCollum, Audrey T. *The Chronically Ill Child: A Guide for Parents and Professionals.* New York: Yale University Press, 1975.

Mills, Joyce C, and Crowley, Richard J. *Therapeutic Metaphors for Children and the Child Within.* New York: Brunner/Mazel, 1986.

Minton, Lynn, *Movie Guide for Puzzled Parents.* New York: Delacorte/Delta, 1984.*

"Parents, Kids & TV." *Young Viewers* 6 (1), 1983.

Petrillo, Madeline, R.N./M.Ed., and Sanger, Sirgay, M.D. *Emotional Care of Hospitalized Children.* Philadelphia, PA: Lippincott, 1972.

Plank, Emma N. *Working with Children in Hospitals: A Guide for the Professional Team.* Chicago, IL: Year Book Medical Publishers, 1962/71.

"Pre-School Films." *Young Viewers* 6 (2–3), 1983.*

Rothenberg, Michael B., M.D., "Television and Children." *Pediatrics in Review* 1 (10), 1980: 329–332.

Squyers, Wendy D., "Using Media in Hospitals." *The Handbook of Health Education*, edited by P. M. Lazes. Germantown, MD: Aspen Systems Corporation, 1979.

Strasburger, Victor C., M.D., "The Effects of Television on Children and Adolescents." *Pediatric Annals* 14 (12), 1985: 814–820.

"Surveys: A Bibliographic Survey and Two Surveys on Media Use in Hospitals and Museums." *Young Viewers* 7 (2–3), 1984.

_____

\* Asterisked selections feature age-specific (but not hospital-tested) evaluations of short or feature-length films/videos for children.

# RELATED CHILDREN'S BOOKS

Films and tapes are forms of communication which have immense appeal to youngsters and we use them as a means of providing small groups of children with a pleasurable and shared experience. We do not, however, use media to explain literature. Nor do we use media specifically to stimulate interest in books. If it happens as a result of our programming that is fine, but it is not why we do it. Rather, we use media *and* books to stimulate children's interests, to encourage their self-expression in various art forms, and to promote interpersonal communication.

We are not, however, against the effective and appropriate use of books in conjunction with media programs. In fact, for hospitalized children there are compelling reasons to use literature with media—either to prepare patients for, or to expand and build on, the film/tape experience.

One of the most shocking things MCC staff discovered by working in hospitals was that chronically ill children—especially those with congenital illnesses such as kidney disease—were growing up in the hospital without the richness of human interaction that preschoolers need in order to develop emotionally, physically, and intellectually. Not only was their range of activities restricted, but they spent an inordinate amount of time (far more than children outside the hospital) watching television, and people seldom talked to them about it or helped them label/identify what they saw. Since their life experience was severely circumscribed by hospitalization and few, if any, were enrolled in an organized school/preschool learning program (which, given the fluctuating hospital population alone, would have been difficult), some of them were not clear about the difference between a fox and a bird. Thus, certain books could be very useful in preparing young children—preschoolers in particular—for understanding and enjoying the films described in this handbook.

Another good reason for using literature in conjunction with films is that many of the works we used had direct or analogous correlations to books or poems. A number of titles were actually adapted from children's books, and some of the lyric works were suggestive of poems.

Using literature as follow-ups is not only a good way to enrich and deepen children's media experience, it is also an excellent way to actively involve professional staff, volunteers, older patients, and parents.

For these reasons, we made the connections explicit and mentioned the titles of the works listed below in the context of our film/tape annotations under "Related Reading."

## Selection Criteria

With one or so exceptions, the books below were not tested with hospitalized children, but we believe—based on what we learned from testing films and tapes—that the selections will appeal to this audience. However, the reader must judge what will work for his/her children in her/his situation.

Our criteria in selecting them were that they related in both *subject* and *mood* to what hospitalized children experienced in the film; they related to both *urban* and *exurban* experiences; they were *brief*; and they were *upbeat* or *uplifting* and avoided references to death.

(In looking at dozens of poetry anthologies, we were surprised at how often death appeared as a subject, even in poems for children. Although the topic could be used quite therapeutically in the right context with a ready child and an understanding adult, we did not believe such works would be suited for general pediatric programming. Thus, we did not include poems or books that mention death.)

*Anansi the Spider: A Tale from the Ashanti* by Gerald McDermott. New York: Penguin/Puffin Books, 1977.

*Animation Book: A Complete Guide to Animated Filmmaking—from Flip-books to Sound Cartoons* by Kit Laybourne. New York: Crown Publishers, 1979.

*Arrow to the Sun: A Pueblo Indian Tale* by Gerald McDermott. New York: Penguin/Puffin Books, 1977.

*Big Brother* by Charlotte Zolotow. New York: Harper & Row, 1960.

*Book of the Pig* by Jack Denton Scott. New York: G. P. Putnam's Sons, 1981.

*Bronzeville Boys and Girls* by Gwendolyn Brooks. New York: Harper & Row, 1956.

*Case of the Elevator Duck* by Polly Berrien Berends. New York: Dell Publishing, 1973.

*Chinese Papercuts: Their Story and How to Make and Use Them* by Florence Temko. San Francisco: China Books, 1982.

*Circle of Seasons* by Myra Cohn Livingston. New York: Holiday House, 1982.

*Circles, Triangles and Squares* by Tana Hoban. New York: Macmillan Publishing, 1974.

*Cricket Sings* by Federico Garcia Lorca. New York: New Directions, 1980.

*Curious George Goes to the Hospital* by Margret and H. A. Rey. Boston: Houghton Mifflin, 1966.

*Curly the Piglet* by Cynthia Overbeck. Minneapolis, MN: Carolrhoda Books, 1976.

*Cut-Outs of Henri Matisse* by John Elderfield. New York: Braziller, 1978.

*Dragon's Tears* by Hirosuke Hamada. Rutland, VT: Charles E. Tuttle, 1964.

*Egg to Chick* by Millicent E. Selsam. New York: Harper & Row, 1946/70.

*Eighth Book of Tan: 700 Tangrams* by Sam Loyd. New York: Dover Publications, 1968.

*Elephant Jam* by Sharon, Lois and Bram. Toronto: McGraw-Hill Ryerson, 1980.

*Elizabeth Gets Well* by Alfons Weber, M.D. New York: Thomas Y. Crowell, 1970.

*Far and Few* by David McCord. Boston: Little Brown, 1952.

*Finger Plays for Nursery and Kindergarten* by Emilie Poulsson. New York: Dover Publications, 1971.

*Fortunately* by Remy Charlip. New York: Parents' Magazine Press, 1964.

*Frederick* by Leo Lionni. New York: Pantheon, 1967.

*Free to Be...You and Me* by Marlow Thomas. New York: McGraw-Hill Book Company, 1974.

*Fun with Tangrams Kit: 120 Puzzles with Two Complete Sets of Tangram Pieces* by Susan Johnston. New York: Dover Publications, 1977.

*Good Morning, Chick* by Mirra Ginsberg. New York: Greenwillow Books, 1980.

*Gunniwolf* by Wilhelmina Harper. New York: E. P. Dutton, 1918/67.

*Hailstones and Halibut Bones: Adventures in Color* by Mary O'Neill. Garden City, NY: Doubleday, 1961.

*Harold and the Purple Crayon* by Crockett Johnson. New York: Harper & Row, 1955.

*Harold's ABC* by Crockett Johnson. New York: Harper & Row, 1963.

*Harold's Fairy Tale* by Crockett Johnson. New York: Harper & Row, 1956.

*Henri Matisse: Paper Cut-Outs* by J. Cowart, J. D. Flam, D. Fourcade, and J. H. Neff. St. Louis Art Museum & Detroit Institute of Arts, 1977.

*Hi, Cat!* by Ezra Jack Keats. New York: Collier/Macmillan, 1970.

*How Summer Came to Canada* by William Toye. Toronto/New York: Oxford University Press, 1969.

*Howard* by James Stevenson. New York: Greenwillow, 1980.

*I Thought I Heard the City* by Lilian Moore. New York: Atheneum, 1969.

*Inside an Egg* by Sylvia A. Johnson. Minneapolis, MN: Lerner Publications, 1982.

*Ira Sleeps Over* by Bernard Waber. Boston: Houghton Mifflin, 1972.

*Jack and the Beanstalk* by Tony Ross. New York: Delacorte Press, 1980.

*Jazz* by Henri Matisse. New York: Braziller, 1985.

*Jenny's in the Hospital* by Seymour Reit. New York: Golden Books/Western, 1984.

*Jessie the Chicken* by Margaret Sanford Pursell. Minneapolis, MN: Carolrhoda Books, 1977.

*Juniper Tree and Other Tales from Grimm* translated by Lore Segal and Randall Jarrell. New York: Farrar, Straus & Giroux, 1973.

*Kittens Are Like That* by Jan Pfloog. New York: Random House, 1976.

*Knight and the Dragon* by Tomie de Paola. New York: G. P. Putnam's Sons, 1980.

*Listen, Children, Listen: An Anthology of Poems for the Very Young* edited by Myra Cohn Livingston. New York: Harcourt Brace Jovanovich, 1972.

*Little Chicken* by Margaret Wise Brown. New York: Harper & Row, 1943.

*Little Duck* by Judy Dunn. New York: Random House, 1976.

*Look Again!* by Tana Hoban. New York: Macmillan Publishing, 1971.

*Madeline* by Ludwig Bemelmans. New York: Penguin Books, 1939.

*Madeline and the Gypsies* by Ludwig Bemelmans. New York: Penguin Books, 1958/77.

*Mary of Mile Eighteen* by Ann Blades. Toronto: Bodley Head, 1971.

*Noodles, Nitwits and Numbskulls* by Maria Leach. Cleveland, OH: Collins, 1961.

*Old-Fashioned Storybook* by Betty Ann Schwartz and Leon Archibald. New York: Simon & Schuster, 1985.

*One Little Kitten* by Tana Hoban. New York: Greenwillow Books, 1979.

*Over in the Meadow* by Ezra Jack Keats. New York: Scholastic Book Services, 1971.

*Paper Movie Machines: Mini-Movies Ready to Make* by Budd Wentz. San Francisco: Troubadour Press, 1975.

*Peter's Chair* by Ezra Jack Keats. New York: Harper & Row, 1967.

*Petronella* by Jay Williams. New York: Parents' Magazine Press, 1973.

*A Picture for Harold's Room* by Crockett Johnson. New York: Harper & Row, 1960.

*Pierre: A Cautionary Tale* by Maurice Sendak. New York: Harper & Row, 1962.

*Poems Children Will Sit Still For: A Selection for the Primary Grades* compiled by Beatrice Schenck de Regniers, Eva Moore, and Mary Michaels White. New York: Citation Press, 1969.

*Poems for Children* by Eleanor Farjeon. New York: J. B. Lippincott, 1926/51.

*Poesia Espanola para Ninos* compiled by Ana Maria Pelegrin. Madrid: Taurus Ediciones, 1969.

*Princess and the Pea* by Hans Christian Andersen; illustrated by Paul Galdone. New York: Seabury Press, 1978.

*Puppets: Friends at Your Finger Tips* by Imogene Forte. Nashville: Incentive Publications, 1985.

*Random House Book of Poetry for Children* compiled by Jack Prelutsky. New York: Random House, 1983.

*Rosie's Walk* by Pat Hutchins. New York: Collier/Macmillan, 1968.

*Shapes and Things* by Tana Hoban. New York: Macmillan Publishing, 1970.

*Sleeping Ugly* by Jane Yolen. New York: Coward-McCann, 1981.

*Snowy Day* by Ezra Jack Keats. New York: Penguin Books, 1962/76.

*Something Queer at the Ball Park* by Elizabeth Levy. New York: Dell Publishing, 1975.

*Something Queer at the Haunted School* by Elizabeth Levy. New York: Dell Publishing, 1982.

*Something Queer at the Lemonade Stand* by Elizabeth Levy. New York: Dell Publishing, 1982.

*Something Queer at the Library* by Elizabeth Levy. New York: Dell Publishing, 1977.

*Something Queer is Going On* by Elizabeth Levy. New York: Dell Publishing, 1973.

*Something Queer on Vacation* by Elizabeth Levy. New York: Dell Publishing, 1980.

*Stonecutter* by Gerald McDermott. New York: Penguin Books, 1975.

*Stories for Free Children* edited by Letty Cottin Pogrebin. New York: McGraw-Hill, 1982.

*A Story, A Story* by Gail E. Haley. New York: Atheneum, 1970.

*Storybook* by Tomi Ungerer. New York: Franklin Watts, 1974.

*Take Another Look* by Tana Hoban. New York: Greenwillow Books, 1981.

*Take Sky* by David McCord. Boston: Little Brown, 1962.

*Tangram: The Ancient Chinese Shapes Game* by Joost Elffers. New York: Penguin Books, 1976.

*Tangrams: Picture-Making Puzzle Game* by Peter Van Note. Rutland, VT: Charles E. Tuttle, 1966.

*Tangrams: 330 Puzzles* by Ronald C. Read. New York: Dover Publications, 1965.

*Tangrams ABC Kit* by Susan Johnston. New York: Dover Publications, 1979.

*Thread One to a Star: A Book of Poems* edited by Lee Bennett Hopkins and Misha Arenstein. New York: Four Winds Press, 1976.

*What Do You See?* by Janina Domanska. New York: Macmillan Publishing, 1974.

*What Good Luck! What Bad Luck!* by Remy Charlip. New York: Scholastic Book Services, 1969.

*Where the Wild Things Are* by Maurice Sendak. New York: Harper & Row, 1963.

*William's Doll* by Charlotte Zolotow. New York: Harper & Row, 1972.

## Related Records and Audiocassettes

*Free to Be...You and Me* by Marlo Thomas & Friends. Arista Records, 1972.

*One Elephant, Deux Elephants: A Children's Record for the Whole Family* by Sharon, Lois and Bram. Elephant Records, 1978.

*Really Rosie* by Carole King. Epic/Ode Records, 1975.

*Smorgasbord* by Sharon, Lois and Bram. Elephant Records, 1979.

# FILM/TAPE DISTRIBUTORS

**Aims Instructional Media**
6901 Woodley Ave
Van Nuys, CA 91406
(800) 367-2467

**Barr Films**
3490 East Foothill Blvd
Pasadena, CA 91107
(800) 423-4483

**Beacon Films**
1250 Washington Street
Norwood, MA 02062
(617) 762-0811

**Bill Budd Films**
235 East 57th Street
New York, NY 10022
(212) 755-3968

**CBC Enterprises/FSD**
PO Box 1600
Montreal, Quebec H3C 3A8
(514) 285-3211

**Churchill Films**
662 North Roberston Blvd
Los Angles, CA 90069
(800) 334-7830

**Coronet/MTI**
108 Wilmot Road
Deerfield, IL 60015
(800) 621-2131

**Davenport Films**
Box 527, Route #1
Delaplane, VA 22025
(703) 592-3701

**Encyclopedia Britannica**
    **Educational Corporation**
425 North Michigan Ave
Chicago, IL 60611
(800) 558-6968

**Films Incorporated/PMI**
5547 North Ravenswood Ave
Chicago, IL 60640
(800) 323-4222

**Hill-Gatu Productions**
703 Tupper Street
Santa Rosa, CA 95404
(707) 578-5535

**International Film Bureau**
332 South Michigan Ave
Chicago, IL 60604
(312) 427-4545

**International Film Foundation**
PO Box 20115
Cathedral Finance Station
New York, NY 10025
(212) 508-1111

**Karen Johnson**
10118 Aldeo Ave
Northridge, CA 91325
(818) 349-4573

**Karol Media**
22 Riverview Drive
Wayne, NJ 07470
(201) 628-9111

**Made-to-Order Library**
345 Fullerton Pkwy (1101)
Chicago, IL 60614
(312) 525-7703

**Museum of Modern Art**
11 West 53rd Street
New York, NY 10019
(212) 708-9530

**National Film Board of Canada**
1251 Avenue of Americas
New York, NY 10020
(212) 586-2400

**Noyes & Laybourne**
77 Hudson Street
New York, NY 10013
(212) 406-7377

**Phoenix Film & Video**
468 Park Ave South
New York, NY 10016
(800) 221-1274

**Pyramid Film & Video**
Box 1048
Santa Monica, CA 90406
(800) 421-2304

**Susan Rubin Films**
161 Remsen Street (#7B)
Brooklyn, NY 11201
(718) 624-1342

**Charles Samu Productions**
1318 Fulton Street
Rahway, NJ 07065
(201) 382-9437

**A. Wallace Estate**
420 Riverside Drive
New York, NY 10025
(212) 865-8817

**Weston Woods**
Weston, CT 06883
(800) 243-5020

**Wombat Film & Video**
250 West 57th Street (#916)
New York, NY 10019
(212) 315-2502

# Indexes

# INDEX OF FILM/TAPE TITLES BY AGE

# INDEX OF FILM/TAPE THEMES

**Perseverance**
THE CASE OF THE ELEVATOR
   DUCK
A CHAIRY TALE
FELIX GETS THE CAN
KUUMBA
L'AGE DOOR
THE MOLE AND THE EGG
RUSSIAN ROOSTER

**Point of view**
A CHAIRY TALE
THE MOLE AND THE TELEPHONE
WHAZZAT?

**Pooling resources**
THE FABLE OF HE AND SHE
WHAZZAT?

**Preadolescence**
BEING BY MYSELF
MY BIG BROTHER
SOMETHING QUEER AT THE
   LIBRARY
TALEB AND HIS LAMB

**Privacy**
BEING BY MYSELF

**Puzzles**
ANANSI THE SPIDER
CURIOUS GEORGE GOES TO THE
   HOSPITAL
FELIX GETS THE CAN
L'AGE DOOR
THE MOLE AND THE EGG
THE MOLE AND THE TELEPHONE
TANGRAM

**Reciprocity**
THE BEAR AND THE MOUSE
A CHAIRY TALE
LITTLE GRAY NECK
OH BROTHER, MY BROTHER

**Reneging on a promise**
THE FROG KING OR FAITHFUL
   HENRY

**Rescue**
ANANSI THE SPIDER
BALTHAZAR THE LION
THE BEAR AND THE MOUSE
MADELINE AND THE GYPSIES
THE SKY IS BLUE

**Resolution of a problem through
   fantasy**
HAROLD AND THE PURPLE
   CRAYON
HAROLD'S FAIRY TALE
WHERE THE WILD THINGS ARE

**Resolving a difference of opinion**
A CHAIRY TALE
WHAZZAT?

**Retribution**
THE MAGIC PEAR TREE
RUSSIAN ROOSTER
SOMETHING QUEER AT THE
   LIBRARY
SOPHIE AND THE SCALES
TALEB AND HIS LAMB

**Returning safely home**
ANANSI THE SPIDER
ARROW TO THE SUN
CURIOUS GEORGE GOES TO THE
   HOSPITAL
HAROLD AND THE PURPLE
   CRAYON

HAROLD'S FAIRY TALE
JACK AND THE BEANSTALK
A LITTLE GIRL AND A GUNNY
   WOLF
MADELINE AND THE GYPSIES
ROSIE'S WALK
THE SKY IS BLUE
A STORY, A STORY
A VISIT FROM SPACE
WHERE THE WILD THINGS ARE

**Reunion with family**
GERALD McBOING BOING
LITTLE GRAY NECK
THE MOLE AND THE EGG
PIERRE

**Role reversal**
A CHAIRY TALE
THE FABLE OF HE AND SHE
RUSSIAN ROOSTER
THE STONECUTTER

**Romance**
ISLE OF JOY
THE PRINCESS AND THE PEA

**Running away from home**
GERALD McBOING BOING
A LITTLE GIRL AND A GUNNY
   WOLF
MADELINE AND THE GYPSIES
TALEB AND HIS LAMB

**Rural farm life**
MARY OF MILE EIGHTEEN

**Scientific method**
THE MOLE AND THE TELEPHONE

**Search for identity**
ARROW TO THE SUN

**Seasons**
THE CREATION OF BIRDS
HOMMAGE A FRANCOIS
   COUPERIN
ISLE OF JOY
LITTLE GRAY NECK
MARY OF MILE EIGHTEEN
NEW FRIENDS
THE SNOWY DAY

**Secrets**
SOPHIE AND THE SCALES

**Seeming liability is a talent**
GERALD McBOING BOING

**Self-acceptance**
GERALD McBOING BOING
THE STONECUTTER

**Self-assertion**
A CHAIRY TALE
THE FROG KING OR FAITHFUL
   HENRY
OH BROTHER, MY BROTHER
PIERRE
TALEB AND HIS LAMB

**Self-esteem**
ARROW TO THE SUN
SOPHIE AND THE SCALES
THE STONECUTTER

**Self-reliance**
HAROLD AND THE PURPLE
   CRAYON
HAROLD'S FAIRY TALE
JACK AND THE BEANSTALK
KEITH
LITTLE GRAY NECK

**Selfishness**
THE MAGIC PEAR TREE

**Separation**
ANANSI THE SPIDER
ARROW TO THE SUN
CURIOUS GEORGE GOES TO THE
   HOSPITAL
GERALD McBOING BOING
IRA SLEEPS OVER
A LITTLE GIRL AND A GUNNY
   WOLF
LITTLE GRAY NECK
MADELINE
MADELINE AND THE GYPSIES
THE MOLE AND THE EGG
NEW FRIENDS
PIERRE
A VISIT FROM SPACE

**Shapes**
ISLE OF JOY
TANGRAM
WORM DANCES

**Siblings**
BEING BY MYSELF
IRA SLEEPS OVER
MY BIG BROTHER
OH BROTHER, MY BROTHER

**Silly songs**
A LITTLE GIRL AND A GUNNY
   WOLF

**Small town life**
BEING BY MYSELF

**Social acceptance**
GERALD McBOING BOING

**Social change**
THE FABLE OF HE AND SHE

**Some bad deals work out okay**
THE FROG KING OR FAITHFUL
   HENRY

**Sound-making**
GERALD McBOING BOING
KUUMBA
THE MOLE AND THE TELEPHONE

**Suburban life**
IRA SLEEPS OVER
OH BROTHER, MY BROTHER

**Survival**
LITTLE GRAY NECK
NEW FRIENDS
SOLO
TALEB AND HIS LAMB

**Surviving disasters with teamwork**
THE FABLE OF HE AND SHE
WHAZZAT?

**There's more than one side to an
   issue**
A CHAIRY TALE
WHAZZAT?

**Things are better if shared**
THE SNOWY DAY

**Trapped in a cage or box**
THE BEAR AND THE MOUSE
KEITH

**Two heads are better than one**
SOMETHING QUEER AT THE
   LIBRARY
WHAZZAT?

# INDEX OF PROGRAMS BY AGE LEVEL

**Young Children
(Ages 3-8)**

**Film Programs**

#1
#2
#3
#4
#5
#6
#7
#8

**CCTV Programs**
#2
#4

**Video Programs**
#1
#2
#9
12
13
17

**Middle Children
(Ages 5–10)**

**CCTV Programs**
#3
#8
11
12

**Video Programs**
10
11
14
15
18
19
21
22

**Older Children
(Ages 7-12)**

**Film Programs**
#9
10
11
12
13
14
15
16

**CCTV Programs**
#1
#5
#6
#7
#9
10
13

**Video Programs**
#3
#4
#5
#6
#7
#8
16
20
23
24

# INDEX OF FOLLOW-UP ACTIVITIES

# INDEX OF FILM/TAPE TITLES IN EACH PROGRAM

## PLAYROOM FILM PROGRAMS

**Playroom Film Program #1**
ROSIE'S WALK
PIGS

**Playroom Film Program #2**
ONE LITTLE KITTEN
THE BEAR AND THE MOUSE

**Playroom Film Program #3**
A LITTLE GIRL AND A GUNNY
WOLF
THE SKY IS BLUE

**Playroom Film Program #4**
TANGRAM
THE SNOWY DAY

**Playroom Film Program #5**
THE MOLE AND THE EGG
TCHOU TCHOU

**Playroom Film Program #6**
PIERRE
THE FROG KING OR FAITHFUL
HENRY

**Playroom Film Program #7**
WORM DANCES
WHAZZAT?

**Playroom Film Program #8**
LITTLE GRAY NECK
HAROLD'S FAIRY TALE

**Playroom Film Program #9**
THE CREATION OF BIRDS
KUUMBA

**Playroom Film Program #10**
THE LATE GREAT AMERICAN PICNIC
CAPTAIN SILAS

**Playroom Film Program #11**
A CHAIRY TALE
NEW FRIENDS

**Playroom Film Program #12**
IRA SLEEPS OVER
TALEB AND HIS LAMB

**Playroom Film Program #13**
ARROW TO THE SUN
THE CASE OF THE ELEVATOR DUCK

**Playroom Film Program #14**
ISLE OF JOY
A STORY, A STORY

**Playroom Film Program #15**
SOLO
THE FABLE OF HE AND SHE

**Playroom Film Program #16**
A QUEST
GERALD McBOING BOING

## CCTV PROGRAMS

**CCTV Program #1**
THE CREATION OF BIRDS
ANANSI THE SPIDER

**CCTV Program #2**
CHICKS AND CHICKENS
ROSIE'S WALK

**CCTV Program #3**
THE SNOWY DAY
THE CASE OF THE ELEVATOR DUCK

**CCTV Program #4**
THE SKY IS BLUE
MADELINE

**CCTV Program #5**
ISLE OF JOY
A STORY, A STORY

**CCTV Program #6**
KEITH
A QUEST

**CCTV Program #7**
TANGRAM
THE STONECUTTER

**CCTV Program #8**
BALTHAZAR THE LION
CAPTAIN SILAS

**CCTV Program #9**
A CHAIRY TALE
THE FABLE OF HE AND SHE

**CCTV Program #10**
NOVEMBER 1977
MARY OF MILE EIGHTEEN

**CCTV Program #11**
HAROLD'S FAIRY TALE
FELIX GETS THE CAN

**CCTV Program #12**
WORM DANCES
WHAZZAT?

**CCTV Program #13**
KUUMBA
SOMETHING QUEER AT THE LIBRARY

## PLAYROOM VIDEO PROGRAMS

**Playroom Video Program #1**
CHICK CHICK CHICK
ROSIE'S WALK

**Playroom Video Program #2**
HAROLD AND THE PURPLE CRAYON
A VISIT FROM SPACE

**Playroom Video Program #3**
L'AGE DOOR
THE CASE OF THE ELEVATOR DUCK

**Playroom Video Program #4**
RUSSIAN ROOSTER
THE CASE OF THE ELEVATOR DUCK

**Playroom Video Program #5**
RUSSIAN ROOSTER
SOLO

**Playroom Video Program #6**
THE CREATION OF BIRDS
A STORY, A STORY

**Playroom Video Program #7**
THE CREATION OF BIRDS
THE MAGIC PEAR TREE

**Playroom Video Program #8**
HOMMAGE A FRANCOIS
COUPERIN
THE CREATION OF BIRDS

**Playroom Video Program #9**
MADELINE AND THE GYPSIES
ANANSI THE SPIDER

**Playroom Video Program #10**
ISLE OF JOY
ANANSI THE SPIDER

**Playroom Video Program #11**
THE STORY OF CHRISTMAS
THE SNOWY DAY

**Playroom Video Program #12**
THE SNOWY DAY
THE SKY IS BLUE

**Playroom Video Program #13**
TANGRAM
THE SKY IS BLUE

**Playroom Video Program #14**
TANGRAM
JACK AND THE BEANSTALK

**Playroom Video Program #15**
PIERRE
A CHAIRY TALE

**Playroom Video Program #16**
HANDS
THE PRINCESS AND THE PEA

**Playroom Video Program #17**
THE MOLE AND THE TELEPHONE
TCHOU TCHOU

**Playroom Video Program #18**
KUUMBA
GERALD McBOING BOING

**Playroom Video Program #19**
THE MASKMAKER
WHERE THE WILD THINGS ARE

**Playroom Video Program #20**
BEING BY MYSELF
OH BROTHER, MY BROTHER

**Playroom Video Program #21**
MY BIG BROTHER
OH BROTHER, MY BROTHER

**Playroom Video Program #22**
WORM DANCES
WHAZZAT?

**Playroom Video Program #23**
SOPHIE AND THE SCALES
THE FABLE OF HE AND SHE

**Playroom Video Program #24**
CAPTAIN SILAS
CURIOUS GEORGE GOES TO THE HOSPITAL

# INDEX OF PROGRAMS FOR EACH TITLE

MAUREEN GAFFNEY is the founder and current director of the Media Center for Children, a not-for-profit information resource on educational media. She is editor of *Young Viewers,* author of *More Films Kids Like* (ALA, 1977), co-author with Gerry Bond Laybourne of *What to Do When the Lights Go On* (Oryx Press, 1981), and author of numerous articles on short films for children. Before launching the Media Center in 1976, Gaffney directed the Children's Film Theater Project for the Center for Understanding Media, coordinated the American Film Festival for the Educational Film Library Association, made filmstrip adaptations of children's picturebooks for *Parents Magazine,* and worked as a freelance media producer/director. Prior to that, Gaffney taught art and reading in elementary schools in Bogota, Colombia and New York City. She majored in theater and communication at Marymount Manhattan College.